⊰ CATO ⊱
SUPREME COURT
REVIEW
2005 — 2006

⋐ C A T O ⋑
SUPREME COURT
REVIEW
2 0 0 5 — 2 0 0 6

ROGER PILON
Publisher

MARK K. MOLLER
Editor in Chief

ROBERT A. LEVY
Associate Editor

TIMOTHY LYNCH
Associate Editor

CENTER FOR CONSTITUTIONAL STUDIES

INSTITUTE
Washington, D.C.

THE CATO SUPREME COURT REVIEW
(ISBN 1-933995-01-7) is published annually at the close
of each Supreme Court term by the Cato Institute, 1000
Massachusetts Ave., N.W., Washington, D.C. 20001-5403.

CORRESPONDENCE. Correspondence regarding subscriptions,
changes of address, procurement of back issues, advertising and
marketing matters, and so forth, should be addressed to:

Publications Department
The Cato Institute
1000 Massachusetts Ave., N.W.
Washington, D.C. 20001

All other correspondence, including requests to quote or
reproduce material, should be addressed to the editor.

CITATIONS. Citation to this volume of the *Review* should
conform to the following style: 2005-2006 Cato Sup. Ct. Rev. (2006).

DISCLAIMER. The views expressed by the authors of the articles
are their own and are not attributable to the editor, the editorial
board, or the Cato Institute.

INTERNET ADDRESS. Articles from past editions are available to
the general public, free of charge, at www.cato.org/pubs/scr.

ISBN 1-933995-01-7

Printed in the United States of America.

Cato Institute
1000 Massachusetts Ave., N.W.
Washington, D.C. 20001
www.cato.org

Contents

CONTENTS

FOREWORD

Politics and Law, Again

*Roger Pilon**

The Cato Institute's Center for Constitutional Studies is pleased to publish this fifth volume of the *Cato Supreme Court Review*, an annual critique of the Court's most important decisions from the term just ended, plus a look at the cases ahead—all from a classical Madisonian perspective, grounded in the nation's first principles, liberty and limited government. We release this volume each year at Cato's annual Constitution Day conference. And each year in this space I discuss briefly a theme that seemed to emerge from the Court's term or from the larger setting in which the term unfolded.

A year ago, with the Roberts hearings looming immediately before us and several stormy years of appellate court confirmation hearings just behind us, I focused on *Politics and Law,* arguing that our judicial confirmation hearings had become so "political" because so much of the twentieth century's constitutional jurisprudence had amounted to politics trumping law. With that politicization of the Constitution—illustrated by several cases that term—we should expect nothing less than politicized confirmation hearings.

In the year since then, much has happened, of course. The ink was hardly dry on last year's *Review* when Chief Justice Rehnquist died. Judge Roberts was then nominated to be chief justice, and Judge Alito was nominated to fill the O'Connor seat for which Roberts had originally been nominated. Their hearings followed, with some delay in the case of Judge Alito's. The hearings were long and stormy, unlike most hearings in the past, and they served to illustrate again how politics today so dominates law.

*Vice President for Legal Affairs; B. Kenneth Simon Chair in Constitutional Studies; Director, Center for Constitutional Studies, Cato Institute.

But a brief lamenting of the advance of politics and retreat of law should not be confused with one arguing that all in our system should be law and little politics. To the contrary, our Constitution is a subtle blend of both politics and law. Thus, there is an important, seemingly opposite variation of today's main problem of turning so much over to politics: it arises when "law" contrary to the Constitution is allowed to trump—in fact, to replace—politics. I say "seemingly" because, in truth, when "law" and the courts that enforce it intrude into areas that were meant to be left to politics, we still have politics trumping law—the politics that creates and enforces that "law." Two of the Court's more important cases this term, involving campaign finance and executive power, illustrate that other side of the modern problem. But first a few lines from last year's Foreword to put the issue in context.

The Constitution contemplates that in a republic like ours, the relation between politics and law is set, for the most part, by law— by the law of the Constitution. Reflecting the will of the founding generation, yet grounded largely in reason, the Constitution was made law through the political act of ratification. As amended by subsequent acts of political will, it authorizes the political branches to act pursuant only to their enumerated powers or to enumerated ends. It further limits the exercise of those powers and the powers of the states either explicitly or by recognizing, with varying degrees of specificity, rights retained by the people. And, by fairly clear implication, made explicit in the *Federalist* and shortly thereafter in *Marbury v. Madison*, the Constitution authorizes the judiciary to declare and enforce that law of authorizations and restraints consistent with the document itself.

Thus, the scope for "politics," in its several significations, is limited. Consistent with constitutional rules and limits, the people may act politically to fill elective offices. And those officers may in turn act politically to fill nonelective offices. But once elected or appointed, those officials may act politically only within the scope and limits set by the Constitution. In particular, not everything in life was meant to be subject to political or governmental determination. In fact, the founding generation wanted most *private* affairs to be beyond the reach of politics, yet under the rule of law. At the same time, they wanted some *public* affairs to be subject mainly to politics, as opposed to comprehensive or rigid legal ordering. And it falls to the judiciary, the nonpolitical branch, to enforce those distinctions, thereby securing the rule of law.

The aim in all of that is to both constrain and authorize the rule of man—and politics—by the rule of law, the law of the Constitution. The Framers understood that legitimacy begins with politics, with the people. Thus, "We the people . . . do ordain and establish this Constitution." But once ratification establishes the rule of law, that law regulates politics thereafter. For the arrangement to work, however, judges charged with declaring and enforcing that law must discern the often subtle relationships between politics and law, restraining politics where it was meant to be restrained and allowing it to reign where it was meant to reign.

Our main problem today, of course, is that much of what once was subject mainly to private ordering, through private law, is now ordered politically, through statutory "law." In everything from marketplace arrangements to retirement security, health care, and on and on, private law has been replaced largely by public law. We all know the source of that change. It came from the Progressive mindset that was institutionalized by the New Deal Court's constitutional revolution. It was then that we were all thrown into the common pot, so to speak, stirred by government planners. Today we live under voluminous "law" not remotely authorized by the Constitution—the product of mere politics. And we do because the New Deal Court opened constitutional barriers, allowing politics to run roughshod over the Constitution's law of liberty.

But that political activism—the mindset of the Progressive Era planner, endowed with a superior understanding of the public good—did not limit itself to zoning, social welfare, economic regulation, and the like. With the New Deal agenda largely completed by the Great Society in the 1960s, Progressives sought new areas to regulate, and they found ready candidates in the aftermath of the Nixon political scandals and the Vietnam War. The Constitution had left campaign finance, as a form of political speech, to be regulated largely by the First Amendment and "politics," understood as the give and take of public opinion operating in the political arena. And it had left foreign affairs largely in the hands of the executive branch, subject to the limited foreign affairs powers vested in Congress and, again, to "politics" in the same sense.

For the activists of the 1970s, however, that left too much to "politics." Much like their forebears in the 1930s who found that the Constitution had left too much to private ordering, the '70s activists sought to impose "law" on what the Constitution had left mainly to political ordering. Thus, in a political exercise aimed at creating "law" seemingly prohibited by the First Amendment, they enacted the Federal Election Campaign Act of 1971 (FECA), designed to regulate the financing of federal campaigning. Two years later, stretching the Constitution's Necessary and Proper Clause, they passed the War Powers Resolution, a detailed scheme for regulating the executive's use of military force, thus intruding on what until then had been thought to be the inherent power of the executive, restrained only by Congress' limited foreign affairs powers, especially the power of the purse, and politics. A year after that Congress amended FECA, enacting comprehensive regulations of federal campaign financing, including severe limits on contributions and expenditures. And in 1978 Congress enacted the Foreign Intelligence Surveillance Act, a complex scheme for regulating what again had long been thought to be the inherent power of the executive to gather foreign intelligence, restrained again only by Congress' limited foreign affairs powers and politics.

Despite the different eras and domains of that political activism leading to law, the underlying principle and pattern should not go unnoticed. Law is a safeguard against the rule of man, to be sure; but overdone it is itself tyrannical. The social engineers of the '30s sowed the seeds of the modern regulatory and redistributive state under which so many today are suffocating. The same hubris, as F.A. Hayek used that term, drove the activists of the '70s to believe that they too could order and micromanage campaign finance and foreign affairs through comprehensive regulatory schemes, and here too the predictable and predicted results are before us.

In her essay below, Allison Hayward discusses some of those results as she only broaches the monstrous web of regulations that constitute today's campaign finance law. In *Wisconsin Right to Life v. FEC* we find a group that owes its existence, ironically, to the Court's failure in 1973 to let state politics work its course, now asking the Court to exempt it from the law's "electioneering communications" ban so that it may run grassroots lobbying advertisements that mention a candidate's name thirty days before a primary election and sixty days before a general election. The Court rejected the FEC's contention that the plaintiff was barred from making an as-applied challenge to the ban, then sent the case back for consideration on the merits—now some two years after the plaintiff had originally asked for a preliminary injunction.

In the other campaign finance case this term, *Randall v. Sorrell*, the Court rejected, inter alia, Vermont's draconian contribution and expenditure limits. That it took no fewer than six opinions to do so speaks volumes about this body of "law." Professor Hayward considers whether *Buckley v. Valeo*, the 1976 decision on which *Randall* turned, should be considered a "superprecedent," a term that surfaced prominently during the Roberts hearings. It is a "poor contender" for that title, she concludes, and not without reason. Far from having plumbed the constitutional principles of the matter, *Buckley* set the stage for the legislation, litigation, and confusion that have followed. But without *Buckley*, would not huge contributions be flowing to candidates, corrupting politics in the process? Perhaps, but under our Constitution, that is for politics, not law, to police. A candidate who discloses his contributions and contributors will "compel" others to do the same, enabling the give and take of public opinion—"politics"—to do the work that no legal compulsion can possibly do without turning that compulsion into the legal quagmire and incumbent protection scheme that our campaign finance law has become.

But if regulating campaign finance through law rather than politics has proven pernicious, regulating foreign affairs through law rather than politics has arguably proven disastrous. To begin, the 1973 War Powers Resolution is today essentially a dead letter. Since its enactment, no president has acknowledged its constitutionality, and all since President Reagan have effectively ignored it, none more so than President Clinton in the Kosovo conflict. By contrast, the 1978 Foreign Intelligence Surveillance Act (FISA) has not been ignored. In fact, it led to the "wall" between foreign and domestic intelligence gathering and to the diminished communications between the agencies charged with each that many who are close to the matter believe contributed to the disaster of 9/11. Since then, of course, the administration has argued both that the authorization to use military force that Congress passed shortly after 9/11 supersedes certain FISA restrictions and that the executive has inherent constitutional authority in any event to engage in foreign intelligence gathering, a contention the FISA Court of Appeals defended in the most definitive opinion on the statute yet to appear. At this writing, however, a U.S. district court has just ruled otherwise in an opinion so thin (it does not even cite the FISA Court of Appeals opinion) that even many of those who agree with its conclusion are distancing themselves from it.

That brings us to the case that drew the most attention this term, *Hamdan v. Rumsfeld*. This is not the place to delve into its complexities, except to say that here too Congress had acted, but unlike with its war powers or foreign intelligence statutes, which might in principle be adjudicated by the Supreme Court, Congress here had moved to strip the Court of jurisdiction, pursuant to its power under Article III, Section 2, Clause 2 of the Constitution. As John Yoo writes below, "Congress spoke in clear terms, using language that the Court had previously interpreted to immediately terminate jurisdiction over pending and future cases." Writing for a bare majority, and overturning a unanimous panel below, Justice Stevens ignored "an ancient and unbroken line of authority," as Justice Scalia put it in dissent. What followed was an unprecedented intrusion by the Court into an area that had always been reserved to the political branches.

But don't take my word for that, or Professor Yoo's, or Justice Scalia's. Here is a noted critic of the administration, writing in the August 10 issue of *The New York Review of Books*:

> The Supreme Court has said in the past that foreign nationals who are outside US borders, like Hamdan, lack any constitutional protections. Hamdan was a member of the enemy forces when he was captured, and courts are especially reluctant to interfere with the military's treatment of "enemy aliens" in wartime. He filed his suit before trial, and courts generally prefer to wait until a trial is completed before assessing its legality. And as recently as World War II, the Supreme Court upheld the use of military tribunals, and ruled that the Geneva Conventions are not enforceable by individuals in US courts but may be enforced only through diplomatic means. . . . [Finally,] [t]he Detainee Treatment Act of 2005 required defendants in military tribunals to undergo their trials before seeking judicial review, and prescribed the D.C. Circuit as the exclusive forum for such review.

Notwithstanding that history of law, the author saw fit to heap effusive praise on the Court for an opinion "equal parts stunning and crucial."

What we have here, then, is not an intrusion by Congress on authority the Constitution vests in the executive, but rather an intrusion by the Court on the shared authority the Constitution vests in the executive and the Congress. And ironically, the Court seemed to be enhancing Congress' power by finding that it needed to authorize the military tribunals at issue, even as it was ignoring, in effect, Congress' express power under the Constitution to limit the Court's jurisdiction. Stunning indeed.

And so here too we have an effort—not by Congress, this time, but by the Court—to introduce a complex web of "law" into an area that the Constitution left to the political branches to manage. And the result, in this area too, is predictable and predicted. Just as Congress, since the post-9/11 NSA surveillance program came to light last December, has been unable to agree yet on any statutory "fix" for the matter, so too it is unclear what, if anything, Congress will do in response to the *Hamdan* decision. That should not surprise. It is in the nature of the matter. As the Framers understood, foreign affairs, involving the often dangerous relationship between the nation and the rest of the world, are ever fluid, requiring the "secrecy, dispatch, and decision" that only the executive can provide, with the assistance or opposition of Congress as constitutionally authorized under its enumerated powers. A rare point of agreement between Jefferson and Hamilton, that insight drew, not surprisingly, from Locke, who understood that foreign, unlike domestic, affairs are "much less capable to be directed by antecedent, standing, positive laws." Lawyers and judges are essential for liberty under law, but so too is politics, the place for which we ignore at our peril.

Introduction

Mark Moller*

The fifth volume of the *Cato Supreme Court Review* arrives during a transitional time on the Court, evidenced by the cacophony of conflicting predictions about where the Court, under its new chief justice, is headed. Will it be a "Kennedy Court," dominated by the new Court's new power-brokering swing vote, as *Slate*'s Dahlia Lithwick suggests;[1] a humble, minimalist Court—the qualities prized by Chief Justice John Roberts; or something entirely unforeseen? This edition of the *Review* probes several points of doctrinal uncertainty and change—from the ongoing debate over executive and judicial power in wartime, to the aftermath of *Gonzales v. Raich*, to the internal debate among advocates of religious liberty over the direction of Free Exercise and Establishment Clause jurisprudence, to the scope of federal statutory preemption, the future of the exclusionary rule, and the politically and morally charged debate over capital punishment.

Nadine Strossen, the president of the American Civil Liberties Union, focuses on one example of change and uncertainty: the drift of the Court's reading of the Establishment and Free Exercise Clauses. Specifically, her article, adapted from her 2005 B. Kenneth Simon lecture at the Cato Institute, argues that the Court in the last forty years has re-interpreted the Religion Clauses in a way that renders them redundant of equal protection principles by treating religious liberty as synonymous with the right to be free from religious discrimination. As a result, the Court has muddied the bright line between church and state and obscured the content of individual First Amendment rights to freedom of conscience in ways contrary, she argues, to the intent of the Framers.

*Editor-in-Chief, *Cato Supreme Court Review*.

[1]Dahlia Lithwick, Swing Time, Slate (Jan. 17, 2006), available at http://www.slate.com/id/2134421.

Professors Martin Flaherty and John Yoo begin review of the term by focusing on a divided, important legal decision: *Hamdan v. Rumsfeld*, which struck down the Bush administration's framework for trying captured enemy combatants held in Guantanamo, Cuba. In separate articles, Yoo and Flaherty take opposing positions on the case. Professor Flaherty argues that *Hamdan*'s result, while imposing a welcome curb on presidential excess, didn't pick the right tools to do the job. Precedent, constitutional structure, and the comparative experience of other countries all argue, he contends, for a far more robust conception of legislative and judicial power in the realm of national security than the Court was willing to forthrightly acknowledge.

Professor Yoo, by contrast, argues that *Hamdan* represents an unprecedented, and dangerous, power grab by the Supreme Court. The president, he argues, has acted with restraint: The military commissions used in Guantanamo are sanctioned by Congress, tradition, and the customary laws of war and are constituted with a scope narrower than that employed by presidents in past wars. By comparison, says Yoo, the Supreme Court has acted imperially, not only ignoring clear legislative restraints on its power to hear the appeal in *Hamdan*, but also departing from a long tradition of judicial deference to presidents in wartime sanctioned by precedent, constitutional text, and structure.

Presidential power is not the only difficult fault line in the Court this term. In *Gonzales v. Oregon* and *Rapanos v. United States*, the Court struggled with the fallout from *Gonzales v. Raich*, the 2005 decision that appeared, to many commentators, to gut the Rehnquist Court's halting efforts to revive a restraining reading of the Commerce Clause. Many had hoped *Oregon* and *Rapanos* would reaffirm and extend the federalism-respecting "clear statement" rules that the Court has from time to time imposed on Congress when it acts at the edge of its constitutional power. Ilya Somin finds no evidence of any such determination on the part of the Court in either case. Moreover, he argues, even if the Court had reinvigorated clear statement rules in one of these cases, the payoffs for federalism would have been uncertain at best.

Defenders of federalism paid relatively little attention to the Court's decision in *Merrill Lynch v. Dabit*, in which it upheld federal statutory preemption of a subset of securities fraud claims under state securities laws. But, as constitutional limits on federal power recede in the wake of *Raich*, the battleground over federalism will shift to the realm of statutory interpretation. Unfortunately, the Court's preemption caselaw is applied inconsistently—a trend evident in securities regulation and corporate governance. Bucking conventional wisdom, Professor Larry Ribstein argues that the Court can promote better regulatory outcomes in the long term in the realm of corporate and securities law if it applies a stronger presumption against preemption across the board.

Balancing state autonomy and national interests are, of course, also the province of the Dormant Commerce Clause, considered this term in *DaimlerChrysler Corp. v. Cuno*, a closely-watched challenge to preferential state tax incentives for in-state investment. *Cuno* was dismissed on standing grounds, leaving the constitutional status of state tax incentives in doubt. Professor Brannon Denning argues that the narrow ruling in *Cuno* stems from the difficulty the Court has had defining when state laws impermissibly "discriminate" against out-of-state goods or out-of-state economic actors. To resolve this conundrum, he suggests the Court must reexamine the rationale behind the doctrine, which, he argues, was driven by the Framers' concerns about political disharmony caused by economic competition during the Articles of Confederation era, rather than by an ideological affinity for free trade.

Professors Allison Hayward, Dale Carpenter, and co-authors Richard Garnett and Joshua Dunlap separately examine three of the Court's high-profile First Amendment rulings. Hayward takes on the free speech challenges to campaign finance regulations in *Wisconsin Right to Life v. FEC* and *Randall v. Sorrell*. In both cases, the Court ruled in favor of the challenger. But Hayward argues that both decisions have a dark side: In each case, the Court kept within the framework of *Buckley v. Valeo*, the flawed fount of the Court's modern First Amendment law governing campaign finance regulation. Indeed, in *Randall* the Court went out of its way to explain why fidelity to *Buckley* is necessary, promoting Hayward to consider whether *Buckley* has now become a "superprecedent"—a precedent immune to overruling.

In *Rumsfeld v. FAIR*, the Supreme Court unanimously rejected a First Amendment challenge mounted by law schools against the Solomon Amendment, a law conditioning federal funding on the schools' acceptance of military recruiters on campus. Many right-leaning commentators applauded the decision. But, says Dale Carpenter, that applause is misplaced. In *FAIR*, the Supreme Court weakened key free-speech restraints on government power defended by many right-of-center commentators, including the compelled speech doctrine and the right of expressive association recognized in *Boy Scouts of America v. Dale*.

Richard Garnett and Joshua Dunlap consider what they call a deceptive "mid term sleeper": *Gonzales v. O Centro Espirita Beneficiente Uniao do Vegetal*, a unanimous decision interpreting the Religious Freedom Restoration Act. In an article that provides a though-provoking contrast to Professor Strossen's, Garnett and Dunlap argue that *O Centro* is worth our attention because it marks the definitive emergence of a consensus on the Court that the Constitution allows—even invites—governments to ease the burdens on religious exercise that a neutral official can impose. *O Centro*, they argue, therefore decisively puts to rest the notion that legislative religious accommodations unconstitutionally privilege, endorse, or establish religion.

In the realm of criminal law, the Court created confusion in two areas: First, by throwing doubt on the scope of the exclusionary rule in *Hudson v. Michigan*, and, second, by opening lethal injection to a wave of new Eighth Amendment challenges in *Hill v. McDonough*. Professor David Moran, who argued *Hudson v. Michigan* before the Court, surveys the term's Fourth Amendment cases with a special focus on *Hudson*. He shows how the Court's opinion in that case calls into question the entire rationale of the exclusionary rule, not just in the knock-and-announce context before the Court in *Hudson*, but in all types of Fourth Amendment violations.

Next, criminal procedure guru Douglas Berman dissects *Hill v. McDonough*, in which the Court considered whether the federal constitutional tort statute, 42 U.S.C. § 1983, may be used to challenge a state's method of execution. Because the Court has previously decided this question in the affirmative, the Court's cert. grant seems like a waste of time. But, argues Berman, the Court's cert. grant and ruling in *Hill* yield two benefits: (1) the cert. grant triggered greater scrutiny of the particulars of lethal injection protocols, while (2) the narrow ruling gave state political branches space to deliberate about capital punishment generally. As such, Berman suggests, *Hill* is an example of what Alexander Bickel called the Court's "passive virtues"—its ability to use appellate procedure to provoke legislative deliberation about a politically and morally contested issue.

Turning to regulatory law, Professor Joshua Wright explores the Court's missed opportunity in *Illinois Tool Works Inc. v. Independent Ink, Inc.* There, the Court rejected a presumption of antitrust market power in patent tying cases, eliminating threat of unnecessary liability hanging over firms that invest in intellectual property. The economic logic underlying the Court's result, says Wright, also suggests that price discrimination does not imply antitrust market power and, by itself, does not threaten consumer welfare. By failing to squarely address the economic logic behind its decision, the Court missed a tailor-made opportunity to end the misguided view that price discrimination is anticompetitive.

Finally, Professor Peter Bowman Rutledge examines the coming Supreme Court term, in light of the voting trends revealed in the term just ended. Rutledge focuses on five areas that will be hotly litigated next term—constitutional limits on punitive damages, equal protection implications of affirmative action in public high schools, partial birth abortion, criminal procedure, and environmental law. He examines what the decisions on the Court's docket in each these areas may reveal about the changing dynamics of the new Roberts Court.

A round of heartfelt thanks are in order. First, and foremost, thanks go to Marla Kanemitsu, my miraculous, long suffering partner, who generously donated her time and sage advice to this edition of the *Review*. Without her, this *Review* would not have been completed.[2] Second, thanks to Anne Marie Dao, my research assistant, and to interns Michael Shiba, Alex Harris, Andrew Perraut, and Kari DiPalma.

We hope you enjoy the fifth volume of the *Cato Supreme Court Review*.

---

[2]"Love is too weak a word for what I feel—I luuurve you, you know, I loave you, I luff you, two F's ... " Woody Allen & Marshall Brinkman, Annie Hall (United Artists 1977).

Religion and the Constitution: A Libertarian Perspective

*Nadine Strossen**

I. Introduction

I am so honored to deliver this lecture, named after a generous supporter of individual liberty, B. Kenneth Simon. Roger Pilon, who holds the chair in constitutional studies that Ken Simon so generously endowed, has told me about Ken's inspiring commitment to the Constitution and the ideals of the Founders. Ken was an entrepreneur, but he also devoted much time to studying issues of constitutional law and history. In Roger's words, Ken had a "life-long love" for those topics. And thanks to his generosity that love is bearing fruit today.

It is also an honor to follow in the footsteps of my distinguished predecessors in this lecture series, including Chief Judge Douglas Ginsburg of the U.S. Court of Appeals for the D.C. Circuit, who is gracing us with his presence today. Along with the Cato Institute, the ACLU is strictly non-partisan. We neutrally advocate civil liberties principles. Therefore, I applaud and thank Roger for inviting libertarians with diverse ideological views to deliver the Simon Lecture.

Of course, even those of us who agree on basic libertarian principles do not necessarily agree on how they apply in particular contexts. That is why I have entitled my presentation, *A Libertarian Perspective on Religion and the Constitution.* I fully realize that no two thinking libertarians are likely to agree on the whole range of complex issues involved.

*Professor of Law, New York Law School; President, American Civil Liberties Union. For assistance with the footnotes for this piece, Professor Strossen gratefully acknowledges her chief aide, Steven C. Cunningham (NYLS '99), and her assistant, Danica Rue (NYLS '09); they bear most of the responsibility, as well as the credit, for most of the footnotes.

A. Definition of a Libertarian

Before going any further, I should make some observations about that key term, "libertarian." I have always thought of myself as both a libertarian and a civil libertarian. Accordingly, I will usually use these terms interchangeably throughout this presentation. Before preparing this lecture, though, I was curious to see if the dictionary definitions of both terms corresponded with my own, largely overlapping, concepts. In fact, the dictionary definitions of both terms are quite similar,[1] but they do correctly note that civil libertarians are not necessarily fiscal libertarians.[2]

My favorite definitions of these terms came from *Libertarian Lexicon*, published by Jacob's Libertarian Press. Here at the Cato Institute, you should all be proud of Jacob's definition of "Libertarian Establishment": "The body of 'mainstream' libertarian thought, as expounded by the Cato Institute and the Reason Public Policy Institute."[3] Correspondingly, here is Jacob's definition of "left-libertarian," which it describes as synonymous with "civil libertarian": "a libertarian who thinks the ACLU is a good thing."[4] Since Roger often calls himself a "classical liberal," I was amused by Jacob's definition of that term: "a libertarian who does not like being called a libertarian."[5]

B. Despite Shared Core Values, Libertarians May Well Disagree about Enforcing Them in the Context of Religion

Even though all of us libertarians and civil libertarians share core commitments to maximizing individual freedom and minimizing government power, it is not at all clear how those commitments play out when it comes to construing the Constitution's provisions concerning religion, which are far from self-explanatory. Certainly,

---

[1] See, e.g., Webster's Third New International Dictionary 1303 (1986) ("Libertarian: 1. An advocate of the doctrine of free will; 2. One who upholds the principles of liberty. . . ."); *id.* at 412 ("Civil Libertarian: one who upholds the principles of civil liberty; *esp.*: one who defends civil liberties against invasion.").

[2] "Libertarianism," at www.answers.com/topic/libertarianism (accessed June 8, 2006).

[3] Jacob Halbrooks, A Libertarian Lexicon (2001), available at www.geocities.com/libertarian_press/lexicon.html (accessed June 7, 2006).

[4] *Id.*

[5] *Id.*

among ACLU leaders, we have had some heated debates and dissent about particular issues and cases in this broad area of religious liberty, and I always consider such vigorous discussion positive. No issue should be treated in a reflexive fashion, and that is particularly true of issues in this highly sensitive area. Roger has told me that Cato has not often waded into this area, and the last time Cato filed a Supreme Court brief in a religion case, it was a close call as to what position that brief would advocate.[6]

Among other difficulties, the First Amendment's two Religion Clauses are at least occasionally in tension with each other. Therefore, if we enforced either provision to its logical extreme, that would violate the other one. Since I will be focusing on those two clauses, let me remind you of their exact language: "Congress shall make no law respecting an establishment of religion, or prohibiting the free exercise thereof."[7]

If we read the Establishment Clause as barring *any* government support for religion, including even police and fire protection, then that would at least arguably violate the Free Exercise Clause, because it would discriminatorily disfavor religious individuals and institutions, denying them essential public services that government provides for everyone else. Conversely, if we read the Free Exercise Clause as barring *any* government regulation of religion, including even regulation that is necessary to protect public safety, then that would at least arguably violate the Establishment Clause, because it would discriminatorily favor religious individuals and institutions, exempting them from obligations that government imposes on everyone else. However, if neither clause should be read to its logical extreme, that means we must engage in the always difficult process of line-drawing. This line-drawing process is especially difficult given government's growing role, with increasing government regulation and increasing government funding of formerly private undertakings.

Libertarians should agree about the general, bottom-line principle at stake: that government regulatory and funding programs must

---

[6] Roger was referring to the brief that the Cato Institute filed in *Locke v. Davey*, 540 U.S. 712 (2004). See Brief of the Institute for Justice, et al. as Amici Curiae in Support of Respondent, Locke v. Davey, 540 U.S. 712 (2004) (No. 02-1315).

[7] U.S. Const. amend. I.

not constrain or channel individual choices regarding religion and conscience. However, we may disagree about how to honor that principle in the context of particular government programs. In other words, we may well disagree about whether particular government programs do in fact constrain or channel individual religious or conscientious choices.

I will cite two specific recent cases to illustrate diverging libertarian views about how the general principles at stake apply to particular factual circumstances. The ACLU opposed the Cleveland, Ohio, school voucher program that the Supreme Court narrowly upheld in 2002 precisely because we concluded that this program, in effect, steered individual students and parents toward certain parochial schools. In contrast, the Cato Institute—and five justices—disagreed with that assessment.[8] Conversely, the Cato Institute opposed a Washington State scholarship program, which the Supreme Court upheld in 2004,[9] because that program did not fund students who were studying for the ministry. Cato argued that this program, in effect, steered individual students away from certain theology majors. In contrast, the ACLU—and seven justices—disagreed with that assessment.

The challenging line-drawing process that is required to enforce both of the First Amendment Religion Clauses has led to increasingly fractured Supreme Court decisions. Consider the Court's most recent pronouncements on point: its two decisions concerning government-sponsored Ten Commandments displays, issued in June 2005—one of which was an ACLU case, I should note.[10] In those rulings, the justices issued a total of ten separate opinions (one for each Commandment?).[11] As then-Chief Justice Rehnquist quipped, after he

---

[8] Zelman v. Simmons-Harris, 536 U.S. 639 (2002).

[9] Locke, 540 U.S. 712.

[10] Van Orden v. Perry, 125 S. Ct. 2854 (2005); McCreary County v. ACLU of Ky., 125 S. Ct. 2722 (2005).

[11] Van Orden v. Perry, 125 S. Ct. 2854 (2005) (Rehnquist, C.J., announcing the judgment of the Court and delivering an opinion, in which Scalia, Kennedy, and Thomas, JJ., join. Scalia, J., and Thomas, J., filing concurring opinions. Breyer, J., filing an opinion concurring in the judgment. Stevens, J., filing a dissenting opinion, in which Ginsburg, J., joins. O'Connor, J., filing a dissenting opinion. Souter, J., filing a dissenting opinion in which Stevens and Ginsburg, JJ., join); McCreary County v. ACLU of Ky., 125 S. Ct. 2722 (2005) (Souter, J., delivering the opinion of the Court, in which Stevens, O'Connor, Ginsburg, and Breyer, JJ., join. O'Connor, J., filing a concurring opinion. Scalia, J., filing a dissenting opinion, in which Rehnquist, C.J., and Thomas, J., join, and in which Kennedy, J., joins as to Parts II and III).

had announced the rulings from the bench: "I didn't know we had that many people on our court."[12]

C. We Must Clearly Address These Issues to Dispel the Prevalent Misunderstandings

Given the current turmoil in this crucial area of constitutional law, we libertarians must address these issues in a clear and comprehensible way. This challenging task is more urgent than ever because these issues are becoming increasingly dominant and divisive in our politics and culture, and because the constitutional principles and libertarian perspectives are so widely misunderstood—a misunderstanding that results in substantial part from demagogic distortion by too many politicians and pundits.

As for the increasing importance of the issues, I can cite the proliferating controversies all over the country that involve contested interactions between government and religion. Recent headline-grabbing examples include: the Terry Schiavo case;[13] reports about religious indoctrination and harassment at the U.S. Air Force Academy;[14] controversies about the availability of emergency contraception, widely known as the "morning after pill;"[15] steeply increased penalties for, and self-censorship of, broadcast material that the FCC might deem "indecent" or "profane," in response to pressure from certain influential religious conservatives; [16] and efforts to restrict

[12] Linda Greenhouse, The Supreme Court: Overview; Justices Allow a Commandments Display, Bar Others, N.Y. Times, June 28, 2005, at A1.

[13] Abby Goodnough, The Schiavo Case: The Overview; U.S. Judge Hears Tense Testimony in Schiavo's Case, N.Y. Times, March 22, 2005, at A1.

[14] Robert Weller, Religious Prejudice Cited at Academy, Albany Times Union, June 23, 2005, at A6; Robert Weller, Air Force Academy Releases New Guidelines that Discourage, but Don't Ban, Prayer, Baton Rouge Advocate, August 13, 2005, at 12; Air Force Academy Guidelines (August 2005), at www.af.mil/library/guidelines2005.pdf (accessed June 6, 2006); Revised Interim Guidelines (February 9, 2006), at www.af.mil/library/guidelines.pdf (accessed June 11, 2006).

[15] Gardiner Harris, U.S. Again Delays Decision on Sale of Next-Day Pill, N.Y. Times, August 27, 2005, at A1; Editorial, Morning After in America, L.A. Times, March 26, 2006, at 4; Gardiner Harris, F.D.A. Gains Accord on Wider Sales of Next-Day Pill, N.Y. Times, August 9, 2006, at A13.

[16] Senate Passes Indecency Bill, Sends it to House (Public Broadcasting Report May 26, 2006) (transcript on file with author); Bill Carter, WB, Worried About Drawing Federal Fines, Censors Itself, N.Y. Times, March 23, 2006, at E1.

the teaching of evolution and promote the teaching of "Intelligent Design" in public schools.[17]

As for the misunderstanding and distortion that mar debates in this area, I can cite as all-too-typical the widespread mischaracterization of the Supreme Court's two recent Ten Commandments rulings. Just three days after the decisions were handed down, for example, Congressman Ernest Istook held a press conference to announce his proposed constitutional amendment,[18] co-sponsored by more than 100 members of Congress, to reverse one of these rulings as well as other Supreme Court decisions concerning the relationship between religion and government.[19] Istook's rationale for the amendment reflects basic misconceptions about how the Court actually ruled in those cases. In particular, he said that "the courts are using the First Amendment to attack religion,"[20] a view shared by too many politicians as well as members of the public and the press. That view reflects the familiar but false assumption that strong enforcement of the First Amendment's Establishment Clause is somehow hostile to religion.[21] Yet, as the Court consistently explains when striking down a measure under the Establishment Clause, the clause is designed to *protect* religion and religious liberty,[22] which is why many devout

---

[17] Brenda Goodman, Teaching the Bible in Georgia's Public Schools, N.Y. Times, March 29, 2006, at B7; Kirk Johnson, Evolution Measure Splits State Legislators in Utah, N.Y. Times, February 5, 2006, at 18; Laurie Goodstein, Schools Nationwide Study Impact of Evolution Ruling, N.Y. Times, December 22, 2005, at A20; Michael Powell, Judge Rules Against Intelligent Design, Wash. Post, Dec. 21, 2005, at A3.

[18] News Release, Istook Heads Coalition to Protect Public Displays of Religious Expression (June 30, 2005), available at www.house.gov/istook/religiousfreedom/documents/rel_063005.pdf (accessed June 11, 2006) (hereinafter Istook News Release).

[19] Religious Protection Amendment, H.J. Res. 57, 109th Cong., 1st Sess. (2005).

[20] Istook News Release, *supra* note 18.

[21] See, e.g., McCreary County v. ACLU of Ky., 125 S. Ct. 2722, 2757 (2005) (Scalia, J., dissenting) (describing the majority opinion, striking down a government-sponsored courthouse display of the Ten Commandments, as "ratchet[ing] up the Court's hostility to religion").

[22] *Id.* at 2746–47 (O'Connor, J., concurring) ("When we enforce [the Establishment Clause], we do so for the same reason that guided the Framers—respect for religion's special role in society. . . . Voluntary religious belief and expression may be as threatened when government takes the mantle of religion upon itself as when government directly interferes with private religious practices.").

believers and religious leaders ardently advocate strong separation between government and religion.[23]

Congressman Istook's false charge that the Supreme Court has been attacking religion overlooks both the Court's many rulings that uphold and enforce the Free Exercise Clause[24] and its rulings that enforce statutes protecting religious freedom, such as the Religious Land Use and Institutionalized Persons Act (RLUIPA).[25] Only a month before the Supreme Court's recent Ten Commandments decisions, for example, the Court ruled unanimously that RLUIPA was constitutional. In that case, *Cutter v. Wilkinson,*[26] the Court held that RLUIPA was an appropriate accommodation of the religious freedom rights of prisoners and other institutionalized persons, rejecting a claim that it violated the Establishment Clause. Unfortunately, that overtly pro-religion ruling received far less attention from politicians and the press than the Ten Commandments decisions, which were too often wrongly portrayed or perceived as anti-religion. But while *Cutter* was being ignored by Congressman Istook and his allies, other critics of the Court[27] were complaining that the Court was too *protective* of religion in *Cutter* and in many other cases under the Free Exercise Clause.[28]

The general misunderstanding about the courts' alleged "attacks" on religion is also reflected in many specific misstatements about religious activities that the Supreme Court purportedly has outlawed, when in fact it has done no such thing. To illustrate this

---

[23] See Nadine Strossen, Religion and Politics: A Reply to Justice Antonin Scalia, 24 Fordham Urb. L.J. 427, 448 (1997).

[24] See, e.g., Church of the Lukumi Babalu Aye, Inc. v. Hialeah, 508 U.S. 520 (1993).

[25] 42 U.S.C. §§ 2000cc et seq.

[26] 544 U.S. 709 (2005).

[27] A prominent example is Marci Hamilton, God vs. the Gavel (2005).

[28] See, e.g., City of Boerne v. Flores, 521 U.S. 507, 536–37 (1997) (Stevens, J., concurring); Philip B. Kurland, Religion and the Law (1962); Frederick Mark Gedicks, An Unfirm Foundation: The Regrettable Indefensibility of Religious Exemptions, 20 U. Ark. Little Rock L.J. 555 (1998); Christopher L. Eisgruber & Lawrence G. Sager, The Vulnerability of Conscience: The Constitutional Basis for Protecting Religious Conduct, 61 U. Chi. L. Rev. 1245, 1315 (1994); Steven G. Gey, Why Is Religion Special?: Reconsidering the Accommodation of Religion Under the Religion Clauses of the First Amendment, 52 U. Pitt. L. Rev. 75 (1990).

widespread pattern, including among policymakers, let me again cite Congressman Istook. In advocating his proposed constitutional amendment, he said that it "will protect the ability [of] schoolchildren to pray at school, individually or together."[29] But no constitutional amendment is needed for that purpose. The Supreme Court has consistently upheld the rights of students to pray at school, either alone or in groups.[30] In fact, student-initiated Bible clubs are flourishing at schools all over the country.[31]

It is also noteworthy that the many Supreme Court decisions and other legal developments that overtly protect religion and religious liberty have all been championed by civil libertarians as well as courts. For example, the religious liberty statute that the Court upheld in *Cutter* was spearheaded in Congress and defended in the courts by both the ACLU and Americans United for Separation of Church and State.[32] Yet, in many circles, both organizations are far better known for staunchly defending the Establishment Clause than for equally staunchly defending the Free Exercise Clause.

In addition to the Istook constitutional amendment, many other policy initiatives are premised on similar misunderstandings about what the courts actually have held concerning religion. Therefore, for a rational policymaking process in this crucial area, it is essential to dispel those misunderstandings and, to get beyond the rhetoric and the pandering, to examine the actual judicial rulings and the underlying constitutional principles. The ACLU is so concerned about these growing controversies and associated misunderstandings that we recently launched a new "Program on Freedom of

[29] Istook News Release, *supra* note 18.

[30] See, e.g., Board of Education of Westside Community Schools v. Mergens, 496 U.S. 226 (1990); Widmar v. Vincent, 454 U.S. 263 (1981).

[31] Court Ruling Has Been "Good News" For School Bible Clubs, Religionlink (August 26, 2002), at www.religionlink.org/tip_020826a.php (accessed June 7, 2006).

[32] Brief of Americans United for Separation of Church and State et al. as Amici Curiae Supporting Petitioners, Cutter v. Wilkinson, 544 U.S. 709 (2005) (No. 03-9877) ("Amici served as active members of a broad coalition of religious, civil-rights, labor, and other organizations that advocated for the Religious Land Use and Institutionalized Persons Act ('RLUIPA'). Thus, amici have a significant interest in having this Court reject respondents' facial challenge to the constitutionality of Section 3 of RLUIPA.").

Religion and Belief" to coordinate our many efforts in this area.[33] In particular, we aim to complement our traditional litigation and legislation strategies with efforts to communicate more clearly and effectively to the public and the media. The director of this new initiative, Dr. Jeremy Gunn, is not only a lawyer but also a theologian.[34] Thus, I welcome this opportunity today to address this important audience as part of the ACLU's more general outreach effort.

For all those on the so-called Religious Right who demonize the ACLU as the "Anti-Christian Litigation Union," to quote some fundraising letters I have seen,[35] I urge you to read Cardozo Law School Professor Marci Hamilton's recent book, *God vs. the Gavel*,[36] which criticizes the ACLU for what she contends is our excessive defense of the rights of Christians and other religious believers.[37] Actually, I am quite fond of collecting various twists that ACLU critics have given to our acronym, ranging from "All Criminals Love Us," to "Always Causing Legal Unrest." My own personal favorite is: "Aw, C'mon, Lighten Up!"

My favorite story about a politician unfairly attacking the ACLU's positions concerning religion arose from a Pawtucket, Rhode Island, case that led ultimately to an important 1984 Supreme Court decision.[38] Our clients had complained that the city's nativity scene included, to quote the Court's opinion, "a Santa Claus house, reindeer pulling Santa's sleigh, candy-striped poles, a Christmas tree, carolers, . . . a clown, an elephant, and a teddy bear."[39] (No wonder

---

[33] Dr. Jeremy Gunn, Expert on Religious Freedom, to Lead New ACLU Program on Freedom of Religion and Belief (July 14, 2005), available at www.aclu.org/about/staff/20074prs20050714.html (accessed June 7, 2006).

[34] *Id.*

[35] The "Anti-Christian Liberties" Union (ACLU), Traditional Values Coalition Special Report, at www.traditionalvalues.org/pdf_files/ACLU.pdf (accessed June 8, 2006); ACLU vs. America: Exposing the Agenda to Redefine Moral Values, available at www.acluvsamerica.com/main/default.aspx (quoting D. James Kennedy, Coral Ridge Ministries) (accessed June 8, 2006); Charles R. Hosler, ACLU: Anti-Christian Litigation Union, The North Carolina Conservative (August 9, 2005), available at www. northcarolinaconversative.com/archives.php?subaction = showfull&id = 1123596165 &archive = 1123598799&start_from = &ucat = & (accessed June 8, 2006).

[36] Marci Hamilton, God vs. the Gavel, *supra* note 27.

[37] *Id.* at 180.

[38] Lynch v. Donnelly, 465 U.S. 668 (1984).

[39] *Id.* at 671.

some sincere Christians considered this display to be degrading to their beliefs![40]) In attacking the ACLU and our clients, the Pawtucket mayor at least showed some humor. Jealousy motivated us, he said: "They don't have three Wise Men and a virgin in their whole organization."[41]

D. Two Major Aspects of My Libertarian Perspective: Summary

Against that political background, let me now discuss two major aspects of my libertarian perspective on religion and the Constitution. First, I will critique a general pattern in the Supreme Court's recent jurisprudence concerning both Religion Clauses, which unjustifiably saps them of their libertarian force, substituting instead only a weakened egalitarian protection. Second, and interrelatedly, I will explain why strong enforcement of both Religion Clauses promotes religious liberty and freedom of conscience.

II. The Supreme Court's Substitution of Weak Egalitarianism for Strong Libertarianism as a General Pattern in Several Areas of Constitutional Law

In recent years, the Court has radically revised both Religion Clauses through the same general approach. It has devalued the central libertarian concern of each clause and instead has over-emphasized peripheral egalitarian concerns. In this important

---

[40] *Id.* at 711–12 (Brennan, J., dissenting) ("To suggest, as the Court does, that [the creche] is merely 'traditional' and therefore no different from Santa's house or reindeer is not only offensive to those for whom the creche has profound significance, but insulting to those who insist for religious or personal reasons that the story of Christ is in no sense a part of 'history' nor an unavoidable element of our national heritage."); *id.* at 727 (Blackmun, J., dissenting) ("The creche has been relegated to the role of a neutral harbinger of the holiday season, useful for commercial purposes, but devoid of any inherent meaning and incapable of enhancing the religious tenor of a display. . . . The import of the Court's decision is to encourage use of the creche in a municipally sponsored display, a setting where Christians feel constrained in acknowledging its symbolic meaning. . . .").

[41] Editorial, Short Circuits, Boston Globe, December 12, 1982 (no page number available).

respect, the Court's Religion Clause jurisprudence parallels its rulings concerning two other key constitutional rights that I have examined in a prior article:[42] rights protected by the Fourth Amendment[43] and by the First Amendment's Free Speech Clause.[44] I will briefly outline the Court's regressive rulings in those other areas too since they shed light on the similar trends concerning the Religion Clauses.

A. The Modern Court Previously Enforced Absolute Liberties in Those Areas

In all of those areas, the modern Court previously enforced a certain absolute baseline of liberty for everyone, subject to only narrow exceptions, such as when the government can show that a restriction satisfies "strict scrutiny" because it advances a compelling governmental interest by narrowly tailored means.[45] Under the Fourth Amendment, prior to the Rehnquist Court's revisionism, the modern Court enforced our right to be free from searches and seizures absent individualized suspicion.[46] Under the First Amendment's Free Speech Clause, invoking the "public forum doctrine," the Court enforced our right to engage in expressive activities on public property that was physically compatible with such activities.[47] Under the Free Exercise Clause, the Court enforced our right

[42] Nadine Strossen, Michigan Department of State Police v. Sitz: A Roadblock to Meaningful Judicial Enforcement of Constitutional Rights, 42 Hastings L.J. 285 (1991).

[43] U.S. Const. amend. IV ("The right of the people to be secure in their persons, houses, papers, and effects, against unreasonable searches and seizures, shall not be violated, and no Warrants shall issue, but upon probable cause, supported by Oath or affirmation, and particularly describing the place to be searched, and the persons or things to be seized.").

[44] U.S. Const. amend. I ("Congress shall make no law . . . abridging the freedom of speech.").

[45] Erwin Chemerinsky, Constitutional Law 673 (3d ed. 2006).

[46] See, e.g., Florida v. Royer, 460 U.S. 491, 498 (1983); United States v. Ortiz, 422 U.S. 891, 896 (1975) ("To protect . . . privacy from official arbitrariness, the Court always has regarded probable cause as the minimum requirement for a lawful search"); Terry v. Ohio, 392 U.S. 1 (1968); Carroll v. United States, 267 U.S. 132, 161 (1925) (according to the classic definition, probable cause exists "[i]f the facts and circumstances before the officer are such as to warrant a man of prudence and caution in believing that the offense has been committed" by the individual who is the subject of the search or seizure).

[47] See, e.g., Southeastern Promotions, Ltd. v. Conrad, 420 U.S. 546 (1976); Grayned v. Rockford, 408 U.S. 104 (1972); Police Department of Chicago v. Mosley, 408 U.S. 92 (1972); Hague v. CIO, 307 U.S. 496 (1939).

to be free from government regulations that substantially burden our religious beliefs or practices.[48] Finally, under the Establishment Clause, the Court enforced our right to be free from government funding of religious institutions.[49]

I will now interject one explanatory comment about the Establishment Clause, and how it fits into this general scheme. Unlike the other constitutional provisions just cited, the Establishment Clause is not expressly phrased in terms of individual freedom. But a central objective of the clause, including its long-enforced ban on government financing of religion, is to protect individual religious liberty and freedom of conscience. Indeed, experts maintain that protecting liberty of conscience was the central objective of both the Establishment Clause itself and its core no-funding principle.[50] That conclusion is espoused, for instance, by N.Y.U. law professor and intellectual historian Noah Feldman in his recent book on church-state issues.[51]

Even before the First Amendment was added to the Constitution, the original unamended Constitution contained one reference to religion, and it too protected freedom of conscience. Article VI, Clause 3 provides that "no religious Test shall ever be required as a Qualification for any Office or public Trust under the United States." Significantly, that provision made religious beliefs, or the lack thereof, completely irrelevant to full and equal participation in the political process. This is especially remarkable, since the Constitution did not make race similarly irrelevant until almost a century

---

[48] See, e.g., Sherbert v. Verner, 374 U.S. 398 (1963).

[49] See, e.g., Roemer v. Board of Public Works of Md., 426 U.S. 736 (1976); Hunt v. McNair, 413 U.S. 734 (1973); Levitt v. Committee for Public Education & Religious Liberty, 413 U.S. 472 (1973); Tilton v. Richardson, 403 U.S. 672 (1971); Lemon v. Kurtzman, 403 U.S. 602 (1971); Board of Education of Central School Dist. No. 1 v. Allen, 392 U.S. 236 (1968); Everson v. Board of Education of Ewing, 330 U.S. 1 (1947).

[50] Zelman v. Simmons-Harris, 536 U.S. 639, 710 (2002) (Souter, J., dissenting).

[51] Noah Feldman, Divided by God: America's Church and State Problem—and What We Can Do About It 49, 50 (2005).

later, after the Civil War,[52] and it did not make gender similarly irrelevant until well into the twentieth century.[53] Our Constitution's initial explicit protection for freedom of belief reflects the Framers' view, strongly influenced by John Locke, that government simply had no legitimate power in this sphere.[54]

Bearing in mind the Establishment Clause's role as a guarantor of individual freedom of conscience, I will now return to the four absolute libertarian precepts the modern Court previously enforced under the Establishment Clause, the Free Exercise Clause, and the two other constitutional provisions I cited. In addition to those four libertarian precepts, the Court also enforced a corollary right to be free from discrimination in exercising those freedoms, which the Equal Protection Clause[55] already guarantees. For example, under the Free Exercise Clause, the Court enforced not only our absolute libertarian right to be free from government regulations that substantially burden our religious beliefs (regardless of whether other religious beliefs are similarly burdened), but also our egalitarian right to be free from government regulations that discriminatorily single out and burden our particular religious beliefs. Then, about two decades ago, around the time that William Rehnquist became chief justice (in 1986), the Court began to overlook the absolute libertarian core of those constitutional rights and to enforce instead only their egalitarian corollaries. Moreover, the Court has enforced only a formal concept of equality that does not provide meaningful protection against actual discrimination in the exercise of constitutional rights. Because the Equal Protection Clause already guarantees de jure equality in the exercise of rights, this reading of specific Bill of Rights guarantees deprives them of independent significance.[56] The result, in terms of our liberties, is equal *non*-protection.

[52]See, e.g., U.S. Const. amend. XV (ratified 1870) ("The right of citizens of the United States to vote shall not be denied or abridged by the United States or by any State on account of race, color, or previous condition of servitude.").

[53]See, e.g., U.S. Const. amend XIX (ratified 1920) ("The right of citizens of the United States to vote shall not be denied or abridged by the United States or by any State on account of sex.").

[54]Feldman, *supra* note 51, at 30.

[55]U.S. Const. amend. XIV ("No State shall . . . deny to any person within its jurisdiction the equal protection of the laws.").

[56]See Hobbie v. Unemployment Appeals Commission, 480 U.S. 136, 141–42 (1987) (rejecting argument that free exercise claims should be subject to rational basis review). *Hobbie* held that "[s]uch a test . . . relegates a serious First Amendment value to the

B. The Court's Reductionist Revision of the Fourth Amendment Illustrates the Trend

In my past writings I have described this rights-reducing pattern most fully concerning the Fourth Amendment's protection against searches and seizures lacking individualized suspicion.[57] I will comment briefly about that Fourth Amendment devolution now, since it sets the stage well for considering the parallel pattern concerning the other rights at issue, including the rights guaranteed by the First Amendment's Religion Clauses.

The Supreme Court first upheld suspicionless searches for criminal law enforcement purposes in 1990, in a radical break from both its longstanding precedents and the Fourth Amendment's intent. In *Michigan Department of State Police v. Sitz*,[58] the Court upheld mass suspicionless searches at "drunk driving roadblocks," stressing that those searches were conducted in a uniform, non-discriminatory fashion. That holding has become the constitutional cornerstone for the proliferating forms of mass searches and seizures to which we are all being subjected,[59] including, beginning in the summer of 2005, in mass transit systems.[60] So long as we are all equally subject to

barest level of minimal scrutiny that the Equal Protection Clause already provides." *Id.* at 141; see also Petition for Rehearing at 11–12, Employment Div. v. Smith, 494 U.S. 872 (1990), reh'g denied, 496 U.S. 913 (1990) (Court's reinterpretation of Free Exercise Clause "drastically restricts [its] meaning . . ., making it a stepchild of the . . . Equal Protection Clause.").

[57] See generally Strossen, *supra* note 42.

[58] 496 U.S. 444 (1990).

[59] See, e.g., A Threat to Student Privacy, N.Y. Times, July 4, 1999, at 10; Linda Greenhouse, Justices Question Georgia Law Requiring Drug Tests for State Candidates, N.Y. Times, January 15, 1997, at A15; ACLU Challenges Detroit Police Over Mass Searches of Public School Students (June 10, 2004), at www.aclu.org/studentsrights/gen/12843prs20040610.html (accessed June 7, 2006).

[60] The ACLU's state-based affiliate in New York, the New York Civil Liberties Union, promptly brought a constitutional challenge to the mass suspicionless searches of New York City subway passengers that were initiated in July 2005. Among other problems, these searches are more intrusive and coercive than other forms of suspicionless searches that the Supreme Court has upheld, including at drunk driving roadblocks. MacWade v. Kelly, No. 05CIV6921RMBFM, 2005 WL 3338573 (S.D.N.Y. Dec. 7, 2005); Alan Feur, Appeals Court Upholds Random Police Searches of Passengers' Bags on Subways, N.Y. Times, August 12, 2006, at B5 ("the ACLU argued that the searches were too infrequent and haphazard to be effective and violated the Fourth Amendment's provision against unreasonable searches and seizures without a specific cause").

government invasions of our privacy, we are told, it does not matter that those invasions are unjustified, based on no individualized suspicion of any wrongdoing.[61]

The first time the Court even suggested that such mass suspicion-less searches and seizures might be constitutional was in 1979, in dicta in *Delaware v. Prouse*.[62] The Court's actual *holding* in *Prouse* was that the Fourth Amendment does bar a suspicionless search of an *individual* motorist.[63] However, the Court noted in dicta that the Fourth Amendment might permit *mass* suspicionless searches of *all* motorists.[64] Then-Justice Rehnquist disagreed with the majority's striking-down of the single suspicionless search at issue in *Prouse*.[65] He also mocked the majority's suggestion that an otherwise-*un*constitutional search could somehow be transformed into a *constitutional* search by being multiplied on a mass scale. To quote his acerbic observation: "The Court . . . elevates the adage 'misery loves company' to a novel role in Fourth Amendment jurisprudence.'"[66] Ironically, under Rehnquist's ideological leadership as chief justice, the Court elevated that adage to an even more exalted status, applying it not only to the Fourth Amendment, but also to other Bill of Rights guarantees, including the First Amendment's twin Religion Clauses.

---

[61] See, e.g., Illinois v. Caballes, 543 U.S. 405 (2005) (upholding use of drug-sniffing dog where lawful traffic stop was not extended beyond time necessary to issue warning ticket and to conduct ordinary inquiries incident to such a stop); Hiibel v. Sixth Judicial District Court of Nevada, 542 U.S. 177 (2004) (holding that arrest of *Terry* stop suspect for refusal to identify himself, in violation of Nevada law, did not violate Fourth Amendment); Board of Education v. Earls, 536 U.S. 822 (2002) (holding that policy requiring all students who participated in competitive extracurricular activities to submit to suspicionless urinalysis drug testing did not violate Fourth Amendment); Vernonia School District 47J v. Acton, 515 U.S. 646 (1995) (holding that policy requiring student intermural athletes to submit to suspicionless urinalysis drug testing did not violate Fourth Amendment); but see Ferguson v. City of Charleston, 532 U.S. 67 (2001) (holding that hospital's reporting results of urinalysis drug tests of pregnant welfare recipients to police violate Fourth Amendment); City of Indianapolis v. Edmond, 531 U.S. 32 (2000) (holding that city's drug interdiction checkpoints for cars, using drug-sniffing dogs, violate Fourth Amendment); Chandler v. Miller, 520 U.S. 305 (1997) (holding that Georgia's requirement that candidates for state office pass urinalysis drug test violates Fourth Amendment).

[62] 440 U.S. 648 (1979).

[63] *Id.* at 663.

[64] *Id.*

[65] *Id.* at 667 (Rehnquist, J., dissenting).

[66] *Id.* at 664 (Rehnquist, J., dissenting).

C. Summary of Rights-Reducing Pattern in These Areas

I will now outline this general pattern of substituting libertarian values with egalitarian ones in four areas of the Court's jurisprudence: its rulings concerning the Fourth Amendment and the First Amendment Free Speech Clause, as well its rulings concerning the First Amendment's Religion Clauses. This repeated general pattern provides a fuller context in which I will then address in more detail the Court's reduced vision of the Religion Clauses specifically.

I can most easily summarize the parallel patterns regarding these four constitutional rights by listing for each one what I call the "libertarian proposition," the "egalitarian corollary," and the "reductionist redefinition." In each case, the "libertarian proposition" is the individual liberty that the Court previously protected, in rulings that I believe were constitutionally correct. The "egalitarian corollary" is the auxiliary guarantee that the Court has inferred from each of these constitutional provisions. I certainly have no quarrel with the Court's rulings that the liberty in question may not be denied on a discriminatory basis. But that unremarkable conclusion is independently supported by the Equal Protection Clause. Therefore, it would sap these other specific constitutional provisions of independent meaning to reduce them only to their egalitarian corollaries, rendering them merely redundant of equal protection principles. Yet that is exactly what the Court has done through what I call its "reductionist redefinitions" of the constitutional rights I am examining.

Set out below are these three stages in the Court's analysis for each of the four rights at issue. I will start with the Fourth Amendment.

Libertarian proposition: Government may *not* conduct suspicionless searches and seizures of anyone.[67]

Egalitarian corollary: Government may not *discriminatorily single out particular individuals for suspicionless searches and seizures.*[68]

Reductionist redefinition: Government *may* conduct suspicionless searches and seizures of anyone so long as it does not *discriminatorily single out particular* individuals.[69]

---

[67] See, e.g., *supra* note 46.

[68] See, e.g., Delaware v. Prouse, 440 U.S. 648 (1979).

[69] See, e.g., Michigan Dept. of State Police v. Sitz, 496 U.S. 444 (1990).

Now let us consider the same regressive pattern under the First Amendment Free Speech Clause regarding what is usually called the "public forum doctrine."[70]

Libertarian proposition: Government may *not* bar expressive activities from public property that is compatible with such activities.[71]

Egalitarian corollary: Government may not *discriminatorily bar particular* speakers or ideas from such public property.[72]

Reductionist redefinition: Government *may* bar all expressive activities from such public property so long as it does not *discriminatorily bar particular* speakers or ideas.[73]

Now consider this pattern as to the Free Exercise Clause.

Libertarian proposition: Government may *not* impose substantial burdens on sincerely held religious beliefs.[74]

---

[70] Erwin Chemerinsky, Constitutional Law 1086 (3d ed. 2006).

[71] See, e.g., United States v. Grace, 461 U.S. 171 (1983) (declaring unconstitutional a broad restriction of speech on the public sidewalks surrounding the Supreme Court's building); Brown v. Louisiana, 383 U.S. 131 (1966) (reversing the conviction of a group of African-Americans who had conducted a silent sit-in as a protest at a racially segregated public library).

[72] See, e.g., Carey v. Brown, 447 U.S. 455 (1980) (declaring unconstitutional an Illinois statute that prohibited picketing or demonstrations around a person's residence unless the dwelling is used as a place of business or is a place of employment involved in a labor dispute); Chicago v. Mosley, 408 U.S. 92 (1972) (declaring unconstitutional an ordinance that prohibited picketing or demonstrations within 150 feet of a school building while the school was in session, except for peaceful picketing in connection with a labor dispute).

[73] See, e.g., Hill v. Colorado, 530 U.S. 703 (2000) (upholding a regulation on protests outside abortion clinics based on the conclusion that the restrictions on speech were content-neutral); United States v. Kokinda, 497 U.S. 720 (1990) (upholding a restriction on solicitations on post office properties); Frisby v. Schultz, 487 U.S. 474 (1988) (sustaining an ordinance that prohibited picketing "before or about" any residence); Cornelius v. NAACP, 473 U.S. 788 (1985) (upholding a federal regulation limiting charitable solicitations of federal employees during working hours); Members of the City Council of the City of Los Angeles v. Taxpayers for Vincent, 466 U.S. 789 (1984) (upholding an ordinance that prohibited the posting of signs on public property); Greer v. Spock, 424 U.S. 828 (1976) (holding that military bases, even parts of bases usually open to the public, are nonpublic forums); Adderly v. Florida, 385 U.S. 39 (1966) (holding that the government could prohibit speech in the areas outside prisons and jails).

[74] See, e.g., Hernandez v. C.I.R., 490 U.S. 680, 699 (1989) ("The free exercise inquiry asks whether government has placed a substantial burden on the observation of a central religious belief or practice and, if so, whether a compelling governmental interest justifies the burden."); Hobbie v. Unemployment Appeals Commission, 480 U.S. 136, 141 (1987) (laws burdening religion "must be subjected to strict scrutiny

Egalitarian corollary: Government may not *discriminatorily single out particular* sincerely held religious beliefs when implementing regulations that impose substantial burdens on them.[75]

Reductionist redefinition: Government *may* impose substantial burdens on sincerely held religious beliefs so long as it does not *discriminatorily single out particular* religious beliefs.[76]

Finally, here is the devolving pattern as to the Establishment Clause.

Libertarian proposition: Government may *not* directly fund religious institutions.[77]

Egalitarian corollary: Government may not *discriminatorily single out* **religious** institutions to receive direct funding.[78]

Reductionist redefinition: Government *may* directly fund religious institutions so long as it does not *discriminatorily single out* **religious** institutions to receive such funding.[79]

Against this backdrop of the Court's general pattern, displacing the absolutist libertarian protection of rights with the relativistic, egalitarian protection, I will next examine more closely how this pattern has infected the Court's Religion Clause rulings in particular.

---

and could be justified only by proof by the State of a compelling interest"); United States v. Lee, 455 U.S. 252, 257–58 (1982) ("The state may justify a limitation on religious liberty by showing that it is essential to accomplish an overriding governmental interest."); Thomas v. Review Board, 450 U.S. 707, 718 (1981) ("The state may justify an inroad on religious liberty by showing that it is the least restrictive means of achieving some compelling state interest."); Wisconsin v. Yoder, 406 U.S. 205 (1972) (holding that free exercise of religion required that Amish parents be granted an exemption from compulsory school laws for their 14- and 15-year old children); Sherbert v. Verner, 374 U.S. 398, 406 (1963) (a generally applicable regulation can be applied to religious objector only if "some compelling state interest . . . justifies the substantial infringement of appellant's First Amendment right").

[75] See generally, Board of Education of Kiryas Joel Sch. Dist. v. Grumet, 512 U.S. 687 (1994); Hernandez v. C.I.R., 490 U.S. 680 (1989); Larson v. Valente, 456 U.S. 228 (1982).

[76] Employment Division v. Smith, 494 U.S. 872 (1990).

[77] Everson v. Board of Education of Ewing, 330 U.S. 1, 18 (1947).

[78] See Mitchell v. Helms, 530 U.S. 793, 881–84 (2000) (Souter, J., dissenting) (summarizing cases); see also Larson v. Valente, 456 U.S. 228, 246 (1982) (striking down law that "grants denominational preferences of the sort consistently and firmly deprecated in our precedents"); Everson, 330 U.S. at 15 (stating that Establishment Clause bars "laws which aid one religion" or "prefer one religion over another").

[79] Zelman v. Simmons-Harris, 536 U.S. 639 (2002); Mitchell v. Helms, 530 U.S. 793 (2000) (plurality opinion).

III. The Court's Reductionist Redefinition of the Free Exercise Clause

In the modern constitutional era, the Court had consistently accorded religious liberty the same high degree of First Amendment protection that it has granted to other First Amendment freedoms, including freedom of speech. Given the fundamental nature of all such rights, any restriction on them is presumptively unconstitutional, and government may justify any such restriction only by satisfying the heavy burden of showing that it is necessary to promote a countervailing goal of compelling importance; this is the "strict scrutiny" standard.[80] Moreover, the Court appropriately has imposed this heavy burden of proof on the government to justify any general measure that has the effect of restricting First Amendment freedoms in a particular context, even if the government did not specifically intend that rights-restricting effect.[81]

A. The Court's Prior Strong Protection of Individual Religious Liberty

In the Court's modern jurisprudence, the Free Exercise Clause was viewed as guaranteeing some absolute degree of freedom from government burdens on religious exercises, regardless of how equally or widely dispersed those burdens might be, and regardless of whether the government imposed those burdens inadvertently rather than intentionally.[82] Consistent with those fundamental First Amendment principles, throughout the modern constitutional law era, the Court required government to make exceptions to generally applicable laws that infringed on religious liberty, just as it required regarding generally applicable laws that infringed on free speech. Specifically, the Court held that if any law imposed a substantial burden on a sincerely held religious belief, the government had to make an exception to accommodate that religious belief unless it

---

[80] See generally Erwin Chemerinsky, Constitutional Law 1252 (3d ed. 2006).

[81] See, e.g., Minneapolis Star and Tribune Co. v. Minnesota Commission of Revenue, 460 U.S. 575, 592 (1983).

[82] See, e.g., Employment Division v. Smith, 494 U.S 872, 894 (1990) (O'Connor, J., concurring) ("The First Amendment . . . does not distinguish between laws that are generally applicable and laws that target particular religious practices. . . . Our free exercise cases have all concerned generally applicable laws that had the effect of significantly burdening a religious practice."); Wisconsin v. Yoder, 406 U.S. 205, 214–20 (1972); Cantwell v. Connecticut, 310 U.S. 296, 304–07 (1940).

could satisfy strict scrutiny by showing that denying the exception was necessary to promote a goal of compelling importance.[83]

A leading early case that enforced this understanding of free exercise rights was *Sherbert v. Verner*, decided in 1963.[84] *Sherbert* held that a state could not enforce one of its general requirements for receiving unemployment compensation, availability for work on Saturday, against a woman who sincerely believed that she had a religious duty not to work on Saturday, but instead to observe it as the Sabbath, a day of rest.[85] The state had not intentionally written its unemployment compensation rules to impose special burdens on Sabbatarians. Rather, the state simply had not considered Sabbatarians and the adverse impact that the Saturday work requirement would have on them.[86] The *Sherbert* Court correctly understood the Free Exercise Clause as ensuring an absolute right to freedom from any substantial burden on the exercise of one's beliefs, no matter how inadvertently the government might have imposed that burden. The government could avoid exempting the religiously burdened individual from the general legal obligation only if it could satisfy the strict scrutiny standard; in this context, the government would have to show that the exemption would prevent it from achieving an objective of compelling importance.[87] After *Sherbert*, the Court

---

[83] See, e.g., Hernandez v. C.I.R., 490 U.S. 680, 699 (1989) ("The free exercise inquiry asks whether government has placed a substantial burden on the observation of a central religious belief or practice and, if so, whether a compelling governmental interest justifies the burden."); Hobbie v. Unemployment Appeals Commission, 480 U.S. 136, 141 (1987) (laws burdening religion "must be subjected to strict scrutiny and could be justified only by proof by the State of a compelling interest"); United States v. Lee, 455 U.S. 252, 257–58 (1982) ("The state may justify a limitation on religious liberty by showing that it is essential to accomplish an overriding governmental interest."); Thomas v. Review Board, 450 U.S. 707, 718 (1981) ("The state may justify an inroad on religious liberty by showing that it is the least restrictive means of achieving some compelling state interest."); Yoder, 406 U.S. at 215 ("[O]nly those interests of the highest order and those not otherwise served can overbalance legitimate claims to the free exercise of religion."); Sherbert v. Verner, 374 U.S. 398, 406 (1963) (generally applicable regulation can be applied to religious objector only if "some compelling state interest . . . justifies the substantial infringement of appellant's First Amendment right").

[84] 374 U.S. 398 (1963).

[85] *Id.* at 403–04.

[86] *Id.* at 406–09.

[87] *Id.* at 408–09.

consistently enforced these Free Exercise Clause principles in many cases.[88]

B. The Court's Radical Revisionism: Employment Division v. Smith

In a widely criticized 1990 decision, *Employment Division v. Smith,*[89] the Rehnquist Court essentially overturned *Sherbert* and all of its progeny, thus gutting the Free Exercise Clause as a guarantor of religious liberty. The Court reduced the Free Exercise Clause to a mere shadow of the Equal Protection Clause, holding that it protects only against government measures that overtly or intentionally single out particular religious beliefs for discriminatory burdens. Under this shrunken remnant of the clause, it does not matter how burdensome the government's regulation is for how many religious observers. Nor does it matter how unnecessary that burden is in terms of advancing any government goal. Under *Smith,* you cannot even state a claim under the Free Exercise Clause—your case is summarily dismissed—unless you can show that the government deliberately discriminated against religion. It is not even enough to show that the government treated religion with reckless indifference.[90]

C. The Court's Abdication of Its Special Responsibility to Protect the Rights of Individuals and Members of Minority Groups

The *Smith* Court's sterile view of the Free Exercise Clause eliminates that clause's historical role as a safety net for members of minority religious groups, whose beliefs are the most likely to be burdened by laws enacted through our majoritarian political processes. Justice O'Connor stressed this fatal flaw in her separate opinion in *Smith,* which excoriated the majority's abandonment of longstanding Free Exercise Clause standards. As she wrote:

---

[88] See *supra* note 74.

[89] 494 U.S. 872 (1990).

[90] *Id.* at 877 ("[T]he 'exercise of religion' often involves not only belief . . . but the performance of (or abstention from) physical acts. . . . [A] state would be 'prohibiting the free exercise [of religion]' if it sought to ban such acts or abstentions only when they are engaged in for religious reasons, or only because of the religious belief that they display. . . . [I]f prohibiting the exercise of religion . . . is not the object . . . but merely the incidental effect of a generally applicable and otherwise valid provision, the First Amendment has not been offended."). *Id.* at 872 (implying that the Free Exercise Clause would prohibit only criminal law that is "specifically directed" at particular religious practice).

> [F]ew States would be so naive as to enact a law directly
> prohibiting or burdening a religious practice as such. . . . If
> the First Amendment is to have any vitality, it ought not
> be construed to cover only the extreme and hypothetical
> situation in which a State directly targets a religious
> practice.[91]

Justice O'Connor aptly concluded that *Smith*'s stunted view of the Free Exercise Clause "relegates a serious First Amendment value to the barest level of minimum scrutiny that the Equal Protection Clause already provides."[92]

The *Smith* majority opinion candidly acknowledged that, henceforth, the Free Exercise Clause would no longer secure religious liberty for adherents of minority religions. Instead, the majority relegated their freedom to the good will of legislative majorities—or the lack thereof.[93] Moreover, the *Smith* majority expressly admitted that "leaving accommodation to the political process will place at a relative disadvantage those religious practices that are not widely engaged in. . . ."[94] Indeed, the majority could hardly deny that fact, considering that *Smith* itself, as well as two other recent cases in which the Court had rejected free exercise claims, all involved formally neutral government measures that just happened to severely undermine the free exercise rights of Native Americans.[95] Likewise,

[91] *Id.* at 894 (O'Connor, J., concurring). Justice O'Connor further observes:
> There is nothing talismanic about neutral laws of general applicability or
> general criminal prohibitions, for laws neutral toward religion can coerce
> a person to violate his religious conscience or intrude upon his religious
> duties just as effectively as laws aimed at religion.

Id. at 901.

[92] *Id.* at 894 (quoting Hobbie v. Unemployment Appeals Commission, 480 U.S. 136, 141–42 (1989) (quoting Bowen v. Roy, 476 U.S. 693, 727 (1986) (O'Connor, J., concurring in part and dissenting in part))).

[93] *Id.* at 890.

[94] *Id.*

[95] Lyng v. Northwest Indian Cemetery Protective Association, 485 U.S. 439 (1988) (rejecting free exercise challenge to federal government's logging and road construction activities on lands sacred to several Native American tribes, even though it was undisputed that these activities "could have devastating effects on traditional Indian religious practices"); Bowen v. Roy, 476 U.S. 693 (1986) (rejecting free exercise challenge to federal benefits statute requiring benefit applicants and recipients to supply their Social Security numbers, despite claim by Native American parents that it would violate their religious beliefs to obtain and provide Social Security number for their daughter).

in another recent case, the Court had rejected the free exercise claims of an Orthodox Jew whose religious beliefs were also violated by a formally neutral government measure.[96]

How did the *Smith* majority justify the admittedly discriminatory impact that its decimated constitutional protection would continue to have upon minority religions? It simply asserted, in conclusory fashion, that such discriminatory deprivation of liberty is the "unavoidable consequence of democratic government."[97] That statement ignores the constitutional role of the Bill of Rights and the constitutional responsibility of the federal courts to enforce it.[98]

In our constitutional system, which does not create a pure democracy, representatives who are elected by majorities may not deprive minorities of their fundamental freedoms, including religious liberty. In this vein, we should recall the memorable words of Justice Jackson in *West Virginia Board of Education v. Barnette*.[99] Notably, this 1943 case was a landmark in establishing not only religious liberty, but also the Supreme Court's special role in protecting constitutional freedoms more generally. *Barnette* overturned the Court's 1940 ruling in *Minersville School District v. Gobitis*,[100] and held that the First Amendment bars public schools from forcing students to pledge allegiance to the flag when they have any conscientious objections. In both cases, the challenge was brought by Jehovah's Witness school children who believed that to salute the flag constituted idolatry and thus violated their religious convictions and duties. A key passage in *Barnette*, which the Court has quoted and relied on many times

---

[96] Goldman v. Weinberger, 475 U.S. 503 (1986) (rejecting challenge to Air Force regulations that forbade the wearing of a yarmulke by an ordained Orthodox Jewish rabbi who was a commissioned Air Force officer working as a clinical psychologist on an Air Force base, despite his sincere belief that he had a religious obligation to wear it).

[97] Employment Division v. Smith, 494 U.S. 872, 890 (1990).

[98] See *id.* at 902 (O'Connor, J., concurring):
In my view . . . the First Amendment was enacted precisely to protect the rights of those whose religious practices are not shared by the majority and may be viewed with hostility. The history of our free exercise doctrine amply demonstrates the harsh impact majoritarian rule has had on unpopular or emerging religious groups such as the Jehovah's Witnesses and the Amish.

[99] 319 U.S. 624 (1943).

[100] 310 U.S. 586 (1940).

since, directly repudiates the assertion by the *Smith* majority, which I quoted above, that members of minority faith groups must endure burdens on their religious practices as the "unavoidable consequence of democratic government." To the contrary, as the *Barnette* Court declared:

> The very purpose of a Bill of Rights was to withdraw certain subjects from the vicissitudes of political controversy, to place them beyond the reach of majorities and officials and to establish them as legal principles to be applied by the courts. One's right to . . . freedom of worship . . . and other fundamental rights may not be submitted to vote; they depend on the outcome of no elections.[101]

In *Smith*, this eloquent statement of central constitutional principle, directly relevant to religious liberty, is not cited by the majority, but instead relegated to Justice O'Connor's separate opinion.[102] Indeed, the *Smith* majority did not even cite the landmark *Barnette* precedent at all. Worse yet, the *Smith* majority opinion twice did cite, and rely on, the Court's 1940 *Gobitis* decision,[103] which had rejected the religious freedom claims of the Jehovah's Witness schoolchildren, and which *Barnette* overturned just three years later. Moreover, both times that the *Smith* majority referred to *Gobitis* in purported support of its reasoning, it did not even acknowledge that this decision had been promptly overruled, and hence had been a binding precedent for only several years, half a century earlier![104] Even the Court's discredited decision in *Plessy v. Ferguson*,[105] which upheld the pernicious "separate but equal" doctrine authorizing racially segregated public facilities, had a much longer, and more recent, pedigree as accepted constitutional doctrine. *Plessy* was not overturned until 1954, in *Brown v. Board of Education*;[106] by then it had been the law of the land for fifty-eight years, fifteen years longer than *Gobitis* had *not*

---

[101] Barnette, 319 U.S. at 638.

[102] Smith, 494 U.S. at 902 (O'Connor, J., concurring).

[103] *Id.* at 879.

[104] Zachary Heiden, Fences & Neighbors, 17 Cardozo Stud. L. & Lit. 255, 230 n.12 (2005) ("At the time, *Gobitis* was generally regarded as completely gone . . . yet Scalia made Justice Frankfurter's *Gobitis* reasoning a central part of his argument.").

[105] Plessy v. Ferguson, 163 U.S. 537 (1896).

[106] Brown v. Board of Education, 347 U.S. 483 (1954).

been the law of the land when the *Smith* Court relied on it. Therefore, in citing *Gobitis* but not the decision that overruled it—*Barnette*—the *Smith* majority opinion blatantly violated the most basic rules for citing legal authorities;[107] more fundamentally, in tandem, it violated the most basic constitutional principles that *Barnette* so eloquently enunciated.

D. Individual Rights Advocates Support Strong Enforcement of Both Religion Clauses

Extraordinarily broad coalitions of civil liberties and religious organizations have pushed for various legislative "fixes" to the *Smith* Court's decimation of the Free Exercise Clause. I am proud that the ACLU has played a leadership role in that process, including by drafting, lobbying for, and defending in court both major federal laws on point: the "Religious Freedom Restoration Act"[108] or "RFRA"; and the "Religious Land Use and Institutionalized Persons Act"[109] or "RLUIPA." I personally testified in support of RFRA in both the House and the Senate, along with spokespersons for a diverse group of coalition partners, including the head of the National Association of Evangelicals. The news media picked up on a shot of the two of us hugging each other, since it apparently had a "strange bedfellows" appeal.

Yet the ACLU's leadership of efforts to revitalize legal protection for religious liberty, post-*Smith,* and our close collaboration with many religious denominations in those efforts, illustrate a fact that is too often obscured by politically motivated distortions: that civil libertarians are as vigorous in our defense of the Free Exercise Clause as in our defense of the Establishment Clause. Professor Marci Hamilton strongly disagrees with the views of the ACLU and other civil libertarians about the Free Exercise Clause, but she would certainly agree that our views strongly support both religious liberty and religion. Indeed, from her perspective, we *too* strongly support both religious liberty and religion.[110]

---

[107] The Bluebook: A Uniform System of Citation 93 (Columbia Law Review Assn. et al. eds., 18th ed. 2005) (Rule 10.7.1(c)).

[108] 42 U.S.C. §§ 2000bb et seq.

[109] *Id.* §§ 2000cc et seq.

[110] Hamilton, God vs. the Gavel, *supra* note 27, at 180.

E. Congressional and Court Reconsideration of Free Exercise Rights Post-Smith

Since my mandate in delivering the Simon Lecture is to focus on constitutional issues, I will not now discuss the legislative responses to the Court's constriction of the Free Exercise Clause in *Smith*, and the Court's replies to those responses,[111] all of which makes for an ongoing, important saga in its own right, involving other constitutional issues, including separation of powers and federalism. For purposes of my present theme, the Constitution's protection of religious liberty, I just want to underscore a basic constitutional reality about any so-called statutory fix: No statute can really "fix" a flaw in the Court's enforcement of constitutional rights. Constitutional rights, by definition, are especially entrenched and are not subject to revocation by a mere majority vote of our elected representatives in Congress with the president's assent.

It is a shame that the Supreme Court never has reconsidered its radical rewriting of the Free Exercise Clause in *Smith*, as several justices have urged it to do.[112] Indeed, in a real sense, the Court never even considered that radical rewriting in the first instance, even in *Smith* itself. In the Supreme Court, the briefs and oral arguments had been confined to the sole issue on which the Court had granted review: whether Oregon had to exempt members of the Native American Church, with its sacramental use of peyote in religious rituals, from its general law criminalizing peyote use.[113] In constitutional law terminology, the issue was whether the state's non-exemption satisfied strict scrutiny.

---

[111] See, e.g., Cutter v. Wilkinson, 544 U.S. 709 (2005) (upholding the constitutionality of one portion of Religious Land Use and Institutionalized Persons Act against contention that it violates Establishment Clause); City of Boerne v. Flores, 521 U.S. 507 (1997) (striking down Religious Freedom Restoration Act, insofar as it applies to state and local governments, as exceeding Congress' power).

[112] Boerne, 521 U.S. at 544–45 (O'Connor, J., dissenting); *id.* at 565 (Souter, J., dissenting); *id.* at 566 (Breyer, J., dissenting); Church of the Lukumi Babalu Aye, Inc. v. Hialeah, 508 U.S. 520, 559 (1993) (Souter, J., concurring in part and concurring in the judgment); *id.* at 578 (Blackmun, J., concurring).

[113] See Petition for Writ of Certiorari, Employment Division v. Smith, 494 U.S. 872 (1990) (No. 88-1213).

Throughout the protracted history of the *Smith* litigation, which the Supreme Court had also reviewed on a previous occasion,[114] no party or judge had argued that any standard other than strict scrutiny should govern. Yet without the benefit of briefs or oral arguments, the *Smith* majority, on its own, refused to assess the state's nonexemption under a strict scrutiny standard. Indeed, it even refused to review that nonexemption under any standard at all. Instead, the Court merely announced a new per se rule that "an individual's religious beliefs [do not] excuse him from compliance with an otherwise valid law prohibiting conduct that the State is free to regulate,"[115] notwithstanding the Free Exercise Clause.[116]

IV. Majoritarian Advocates Support Weak Enforcement of Both Religion Clauses

Before I elaborate on how the Rehnquist Court's equal non-protection approach has eviscerated the Establishment Clause, paralleling what it did to the Free Exercise Clause in *Smith*, I will first develop another, related theme that also links the Court's recent jurisprudence under both clauses: its excessive deference to majoritarian political and religious preferences. I have already addressed this point concerning the Court's Free Exercise analysis in *Smith*. I will now discuss how this majoritarian deference characterizes certain justices' views of both First Amendment Religion Clauses.

---

[114]See Smith, 494 U.S. at 875 (describing procedural history). The Supreme Court's previous decision in *Smith* is reported at 485 U.S. 660 (1988).

[115]Smith, 494 U.S. at 878–79.

[116]The plurality's sweeping revision of Free Exercise Clause jurisprudence was without the benefit of briefs or oral arguments. That was one basis for the petition for rehearing that was jointly filed by a broad array of constitutional scholars, religious organizations, and other individuals and groups. Petition for Rehearing at 5–6, Employment Division v. Smith, 494 U.S. 872 (1990), reh'g denied, 496 U.S. 913 (1990):

> Because the Court's far-reaching holding resolved an issue not briefed by the parties, because recent research on the history of the Free Exercise Clause demonstrates that the broader reading of the Clause rejected by the Court . . . was contemplated by the Framers of the First Amendment, and because assertions that the Court has "never held" that the Free Exercise Clause requires government to justify unintended burdens on free exercise must come as a surprise to the federal and state courts, state attorneys general, and treatise writers who have uniformly read this Court's Free Exercise decisions from as far back as at least *Sherbert v. Verner*, as holding precisely that, a rehearing is appropriate.

A. *Justice Scalia, Who Authored* Smith, *Gutting the Free Exercise Clause, also Advocates a Weakened Version of the Establishment Clause*

For those who falsely equate strong defense of the Establishment Clause with hostility toward religion, and who correspondingly assume that a limited view of the Establishment Clause should be equated with support for religion, the *Smith* decision and its aftermath should be puzzling. I have already noted that the legislative attempts to repair some of *Smith*'s damage to religious freedom have been spearheaded, contrary to stereotypes, by organizations that also strongly support anti-establishment values, including the ACLU and Americans United for Separation of Church and State. The line-up on the Supreme Court should also be puzzling to the too many politicians and pundits who complain that the Court's rulings enforcing the Establishment Clause undermine religion.

How many of those aligned with the so-called Religious Right realize that *Smith*, the decision that gutted the Free Exercise Clause, was authored not by one of the Court's champions of a strong Establishment Clause but rather by the Religious Right's very own poster justice, Antonin Scalia? I hasten to add that Justice Scalia has strongly defended particular constitutional rights and has written some landmark opinions that eloquently espouse libertarian principles.[117] I should also note that he and I are personal friends, despite our disagreements on particular issues.[118] But when it comes to the Religion Clauses, I wish the Religious Right would realize that Justice Scalia is religiously wrong!

Moreover, several other justices join Justice Scalia in their unduly narrow views of both Religion Clauses, in both contexts substituting for a core libertarian protection only a peripheral egalitarian protection, as I outlined earlier. Correspondingly, many justices who have most strongly enforced the Establishment Clause also have most strongly enforced the Free Exercise Clause, objecting to the *Smith* decision's undue constriction of that clause.[119]

---

[117] Nadine Strossen, Tribute to Justice Antonin Scalia, 62 N.Y.U. Ann. Surv. Am. L. 1, 7 (2006).

[118] *Id.*

[119] For example, the following justices have explicitly supported the *Smith* ruling, with its limited view of the Free Exercise Clause, and also have endorsed only a limited view of the Establishment Clause (they are listed in alphabetical order): Justices Kennedy, Rehnquist, Scalia, and White. Conversely, the following justices

B. *Both Religion Clauses Are Anti-Majoritarian*

Those patterns in the justices' rulings—treating both First Amendment Religion Clauses similarly, and either strictly enforcing both, or weakly enforcing both—might at first seem counter-intuitive. However, any impression that these Establishment Clause and Free Exercise Clause rulings are inconsistent with each other only reflects the prevalence of the political rhetoric that the Establishment Clause is anti-religion. Only if one accepts this allegation would one expect an advocate of Establishment Clause values to reject Free Exercise Clause values, and vice versa. Yet the Establishment Clause, far from being averse to religion, is beneficial to it.

Along with all provisions in the Bill of Rights, including the Free Exercise Clause, if the Establishment Clause can fairly be described as anti-anything, it is anti-*government*. Put a bit more elegantly, both Religion Clauses, as well as other Bill of Rights provisions, minimize government power in order to maximize individual liberty. In our democratic republic, every provision in the Bill of Rights constrains the power even of democratically elected representatives to limit the rights of individuals and minority groups in the name of the majority. In short, those provisions are anti-*majoritarian*. Accordingly, the First Amendment Religion Clauses protect individual religious liberty and freedom of conscience in the face of majoritarian religious preferences and the accompanying majoritarian political pressures.

C. *Justice Scalia's Majoritarian Approach to the Establishment Clause*

As discussed above, from a constitutional and libertarian perspective, *Smith's* most fundamental flaw was its suggestion that religious liberty for minority groups must be relegated to the vicissitudes of the majoritarian political process. To all of us who are familiar with Justice Scalia's overall jurisprudence, this is hardly a shocking position for him to take, since he so consistently votes to remit to the

---

have explicitly criticized *Smith's* limited view of the Free Exercise Clause, and also have supported robust enforcement of the Establishment Clause (they are listed in alphabetical order): Justices Blackmun, Brennan, Marshall, O'Connor, and Souter. (Some of the current justices are not included in either list because they have not yet had the occasion to opine expressly on one or both of these issues.)

political process what civil libertarians and libertarians consider to be fundamental constitutional rights.[120]

That same deference to the political branches of government, and that same penchant to uphold laws that reflect majoritarian religious preferences at the expense of religious minorities, carries through to the Establishment Clause rulings of Justice Scalia and others on the current Court. In the Court's most recent Establishment Clause cases, its two Ten Commandments decisions,[121] Justice Scalia, along with three other justices, expressly opined that the Establishment Clause should permit government to sponsor religious displays that promote the religious beliefs of the majority of Americans.[122] In the ACLU's Ten Commandments case, in which the majority struck down the Kentucky courthouse displays, Justice Scalia's opinion actually relied on statistics indicating that 97.7 percent of people living in this country are affiliated with Christianity, Judaism, and Islam, three monotheistic faiths.[123] Given those numbers, he concluded, government officials and agencies should be free to promote a religious belief in a single deity.[124]

That assertion raises factual problems, insofar as Islam apparently does not regard the Ten Commandments as authoritative.[125] It also raises constitutional problems insofar as the Court had always held that the Establishment Clause is most profoundly violated by government measures promoting particular religions or denominations,[126] and all of the Ten Commandments displays at issue in both

---

[120]See, e.g., Lawrence v. Texas, 539 U.S. 558, 586 (2003) (Scalia, J., dissenting); Planned Parenthood of Southeastern Pennsylvania v. Casey, 505 U.S. 833, 979 (1992) (Scalia, J., concurring in the judgment in part and dissenting in part).

[121]Van Orden v. Perry, 125 S. Ct. 2854 (2005); McCreary County v. ACLU of Ky., 125 S. Ct. 2722 (2005).

[122]Van Orden, 125 S. Ct. at 2864 (Scalia, J., concurring).

[123]McCreary, 125 S. Ct. at 2753 (Scalia, J., dissenting).

[124]Id. at 2752 (Scalia, J., dissenting).

[125]Paul Finkelman, The Ten Commandments on the Courthouse Lawn and Elsewhere, 73 Fordham L. Rev. 1477, 1519 (2005); see also Brief of Amici Curiae Anti-Defamation League et al. in Support of Respondent, Van Orden v. Perry, 125 S. Ct. 2854 (2005) (No. 03-1500); Brief of Amici Curiae Anti-Defamation League et al. in Support of Petitioner, McCreary County v. ACLU of Ky., 125 S. Ct. 2722 (2005) (No. 03-1693).

[126]See Larson v. Valente, 456 U.S. 228, 244 (1982); School District of Abington Township v. Schempp, 374 U.S. 203, 226 (1963); Everson v. Bd. of Ed. of Ewing, 330 U.S. 1, 15 (1947); see also Board of Ed. of Kiryas Joel Village School Dist. v. Grumet, 512 U.S. 687, 748 (1994) (Scalia, J., dissenting).

cases featured the same particular version that happens to be espoused by the same particular denominations. Not surprisingly, those were the Protestant denominations that were numerically and politically dominant in the local communities where the challenged Ten Commandments displays were located. Correspondingly, all of those displays were inconsistent with the versions of the Ten Commandments that are espoused by other denominations, including Catholics, Jews, and Lutherans.[127]

Even beyond those serious problems, Justice Scalia's expressly majoritarian analysis is at odds with the general concept of constitutionally entrenched rights that courts should protect, even—indeed, especially—against majoritarian policies and preferences. As Justice O'Connor succinctly put it in her concurring opinion in the ACLU's Ten Commandments case from Kentucky, "We don't count heads in enforcing the First Amendment."[128] To support that assertion she cited *Barnette*.

Just as it is no coincidence that Justice Scalia espoused such narrow views of both Religion Clauses in both *Smith* and the Ten Commandments cases, it is also no coincidence that Justice O'Connor strongly rebuffed those views in the same cases, consistently sounding the same anti-majoritarian, pro-libertarian theme in both. As noted above, Justice O'Connor castigated Justice Scalia's opinion in *Smith* for riding roughshod over the rights of religious minorities, quoting *Barnette*'s key language on point.[129]

When we consider both Religion Clauses, and the array of positions that have been advocated by justices and others, including the ACLU, it should be clear that the critical vectors are not for or against religion, as too many politicians and others contend, but rather for or against individual liberty. In the judicial context, the critical vector is whether one is for or against strict judicial scrutiny of laws reflecting majoritarian religious preferences.

---

[127] The Ten Commandments (a.k.a. The Decalog), Its Text and Grouping, at http://www.religioustolerance.org/chc_10c4.htm (accessed June 13, 2006).

[128] McCreary, 125 S. Ct. at 2747 (O'Connor, J., concurring).

[129] Employment Division v. Smith, 494 U.S. 872, 902–03 (1990) (O'Connor, J., concurring).

V. The Court's Reductionist Redefinition of the Establishment Clause

Now I will return to the first of my two interlinked major points and elaborate on the Court's recent reductionist redefinition of what it had long held to be a core Establishment Clause tenet: its absolute bar on any government funding of any religious institution.

A. Egalitarian Concerns Should Not Trump Libertarian Concerns in the Context of School Vouchers and Other Government Funding Programs

Throughout modern constitutional history, the Supreme Court has consistently held that the Establishment Clause imposes an absolute bar on government funding of any religious institution.[130] As I already noted, Roger Pilon told me that he and others at the Cato Institute are of the view that in this context, equality concerns should at least sometimes trump libertarian First Amendment concerns, so that if government chooses to fund programs run by secular institutions, then religious institutions must be free to apply for that funding as well. To hold otherwise, he said, would be to discriminate against religious institutions and thus burden the free exercise of religion, drawing an analogy to the Court's holding in *Sherbert*. I respect that position, but let me explain why I believe it is wrong.

Most fundamentally, religion is constitutionally distinct from everything else under the First Amendment, because it alone is singled out under the Establishment Clause. Although reasonable libertarians and civil libertarians might well disagree about exactly what limits this clause imposes on government involvement with religion, we surely must all acknowledge that it does indeed impose some such limits specifically and only on religion, and it thus mandates some distinctive—*i.e.*, non-equal—treatment of religion.

---

[130] See Mitchell v. Helms, 530 U.S. 793, 873–99 (2000) (Souter, J., dissenting) (summarizing cases); *id.* at 899 ("This stretch of doctrinal history leaves one point clear beyond peradventure: . . . we have consistently understood the Establishment Clause to impose a substantive prohibition against public aid to religion and, hence, to the religious mission of sectarian schools."); Rosenberger v. Rector & Visitors of the University of Va., 515 U.S. 819, 873–84 (1995) (Souter, J., dissenting) (summarizing cases).

B. The Establishment Clause Absolutely Bars All Government Funding of Religion

Now I will outline the abundant authority for the conclusion that the Establishment Clause's distinctive treatment of religion includes an absolute bar on all government funding, including government funding that is part of an otherwise broadly distributed benefits program. That conclusion is supported by constitutional history, by the purposes underlying the Establishment Clause, by the Court's consistent rulings throughout more than half a century, and by scholars across a broad ideological spectrum.

1. This Absolute Bar is Supported by Constitutional History

The relevant pre-constitutional history is well-summarized by University of Texas Law Professor Douglas Laycock as follows:

> If the debates of the 1780's support any proposition, it is that the Framers opposed government financial support for religion .... They did not substitute small taxes for large taxes; three pence was as bad as any larger sum. The principle was what mattered. With respect to money, religion was to be wholly voluntary. Churches either would support themselves or they would not, but the government would neither help nor interfere.[131]

How could any free market libertarian possibly object to that principle?

Professor Laycock's reference to "three pence," of course, is an allusion to one of James Madison's famous lines in his influential *Memorial and Remonstrance against Religious Assessment*, published in 1785.[132] This *Remonstrance* played the key role in defeating a Virginia

---

[131] Douglas Laycock, Nonpreferential Aid to Religion: A False Claim About Original Intent, 28 Wm. & Mary L. Rev. 875, 921–23 (1986). See also T. Curry, The First Freedoms 217 (1986) (at the time of the framing of the First Amendment Religion Clauses, "the belief that government assistance to religion, especially in the form of taxes, violated religious liberty had a long history"); Jesse Choper, Securing Religious Liberty 16 (1995) ("There is broad consensus that a central threat to . . . religious freedom . . .—indeed, in the judgment of many the most serious infringement upon religious liberty—is posed by forcing them to pay taxes in support of . . . religious activities").

[132] James Madison, Memorial and Remonstrance (June 20, 1785), available at www.worldpolicy.org/globalrights/religion/madison-remonstrance.html (accessed June 12, 2006).

39

bill that would have allowed taxpayers to designate any religious or educational institution as the beneficiary of their assessed taxes. Notably, though, these elements of even-handedness and individual choice did not redeem the tax plan for Madison and his contemporaries, because it still fell afoul of the absolute ban on any government funding of religion. In a central passage, which was widely cited in the founding era and has often been cited in modern Supreme Court decisions,[133] Madison posed this rhetorical question, to underscore the absolute principle at stake, essential to individual liberty:

> Who does not see that . . . the same authority which can force a citizen to contribute three pence only of his property for the support of any one establishment, may force him to conform to any other establishment in all cases whatsoever?[134]

The principles set out in Madison's *Remonstrance* not only led to the defeat of the Virginia tax bill for general support of religious and educational institutions; it also spurred the adoption of the Virginia Bill for Establishing Religious Freedom, written by Thomas Jefferson.[135] Along with Madison's *Remonstrance*, Jefferson's bill is also considered authoritative in shaping and interpreting the First Amendment's Religion Clauses.[136] Two key passages in that famous document, which also have been widely quoted, further demonstrate the primacy of the no-government-funding principle. First, the Bill's Preamble declares that "to compel a man to furnish contributions of money for the propagation of opinions which he disbelieves, is

---

[133] See, e.g., Chicago Teachers Union, Local No. 1 v. Hudson, 475 U.S. 292, 306 n.15 (1986); Abood v. Detroit Bd. of Education, 431 U.S. 209, 235 n.31 (1977); Lemon v. Kurtzman, 403 U.S. 602, 633–34 (1971) (Douglas, J., concurring); Engel v. Vitale, 370 U.S. 421, 436 (1962); International Association of Machinists v. Street, 367 U.S. 740, 779 n.4 (1961) (Douglas, J., concurring).

[134] Madison, *supra* note 132, at paragraph 3.

[135] Virginia Act for Establishing Religious Freedom, Va. Code Ann. § 57-1 (1786).

[136] See, e.g., Everson v. Board of Education of Ewing, 330 U.S. 1, 13 (1947) ("This Court has previously recognized that the provisions of the First Amendment, in the drafting and adoption of which Madison and Jefferson played such leading roles, had the same objective and were intended to provide the same protection against governmental intrusion on religious liberty as the [Virginia Act for Establishing Religious Freedom]"); Watson v. Jones, 80 U.S. (13 Wall). 679 (1871); Davis v. Beason, 133 U.S. 333 (1890).

sinful and tyrannical."[137] Second, its text provides that "no man shall be compelled to . . . support any religious worship, place, or ministry whatsoever."[138]

2. This Absolute Bar is Supported by the Purposes underlying the Establishment Clause

The Framers' absolute opposition to government funding of religion reflected three core objectives that animated the First Amendment's non-Establishment Clause.

a. To Protect Individual Freedom of Conscience

The first such objective is to protect individual freedom of conscience. As I have already noted, some experts consider this to be the clause's foremost objective.[139] This paramount goal certainly resonated throughout Madison's *Remonstrance* and Jefferson's Virginia Bill for Religious Liberty as a key reason for repudiating any taxpayer support for religion. Indeed, in order to protect freedom of conscience, Jefferson maintained that government could not tax individuals even for the purpose of funding religious institutions of their

---

[137] Va. Code Ann. § 57-1.

[138] *Id.* Roger Pilon and other critics of the foregoing historical arguments in favor of the no-funding principle note that, during the founding era, many colonial and state governments had official established religions, and provided government funding to religious institutions; indeed, Massachusetts did not disestablish its state religion until 1836. Far from ratifying these practices, though, the Establishment Clause was expressly designed to repudiate them at the national level. See, e.g., Rosenberger v. Rector & Visitors of the University of Va., 515 U.S. 819, 869 (1995) (Souter, J., dissenting) (quoting Everson v. Board of Education of Ewing, 330 U.S. 1, 10, 11, 13 (1947) (specific citations omitted)):

> Madison wrote [the *Remonstrance*] against a background in which nearly every Colony had exacted a tax for church support, . . . the practice having become "so commonplace as to shock the freedom-loving colonials into a feeling of abhorrence,". . . . Madison's *Remonstrance* captured the colonists' "conviction that individual religious liberty could be achieved best under a government which was stripped of all power to tax, to support, or otherwise to assist any or all religions. . . . ." Their sentiment, as expressed by Madison in Virginia, led not only to the defeat of Virginia's tax assessment bill, but also directly to passage of the Virginia Bill for Establishing Religious Freedom, written by Thomas Jefferson.

[139] Noah Feldman, From Liberty to Equality: The Transformation of the Establishment Clause, 90 Calif. L. Rev. 673, 675 (2002).

own faith, since that would "depriv[e]" the individual "of the comfortable liberty of giving his contributions to the particular pastor, whose morals he would make his pattern."[140]

b. To Preserve the Purity of Religion

A second major Establishment Clause objective was to preserve religion and religious institutions from what Madison decried as the "degrad[ing]"[141] influence of government. Roger Williams and other devout religious leaders in the colonial era recognized that even what might seem to be beneficial government involvement with religion, including tax support, in fact would undermine religion's independence and vitality. As Madison's *Remonstrance* noted, government support of religion "is a contradiction to the Christian Religion itself; for every page of it disavows a dependence on the powers of this world."[142] In 1947, in the Court's first modern Establishment Clause case, Justice Rutledge elaborated on Madison's point as follows: "The great condition of religious liberty is that it be maintained free from sustenance, as also from other interferences, by the state. For when it comes to rest upon that secular foundation it vanishes with the resting."[143]

Many contemporary religious leaders and citizens have echoed that concern, in arguing against government-funded support of religion. For example, vouchers for religious schools and other forms of "faith-based funding" have been opposed by no less staunch a stalwart of the so-called Religious Right than Phyllis Schlafly and her Eagle Forum. The Eagle Forum's newsletter warned: "Because [government funding] brings . . . religion-restricting government regulations, many . . . religions . . . know better than to hand over control of their social service ministries to the government. . . . Government vouchers . . . will just bring more government, not more liberty."[144] Likewise, the Eagle Forum newsletter warned that vouchers would "destroy private education,"[145] including private religious schools, gradually expunging religion from their curricula.

---

[140]Hening, Statutes of Virginia 84 (1823); Henry Steele Commager, Documents of American History 125 (1944).

[141]Madison, *supra* note 132, at paragraph 8.

[142]*Id.* at paragraph 6.

[143]Everson v. Board of Education of Ewing, 330 U.S. 1, 53 (1947) (Rutledge, J., dissenting).

[144]Sue Ella Deadwyler, Eagle Forum of Geogia, Georgia Insight (Jan. 23, 2004), available at http://www.georgiaeagle.org/index.php?where=insight&id=78.

[145]Cathie Adams, Vouchers: The Parent Trap, 6 Torch (March 1999), available at www.texaseagle.org/torch/03-99.html (accessed June 12, 2006).

This objection to "faith-based funding"—that it would subject religious institutions to intrusive government monitoring—has come even from religious leaders who are strong supporters of President Bush, for whom this has been a pet issue. For example, speaking on his *700 Club* television show in 2001, Pat Robertson said that "what seems to be such a great initiative can rise up to bite the [government-funded religious] organizations as well as the . . . government."[146] Robertson further stated: "[F]ederal rules will envelope these [religious] organizations, they'll begin to be nurtured . . . on federal money, and then they can't get off of it. It'll be like a narcotic."[147]

In its many past cases reaffirming the core Establishment Clause ban on government funding of religion, the Court has stressed this goal of avoiding "corrosive secularism."[148] That theme was also stressed in the dissent in the 2002 case in which the Court narrowly upheld a voucher program in Cleveland, Ohio, that systematically channeled massive tax funding into parochial schools, and thus for the first time violated the hitherto absolute no-funding principle. As Justice Souter observed in his powerful dissent from the Court's 5-4 ruling in that case, *Zelman v. Simmons-Harris*: "When government aid goes up, so does reliance on it; the only thing likely to go down is independence. . . . [One] wonder[s] when dependence will become great enough to give the State . . . an effective veto over basic decisions on the content of curriculums?"[149]

The Cleveland voucher program attached regulatory conditions that are typical of conditions we can reasonably anticipate being imposed on other government funding programs, since they reflect widely held secular values in our broader society. But those values are inconsistent with many religious beliefs. Therefore, requiring religious institutions to adhere to them, as a condition of funding, endangers the institutions' religious liberty. Specifically, the Cleveland voucher program barred any religious schools that received

[146] See Rob Boston, Love for Sale: Faith-based Grant Buys TV Preacher's Favor, The Wall of Separation: Official Weblog of Americans United for Separation of Church and State (Feb. 2, 2005), available at http://blog.au.org/2005/02/love_for_sale_f.html (last visited Mar. 2, 2006).

[147] *Id.*

[148] School District of the City of Grand Rapids v. Ball, 473 U.S. 373, 385 (1985).

[149] Zelman v. Simmons-Harris, 536 U.S. 639, 715 (2002) (Souter, J., dissenting).

government funds from "discriminat[ing] on the basis of . . . religion," and also from "teach[ing] hatred of any person or group on the basis of . . . religion."[150] As Justice Souter's dissent noted, the anti-discrimination provision could mean that "a participating religious school may well be forbidden to choose a member of its own clergy to serve as teacher or principal over a layperson of a different religion claiming equal qualification."[151] Likewise, the anti-hate-speech regulation "could be understood . . . to prohibit religions from teaching traditionally legitimate articles of faith as to the error, sinfulness, or ignorance of others. . . ."[152]

c. To Avoid Conflict among Religious Groups

The third major objective underlying the Establishment Clause also supports its categorical ban on government funding; that objective is to avoid the conflict and strife among various religious groups that have torn apart so many societies throughout history and around the world. As Justice Rutledge warned, back in 1947, "Public money devoted to payment of religious costs . . . brings the quest for more. It brings too the struggle of sect against sect for the larger share or for any. Here one [religious sect], by numbers [of adherents] alone will benefit most, there another. This is precisely the history of societies which have had an established religion and dissident groups."[153]

This general danger that Justice Rutledge foretold is clearly evident in the specific context of the Cleveland voucher program at issue in the *Zelman* case. Justice Breyer's dissent in that case underscored this danger through a series of rhetorical questions:

> Why will different religions not become concerned about, and seek to influence, the criteria used to channel this money to religious schools? Why will they not want to examine the implementation of the programs that provide this money— to determine, for example, whether implementation has biased a program toward or against particular sects, or whether recipient religious schools are adequately fulfilling a program's criteria? If so, just how is the State to resolve the

[150] *Id.* at 713.

[151] *Id.* at 712.

[152] *Id.* at 713.

[153] Everson v. Board of Education of Ewing, 330 U.S. 1, 53 (1947) (Rutledge, J., dissenting).

resulting controversies without provoking legitimate fears of the kinds of religious favoritism that, in so religiously diverse a Nation, threaten social dissension?[154]

Justice Souter's dissent in *Zelman* likewise stressed the religious divisiveness that will likely result from government funding of religious schools; he cited many specific examples of religious doctrines that are controversial in our contemporary society:

> Religious teaching at taxpayer expense simply cannot be cordoned from taxpayer politics, and every major religion currently espouses social positions that provoke intense opposition. Not all taxpaying Protestant citizens, for example, will be content to underwrite the teaching of the Roman Catholic Church condemning the death penalty. Nor will all of America's Muslims acquiesce in paying for the endorsement of the religious Zionism taught in many religious Jewish schools. . . . Nor will every secular taxpayer be content to support Muslim views on differential treatment of the sexes, or . . . to fund the espousal of a wife's obligation of obedience to her husband, presumably taught in any schools adopting the articles of faith of the Southern Baptist Convention. Views like these . . . have been safe in the sectarian pulpits and classrooms of this Nation not only because the Free Exercise Clause protects them directly, but [also] because the ban on supporting religious establishment has protected free exercise, by keeping it relatively private. With the arrival of [government financing], that privacy will go, and along with it will go confidence that religious disagreement will stay moderate.[155]

---

[154] Zelman, 536 U.S. at 723–24 (Breyer, J., dissenting).

[155] *Id.* at 715–16 (Souter, J., dissenting). See also *id.* at 724–25 (Breyer, J., dissenting): How are state officials to adjudicate claims that one religion or another is advocating, for example, civil disobedience in response to unjust laws, the use of illegal drugs in a religious ceremony, or resort to force to call attention to what it views as an immoral social practice? What kind of public hearing will there be in response to claims that one religion or another is continuing to teach a view of history that casts members of other religions in the worst possible light? . . . [A]ny major funding program . . . will require criteria. And the selection of those criteria, as well as their application, inevitably pose problems that are divisive.

3. This Absolute Bar is Supported by the Court's Consistent Rulings throughout More than Half a Century

In the Court's first modern Establishment Clause ruling, its 1947 *Everson* decision, the justices unanimously endorsed the centrality of that clause's absolute ban on government funding of religion. Despite their disagreements about other aspects of the Establishment Clause's scope, the justices all concurred that it "means at least this: No tax in any amount, large or small, can be levied to support any religious activities or institutions."[156] In an unbroken string of cases decided between 1947 and 2000, the Court consistently reaffirmed and enforced this principle. As Justice Souter concluded after describing this line of cases: "This stretch of doctrinal history leaves one point clear beyond peradventure: together with James Madison, we have consistently understood the Establishment Clause to impose a substantive prohibition against public aid to religion and, hence, to the religious mission of sectarian schools."[157]

This longstanding principle of no government funding for religion remained firmly entrenched until 2000, when it was rejected by a four-person plurality opinion that Justice Souter, in an opinion joined by two other justices, strongly decried for so sharply diverging from the Court's precedents.[158] Then, in 2002, for the first time ever, a narrow majority of the Court upheld a government program that provided substantial, direct aid to religious institutions—specifically, parochial schools. In the *Zelman* case, which the four dissenters correctly called "a dramatic departure from basic Establishment Clause principle,"[159] the Court upheld Cleveland's voucher program. As Justice Breyer put it, the majority "adopt[ed]" an interpretation of the Establishment Clause that this Court rejected more than half a century ago."[160]

---

[156] Everson, 330 U.S. at 15–16.

[157] Mitchell v. Helms, 530 U.S. 793, 899 (2000) (Souter, J., dissenting).

[158] See *id*. at 900 ("As a break with consistent doctrine the plurality's new criterion [for assessing the permissibility of government aid to religion] is unequalled in the history of Establishment Clause interpretation."); *id*. at 901 n.19 ("Short of formally replacing the Establishment Clause, a cleaner break with prior law [than the plurality's approach] would be hard to imagine."); *id*. at 911 ("The plurality would break with the law. The plurality's notion would be the end of the principle of no aid to the schools' religious mission.").

[159] Zelman, 536 U.S. at 717 (Souter, J, dissenting).

[160] *Id*. at 728 (Breyer, J., dissenting).

Jettisoning the Court's long-enforced absolute bar against government funding of religion, and the associated individual freedom of conscience that depends on that bar, the majority instead substituted only a bar on unequal funding of religion. In thus replacing the Establishment Clause's absolute libertarian guarantee with its egalitarian corollary, the *Zelman* majority countermanded multiple precedents in which the Court had expressly rejected just this substitution. The Court had repeatedly stressed that evenhanded distribution of government aid—as among secular and religious recipients—while certainly a necessary precondition for the constitutionality of any government aid program that benefited religion, was not a sufficient precondition for constitutionality.[161] As the four *Zelman* dissenters noted, "[a]s recently as two terms ago, a majority of the Court recognized that . . . evenhandedness toward aid recipients had never been treated as alone sufficient to satisfy the Establishment Clause."[162] Accordingly, until the 2002 *Zelman* case, the Court regularly struck down government aid programs that had the constitutionally prohibited purpose or effect of financially supporting the religious mission of religious institutions, even when the programs distributed aid broadly and evenhandedly among secular and religious recipients.[163]

---

[161] See *id.* ("An earlier Court found [the majority's] 'equal opportunity' principle insufficient; it read the [Establishment] Clause as insisting upon greater separation of church and state, at least in respect to primary education."); Mitchell, 530 U.S. at 877 (Souter, J., dissenting) ("Evenhandedness of distribution as between religious and secular beneficiaries is a relevant factor, but not a sufficiency test of constitutionality. There is no rule of religious equal protection to the effect that any expenditure for the benefit of religious school students is necessarily constitutional so long as public school pupils are favored on ostensibly identical terms."); Rosenberger v. Rector & Visitors of the University of Va., 515 U.S. 819, 877–80 (1995) (Souter, J., dissenting); *id.* at 877 ("[T]he Court recognizes that evenhandedness is only a 'significant factor' in certain Establishment Clause analysis, not a dispositive one"); *id.* at 880 ("[W]e did not, in any of these cases, hold that evenhandedness might be sufficient to render direct aid to religion constitutional.").

[162] Zelman, 536 U.S. at 696 (Souter, J., dissenting).

[163] See, e.g., School Dist. of Grand Rapids v. Ball, 473 U.S. 373, 395 (1985); Wolman v. Walter, 433 U.S. 229, 254 (1977); Meek v. Pittenger, 421 U.S. 349, 365 (1975); Committee for Public Ed. v. Nyquist, 413 U.S. 756, 774 (1973); Levitt v. Committee for Public Education & Religious Liberty, 413 U.S. 472, 480 (1973); Tilton v. Richardson, 403 U.S. 572, 683 (1971) (plurality opinion).

4. This Absolute Bar is Supported by Scholars across a Broad Ideological Spectrum

It is noteworthy that scholars across a broad ideological spectrum concur that a core meaning of the Establishment Clause today must continue to be its longstanding bar on government financing of religion. That is true, for instance, even of Michael McConnell, now a judge on the U.S. Court of Appeals for the Tenth Circuit, who has famously advocated a substantially narrowed understanding of the Establishment Clause.[164] Yet even his limited concept of government action that violates the Establishment Clause extends to "legal compulsion to support" religious activities through taxes.[165]

Another example is N.Y.U. Law Professor Noah Feldman, who advocates another variation on McConnell's theme of a radically reduced Establishment Clause. Feldman urges shrinking that clause to encompass only two core principles, which "historically lay at the root of" our Constitution's treatment of religion.[166] The first core principle is "no coercion," and the second is "no money."[167] (Those two principles are mutually independent, so government funding would be banned even if it is not coercive.) Concerning the second principle, no money, Feldman advocates the following absolute rule: "[T]he state may [not] expend its resources so as to support religious institutions and practices."[168]

Let me quote one final, important example of a constitutional scholar who also has forcefully defended the "no funding" principle. He has stressed that this principle is essential for minimizing cultural divisiveness in our pluralistic, diverse society. That last persuasive expert is none other than Cato's Roger Pilon himself! As Roger put it in 1997:

> [T]he more of life we try to live collectively, through the forced association that is government, the more we invite cultural clashes that in the end are irreducible clashes over values. Suppose, for example, that we . . . tried to finance private religious institutions through public taxation. . . . In

[164] Michael W. McConnell, Coercion: The Lost Element of Establishment, 27 Wm. & Mary L. Rev. 933 (1986).

[165] *Id.* at 938 ("[L]egal compulsion to support or participate in religious activities would seem to be the essence of an establishment.").

[166] Feldman, *supra* note 51, at 237.

[167] *Id.*

[168] *Id.*

our heterogeneous society, the disputes would be inescapable and endless. And there would be no principled resolution to them.[169]

VI. Conclusion

Libertarians, as well as civil libertarians, should be very concerned about the widespread misunderstandings of the core libertarian principles embodied in the First Amendment's Religion Clauses, as well as the modern Supreme Court's decisions that have enforced those principles. The Court's more recent, revisionist rulings in the religion area parallel its anti-libertarian rulings regarding the two other constitutional rights that I have also briefly discussed above, under the First Amendment Free Speech Clause and the Fourth Amendment. By elevating ancillary egalitarian concerns over central libertarian precepts, the Court has enforced only a constricted vision of constitutional rights.

I will summarize that constricted vision with a variation on the following famous line by Anatole France: "The law, in its majestic equality, forbids the rich as well as the poor to sleep under bridges, to beg in the streets, and to steal bread."[170] Here is the variation on this theme that captures the critique I have laid out in this article: The law, in its majestic equality, allows all of us alike to undergo suspicionless searches; to be barred from expressive activities on government property that is compatible with such activities; to be forced to choose between honoring our religious beliefs or complying with government regulations, on pain of imprisonment; and to be forced to contribute our tax dollars to religious institutions, in violation of our own beliefs.

---

[169] Roger Pilon, E Pluribus Unum?: A Symposium on Pluralism and Public Policy, The American Jewish Committee, Remarks at the Arthur and Rochelle Belfer Center for American Pluralism 62 (1997) (transcript on file with author).

[170] Anatole France, The Red Lily ch. 7 (1894), reprinted in John Bartlett, Bartlett's Familiar Quotations 550 (Justin Kaplan ed., Little Brown 16th ed. 1992).

More Real than Apparent: Separation of Powers, the Rule of Law, and Comparative Executive "Creativity" in *Hamdan v. Rumsfeld*

*Martin S. Flaherty**

I. Introduction

Rarely has the Supreme Court handed a "wartime" president a greater defeat, or human rights defenders a greater victory, than it did in *Hamdan v. Rumsfeld*.[1] A common view on the winning side is that the Supreme Court pretty much delivered a knockout blow.[2] The Court, first, kept the case, rejecting the argument that Congress had stripped it of jurisdiction to hear pending cases from Guantanamo Bay. Second, *Hamdan* declared that the president had no authority to constitute the special military tribunals he had set up to detain such "enemy combatants" as Salim Ahmed Hamdan, Osama Bin Laden's alleged driver and assistant. Finally, the majority stated that the commissions, as established, violated fundamental protections set out in Common Article 3 of the four Geneva Conventions of 1949. Not since *Youngstown Sheet & Tube Company v. Sawyer*[3] has any decision vindicated law over executive power in more convincing or historic fashion.

All this euphoria makes it easy to overlook the judgment's shortcomings. No one on either side should forget that the margin of victory was in effect no more than one vote. In a historic coincidence, the new chief justice had to recuse himself for having sat on the

*Co-Director, Crowley Program in International Human Rights, Leitner Family Professor of International Human Rights, Fordham Law School. I would like to thank Amber Lewis and Florin Butunoi for their diligent research assistance.

[1] 126 S. Ct. 2749 (2006).

[2] For an approving yet careful initial assessment, see David Cole, Why the Court Said No, 53 N.Y. Rev. of Books 41 (Aug. 10, 2006).

[3] 343 U.S. 579 (1952).

panel that considered the case before the D.C. Circuit, where he voted for nearly all the government's arguments.[4] The majority itself, moreover, pulled several punches. To its credit, it did at least allude to potential constitutional problems that would arise had it decided that Congress had intended to deprive the Court of jurisdiction. But it showed more caution on the merits.[5] Justice Stevens did not mention parallel constitutional problems that would have surfaced had the Court ruled that Congress authorized the tribunals.[6] Nor did the majority hold that the Geneva Conventions are either self-executing or provide individuals with judicially enforceable remedies.[7] The Court's prudence may have been a classic exercise of the "passive virtues," a savvy maneuver to deflect negative reaction, or both. The prudence nonetheless comes at a cost, by concealing the strength of the judgment's foundations.

In truth *Hamdan's* strengths are more real than they are apparent. In every important area, *Youngstown*, along with conventional legal analysis more generally, allows the Court to go at least as far as it did, and to go even further in the future. First, the Court vindicated separation of powers by requiring Congress' focused and deliberate involvement where at best inadvertence had gone before. Far from infringing upon the political branches, the Court did not go as far as its predecessors in exhorting Congress in particular to live up to its responsibilities. Second, the Stevens opinion vindicated the rule of law—above all international law—through its exceptionally close reading of humanitarian custom and the Geneva Conventions. It did not, however, go as far as historical materials would have allowed it, missing an opportunity to reassert the doctrine of self-execution. Finally, the Court again rebuked the executive for its creative attempts to assert a government of men and women rather than laws in the context of the "war on terror." Yet, the Court would have been on stronger ground here, too, had it drawn on examples of executive overreaction in other countries that have confronted domestic or international terror.

This essay will consider *Hamdan* in each of these three areas: separation of powers; the rule of law, especially international law;

[4] Hamdan v. Rumsfeld, 415 F.3d 33 (D.C. Cir. 2005).
[5] Hamdan, 126 S. Ct. at 2773.
[6] *Id.* at 2774–75.
[7] *Id.* at 2793–94.

and the lessons of executive creativity drawn from foreign jurisdictions. In each instance, it will show that *Hamdan* rests upon foundations that could support broader judicial intervention than the Court chose to exercise in the case itself. To make this argument is not to diminish the historic victory that *Hamdan* represents. It is, rather, to help forestall defeat in any of these three areas down a road that the ongoing fight against terrorism will doubtless take us.

II. Separation of Powers

Above all, the Supreme Court's decision in *Hamdan* defended separation of powers. The central part of the Court's ruling not only held that the president lacks authorization to create the military commissions, but also that Congress had prevented him from doing so in the Uniform Code of Military Justice (UCMJ).[8] For the majority, separation of powers arguments were less a means for the assertion of judicial power than an opportunity to fight for the involvement of the legislature, even in dire times. Indeed, the Court fought for legislative involvement with perhaps more obvious resolve than the legislature itself.

Hamdan's insistence on a genuine legislative role finds ample support in sources dating from the Founding through recent wartime precedent. That insistence will matter, however, only to the extent that Congress itself takes advantage of the Court's defense of legislative prerogatives, a point that the Court must now make with the same vigor it has in the past.

A. Hamdan's *Insistence on Focused Legislative Involvement*

Hamdan's first skirmish on the merits established the majority's firm yet circumscribed stance on behalf of meaningful congressional involvement in addressing terrorism. This skirmish involved the claim that the president could establish the military commissions "in cases of controlling necessity" by virtue of Article II, the Executive Vesting Clause, the Commander-in-Chief Clause, or some combination. Claims that executive authority encompasses a broad array of "inherent" foreign affairs powers have gained some currency among academics and in this instance were enough to convince the D.C. Circuit.[9] For their part, Justice Thomas, joined by Justice Scalia, relied

[8] Uniform Code of Military Justice, art. 21, 64 Stat. 115, codified at 10 U.S.C. § 821.
[9] Hamdan v. Rumsfeld, 415 F.3d 33 (D.C. Cir. 2005).

on that claim as a basis for presuming that the president's actions in the area of national security merit substantial deference absent a clear showing of a congressional prohibition.[10] The Court itself did not reject claims of inherent executive authority outright. The majority did, however, bypass it, stating that Congress, when it enacted the UCMJ and predecessor statutes, preserved the president's power to establish military commissions provided that such commissions comport with the laws of war. The Court nonetheless dealt the notion of inherent foreign affairs power a significant blow in two respects. More narrowly, it held that whatever independent power the president may possess to create military commissions in extraordinary circumstances, that power does not trump an act of Congress, pursuant to its own War Powers, that requires the president to observe humanitarian law. More broadly, neither *Hamdan* nor the previous Guantanamo cases[11] show any inclination to accept the president's assertion of military powers in the absence of legislative authorization.

Hamdan also went further than the Guantanamo cases by clarifying that separation of powers requires meaningful, not just arguable, congressional involvement. Justice Stevens made short work of the president's claims that authorization for the military commissions came either from the Authorization of the Use of Military Force (AUMF)[12] or the Detainee Treatment Act (DTA).[13] With regard to the AUMF, the Court assumed that the enactment acted as a declaration of war and "activated the President's war powers."[14] But the majority noted that "there is nothing in the text or legislative history of the AUMF even hinting that Congress intended to expand or alter the authorization set forth" in the UCMJ.[15] Of course one could read the AUMF's language authorizing the president to take "all necessary and appropriate"[16] force to respond to the September 11 attacks to do just that. However, Justice Stevens expressly relied on

---

[10] Hamdan, 126 S. Ct. at 2823–26 (Thomas, J., dissenting).

[11] Hamdi v. Rumsfeld, 542 U.S. 507 (2004); Rasul v. Bush, 542 U.S. 466 (2004).

[12] Pub. L. No. 107-40, 115 Stat. 224, note following 50 U.S.C § 1541 (2001).

[13] Pub. L. No. 109-148, §§ 1001-06, 119 Stat. 2739, codified at 42 U.S.C. § 2000dd.

[14] 126 S. Ct. at 2775.

[15] *Id.*

[16] Pub. L. No. 107-40, *supra* note 12.

the canon against implicit repeal; implicitly relied on the related canon favoring specific enactments over general ones; and, finally, also relied on the Nazi saboteur case, *Ex Parte Quirin*,[17] in which the Court looked beyond Congress' declaration of war when assessing the scope of presidential power.[18]

Justice Stevens made even shorter work of the DTA, which he read to reserve questions about the military commissions' comportment with the Constitution and federal laws.[19] Though different in particulars, the majority's rejection of these statutes as a source for presidential power shares a common theme. Absent "a more specific congressional authorization"—one that indicates Congress truly considered granting the president expanded discretion either in general or in response to particular terrorism threats—the Court will not accept a shift in the established limitations under which all the branches have operated.[20]

Separation of powers, defined as genuine legislative involvement in national security matters that bear upon fundamental rights, is central to *Hamdan*'s consideration of the UCMJ, a congressional enactment. Justice Stevens emphasized the need for this involvement, forcefully yet subtly, when addressing how the president derives the authority to establish military commissions at all. Even today, one searches in vain in the United States Code for a clear or even unclear textual provision authorizing the president to establish military commissions. The closest candidate remains article 21 of the UCMJ, which merely states that the conferral of jurisdiction on courts-martial "shall not be construed as depriving military commissions . . . of concurrent jurisdiction in respect of offenders or offenses that by statute or by the law of war may be tried by such military commissions. . . ."[21] In *Quirin* the Court controversially treated the predecessor version of this elliptical provision under the Articles of War as an authorization.

---

[17] 317 U.S. 1 (1942).

[18] *Id.* at 28–29.

[19] Hamdan, 126 S. Ct. at 2775.

[20] *Id.*

[21] Justice Stevens cites to article 21, while Justice Kennedy prefers to cite the codified provision, 10 U.S.C. § 821 (2000).

The *Hamdan* Court therefore simply could have relied on stare decisis. Or it could have argued that Congress, in reenacting the provision in the UCMJ after World War II, at least implicitly endorsed the *Quirin* reading.[22] It did neither. Instead, the majority pointedly refused to uphold *Quirin*'s treatment of authorization, instead reading the case to do no more than recognize "what power, under the Constitution and the common law of war, the President" previously had.[23] The *Hamdan* majority did not say whether the Constitution actually permitted the institution of military commissions prior to that congressional preservation. It did, however, stress that article 21 expressly requires military commissions to comply with the laws of war.[24] Once more, the Court refused to read more into an enactment than was plainly there, even in the face of presidential calls to err on the side of executive power.

Hamdan's preference for deliberative legislative action culminates in the Court's consideration of limits Congress placed upon the president's authority. In contrast to every enactment and provision considered up to this point, Congress actually had fulfilled the deliberation requirement in UCMJ article 36.[25] Article 36(b) further states that "[a]ll rules and regulations made under this article shall be uniform" with respect to courts-martial, military commissions, and other military tribunals "insofar as practicable."[26] Both Justice Stevens for the majority, and Justice Kennedy in his concurrence, read this text as an express uniformity requirement that in effect sets courts-martial as the baseline.[27] Both Stevens' and Kennedy's opinions also read the practicability determination to require independent judicial assessment rather than deference to the president. On these bases, the Court, critically, rejected the president's assertions that terrorism renders uniformity impracticable.

By contrast, the Court's prior analysis of article 36(a) demonstrates that the Court's search for legislative clarity will not always cut

---

[22] But see Neal K. Katyal and Laurence H. Tribe, Waging War, Deciding Guilt: Trying the Military Tribunals, 111 Yale L.J. 1259, 1288–89 (2002) (arguing that the UCMJ did not incorporate *Quirin*'s position on authorization).

[23] Hamdan, 126 S. Ct. at 2774.

[24] *Id.*

[25] 10 U.S.C. § 836 (2000).

[26] 10 U.S.C. § 836(b) (2000).

[27] Hamdan, 126 S. Ct. at 2790–93; *id.* at 2800–02 (Kennedy, J., concurring).

against the president. *That* text calls for courts-martial and commissions to apply the procedural and evidentiary rules employed in federal district court "as far as [*the president*] considers practicable."[28] Both Stevens and Kennedy read this to expressly require deference to the president's determinations.[29] When Congress clearly commands deference to the president, the Court will likely defer. Conversely, when the two different provisions are juxtaposed, the contrast highlights the majority's grounds for making its own determination about uniformity where, as in article 36(b), Congress has simply set forth an objective standard.

Hamdan's focus on separation of powers also marks its approach to the somewhat different question of jurisdiction. This issue differs from the others, and not just because it precedes the merits. First, it directly implicates the Court's own role. Second, it is a concededly closer question, as witnessed by Justice Scalia's typically strong dissent[30] and a flurry of critiques that appear otherwise resigned to the Court's handling of the substantive issues.[31] Despite these differences, the Court again declined to rely on any constitutional or other argument, other than congressional action or inaction—in this instance the DTA. Citing "ordinary principles of statutory construction," Justice Stevens drew a negative inference from the act's failure to grandfather habeas petitions pending in challenges relating to detention in Guantanamo from its provisions stripping federal courts other than the D.C. Circuit of jurisdiction. As the majority noted, this omission contrasts with Congress' express decision to extend jurisdiction provisions to pending cases challenging final determinations from military commissions and combat status review tribunals.[32]

The Scalia dissent nonetheless rightly noted that the provision omitted from the grandfather clause, with its seeming absolute statement that "no court, justice, or judge" shall have jurisdiction to hear

---

[28] 10 U.S.C. § 836(a) (2000).

[29] 126 S. Ct. at 2791; *id.* at 2801 (Kennedy, J., concurring).

[30] *Id.* at 2810 (Scalia, J., dissenting).

[31] See, e.g., Ramesh Ponnuru, Slate's Hamdan Hoax: Justice Stevens just can't be defended, National Review Online (July 28, 2006), at http://article.nationalreview.com/?q=ZDAxOTBjZmYwYmM4NGEwMDQ2MDliYWRiY2U4NTk2Z-jU=&c=1 (criticizing the majority's reading of the DTA).

[32] Hamdan, 126 S. Ct. at 2769.

Guantanamo cases, can easily be read to preclude the Supreme Court's jurisdiction over even the pending *Hamdan* case.[33] And it is difficult to imagine the Republican Congress passing the DTA desiring much else. That said, the Court's conclusion remains faithful to the more fundamental conception of separation of powers that characterizes its handling of the merits. The Court simply will refuse to interpret Congress' enactments in a way that aggrandizes the executive branch even in the context of terrorism, so long as it leaves any plausible ambiguity. Such ambiguity encompasses no text, unclear text, or, in the DTA, exceptionally sloppy text.

B. Deeper Foundations

The aspects of *Hamdan* considered so far read like a technical exercise in statutory interpretation. Yet the context for the exercise is thoroughly constitutional. The Court did not impose anything as mechanical as a clear statement rule, but a refusal to countenance radical transfers of power to the president without some fairly convincing showing of congressional approval runs through the majority and concurring opinions. As noted, this effective requirement in turn springs directly from an inclusive vision of separation of powers, one squarely at odds with that put forward by the Bush administration. Despite the specter of terror, the Court's vision, among other things, looks skeptically at executive claims of independent power, preserves traditional notions that the Constitution divides power not just to promote efficiency but to safeguard liberty, and sees broad-based democratic participation as ultimately serving efficiency in any case. Far from activist, the Court's increasingly clear post-9/11 conception is profoundly conservative. In each regard, the Court's affirmation of the doctrine reflects conventional sources of text, history, structure, custom, and precedent. These bases in turn support *Hamdan*'s analysis of the president's authority throughout, and would have and likely will allow the Court to go even further.

Start with the president's now apparently receding contention that he possesses wide-ranging foreign affairs authority by virtue of the Executive Vesting Clause, the Commander-in-Chief Clause, or sources less clear. The majority's evident skepticism, and even

---

[33] *Id.* at 2810 (Scalia, J., dissenting).

Justice Thomas's cautious deployment of the claim, at best reflect an appropriate realization that there is no there here. As a matter of textual analysis, these clauses support the substantial unenumerated powers attributed to them only if overread in a manner that would make the New Deal Court's handling of the Commerce Clause seem modest. More conclusively, neither the Founding nor eighteenth century history more generally provides any but the most isolated evidence to support the idea that the Constitution confers upon the president broad, non-textual grants of foreign affairs or military power.[34] As rightly noted in *Youngstown*, a case that presidentialists tend to avoid, neither custom nor precedent provides assistance for the executive's claim.[35]

Hamdan makes clear that the "war on terror" is going to change the way the Court treats the president's claims of direct constitutional authority. As in *Rasul* and *Hamdi*, the *Hamdan* majority looked exclusively to congressional authorization as sanction for presidential action. *Hamdan*, moreover, went further in its repeated presumption against ambiguous delegation, an interpretive stance in direct opposition to both the dissent's contrary presumption and to the dissent's corresponding acceptance of the executive's broad claims of direct constitutional authority. As seen, the Court even went so far as to hold that whatever military authority the president possesses does not trump Congress' valid authority of military matters. The constitutional underpinnings that allowed the Court to do all this could have permitted it to reject the executive's broad claims outright. Though such a statement likely would have appeared as dicta, it would have had the salutary effect of rendering explicit the Court's implicit skepticism. For now, it will suffice that *Hamdan*'s unstated position remains clear enough.

Turn now to *Hamdan*'s presumption against unclear delegation. The Court's doctrinal stance reflects and confirms a functional approach to separation of powers that also rests firmly on conventional interpretive bases. Contrary to many of the judges and commentators who argue for expansive executive authority, neither constitutional text, structure, history, nor even custom suffices to

---

[34] See Curtis A. Bradley & Martin S. Flaherty, Executive Power Essentialism and Foreign Affairs, 102 Mich. L. Rev. 545 (2004).

[35] Youngstown Sheet & Tube Co. v. Sawyer, 343 U.S. 579 (1952).

resolve "concrete problems of executive power as they actually present themselves."[36] Nowhere is this more true than in the history of the Founding, the era presidential advocates assert affords the best guidance. The Founding, in tandem with other interpretive sources, does provide guidance, but at a very general level concerning the functions or purposes of separation of powers.[37] One of these is the efficiency born of the division of labor that the doctrine of separation of powers envisions.[38] Justice Thomas's dissent correctly alludes to this functional goal when noting the Founding view that a single executive would enjoy the advantages of energy, secrecy, and dispatch in discharging its functions.[39] But that is only one part of the story. Founding sources indicate the Founding generation viewed separation of powers as a means to create a balance among the government's branches in the service of liberty—which that generation, in turn, valued no less, and probably much more, than efficiency. No statement reflects this concern better than Madison's famous dictum that "the accumulation of all powers, legislative, executive, and judiciary, in the same hands, whether of one, a few, or many, and whether hereditary, self-appointed, or elective, may justly be pronounced the very definition of tyranny."[40]

It follows as a general matter that Justice Thomas's concerns for efficiency should at least be offset against the benefits that a balance of power among the branches yields, at least absent some specific assignment of authority to one branch or another. It follows further that concern for such a balance cuts against any presumption that a particular branch wields exclusive power in a contested area, particularly one in which fundamental liberty is at stake. Viewed in this light, Justice Jackson's concurrence in *Youngstown*, in which he created his famous framework, keyed to Congress' specific approval, disapproval, or failure to act with regard to presidential assertions, can be understood to promote this functional "balance of power" inquiry.

---

[36] *Id.* at 634 (Jackson, J., concurring).

[37] See Martin S. Flaherty, The Most Dangerous Branch, 105 Yale L.J. 1725 (1996).

[38] *Id.* at 1781–95.

[39] Hamdan, 126 S. Ct. at 2823–24 (Thomas, J., dissenting).

[40] The Federalist No. 47, at 269 (James Madison) (Clinton Rossiter ed., 1961); see Flaherty, The Most Dangerous Branch, *supra* note 37, at 1766–68.

Hamdan's preoccupation with manifest congressional action reflects these same functional concerns. Given the majority's doubts about the president's direct constitutional powers, its approach necessarily focuses on specific legislative authorization, and with it, any specific limitations. Once again, however, the foundation could sustain a greater structure. As Justice Kennedy's concurrence demonstrates, the majority could have easily made *Youngstown* the touchstone for its analysis. In particular, Justice Stevens could have stressed that its reading of the UCMJ placed the president's authority at its "lowest ebb."[41] As it is, *Hamdan's* apparent requirement of specific congressional consideration of a matter outside the president's exclusive control bodes ill for an array of executive claims based upon general authorizations such as the AUMF. As has been noted, *Hamdan* almost certainly has shifted the burden onto those who argue that the AUMF authorizes the NSA phone-tapping program.[42] More express reliance on *Youngstown* would nonetheless have served to make this burden even weightier.

Nor is this all. Eighteenth-century sources indicate that, alongside balance and efficiency, the Founding generation came to view separation of powers as broadly advancing democratic accountability. Such accountability was not seen as the exclusive province of a particular branch, but as a joint conception that mandated participation of both Congress and the president outside their clearly exclusive domains, the better to promote deliberation and reflect genuine societal commitments.[43] Presidential champions such as Justice Thomas, however, argue that when it comes to national security, the need for governmental efficiency matters more, and that any doubts should be resolved on behalf of the executive boasting secrecy, dispatch, and vigor. Not only is this position widely

[41] Hamdan, 126 S. Ct. at 2800 (Kennedy, J., concurring) (citing Youngstown, 343 U.S. at 637).

[42] The Department of Justice provided a controversial defense of the NSA spying program in a letter to the majority and minority leaders of the Senate and House Intelligence Committees dated December 22, 2005 and available at www.nationalreview.com/pdf/12%2022%2005%20NSA%20letter.pdf. For a response from leading academics, see Beth Nolan, Curtis Bradley, David Cole, et al., On NSA Spying: A Letter to Congress, 53 N.Y. Rev. of Books, Feb. 9, 2006, available at http://www.nybooks.com/articles/18650.

[43] See Flaherty, The Most Dangerous Branch, *supra* note 37, at 1767–68.

61

assumed, it probably stands at the core of pro-executive arguments in the wake of September 11. Yet the idea of joint accountability and greater democratic participation furnishes a basis to challenge that assumption. And indeed, many from within the national security establishment have done just that, including JAG lawyers who question presidential assertions on power[44] and NSC veterans who argue that greater democratic input facilitates better security planning.[45]

Neither the *Hamdan* majority, nor even Justice Kennedy, builds upon this particular foundation. Justice Breyer's brief concurrence, however, gets at the conclusion almost exactly. As he puts it: "Where, as here, no emergency prevents consultation with Congress, judicial insistence upon that consultation does not weaken our Nation's ability to deal with danger. To the contrary, that insistence strengthens the Nation's ability to determine—through democratic means—how best to do so."[46]

III. The Rule of (International) Law

After separation of powers, *Hamdan*'s significance lies in its defense of the rule of law, in this case, of international law. Such a defense could not have been more timely in light of numerous assaults, including: recent academic critique stressing the limits of international law;[47] the D.C. Circuit's dismissive treatment of Hamdan's international law claims below;[48] and most of all, the Bush administration's ongoing assertions that international law has little or no applicability to the "war on terror," aimed at creating a "law free zone" in which executive discretion would be absolute. Here as before, *Hamdan* achieved its broader result in a narrow fashion. Technically, all the majority did was hold that Congress adopted one substantive set of limits on the president's power to establish

---

[44] See Adam Liptak, The Struggle for Iraq: Procedures; U.S. Barred Legal Review of Detentions, Lawyer Says, N.Y. Times, May 19, 2004, at A14; Josh White, Military Lawyers Fought Policy on Interrogations, Wash. Post, July 15, 2005, at A1.

[45] See James E. Baker, United States Court of Appeals for the Armed Forces, National Security Process and a Lawyer's Duty: Remarks to the Senior Judge Advocate Symposium, 173 Mil. L. Rev. 124, 130 (2002).

[46] Hamdan, 126 S. Ct. at 2799 (Breyer, J., concurring).

[47] Jack L. Goldsmith & Eric A. Posner, The Limits of International Law (2005).

[48] Hamdan v. Rumsfeld, 415 F.3d 33 (D.C. Cir. 2005); but see *id.* at 44 (Williams, J., concurring).

military commissions, and that these came from Common Article 3 of the Geneva Conventions of 1949. But the Court nonetheless took international law seriously in two regards. Most importantly, it took it seriously in itself, interpreting the conventions' protections carefully and without deference to radical interpretations put forward by the president. In addition, the majority paradoxically used the limitations of international law to permit Congress to render the conventions justiciable. Once again, *Hamdan*'s conclusions rest upon compelling bases, international and domestic, that could have vindicated international law even more extensively, and may yet have an opportunity to do so.

A. Taking International Law Seriously

Overstatement aside, the Court did not quite hold that "[t]he procedures adopted to try Hamdan also violate the Geneva Conventions."[49] Rather, the majority decided only that article 21 of the UCMJ incorporates these treaties by conditioning the establishment of military commissions on adherence to the laws of war, which by the time of the UCMJ's passage included the four Geneva Conventions. *Hamdan* in other words did not determine whether the treaties, which the United States duly ratified, would themselves have given Hamdan a defense as self-executing "supreme Law of the Land"[50] in the absence of Congress' incorporation. Even so, Congress' statutory incorporation of these norms requires judges to interpret treaties and, where the incorporation so extends, to apply customary international law, on the merits. And this the Court did with appropriate respect and care.

Not the first, but by far the most important, issue involved the applicability of Common Article 3. As was once known only to specialists, the four Geneva Conventions provide extensive protections to individuals in cases of armed conflict "between two or more of the High Contracting Parties," that is, sovereign nations that have ratified the treaties.[51] By contrast, Common Article 3, common to all

[49] Hamdan, 126 S. Ct. at 2793.

[50] U.S. Const. art. VI, cl. 2 ("[A]ll treaties made, or which shall be made, under the Authority of the United States, shall be the supreme Law of the Land."); see also Breard v. Greene, 523 U.S. 371, 375 (1998) ("[T]reaties are recognized by our Constitution as the supreme law of the land.").

[51] See, e.g., Convention Relative to the Treatment of Prisoners of War, art. 3, Aug. 12, 1949, 6 U.S.T. 3316, 3318, 75 U.N.T.S. 135, 136.

four conventions, provides lesser but still fundamental rights to persons no longer taking part in hostilities: "[i]n the case of armed conflict not of an international character occurring in the territory of one of the High Contracting Parties."[52] The administration correctly contended that since al-Qaeda was not a sovereign nation and so not a High Contracting Party, the full scope of the convention's protections did not apply. But it also put forward the radical argument that Common Article 3 did not apply since al-Qaeda's terrorist attacks were international in character. A majority of the D.C. Circuit panel below, including then-Judge Roberts, accepted this argument.

With rigor and economy, the majority exposed this government's position for the sophistry it is. Given the extensive protections that the conventions set out to apply to conflicts between sovereigns that have ratified them, reasoned Justice Stevens, Common Article 3's baseline protections apply to any conflicts that do not rise to that level. Textually, the majority noted that "international" has been a term of art since first coined by Jeremy Bentham, literally meaning "between countries."[53] A conflict not of an international character thus simply means hostilities not between two nation states, rather than conflict entirely within national borders. The Court confirmed its interpretation with the persuasive commentaries put out by the International Committee of the Red Cross, the body the conventions accord distinctive implementation powers. Likewise, Justice Stevens found further confirmation for his opinion in the holdings of international tribunals, including the International Court of Justice and the International Tribunal for the Former Yugoslavia.[54]

Not only did the Court interpret Common Article 3 with care, it also sustained its authority "to say what the law is."[55] By contrast, Justice Thomas's dissent argued that the Court had a "duty" to defer to the president's interpretation of the treaty both as a general matter and as a function of his role as commander in chief with regard to treaties dealing with armed conflict. His proposed standard, moreover, approached *Chevron* deference insofar as an executive interpretation need only be "reasonable" or "plausible" to be followed. Not

[52] *Id.*

[53] Hamdan, 126 S. Ct. at 2796.

[54] *Id.* at 2794–96.

[55] Marbury v. Madison, 5 U.S. (1 Cranch) 137 (1803).

surprisingly, he concluded that the president's argument that the "war on terror" was "international" and so beyond the scope of Common Article 3 was sufficiently plausible notwithstanding the textual, structural, persuasive, and comparative evidence to the contrary.[56] For his part Justice Stevens did not address the deference argument expressly, leaving the Court's action to speak for itself.

The Court dealt with Common Article 3's specific requirements more tersely, in part because they are so basic. The violation on which the majority focused centered on the condition that persons be tried "by a regularly constituted court." Relying on analogous treaty provisions and again on the ICRC's commentaries, Justices Stevens and Kennedy both concluded that "[t]he regular military courts in our system are the courts-martial established by congressional statutes."[57] In the light of historic practice, at most the president may convene a commission only when practical need justifies divergence from a court-martial, and no such need had been demonstrated.[58] Justice Stevens argued that the commissions also violated Common Article 3's requirement that the court in question afford "all the judicial guarantees, which are recognized as indispensable by civilized peoples."[59] Of these, he argued, the commissions failed to observe an accused's right to be present at trial and to be privy to the evidence against him or her.[60] This contention, however, commanded only a plurality. Justice Kennedy decided against joining this part of the Stevens opinion—first, because of the possibility that appellate procedures might cure these defects and, second, due to his reluctance to draw upon treaties that the United States has declined to ratify (here Protocol I to the Geneva Conventions), to which Justice Stevens referred.[61]

The other way that the majority took international law seriously was to deem it justiciable. In *Johnson v. Eisentrager*, the Court rejected a claim, made by Nazis tried before a U.S. military tribunal convened in China, that their trial violated the Geneva Conventions on the

---

[56] Hamdan, 126 S. Ct. at 2823 (Thomas, J., dissenting).

[57] *Id.* at 2797; *id.* at 2803 (Kennedy, J., concurring).

[58] *Id.* at 2804 (Kennedy, J., concurring).

[59] *Id.* at 2795–97.

[60] *Id.* at 2798 & n.67.

[61] *Id.* at 2809 (Kennedy, J., concurring).

ground that it impermissibly deviated from a court-martial.[62] In a footnote, however, *Eisentrager* also stated that the only remedies the Geneva Conventions contemplated were diplomatic and political in any case.[63] The Court immediately distinguished this potential hurdle. For the sake of argument, it assumed without deciding that the 1949 conventions, like their 1921 predecessor considered by the *Eisentrager* Court, would not be a basis for judicial enforcement "absent some other provision of law."[64] But here, Justice Stevens argued that the "other provision" was article 21 of the UCMJ, which conditioned its recognition of authority regarding commissions on compliance with the laws of war. Congress, in short, provided a judicially enforceable remedy for the Geneva Conventions by limiting their authority to adherence to the treaties as a matter of domestic law.[65]

B. Stronger Foundations

Hamdan reflects the Court's growing sense of ownership over international law. Both globalization generally, and national security issues more specifically, will continue to provide cases that require interpretation of international legal materials to resolve truly fundamental issues, rather than technical questions about airline liability or illegal drug markets, however important.[66] With questions of basic rights and presidential authority inevitably comes greater focus and

---

[62] 339 U.S. 763 (1950).

[63] *Id.* at 789 n.14.

[64] 126 S. Ct. at 2794.

[65] If anything, Justice Stevens took customary international law of warfare even more seriously than the treaty law of the Geneva Conventions. His opinion in fact devotes its initial and more extensive efforts to demonstrate that the UCMJ's law of war limitation on presidential action precludes the vague conspiracy to commit terrorist acts for which Hamdan was charged. This effort, however, commanded only a plurality. Hamdan, 126 S. Ct. at 2775–86 (opinion of Stevens, J.). The justice's comprehensive effort to articulate often imprecise international custom nonetheless provides further evidence of the Court's commitment to take international law seriously.

[66] Gonzales v. O Centro Espirita Beneficiente Uniao do Vegetal, 126 S. Ct. 1211, 1224–25 (2006) (interpreting the UN Convention on Psychotropic Substances); Eastern Airlines, Inc. v. Floyd, 499 U.S. 530 (1991) (interpreting the term "lésion corporelle" in the (Warsaw) Convention for the Unification of Certain Rules Relating to International Transportation by Air).

deliberation. While the majority opinion reflects these qualities, however, the bases for its conclusions once more are stronger than the arguments it offered, and point to broader conclusions. Entirely conventional methods of treaty interpretation confirm the Court's interpretation of Common Article 3 with almost embarrassing clarity. Yet they also challenge the assumption that the Geneva Conventions only contemplate political enforcement. Beyond the substance of the treaties, international sources combine with Founding understandings about international law to sustain the Court's authority to decide the treaty issues in the first place. The point applies to both the majority's refusal to defer to the executive's interpretations and to its determination that the Geneva Conventions are justiciable.

Nowhere does *Hamdan* make a more convincing case than its holding that Common Article 3 applies in armed conflicts generally. Its persuasiveness rests not only upon an array of sources concisely presented, but also upon the conclusion itself, which reflects as close to a consensus interpretation as is possible outside the White House. At one point, however, Justice Stevens highlighted that one purpose of the provision was to provide protections in civil wars. That mention, fine so far as it goes, could be misread to complement a favorite administration argument that the article was meant to apply to civil wars alone. Although the opinion rejected this view, it did so by reference only to the deletion of a proposed text that would have expressly tied the provision to civil wars, religious wars, and colonial conflicts, wrongly reading the deleted text as a limitation itself.[67]

A broader view of the treaties' context would leave less doubt. The origins of Common Article 3 came from the ICRC's proposal to apply the full protections contemplated for the conventions to conflicts "not of an international character, especially civil wars, religious war, and colonial conflicts."[68] This language was widely understood to mandate coverage in a wide range of conflicts, including insurrections, rebellions, the break-up of states, and brigandage.[69] Various national delegations balked at the prospect of full protection

[67] 126 S. Ct. at 2796.

[68] Convention Relative to the Treatment of Prisoners of War, art. 3, Aug. 12, 1949, 6 U.S.T. 3316, 3318, 75 U.N.T.S. 135, 136.

[69] See Jean Pictet, Commentaries of Geneva Conventions of 12 August 1949 (1952), and International Committee of the Red Cross, Commentary on Additional Protocols of 8 June 1977 to the Geneva Conventions of 12 August 1949 (1987).

in light of such exceptionally broad coverage. The solution therefore became the protection of more basic rights, while retaining the idea of coverage to all armed conflict.[70] Nor, for that matter, would an emphasis on civil war support a conclusion that the article applied only to conflicts within national boundaries. As the *travaux preparatoires* make clear, the paradigmatic civil war on the minds of the delegates shaping the treaties was the Spanish Civil War. While the actual conflict occurred within Spain's borders, the conflict famously attracted fascist and anti-fascist men and materiel from around the world, including the Abe Lincoln Brigade from the United States.[71]

A more thoroughgoing use of international legal materials might also have kept Justice Kennedy with the rest of the majority on the issue of Common Article 3's substantive requirements. Recall that the justice defected based on uncertainty over whether a right to be present at trial and a right to review relevant evidence qualified as fundamental protections "recognized by civilized peoples."[72] That uncertainty stemmed from his concern that a principal source for recognizing these rights was article 75 of Protocol I to the Geneva Conventions, a treaty that the United States has not ratified.[73] Yet, other treaties the nation has ratified do recognize the rights at issue, above all the International Covenant on Civil and Political Rights.[74] So too do measures that the U.S. has supported in the UN Security Council, including: the Statute of International Criminal Tribunal for the Former Yugoslavia[75] and the Statute of the International Criminal Tribunal for Rwanda.[76]

---

[70] *Id.*

[71] See ICRC Commentaries of Convention for the Amelioration of the Condition of the Wounded and the Sick in Armed Forces in the Field 20, 12 August 1944, 6 U.S.T. 3114, T.I.A.S. No. 3362, 75 U.N.T.S. 31 ("Geneva I").

[72] Hamdan, 126 S. Ct. at 2809 (Kennedy, J., concurring).

[73] Protocol Additional to the Geneva Conventions of 12 August 1949, and Relating to the Protection of Victims of International Armed Conflicts ("API"), art. 75, June 8, 1977, 1125 U.N.T.S. 3.

[74] International Covenant on Civil and Political Rights, arts. 9 & 14, 16 December, 1966, 21 U.N. GAOR Supp. (No. 16) at 52, 999 U.N.T.S. 171 (hereinafter ICCPR).

[75] Statute of the International Criminal Tribunal for the Former Yugoslavia, art. 21, S/Res/827, May 25, 1993, U.N. Doc. S/25704 at 36, annex (1993).

[76] Statute of the International Criminal Tribunal for Rwanda, art. 20, S/Res/955, Nov. 8, 1994, U.N. Doc. ITR/3/REV.1 (1995).

Absent specific statutory repeal, moreover, the relevant question is not whether the nation has declined to recognize the rights, but rather the content of the international law that the UCMJ incorporates. On this point, widely-ratified treaties that the U.S. either would not have an opportunity to join, such as the European Convention for Human Rights,[77] or (as with Protocol I) simply has declined to join, such as the American Convention on Human Rights,[78] are just prominent indications of a global consensus showing that "civilized peoples" see the rights at issue as essential. For this reason, President Bush's own former legal advisor at the State Department concludes that article 75 of the unratified Protocol I had achieved the status of customary international law, which requires that type of recognition that Common Article 3 demands.[79]

However well supported, the Court's interpretations of international law matter only so far as it gets to do the interpreting in the first place. The majority asserted this authority both implicitly, by declining to defer to the president's treaty interpretations, and expressly, by finding that the Geneva Conventions are justiciable. International law supports these determinations as well. And in these areas especially, domestic foreign relations law considerations also point to judicial enforcement of treaty obligations absent provisions to the contrary.

The more conventional the sources, the more strongly foreign relations law and international law point away from judicial deference. Or at least they do when deference to the executive interpretations would cause the nation to shirk its international legal obligations or otherwise become a global outlier. Text, evident Founding understandings, and early practice, among other things, confirm this conclusion. First, nothing in constitutional text suggests

[77] Convention for the Protection of Human Rights and Fundamental Freedoms (as amended), arts. 5 & 6, 213 U.N.T.S. 222.

[78] American Convention on Human Rights, arts. 3, 5, 8 & 25, Nov. 21, 1969, O.A.S.T.S. No. 36, 1144 U.N.T.S. 143, 9 I.L.M. 99 (1969).

[79] The U.S. regards "the provisions of article 75 as an articulation of safeguards to which all persons in the hands of an enemy are entitled." William Taft IV, The Law of Armed Conflict After 9/11, 28 Yale J. Int'l L. 319, 322 (2003). See Brief of the Association of the Bar of the City of New York and the Human Rights Institute of the International Bar Association as Amici Curiae at 14–19, Hamdan v. Rumsfeld, 126 S. Ct. 2749 (2006) (No. 05-184).

that the president's views on international law should be privileged.[80] To the contrary, any need to apply law in the context of judicial proceedings falls in the very core of *Marbury's* fundamental holding.[81] Second, an overwhelming mass of historical sources demonstrate that a critical factor that led to the federal constitutional convention was the nation's need to provide domestic judicial enforcement of its international obligations to protect individual rights—specifically, contract and property rights guaranteed to British subjects under the 1783 Treaty of Paris, which ended the Revolutionary War. Among other things, the sources make abundantly clear that this concern led directly to the Supremacy Clause proclaiming treaties to be the "supreme Law of the Land" and to the resulting doctrine of self-execution.[82] It also led to the Supreme Court's recognition of the *Charming Betsy* canon, which holds that a statute should not be interpreted to violate international law if another construction is possible.[83] Third, early practice confirmed the expectation that the courts would apply international law independently, free from executive interference. As fresh research by Professor David Sloss shows, between 1789 and 1838, the Supreme Court considered nineteen individual rights claims under treaties in which the U.S. government argued against the claimant on the merits. Despite the executive's position, the Court held for the aggrieved party against the government fourteen times and was evenly divided in another two.[84]

Hamdan's return to first principles, moreover, appears to be the way of the future. Despite various and recent statements in dicta paying lip service to the idea of judicial deference in foreign affairs,

---

[80] This is a different matter from the president lawfully terminating a treaty.

[81] Marbury v. Madison, 5 U.S. (1 Cranch) 137, 173 (1803).

[82] For accounts summarizing this near consensus view, see Martin S. Flaherty, History Right?: Historical Scholarship, Original Understanding, and Treaties as "Supreme Law of the Land," 99 Colum. L. Rev. 2095 (1999); Carlos Manuel Vazquez, Laughing at Treaties, 99 Colum. L. Rev. 2154 (1999). But see John C. Yoo, Globalism and the Constitution: Treaties, Non-Self-Execution, and the Original Understanding, 99 Colum. L. Rev. 1955 (1999).

[83] Murray v. The Schooner Charming Betsy, 6 U.S. (2 Cranch) 64, 82 (1804).

[84] David Sloss, Judicial Deference to Executive Branch Treaty Interpretations: A Historical Perspective, 62 NYU Annual Survey of Am. L. (forthcoming 2006), available at http://ssrn.com/abstract=889924.

the Court this past term further staked out its domain in *Sanchez-Llamas v. Oregon*.[85] There, the justices declined to accord deference to the International Court of Justice and rejected a claim that the Vienna Convention on Consular Relations, a self-executing treaty signed and ratified by the United States, foreclosed use of the state procedural default rules to bar domestic judiciaries from resolving the underlying treaty issues on the merits.[86] The Court's specific interpretation is debatable. The decision, however, helps demonstrate that *Hamdan*'s refusal to defer is not idiosyncratic. Chief Justice Roberts, writing for the majority, engaged in extended and careful international law analysis, as did Justice Breyer in dissent.[87] They did so, moreover, on their own terms, rather than following the lead of the ICJ, the president, or any other pretender to assertions of deference.

The same, likewise understated, combination of international law and internationalist domestic law would have permitted the Court to speak with far greater confidence concerning justiciability. The analysis here begins on the international side. The majority should not have assumed, with the *Eisentrager* Court, that the Geneva Conventions themselves contemplated a scheme of diplomatic and political enforcement exclusively, or even that such a scheme would preclude domestic judicial enforcement absent some other provision of law. At worst, all the treaties do is leave the decision regarding whether a sovereign government should add complementary domestic remedies or defenses to the sovereign national government. In this, the treaties reflect an older conception of international law, which generally did not address how a domestic legal system should provide remedies or otherwise be ordered.[88] Even here, though, our nation's early peacetime treaties often cut the other way, as exemplified by the Treaty of Paris itself, which clearly contemplated some form of domestic judicial enforcement, even if its express terms did not so mandate.[89]

---

[85] Sanchez-Llamas v. Oregon, 126 S. Ct. 2669 (2006).

[86] *Id.* at 2674.

[87] *Id.* at 2675–88 (Roberts, C.J., concurring); *id.* at 2691–09 (Breyer, J., dissenting).

[88] Bradley & Flaherty, Executive Power Essentialism, *supra* note 34, at 570–71.

[89] Article 4 of the treaty stated that "creditors on either side shall meet with no lawful impediment to the recovery of the full value in sterling money of all bona fide debts heretofore contracted," while article 6 declared that there "shall be no future confiscations made nor any prosecutions commenced" against former loyalists.

Today, however, a requirement that states provide meaningful domestic remedies for individual treaty rights has become a general feature of international law, both as treaty and arguably as custom. In the aftermath of Word War II, the Universal Declaration of Human Rights proclaimed: "Everyone has the right to an effective remedy by the competent national tribunals for acts violating the fundamental rights granted him by the constitution or by law."[90] The ICCPR, which the U.S. has ratified, calls for states to ensure effective remedies before "competent judicial, administrative or legislative authorities" and further calls on states "to develop the possibilities of judicial remedy."[91]

Combine modern international law's general orientation toward effective and ideal remedies with U.S. law's similarly directed historic stance. Here, at worst, one might concede that the Congress that passed the UCMJ likely did not contemplate domestic judicial enforcement. Even here, the Court's post-World War II considerations of individual claims under the Geneva Conventions' predecessor treaty in *In re Yamashita*[92] and, for that matter, in *Eisentrager* itself suggest otherwise. Congress in 1950 had these precedents before it and offered no statutory language precluding judicial enforcement.

But even assuming no clear legislative guidance one way or the other, an interpretation permitting judicial enforcement better comports with traditional domestic law principles in at least two regards. For one, it accords with the general Founding commitment of vindicating individual treaty claims, as reflected in text and early practice.

The Definitive Treaty of Peace (1783), available at http://www.yale.edu/lawweb/ avalon/diplomacy/britain/paris.htm.

[90] Universal Declaration of Human Rights, art. 8, G.A. res. 217A (III), U.N. Doc A/ 810 at 71 (1948).

[91] ICCPR, art. 2(3)(b), *supra* note 74. Notwithstanding this provision, the U.S. had announced a declaration to the effect that the ICCPR shall not be self-executing. See 138 Cong. Rec. S4781-01 (daily ed., April 2, 1992). This does not change my general point: that international law now generally requires effective domestic remedies of international rights claims and further calls for judicial remedies as the best means toward this end.

[92] In re Yamashita, 327 U.S. 1 (1946). As Justice Kennedy noted, that case also dealt with a claim challenging military commission proceedings, yet there "the Court likewise considered . . . the merits—without any caveat about remedies under the Convention—a claim that an alleged violation of the 1929 Convention 'establish[ed] want of authority in the commission to proceed with the trial.'" *Id.* at 23–24 (citation omitted).

This point applies with additional force given that *Hamdan* relied on the treaties merely to impose a defense to an illegal trial by way of a habeas petition, a reliance on international law that could scarcely be more modest or circumscribed. For another, interpreting the UCMJ to allow justiciability further comports with the related commitment to follow international law more generally. In this instance, that commitment could be realized through an interpretation that better reflects international law's basic stance in favor of domestic, and ideally, judicial remedies. This second point itself applies with added force given a now largely forgotten international law principle that called for a "denial of justice" claim where a nation could not or would not vindicate its citizens' interests through diplomatic means.[93] Since no nation or organization exists to assert the rights of someone in Hamdan's position, his claims fall squarely within this historic paradigm.

IV. Comparative Law

The *Hamdan* decision finds further support in still one more significant source, one on which it barely relied. This source is comparative law. As we have seen, separation of powers principles more than justify the Court's treatment of authorization. International law readily supports the majority's consideration of the rights at issue. Comparative law adds further support for *Hamdan*'s decision to reject deference to the executive as a constitutional mandate not just in treaty interpretation, but in foreign affairs generally.

The battle over comparative law was fought mainly on the margins and between the lines. Justice Thomas's dissent takes the Court to task for hamstringing the president.[94] Outside the Court, so too did Professor Yoo, who bemoaned what the decision would do to undermine the president's "creativity" in fighting terrorism.[95] Of course, the first response to these arguments must be that separation of powers and the rule of law in large part exist to check overly creative executives. This argument, however, leaves unchallenged the basic assumption that the executive should get a substantial

---

[93] See Thomas H. Lee, The Safe-Conduct Theory of the Alien Tort Statute, 106 Colum. L. Rev. 830, 881 n.265 (2006).

[94] Hamdan v. Rumsfeld, 126 S. Ct. 2749, 2823–26 (2006) (Thomas, J., dissenting).

[95] Adam Liptak, The Court Enters the War, Loudly, N.Y. Times, July 2, 2006, at § 4, 1.

benefit of any doubt in the application of these doctrines since it knows more about foreign affairs, especially security, and above all the global terrorist threat. But a survey of other jurisdictions suggests that there is another side to this issue. Faced with terror, governments around the world tend to overreact and trample basic liberties. Over-reaction may also lead to policies that are easy, sloppy, and counter-productive. For all these reasons, future courts would do well to follow Justice Jackson's example in *Youngstown*, look abroad, and decline the invitation of automatic deference to the president expressly.

A. Executive "Creativity" and Terrorism

Neither Justice Stevens nor Justice Kennedy showed any inclination to hold the judiciary back in the face of the executive's foreign affairs competence. Unlike the questions concerning authorization and rights, the issue of possible deference did not receive its own rubric, section, or analyses. Instead, the matter runs through the opinions, cropping up at points in which opportunities for the Court to defer arose and were bypassed. Having agreed that the UCMJ requires some practical justification for the creation of military commissions, the majority and concurrence refuse to take the executive's mere establishment of them as a fulfillment of this requirement.[96] As noted, both opinions similarly refuse to give any apparent weight to the president's imaginative interpretation of Common Article 3.[97]

Neither the Stevens nor Kennedy opinion defends its failure to defer. Where they refer to deference at all, the discussion relates purely to a statutory duty to defer imposed by Congress, not a general constitutional imperative. In this regard, each justice notes that UCMJ article 36(a) appeared to call for genuine deference to a presidential determination that practical considerations justify courts-martial and military commissions diverging from procedures in federal district courts.[98] Each opinion also mentioned in passing that "some deference" would be owed an actual presidential attempt to justify commission rules diverging from courts-martial under article 36(b).[99] At no point, however, did either one refer to the

---

[96] Hamdan, 126 S. Ct. at 2790–93; *id.* at 2800–02 (Kennedy, J., concurring).

[97] *Id.* at 2795–97; *id.* at 2802–05 (Kennedy, J., concurring).

[98] *Id.* at 2791–92; *id.* at 2807–08 (Kennedy, J., concurring).

[99] *Id.* at 2791 n.51; *id.* at 2801 (Kennedy, J., concurring).

possibility that the executive's peculiar foreign affairs expertise, as a constitutional matter, should influence the extent of statutory deference or the adequacy of the president's justifications. With regard to this kind of deference, the Court was simply silent.

This silence places *Hamdan* on one of two possible places along an analytic spectrum. At one end is an acknowledged constitutional duty to accord the executive some measure of deference in foreign affairs matters. Next comes a silent acceptance of this imperative. Silence in this instance may be useful should the Court determine that the relevant legal materials rebut any claim of deference, but do not do so compellingly, so any requirement to defer is best left unstated. The point after this is silent rejection of any requirement to give special weight to presidential determinations. Silence here might be advisable to keep on board a justice who is skeptical of the doctrine, but does not yet want to announce its demise in light of previous dicta. The point after this on the spectrum is an express rejection of deference. Beyond this point, finally, lies a reverse presumption, such as the application of a higher level of scrutiny, in which the president must offer a higher than usual justification for his actions. Without more, *Hamdan*'s silence may indicate simply that deference is alive and well, but that separation of powers and international law were strong enough to trump it in this case. Or it might mean that deference itself is in trouble.

Hamdan's context gives reason to suppose that at least five justices are not in the mood to err on the side of the president. First, the Court's silence comes in the face of Justice Thomas's dissent, which speaks of "our duty to defer to the Executive's military and foreign policy judgment," based upon various textual grants of foreign affairs authority to the president, quotations from the Founders, the executive's structural advantages of decisiveness, and dicta culled from case law.[100] Second, the Court's silence extends to its own previous dicta, in cases where it had alluded to the need to defer in matters such as treaty interpretation.[101] Third, *Hamdan* comes in

[100] *Id.* at 2825, 2823–26 (Thomas, J., dissenting).

[101] See, e.g., El Al Israel Airlines, Ltd. v. Tsui Yuan Tseng, 525 U.S. 155, 168 (1999) (quoting Sumitomo Shoji American, Inc. v. Avagliano, 457 U.S. 176, 184–85 (1982)). See also United States v. Stuart, 489 U.S. 353, 369 (1989) (same); Kolovrat v. Oregon, 366 U.S. 187, 194 (1961) ("While courts interpret treaties for themselves, the meaning given them by the departments of government particularly charged with their negotiation and enforcement is given great weight.").

the wake of the attacks of September 11. Whether President Bush qualifies as a war time commander in chief, his actions respond to a grave national security threat. Finally, and relatedly, there has been no shortage of imaginative, presidentialist lawyers and scholars who have sought to push the envelope of executive power for these and other reasons.[102] Not least in this regard is Professor Yoo himself, who has consistently argued that the novelty of the terrorist threat compels a broad conception of executive power in order to enable the president to respond to terrorism in effective and creative ways.

Amidst this array of pro-executive assertions, the Court's reticence on deference must rest on something more than the strength of Hamdan's arguments on the UCMJ and Common Article 3 in this specific case. The majority's general avoidance of deference rhetoric—giving no indication that it regretfully must countermand the president because the law gives the court no other choice, for example—suggests that skepticism about deference itself silently drives the opinion. But if *Hamdan* does signal a move in that direction, it should say as much and say why. Comparative law would help it to do so.

B. Wider Foundations

The specific yet still vast area of comparative law that bears upon post 9/11 deference centers upon executive responses to terrorism. Currently, the International Commission of Jurists is undertaking a study of just this topic under the direction of Arthur Chaskelson, former chief justice of the South African Constitutional Court.[103] Pending this comprehensive study, a mountain of information remains available concerning governmental responses to terrorism in reports by bar associations, human rights NGOs, and academic programs. Together, these sources point to the darker side of executive decisiveness, activity, secrecy, and dispatch.[104] They first show that a consistent cost of responding to terrorism is systemic violations

[102] See John C. Yoo, Rejoinder: Treaty Interpretation and the False Sirens of Delegation, 90 Calif. L. Rev. 1305 (2002); John C. Yoo, Politics as Law?: The Anti-Ballistic Missile Treaty, the Separation of Powers, and Treaty Interpretation, 89 Calif. L. Rev. 851 (2001).

[103] Information on the panel conducting this study may be found at: http://ejp.icj.org/article.php3?id_article=6.

[104] Cf. Hamdan, 126 S. Ct. at 2823 (Thomas, J., dissenting) (citations omitted).

of the most basic rights. They further give grounds to question that this cost brings any countervailing pay-off in the form of effective security responses.

Comparative law first of all suggests that governments confronting terror, above all executives, habitually err on the side of violating fundamental rights. One contemporary and useful measure of this cost comes via international human rights law. A few examples drawn from personal experience must suffice to illustrate how. Of these, perhaps the most pertinent to the United States is the United Kingdom's experience in Northern Ireland. There, for thirty years the U.K. faced a deadly yet relatively small threat from nationalist and loyalist paramilitary groups. Successive U.K. governments responded by obtaining parliamentary enactment of a series of emergency laws and installing a massive security presence of police and army. While the level of violence ebbed and flowed, these policies resulted in violations of international human rights laws across the board. For example, the right against arbitrary arrest and detention fell prey to internment policies and standards permitting seven-day detention without a hearing. The right not to endure torture or cruel, inhuman, or degrading treatment suffered from various extreme techniques applied in prison as well, standards allowing admission of coerced confessions, and a failure to provide preventative monitoring. The right to life itself bowed before well-documented shoot-to-kill policies as well as also well-documented collusion between the security forces and loyalist paramilitaries, including the use of death squads.[105]

The U.K. is one of the more benign examples of executive overreach. Britain also bequeathed to its former colonies the type of emergency response that it employed to deal with earlier bouts of Northern Ireland violence. Further personal experience here includes Malaysia, Kenya, South Africa,[106] and Hong Kong.[107] Whenever governments in

[105] Over a decade of personally documenting these violations in country through numerous human rights missions appear in Lawyers Committee for Human Rights, Human Rights and Legal Defense in Northern Ireland (1993); Lawyers Committee for Human Rights, At the Crossroads: Human Rights and the Northern Ireland Peace Process (1996); Crowley Program in International Human Rights & Lawyers Committee for Human Rights, Obstacles to Reform: Human Rights in Turkey (1999).

[106] See Martin S. Flaherty, Human Rights Violations against Defense Lawyers: The Case of Northern Ireland, 7 Harv. Hum. Rts. J. 87, 88–89 (1994).

[107] Hong Kong stands out as mainly a potential example, since it has not had the occasion to put its colonial security laws in operation to the extent of the other

these jurisdictions perceived a terrorist threat or some equivalent, their reactions led to the same types of human rights violations, often on a larger scale. The pattern of violations in some of these countries led to more entrenched violations of certain rights, including the use of counter-terror measures to target political opponents and restrictions on democracy itself. Malaysia, for example, has made detention without trial a permanent feature of its legal landscape with its infamous Internal Security Act. It has used this and other laws to break otherwise lawful opposition movements or parties. It has also used the threat of terror to perpetuate restrictions on freedom of the press and democratic self-government in which the opposition has a meaningful chance to win executive power.[108] And the account can go on. To take just one more example, Turkey's response to Kurdish violence entailed all of the above restrictions, and added a direct assault on judicial independence through the establishment of special state security courts to handle terrorist defendants.[109]

Comparative law's lesson that executives rush to sacrifice rights in the name of security may appear obvious. But proponents of deference to the executive in the "war on terror" fail to draw the obvious lesson. It may well be that in any well-ordered government, the executive uses institutional strengths to err on the side of security in the face of threat or attack. Yet the other side of the equation is that it is equally the job of the judiciary to defend fundamental rights that the domestic system has either entrenched or incorporated from international law against executive, or for that matter against legislative, pathologies. Domestic materials may suffice to remind us of this lesson. Foreign materials nonetheless remind us of the need for the courts to play their assigned role in the present context.

Comparative study challenges a submissive attitude to the president in a second way by challenging the assumption that executive

former colonies. See Report of the Committee on International Human Rights of the Association of the Bar of the City of New York and Joseph R. Crowley Program in International Human Rights at Fordham Law School, Legal Analysis of Certain Provisions of the National Security (Legislative Provision) Bill Pending before the Legislative Council of the Hong Kong Special Administrative Region, available at http://www.abcny.org/pdf/report/30637027.pdf (accessed August 9, 2006).

[108] See Nicole Fritz & Martin Flaherty, Unjust Order: Malaysia's Internal Security Act (Crowley Program in International Human Rights 2003).

[109] See Obstacles to Reform, *supra* note 105.

creativity, left to its own devices, will produce the most effective results. To be sure, lawyers have little valuable to say on this point either pro or con. Whether executive authority on its own will be the best means to stop future terrorist attacks, secure vital intelligence, undermine the conditions that allow terrorism to breed, or identify the weapon of mass destruction that terrorists might use are all questions better addressed by political scientists, the police, the military, and security experts. Lawyers can identify violations of constitutional or international rights. Their views on whether the typical actions of an unchecked executive will end violence or backfire and foment it tend to be derivative or plain speculation.

With this caveat in mind, the experience of other jurisdictions can still undercut certain ready assumptions. Mexico, for another example observed first-hand, possesses a criminal justice system that in many relevant respects mimics an emergency law regime, including ease of arrest, unmonitored detention, admissibility of problematic confessions, and a comparatively free hand for police and prosecutors. The net effect has been not merely rights violations, but a phenomenon of "rounding up the usual suspects," in part resulting in the innocent going to jail, the guilty going free, and consistently high crime rates.[110] Northern Ireland illustrates an even more counterproductive example of internment without trial during the early 1970s. Under U.K. policy toward Northern Ireland, employed by an aggressive executive under a longstanding parliamentary authorization, hundreds of mainly young Catholic men were rounded up and interned, ostensibly to defuse the threat posed by the Irish Republican Army. Far from eliminating this threat, the conventional wisdom is that the resentment internment produced proved to be an IRA recruitment boon.

Perhaps not surprisingly, these foreign examples echo domestic voices that question the efficacy of granting the executive too much power. As some security experts have argued, unaccountable executive power, among other things, can lead to a reliance on easy options, such as detention of unpopular individuals, at the expense

[110] Crowley Program in International Human Rights & Centro de Derechos Humanos Agustín Pro Juárez, Presumed Guilty? Criminal Justice and Human Rights in Mexico 805–07 (2000).

of the harder work of coordinating and analyzing intelligence.[111] Justice Breyer appears to have had something like these tendencies in mind when he stated that "judicial insistence upon that consultation does not weaken our Nation's ability to deal with danger," but rather "strengthens the Nation's ability to determine—through democratic means—how best to do so."[112]

Lest actual Supreme Court reliance on comparative law appears fanciful, return to Justice Jackson's robust performance in *Youngstown*. Professor Vicki Jackson (no relation) has usefully recaptured the concurrence's neglected yet timely reliance on foreign constitutional experience.[113] As she notes, Justice Jackson surveyed German, French, and British constitutional practice in the period leading up to World War II.[114] The lesson he drew was that unchecked executive power will threaten freedom, particularly in perceived emergencies. In the words of the concurrence:

> This contemporary foreign experience may be inconclusive as to the wisdom of lodging emergency powers somewhere in a modern government. But it suggests that emergency powers are consistent with free government only when their control is lodged elsewhere than in the Executive who exercises them. . . . Nothing in my experience convinces me that such risks are warranted by any real necessity, although such powers would, of course, be an executive convenience.[115]

For Jackson, the first line of defense was the legislature. Without it, he famously doubted the ability of the courts to stand in the way. "I have no illusion," he wrote, "that any decision by this Court can keep power in the hands of Congress if it is not wise and timely in meeting its problems."[116]

The neglected discussion of foreign experience in the Jackson concurrence shows how much further the current Court could go in

---

[111] Baker, National Security Process, *supra* note 45.

[112] Hamdan v. Rumsfeld, 126 S. Ct. 2749, 2799 (2006) (Breyer, J., concurring).

[113] See generally Vicki C. Jackson, Constitutional Law and Transnational Comparisons, The Youngstown Decision and American Exceptionalism, 29 Harv. J.L. & Pub. Pol'y (forthcoming 2006).

[114] *Id.*

[115] Youngstown Sheet & Tube Co. v. Sawyer, 343 U.S. 579, 652 (1952) (Jackson, J., concurring).

[116] *Id.* at 678.

substance and method. On the merits, what matters is that Jackson's analysis of executive power during emergencies prompted him to exhort the active use of checks upon the president in the first place. With this exhortation, Jackson lands fairly close to the opposite end of the spectrum from express deference, by adopting something like a presumption against the executive with regard to claims of inherent powers. The point is not that this position is correct. It is, rather, that Jackson rightly weighs the less benign aspects of executive authority in the balance. At the very least, to use language Jackson used in another context, insight about the abuse of executive power and the modern praise of executive decisiveness should "largely cancel each other."[117] Either way, a better understanding of both the value and dangers of an executive facing a grave security threat necessarily follows from a wider study, including comparative study. As *Youngstown* shows, the Court can and has undertaken exactly this kind of analysis.[118]

V. Conclusion

Hamdan, like *Rasul* and *Hamdi* before it, will be just one legal battle in a long struggle. All concerned in this struggle, regardless of viewpoint, agree that the threat from terrorism is real and grave. All agree that the stakes in responding to this threat are uniquely high. All agree that there is no end to this threat in sight, either soon or ever. Where company parts is that some view terrorism's only casualty to be national security. Others see another target of terrorism to be our systems of ordered liberty and fundamental freedom.

---

[117] *Id.* at 635.

[118] Comparative law points to another, and more novel, source of concern about executive power by way of globalization. As Anne-Marie Slaughter has demonstrated, international relations increasingly consists of executive officials, judges, and legislators dealing with counterparts from other countries directly rather than in state to state dealings mediated by professional diplomats. See Anne-Marie Slaughter, A New World Order (2004). In this process of direct political contacts, executive officials are far in the lead. The net result in any particular country is the relative enhancement of executive power at the expense of legislatures and courts. Globalization, in short, undermines the inter-branch balance that separation of powers presupposes. In this context, deference doctrines exacerbate a growing problem. For a treatment of this phenomenon with a focus on ways the judiciary might respond, see Martin S. Flaherty, Judicial Globalization in the Service of Self-Government, 20 Ethics & Int'l Affairs (forthcoming 2006).

The brutal truth, though, is that the fear bred of danger almost always trumps any other concern, particularly about liberty. Benjamin Franklin had exactly this truth in mind when he stated that "any country that would sacrifice its liberty for a little security deserves neither liberty nor security."[119]

All of which makes *Hamdan* appear even more as an act of courage. But it is a fragile one. The Court is but one appointment away from an opposite result in related cases. The Court itself, not to mention individual justices, has been less than exemplary during times of perceived crisis—from Justice Chase's jury charges on the Alien and Sedition Acts,[120] to *Ex Parte McCardle*,[121] *Schenck v. United States*,[122] *Hirabayashi v. United States*,[123] *Korematsu v. United States*,[124] and *United States v. Dennis*.[125] As many of these cases show, Congress' own record has been just as spotty.[126] To paraphrase Brandeis, the executive feared evildoers and persecuted scapegoats.[127] Too often Congress and the courts went along.

Of course there have been many victories as well, *Hamdan* not least. But to sustain these, the branches constituted to check executive excess will continue to need all the resources that the struggle will require. Some will be familiar, such as separation of powers. Others, such as international law and comparative law, will seem novel, yet are also part of our legal tradition, properly understood. The struggle to prevent liberty as well as security from succumbing to terror will require every one.

[119] Benjamin Franklin, An Historical Review of the Constitution and Government of Pennsylvania, From Its Origin (1759).

[120] See Richard E. Ellis, The Jeffersonian Crisis: Courts and Politics in the Young Republic 78–81 (1974).

[121] 74 U.S. 506 (1869).

[122] 249 U.S. 247 (1919).

[123] 320 U.S. 81 (1943).

[124] 321 U.S. 760 (1944).

[125] 341 U.S. 494 (1951).

[126] As with the Court, Congress will also continue to be a battleground, as witness various proposals for authorization of military commissions in response to *Hamdan*. See David S. Cloud & Sheryl Gay Stolberg, Rules Debated for Trials of Detainees, N.Y. Times, July 27, 2006, at 20A.

[127] Cf. Whitney v. California, 274 U.S. 357, 372 & 375 (1927) (Brandeis, J., concurring).

An Imperial Judiciary at War: *Hamdan v. Rumsfeld*

*John Yoo**

A president responds to a war like no other before with unprecedented measures that test the limits of his constitutional authority. He suffers setbacks from hostile Supreme Court justices, a critical media, and a divided Congress, all of which challenge his war powers.

Liberal pundits and editorial pages believe this describes George W. Bush after the Supreme Court's decision in *Hamdan v. Rumsfeld* rejected the Bush administration's regulations governing military commissions for the trial of terrorists.[1] But the narrative of an executive wielding "unchecked" executive branch powers just as easily fits Abraham Lincoln when he issued the Emancipation Proclamation and freed the slaves, or FDR when he made the United States the great "arsenal of democracy" in the lead-up to World War II.[2]

While the Court's intervention into war will be greeted in some quarters as a vindication of the "rule of law," the *Hamdan* decision ignores the basic workings of the American separation of powers and will hamper the ability of future presidents to respond to emergencies and war with the forcefulness and vision of a Lincoln or an FDR. Instead of heralding a return to checks and balances, *Hamdan* signals an unprecedented drive by a five-justice majority on the Supreme Court to intervene in military affairs while war is still

*Professor of Law, University of California at Berkeley School of Law (Boalt Hall); Visiting Scholar, American Enterprise Institute. As an official in the Office of Legal Counsel at the U.S. Department of Justice from 2001 to 2003, the author worked on issues related to the military commissions at issue in this essay. A broader treatment of those events can be found in the author's forthcoming book, *War by Other Means: An Insider's Account of the War on Terrorism* (2006). The author thanks Patrick Hein for his excellent research assistance.

[1] Hamdan v. Rumsfeld, 126 S. Ct. 2749 (2006).

[2] FDR's Fireside Chats 170–72 (Russell D. Buhite & David W. Levy eds., 1992).

ongoing. Bush administration critics no doubt believe that the justices are restoring the separation of powers after a five-year period in which the president exercised unilateral discretion to respond to the 9/11 attacks. But they are proceeding on the mistaken assumption that the separation of powers works in the same way in foreign affairs as it does in domestic affairs. What makes *Hamdan* remarkable is not the actions of the president and Congress, but the intrusive role of the Supreme Court in attempting to superimpose a domestic lawmaking framework upon the management of national security matters.

To develop these points more fully, Part I of this essay examines the character of military commissions and sets forth a brief history of their use by previous administrations. Part II discusses the Court's refusal to obey the directive of Congress and the president that it not decide pending habeas cases from Guantanamo Bay. Part III explains that *Hamdan* misconstrued statutes, treaties, and Supreme Court precedent to essentially overturn decades, if not centuries, of judicial practice in deferring to the president and Congress on wartime policy.

I. Character and History of Military Commissions

Contrary to the claims of critics, policy on military commissions is not a story of a unilateral power-grab by President Bush. Rather, military commissions are the product of a consistent constitutional practice and cooperation between the political branches of government. Until *Hamdan*, the Supreme Court remained respectful of the president and Congress' efforts to set wartime policy on the prosecution and punishment of enemy war crimes. Rather than attempting to require that Congress issue a clear statement regulating every aspect of military commissions, the Court deferred to the working arrangement between the other branches to protect national security and carry out war.

Long American practice recognizes that the president, as commander-in-chief, plays the leading role in wartime. Presidents have started wars without congressional authorization, and they have exercised complete control over military strategy and tactics.[3] Of

---

[3]See generally John Yoo, The Powers of War and Peace: The Constitution and Foreign Affairs after 9/11 (2006).

course, whether the president has the constitutional authority to begin wars has been one of the most controversial academic subjects, one on which I have written. But even those who argue that wars that do not receive congressional approval are unconstitutional do not and cannot seriously dispute that presidents have often used force abroad on their own authority. The two bookends to the Cold War—the Korean War and the Kosovo War—were both waged by presidents without any declaration of war or other congressional authorization.

The advantages of executive control over war have been understood as far back as British political philosopher John Locke, who argued that foreign affairs are "much less capable to be directed by antecedent, standing, positive laws," while the executive could act quickly to protect the "security and interest of the public."[4] Presidents can act with a speed, unity, and secrecy that the other branches of government cannot match. Because executives are always on the job, they can adapt quickly to new situations. By contrast, legislatures are large, diffuse, and slow. Their collective design may make them better for deliberating over policy, but at the cost of delay and lack of resolve.

September 11, 2001, was exactly such a moment. The September 11 attacks succeeded in part because our government was mired in a terrorism-as-crime approach[5] that worried less about preventing terrorist attacks and more about hypothetical threats to civil liberties—hence the "wall" that prevented our law enforcement and intelligence agencies from sharing information. Our laws considered war as conflict only between nations and failed to anticipate the rise of a non-state terrorist organization that could kill 3,000 Americans, destroy the World Trade Center, and damage the Pentagon in a single day.

In response to the 9/11 attacks, President Bush ordered the creation of military commissions to try members of the enemy who commit war crimes.[6] Military commissions are an example of the

[4] John Locke, Second Treatise on Government § 147 (1690).

[5] See John Yoo, National Security and the Rehnquist Court, 74 Geo. Wash. L. Rev. 1701, 1726 (2006).

[6] Military Order of Nov. 13, 2001, Detention, Treatment, and Trial of Certain Non-Citizens in the War Against Terrorism, 66 Fed. Reg. 57,833, § 4 (Nov. 13, 2001) (hereinafter "Bush Military Order").

laws and institutions needed to adapt to the war against al Qaeda. Unlike regular courts, military commissions can close portions of proceedings when classified material is involved or an enemy leader might testify.[7] A fair trial is still guaranteed because the defense attorneys are present.[8] Defense attorneys must have appropriate security clearances. Assurances are obtained that neither they nor the defendant will leak any classified information.

A military commission can also use more flexible rules of evidence.[9] Our criminal trials impose a very high standard on what information reaches a jury. Witnesses generally must testify in person, hearsay evidence typically must be excluded, and the reliability of evidence must meet high procedural hurdles. That is because our jury is supposed to be kept ignorant of certain types of evidence that might sway the novice. Juries are not trusted to make difficult judgments about the reliability of broad, contextual information. Military commissions, however, are staffed by professionals versed in the reliability of hearsay evidence, or whether an item of evidence is more probative than prejudicial.[10] Rules of courtroom procedure like the exclusionary rule's bar on evidence that was obtained without a warrant seek to discipline police conduct and have less to do with the relevance or credibility of evidence. We should not apply those rules to war because courtroom outcomes should not "discipline" or affect how the military does its job on the battlefield.

Our military does not play the same role in our society that the police do. Police must follow the exclusionary rule and the Miranda warnings or courts let the suspect go free. Courts use those rules to encourage the police and prosecutors to respect the defendant's rights and because the costs to society of the occasional error are deemed low. Those rules make no sense in the war situation, where the primary purpose of the armed forces is to defeat the enemy. If the military had to abide by a host of legal rules, it would interfere drastically with their ability to fight effectively. As has been said, the job of the 82nd Airborne is to vaporize, not Mirandize.

---

[7] *Id.* § 4(c)(4).
[8] See, e.g., *id.* §§ 4(c)(2), (5).
[9] See, e.g., *id.* §§ 1(f), (4)(c)(3)–(4).
[10] See, e.g., *id.* § 4(c)(3).

Civilian courts would not allow important military evidence in at least two cases.[11] Suppose Osama bin Laden called his mother to warn her of the 9/11 attacks and she told a friend. A civilian court would exclude that as hearsay testimony. But a military commission could allow it. A *Wall Street Journal* reporter found a hard drive filled with al Qaeda documents in a Kabul market. That information would likely not be admitted in civilian court because its chain of custody from al Qaeda to the Kabul market could not be verified. A military commission could review the information if it thought it was reasonably reliable.[12] Another example is information gained through interrogations, intelligence intercepts, and informants. None of that information complies with the Fourth Amendment's warrant requirement or Miranda, but if it is reasonably relevant, the military will act upon it.

In fact, thoughtful civil libertarians ought to welcome military commissions. Military commissions have the benefit of limiting to enemy combatant cases any compromises between national security and civil liberties. Civil libertarians, most recently Geoffrey Stone in his *Perilous Times*, warn that courts historically bend too far to accommodate the needs of national security in wartime.[13] Such patterns drawn from the past don't necessarily describe the present or predict the future, of course, particularly in the face of unprecedented change. The main worry ought to be, however, that compromises that favor national security will permanently affect our domestic criminal law in time of peace. Military commissions, in fact, have a civil libertarian function, by confining the more flexible rules for national security cases where they will not seep over to civilian cases. Trying enemy combatants in civilian courts could have the opposite effect, particularly in periods just after a major enemy assault like 9/11.

Military commissions are also more secure. Civil trials of terrorists in the U.S. make an inviting target for al Qaeda. Even before 9/11, our government recognized the threat to judicial personnel by placing heavy security in the New York City federal court building and

---

[11] Ruth Wedgwood, Al Qaeda, Terrorism, and Military Commissions, 96 Am. J. Int'l L. 328, 330–31 (2002).

[12] *Id.*

[13] Geoffrey Stone, Perilous Times: Civil Liberties in Wartime (2004).

putting federal judges who tried the al Qaeda cases of the 1990s under constant protection.[14] Civilian trials tend to be in major cities, such as New York City or Washington, D.C., compounding potential loss of life if they were targeted for attack. In this war military tribunals are conducted at Guantanamo Bay, a well-defended military site beyond our shores.

Some critics believe the military can't run a fair trial. They claim that they are too secretive and unfair because they operate without juries and presume the guilt of the defendant.[15] Civil libertarians think military officers can't be effective defense attorneys because they are susceptible to "command influence"—swayed by their superior officers' desire to convict. In short, they argue that military commissions are inherently flawed because their rules and procedures are just too different from the standard criminal trial system.

That view displays a serious lack of understanding of the military justice system. Millions of American servicemen and women serve today under the Uniform Code of Military Justice (UCMJ).[16] That system, developed over many decades, provides a fair and open trial. Unlike our criminal trials, in which jurors are selected for their ignorance, military tribunals are staffed by officers who are college graduates with extensive professional knowledge. The system requires defense attorneys to do their best to represent their clients free from command influence. On the military commissions to date, defense attorneys have succeeded in challenging the very constitutionality of the commissions all the way to the Supreme Court. President Bush did not order the military to convict whomever he wanted but to provide each defendant a "full and fair trial."[17] The military is bound to carry out his orders.

Civil libertarians, members of the media, and academics portray military commissions as some Frankenstein creation of the Bush administration. According to the *New York Times*, "[i]n the place of

[14] Wedgwood, *supra* note 11, at 331.

[15] See, e.g., Barbara Olshansky, Secret Trials and Executions: Military Tribunals and the Threat to Democracy (2006); Jordan J. Paust, Post-9/11 Overreaction and Fallacies Regarding War and Defense, Guantanamo, the Status of Persons, Treatment, Judicial Review of Detention, and Due Process in Military Commissions, 79 Notre Dame L. Rev. 1335, 1362–64 (2004).

[16] 10 U.S.C. §§ 801–946 (2006).

[17] See Bush Military Order, *supra* note 6, § 4(c)(2).

fair trials and due process," President Bush "has substituted a crude and unaccountable system that any dictator would admire."[18] They are anything but. Only pundits with little knowledge of American history or no contact with the military and its legal system would voice such a view.

Military commissions are the customary form of justice for prisoners who violate the laws of war. They have also served as courts of justice during occupations and in times of martial law. American generals have used military commissions in virtually every significant war from the Revolutionary War through World War II.[19] As commander of the revolutionary armies, George Washington put John Andre on trial for spying in 1780 before a military commission.[20] Major Andre had been found, out of uniform, carrying the plans for West Point that he had received from Benedict Arnold. Washington's military "Court of Inquiry" convicted Andre and sentenced him to hanging. During the War of 1812, General Andrew Jackson employed military commissions in the areas under his command and used them again in an 1818 Indian War. These special military courts did not assume the name "commission" until the Mexican-American War, when General Winfield Scott established two types, one to help maintain law and order in the occupied parts of Mexico, the other to try violations of the laws of war, such as guerrilla warfare.

Military commissions were heavily used in the Civil War. Union generals established military commissions in early 1862 to try suspected Confederate operatives behind Union lines, to prosecute violations of the laws of war, and to administer justice in occupied areas. Later that year, President Lincoln proclaimed that "all rebels

[18]Editorial, A Travesty of Justice, N.Y. Times, Nov. 16, 2001, at A24.

[19]For a critical review of the history, see Louis Fisher, Military Tribunals & Presidential Power: American Revolution to the War on Terrorism (2005). A valuable source is Brian C. Baldrate, The Supreme Court's Role in Defining the Jurisdiction of Military Tribunals: A Study, Critique, & Proposal for Hamdan v. Rumsfeld, 186 Mil. L. Rev. 1 (2005). See also American Bar Association Task Force on Terrorism and the Law, Report and Recommendations on Military Commissions (Jan. 4, 2002). Law professors have written on both sides of the issue. See, e.g., David J. Bederman, Article II Courts, 44 Mercer L. Rev. 825 (1993); Curtis A. Bradley & Jack L. Goldsmith, The Constitutional Validity of Military Commissions, 5 Green Bag 2d 249 (2002); Harold Hongju Koh, The Case Against Military Commissions, 96 Am. J. Int'l L. 337 (2002).

[20]William Winthrop, Military Law and Precedents 832 (2d ed. 1920).

and insurgents, their aiders and abettors within the United States," and anyone "guilty of any disloyal practice affording aid and comfort to rebels" would be subject to martial law "and liable to trial and punishment by courts martial or military commissions."[21] Congress gave the commissions jurisdiction over several other violations of law in the following year. After the North prevailed, Congress authorized the use of military commissions as courts of occupation in the military districts of the conquered South. Military commissions were used most notably to try Lincoln's assassins and the commander of the Andersonville prisoner of war camp. According to a definitive study of military law, military commissions tried about 2,000 cases during the Civil War, and about 200 during Reconstruction.[22]

Several cases involving military commissions made their way to the Supreme Court during the Civil War. In *Ex Parte Vallandigham*,[23] the Supreme Court held that it did not have the jurisdiction to hear a challenge to a sentence imposed by a military commission,[24] and the Supreme Court did not hear another such challenge while the war went on. In *Ex Parte Milligan*,[25] the Court also addressed the legality of military commissions. The Court held that the government could not try civilians on loyal Union territory by military commission, if the civil courts were open and if the civilians had not associated with the enemy.[26] By implication, if Milligan had been an enemy combatant, not a civilian, a military commission *could* have tried him for war crimes. Lincoln's assassins were tried by a military commission convened by President Andrew Johnson and approved by an opinion of the attorney general, and a federal court rejected a challenge to its use.[27] The attorney general's opinion stated that

---

[21] Proclamation Suspending the Writ of Habeas Corpus Because of Resistance to Draft (Sept. 24, 1862), in 6 Life & Works of Abraham Lincoln 203 (Marion Mills Miller ed., 1907).

[22] Winthrop, *supra* note 20, at 834, 853.

[23] 68 U.S. (1 Wall.) 243 (1863).

[24] *Id.* at 251–53.

[25] 71 U.S. (4 Wall.) 2 (1866).

[26] *Id.* at 118–24.

[27] Ex Parte Mudd, 17 F. Cas. 954 (S.D. Fla. 1868) (unreported).

long practice under the rules of warfare permitted assassins to be tried and executed by military commission.[28]

With the end of Reconstruction, military commissions disappeared, though they were used sporadically in the Spanish-American War and World War I. World War II, however, witnessed the use of military commissions on an unprecedented scale, both to try war criminals and administer justice in occupied Germany and Japan. Military commissions administering law and order in occupied Germany heard hundreds of thousands of cases.[29] Military commissions were also extensively used to try enemy combatants for violating the laws of war, the most famous examples being the Nuremburg Tribunal that tried Nazi leaders after the war, and the International Military Tribunal for the Far East that tried Japanese leaders for war crimes. American military commissions tried 3,000 defendants in Germany and 1,000 defendants in Japan for war crimes.[30] Military commissions tried members of the enemy for "terrorism, subversive activity, and violation of the laws of war."[31]

It is important to note that World War II military commissions operated both abroad and in the United States. FDR's commission order sparked a lawsuit, and the resulting Supreme Court opinion supports the Bush military commissions today.[32] Indeed, FDR took far more liberties with the constitutional law of the day than the current administration.

In June 1942, eight Nazi agents with plans to sabotage factories, transportation facilities, and utility plants landed in Long Island, New York, and Florida.[33] All had lived in the United States before

---

[28] Military Commissions, 11 Op. Att'y Gen. 297 (1865).

[29] See Eli E. Nobleman, Military Government Courts: Law and Justice in the American Zone of Germany, 33 A.B.A. J. 777, 777–80 (1947); Pitman B. Potter, Legal Bases and Character of Military Occupation in Germany and Japan, 43 Am. J. Int'l L. 323 (1949).

[30] War Crimes, War Criminals, and War Crimes Trials 5–6 (Norman E. Tutorow ed., 1981).

[31] A. Wigfall Green, The Military Commission, 42 Am. J. Int'l L. 832, 833 (1948).

[32] Ex Parte Quirin, 317 U.S. 1 (1942).

[33] The facts of the Nazi saboteur case are recounted in *id.* at 19–22; Louis Fisher, Nazi Saboteurs on Trial: A Military Tribunal & American Law (2003); Eugene Rachlis, They Came to Kill: The Story of Eight Nazi Saboteurs in America (1961); Michael R. Belknap, The Supreme Court Goes to War: The Meaning and Implications of the Nazi Saboteur Case, 89 Mil. L. Rev. 9 (1980); David Danelski, The Saboteurs' Case, 1 J. S. Ct. Hist. 61 (1996).

the war, and two were American citizens. One decided to turn informer. After first dismissing his story, the FBI soon arrested the plotters.[34] When their capture was revealed, members of Congress and the media demanded the death penalty, even though no law authorized capital punishment for their crime. FDR decided to try them by military commission.[35] He issued executive orders establishing the commission, defining the crimes, appointing its members, and excluding federal judicial review. The first executive order created the commission and defined its jurisdiction over aliens or foreign residents "who give obedience to or act under the direction of" an enemy nation, and attempt to enter the United States "preparing to commit sabotage, espionage, hostile or warlike acts, or violations of the law of war."[36] He also ordered that the Nazis be barred from any other court.[37] FDR's second order established the procedures for the military commissions. It was only one paragraph long. It required "a full and fair trial," allowed the admission of evidence that would "have probative value to a reasonable man," and required a two-thirds vote for conviction and sentence.[38]

Because the Bush administration patterned its order on FDR's, the critics of military commissions only have FDR to blame. But in truth, FDR's handiwork intruded more on civil liberties than Bush's, and under the law of the time was of more questionable constitutionality. In 1942, the governing case on the books was *Ex Parte Milligan*, requiring the government to use federal courts if the defendant had not associated with the enemy and the civilian courts were open.[39] Military counsel for the Nazi saboteurs challenged the commissions on just that ground—that the military commission could not exercise jurisdiction because courts were open, the defendants were not in a war zone, and a military commission violated the Articles of War enacted by Congress.[40]

---

[34] See Danelski, *supra* note 33, at 64–65.

[35] *Id.* at 65.

[36] 7 Fed. Reg. 5,101 (1942).

[37] *Id.*

[38] *Id.* at 5,103.

[39] See Ex Parte Milligan, 71 U.S. (4 Wall.) 2, 118–24 (1866).

[40] See Danelski, *supra* note 33, at 68–69.

After two days of oral argument, the justices decided to uphold trial of the prisoners by military commission. The great pressure on the Court was reflected in its decision to deliver a unanimous opinion on July 31, the day after oral argument, while its opinion would not appear until later. The military commission began its trial the next day. Three days later it convicted and sentenced the defendants to death. Five days later, FDR approved the verdict but commuted the sentences of two of the defendants.[41]

FDR's commissions operated under his two executive orders alone. There were no regulations such as those recently developed by the Bush Defense Department to define the elements of the crimes that a commission can hear.[42] A separate Bush Defense Department regulation has established rules on the admissibility of evidence, the right of cross-examination, the right against self-incrimination, proof beyond a reasonable doubt as the standard for conviction, and the right of defense counsel to examine any exculpatory evidence the prosecution possesses. And under the Bush commissions, unlike FDR's, a unanimous vote is required to impose the death penalty.[43]

What concerns today's civil libertarians is that military commissions do not afford as much due process as domestic criminal trials. But the truth is that the military commission rules under the Bush administration are far closer to the standards governing courts-martial of American soldiers than those set out by FDR, and they recognize many more procedural rights. Defense Department regulations specifically detail the crimes that can be tried.[44] FDR stated only the general prohibition of "sabotage, espionage, hostile or war-like acts, or violations of the law of war," which could be interpreted to mean many things.[45] Spying today, for instance, includes four

---

[41] *Id.* at 71–72.

[42] See Crimes and Elements of Trials by Military Commission, 68 Fed. Reg. 39,381–401 (July 1, 2003) (codified at 32 C.F.R. § 11.6).

[43] For a full description of the rights accorded the accused under the DOD regulations, see, e.g., U.S. Department of Defense, Military Commission Order No. 1, Procedures for Trials by Military Commissions of Certain Non-United States Citizens in the War Against Terrorism ¶ 5 ("Procedures Accorded the Accused") and ¶ 6 ("Conduct of the Trial") (Mar. 21, 2002), available at http://www.defenselink.mil/news/Mar2002/d20020321ord.pdf (codified at 32 C.F.R. §§ 11.5–.6).

[44] See *id.*

[45] See 7 Fed. Reg. 5,101 (1942).

different required elements—that the defendant in wartime sought to "collect certain information," convey it to the enemy, and was "lurking or acting clandestinely, while acting under false pretenses."[46] Extensive comments explain different terms and situations that might arise.[47] Civil libertarians might cavil about the details, but the Bush administration's effort goes much farther than FDR's orders to protect defendants' civil liberties.

When the Court issued its unanimous opinion in *Ex Parte Quirin* months later, it narrowed *Milligan* and upheld FDR's use of military commissions.[48] Unlike in *Milligan*, the saboteurs clearly had joined the Nazi armed forces.[49] Chief Justice Stone's opinion found that Congress' creation of the existing courts-martial system, and the lack of any legal code specifying the laws of war, did not preclude the use of military commissions.[50] He read the Articles of War—the precursor to today's UCMJ—as authorization for military commissions, but didn't reach the question whether FDR could have created them on his own. "By the Articles of War, and especially article 15, Congress has explicitly provided, so far as it may constitutionally do so, that military tribunals shall have jurisdiction to try offenders or offenses against the law of war in appropriate cases."[51]

In later World War II cases, the Supreme Court continued to approve of military commissions. In *In re Yamashita*, General McArthur ordered a military commission to try the commanding Japanese general in the Philippines for failing to prevent his troops from committing brutal atrocities and war crimes.[52] Appealing his conviction, General Yamashita sought a writ of habeas corpus from the Supreme Court, as he could because the trial was held on American territory in the Philippines. In 1946, Chief Justice Stone again rejected the challenge and found military commissions authorized by Congress in the Articles of War.[53] In two other cases, the Supreme Court

---

[46] 32 C.F.R. § 11.6(b)(6).

[47] *Id.* § 11.6.

[48] Ex Parte Quirin, 317 U.S. 1, 45–48 (1942).

[49] *Id.* at 21.

[50] *Id.* at 25.

[51] *Id.* at 28.

[52] In re Yamashita, 327 U.S. 1 (1946).

[53] *Id.* at 11–12.

refused to step in to review the convictions of Japanese leaders by an international war crimes tribunal run by McArthur, or to review the sentences of Germans captured in China after the end of hostilities and tried by military commission.[54]

Several issues decided in *Ex Parte Quirin, In re Yamashita,* and *Johnson v. Eisentrager* are worth noting because they bear on the Court's opinion in *Hamdan.*

First, claims that Bush's military commissions violate the Constitution because Congress has not approved them have little merit. It is true that Congress has not passed a law specifically authorizing military commissions in the war on terrorism, but it never did in World War II either. Instead, the *Quirin* Court relied on article 15 of the Articles of War, which Congress enacted in a 1916 overhaul of the rules of military justice. Article 15 is still on the books today and continues to authorize military commissions.[55] Now section 821 of the UCMJ, article 15 declared that the creation of courts-martial for the trial of American servicemen for violating military rules of discipline did not "deprive military commissions . . . of concurrent jurisdiction with respect to offenders or offenses that . . . by the law of war may be tried by military commissions."[56] In enacting section 821 in 1916 and again in 1950 as part of the UCMJ, Congress probably meant nothing more than to reserve to the president his existing authority to establish military commissions, rather than to specifically authorize them. Nonetheless, the *Quirin* Court read article 15 as direct congressional authorization of commissions. Congress

[54] See Hirota v. McArthur, 338 U.S. 197 (1948); Johnson v. Eisentrager, 339 U.S. 763 (1950). In a 1952 case in which a wife of an American serviceman in occupied Germany was tried by military tribunal for murdering her husband, the Supreme Court again upheld military commissions as authorized by Congress. See Madsen v. Kinsella, 343 U.S. 341, 348–49 (1952).

[55] In fact, Congress reiterated the point again in 1996 in the legislative history to the War Crimes Act. The act, Congress observed, "is not intended to affect in any way the jurisdiction of any court-martial, military commission, or other military tribunal under any article of the Uniform Code of Military Justice or under the law of war or the law of nations." H.R. Rep. No. 104-698, at 12 (1996), reprinted in 1996 U.S.C.C.A.N. 2166, 2177.

[56] 10 U.S.C. § 821 (1956) ("The provisions of this chapter conferring jurisdiction upon courts-martial do not deprive military commissions, provost courts, or other military tribunals of concurrent jurisdiction with respect to offenders or offenses that by statute or by the law of war may be tried by military commissions, provost courts, or other military tribunals.").

chose not to disturb *Quirin* when it re-enacted article 15 as part of the UCMJ.

Second, *Yamashita* rejected a claim that the federal courts ought to review whether military commissions, and their procedures, were militarily "necessary." This claim arose in two ways. General Yamashita claimed that his military commission trial was illegal because it took place away from the battlefield and after active hostilities had ceased. The Court held that the decision whether to proceed with a military commission in those circumstances was a decision for the political branches.[57] Yamashita then argued that the procedures used in his trial were so different from those used in courts-martial as to be illegal. He relied on article 38 of the Articles of War, later re-enacted as section 38 of the UCMJ, which requires that procedures used in military commissions, "in so far as [the president] shall deem practicable," use the rules of evidence used in federal district court. The *Yamashita* Court rejected this claim because the Articles of War did not apply to members of the enemy on trial for war crimes.[58] More important, the Court found that judicial review did not extend to the president's determination of procedural rules for military commissions.[59]

Third, *Eisentrager* rejected the claim that the Geneva Conventions governed the operation of military commissions. In their petition for a writ of habeas corpus, the German prisoners claimed that their trial violated the provisions of the 1929 Geneva Conventions. While the Court observed that the petitioners might be entitled to rights under the conventions, it found that "the obvious scheme of the Agreement is that responsibility for observance and enforcement of these rights is upon political and military authorities."[60] The Geneva Conventions, according to the *Eisentrager* majority, could not be enforced by the federal courts. "Rights of alien enemies are vindicated under [the Geneva Conventions] only through protests and intervention of protecting powers as the rights of our citizens against foreign governments are vindicated only by Presidential intervention."[61]

---

[57] See Yamashita, 327 U.S. at 12–13.

[58] *Id.* at 18–19.

[59] *Id.* at 23.

[60] Johnson v. Eisentrager, 339 U.S. 763, 789 n.14 (1950).

[61] *Id.*

Bush administration critics who are fans of *Youngstown*[62] have yet to explain their constitutional problems with military commissions. They believe that presidential power is at its height when acting with congressional support, which is clearly present in the UCMJ and then in Congress' Authorization for Use of Military Force (AUMF)[63] enacted in the days after 9/11. If the latter implicitly authorizes the detention of enemy combatants, it should also permit their trial. Congress supplemented those two sources of approval with the 2005 Detainee Treatment Act,[64] which allows an appeal to the federal appeals court in Washington, D.C., of the verdict of a military commission.[65] If Congress never approved of commissions in the first place, why would it create a review process for them? Congress has never shown any hostility toward military commissions, either historically, or in the war on terrorism.

Even if Congress had not authorized military commissions in the UCMJ, President Bush would still have authority to establish them under his constitutional authority as commander-in-chief.[66] Congress, of course, has its own authority to establish military courts under its constitutional authority to "define and punish . . . Offences against the Law of Nations" and to "make Rules for the Government and Regulation of the land and naval Forces."[67] Article II of the Constitution grants the president the "executive Power" and the job of commander-in-chief. While Congress has sometimes authorized military commissions itself, American history affords many examples of presidents and our military commanders creating them without congressional legislation.

The purpose of military commissions makes clear that they should remain within the discretion of the commander-in-chief. Waging war is not limited only to ordering which enemy formations to strike and what targets to bomb. It also involves forming policy on how to fight, how to detain enemy combatants, and how to sanction the

---

[62] See Youngstown Sheet & Tube Co. v. Sawyer, 343 U.S. 579, 869 (1952) (Jackson, J., concurring).

[63] Authorization for Use of Military Force, Pub. L. No. 107-40, 115 Stat. 224 (2001).

[64] Detainee Treatment Act of 2005, Pub. L. No. 109-148, § 1005(e)(1), 119 Stat. 2739, 2742 (2005).

[65] *Id.* § 1005(e)(3)(A).

[66] U.S. Const. art. II, § 2, cl. 1.

[67] *Id.* art. I, § 8, cl. 10, 14.

enemy if it violates the rules of civilized warfare. Allowing military commanders to try and punish violators creates incentives for the enemy to follow the rules in the future and assures our own troops that war crimes will not be tolerated. As the Supreme Court recognized in *Yamashita*, "An important incident to the conduct of war is the adoption of measures by the military commander, not only to repel and defeat the enemy, but to seize and subject to disciplinary measures those enemies who, in their attempt to thwart or impede our military effort, have violated the law of war."[68] Military commissions also help commanders properly restore order in the aftermath of a conflict, and this can be an important way of making sure fighting does not flare up again.

This is not to license an anything-goes attitude, by any means. Important limitations restrict the scope of military commissions. The most significant is the limitation of their jurisdiction to war crimes. Military commissions have no constitutional authority to try Americans or non-Americans for garden variety crimes, civil wrongs, or any other offense unrelated to war. They can hear only prosecutions for violations of the laws of war. President Bush also exempted American citizens—previous military commissions tried everyone who violated the laws of war.[69] In *Quirin*, at least one of the Nazi saboteurs was an American citizen, but recall that the Supreme Court concluded that "[c]itizenship in the United States of an enemy belligerent does not relieve him from the consequences of a belligerency which is unlawful."[70] President Bush consciously chose to reject the breadth of military commissions as used in World War II and the Civil War.

This landscape changed when *Rasul v. Bush*[71] reversed *Eisentrager* and held that federal jurisdiction extended to petitions for writs of habeas corpus brought by alien enemy combatants held abroad.[72] But *Rasul* ultimately only served to illustrate the level of cooperation between the executive and legislative branches. In late 2005, pursuant to its authority to regulate the jurisdiction of the federal courts,[73]

---

[68] In re Yamashita, 327 U.S. 1, 11 (1946) (citing Ex Parte Quirin, 317 U.S 1, 28 (1942)).

[69] See Bush Military Order, *supra* note 6, § 2(a).

[70] Quirin, 317 U.S. at 37.

[71] Rasul v. Bush, 542 U.S. 466 (2004).

[72] *Id.* at 483–84.

[73] U.S. Const. art. III, § 2, cl. 2.

Congress enacted the Detainee Treatment Act, part of which expressly overruled *Rasul*.[74] The act declared that "no court, justice, or judge shall have jurisdiction to hear or consider" any habeas or other actions that "related to any aspect of detention" of an alien detained at Guantanamo Bay, Cuba.[75]

Instead, the Detainee Treatment Act created an appeals process for military commissions to civilian federal courts. It allows a defendant to appeal a verdict to the federal appeals court in Washington, D.C., and presumably from there to the Supreme Court.[76] If a defendant is sentenced to ten years or more, he can appeal as a matter of right; if the sentence is lower, the D.C. Circuit may take the appeal as a matter of its own discretion. But the act only allows for reversal if a military commission disobeys Defense Department regulations, and it permits challenges to the legality of the procedures themselves.[77] Congress ordered that the review procedures would apply to all cases "pending on or after the date of the enactment of this Act."[78]

II. Jurisdiction-Stripping and Military Commissions

Constitutional practice shows that there has been a substantial history of political branch interaction and cooperation on the subject of military commissions. Rather than a story of unilateral executive branch action, Congress has supported presidential use of commissions in at least three different ways: a) section 821 of the UCMJ, which recognizes military commissions;[79] b) the AUMF enacted on September 18, 2001, which authorized the president to use all necessary and appropriate force against those responsible for the September 11 attacks;[80] and c) the Detainee Treatment Act of 2005,[81] which created a carefully crafted review process for military commission verdicts. Again, that is not to say that President Bush could not use

---

[74] Detainee Treatment Act, *supra* note 64, § 1005(e)(1).

[75] *Id.*

[76] *Id.* § 1005(e)(3)(A).

[77] *Id.* § 1005(e)(3)(D).

[78] *Id.* § 1005(h)(2).

[79] See 10 U.S.C. § 821.

[80] See *supra* note 63.

[81] See *supra* note 64.

military commissions on his own authority once war broke out; several presidents had employed them as a wartime measure without any specific congressional authorization. But it was unnecessary for the Court to reach the issue of the president's constitutional powers since Congress was on record as supporting military commissions.

And until this year, the courts have generally deferred to the political branches in the use of military commissions. To summarize, in *Quirin*, the Court construed the identical predecessor to section 821 of the UCMJ as an affirmative congressional authorization for military commissions,[82] which Congress could have changed when it enacted the UCMJ after World War II. In *Yamashita*, the Court held it could not review the procedures used by military commissions.[83] In *Eisentrager*, the Court found that any standards imposed by the Geneva Conventions were not to be enforced by the federal courts, but by the political branches.[84] And in *Hamdi*, the Court had even read the AUMF in a broad manner to include the detention of enemy combatants without criminal trial until the end of hostilities, even though its authorization to use force did not specifically enumerate the power to detain.[85] If the power to use force against the enemy includes the power to detain, certainly it would include the authority to conduct a war crimes trial by military commission.

Nevertheless, the Supreme Court in *Hamdan* rejected all of that history, political branch cooperation, and judicial precedent. Here, I wish to focus on the extent to which the Court was so intent on blocking military commissions that it exercised its judicial power in unprecedented ways. A sign of how "activist" or outcome oriented a decision is might be seen in the violence it does to the existing body of constitutional principles and precedents. On this score, the *Hamdan* Court displayed a lack of judicial restraint that would have shocked its predecessors, signaling a dangerous judicial intention to intervene in wartime policy.

The first area where the Court put its intentions on display was its treatment of the Detainee Treatment Act's effort to remove federal

[82] Ex Parte Quirin, 317 U.S. 1, 28 (1942).

[83] In re Yamashita, 327 U.S. 1, 23 (1946).

[84] Johnson v. Eisentrager, 339 U.S. 763, 789 n.14 (1950).

[85] Hamdi v. Rumsfeld, 542 U.S. 507, 517 (2004).

jurisdiction over habeas cases, like Hamdan's, originating from Guantanamo Bay. Congress spoke in clear terms, using language that the Court had previously interpreted to immediately terminate jurisdiction over pending and future cases. A removal of jurisdiction eliminates the power of the Court to issue a final judgment in a case. If a case is still pending at any level of trial or appeal when Congress strips jurisdiction, a court must immediately dismiss it. In "an ancient and unbroken line of authority," in Justice Scalia's words, the Court had customarily applied provisions removing jurisdiction immediately to pending cases.[86] Rather than presume jurisdiction to remain in such cases, the Court has usually required Congress to clearly reserve when it wishes the courts to continue to exercise jurisdiction in pending cases. As the Court had said in dismissing a case where a jurisdiction-stripping provision was enacted after the Court had granted certiorari, "[t]his rule—that, when a law conferring jurisdiction is repealed without any reservation as to pending cases, all cases fall with the law—has been adhered to consistently by this Court."[87]

Ex Parte McCardle remains the foundational case in this area, one with clear analogies to the Detainee Treatment Act. McCardle had been imprisoned during Reconstruction by the military government in Mississippi for publishing libelous and incendiary articles that incited violence.[88] In 1867, before McCardle's imprisonment, Congress had vested the federal courts with the authority to issue writs of habeas corpus when a petitioner was detained in violation of federal law. McCardle appealed to the circuit court, where he lost, and to the Supreme Court. After the Supreme Court heard argument but before any decision had issued, Congress enacted a statute repealing the Supreme Court's appellate jurisdiction over cases brought under the 1867 Act.[89] Congress was concerned that the Court might use *McCardle* as the vehicle for finding Reconstruction

---

[86] Hamdan v. Rumsfeld, 126 S. Ct. 2749, 2810 (2006) (Scalia, J., dissenting) (citing Bruner v. United States, 343 U.S. 112, 114–17 (1952)).

[87] Bruner, 343 U.S. at 116–17.

[88] Ex Parte McCardle, 74 U.S. (7 Wall.) 506 (1868).

[89] See *id.* at 512.

unconstitutional, a result hinted at by its decision in *Ex Parte Milligan*.[90] The Court dismissed the case, with Chief Justice Chase writing that "Jurisdiction is power to declare the law, and when it ceases to exist, the only function remaining to the court is that of announcing the fact and dismissing the cause."[91]

What was good enough for the Court in *McCardle*, and every Supreme Court since, apparently was not good enough for the *Hamdan* majority. Justice Stevens found that the removal of jurisdiction was ambiguous, because the provision in the Detainee Treatment Act creating the new appeals process for military commissions and detention decisions expressly applied to all cases "pending on or after the date of . . . enactment."[92] Stevens held that Congress' failure expressly to apply this language to the stripping of jurisdiction over habeas claims originating from Guantanamo Bay amounted to a rejection of this language.[93] If Congress had really wanted to strip jurisdiction over Hamdan's case, Justice Stevens' logic went, then it should have included the "pending on or after the date of enactment" language to all three provisions: jurisdiction stripping; review of military commission appeals; and review of detention decisions.

The problem is that the Court had never imposed such a requirement before on a jurisdiction-stripping provision. In an unchallenged line of cases, the Court had required a clear statement when Congress chose to *exclude* pending cases from a jurisdiction-stripping provision, rather than the opposite presumption favored by Justice Stevens.[94] As Justice Scalia observed, there does not appear to be a single case in Anglo-American legal history in which a court refused to give immediate effect to a jurisdiction-stripping statute in pending cases.[95] Ironically, Justice Stevens had written in one of the Court's more recent jurisdiction-stripping discussions that "[w]e have regularly applied intervening statutes conferring or ousting jurisdiction,

[90] See Jesse H. Choper et al., Constitutional Law—Cases, Comments, Questions 42 (10th ed. 2006).

[91] McCardle, 74 U.S. at 514.

[92] See Detainee Treatment Act, *supra* note 64, §§ 1005(h)(2), (e)(2)–(3).

[93] See Hamdan v. Rumsfeld, 126 S. Ct. 2749, 2762–69 (2006).

[94] See Landgraf v. USI Film Products, 511 U.S. 244, 274 (1994) (citing Bruner v. United States, 343 U.S. 112, 116–17 (1952)); Hallowell v. Commons, 239 U.S. 506 (1916); Republic of Austria v. Altmann, 541 U.S. 677, 693 (2004).

[95] Hamdan, 126 S. Ct. at 2812 (Scalia, J., dissenting).

whether or not jurisdiction lay when the underlying conduct occurred or when the suit was filed."[96] The better view, it seems to me, is that Congress included the "pending on or after the date of enactment" language because there was no settled case law, as there was for jurisdiction-stripping, on whether the creation of a new appellate review system would apply to pending as well as future cases.

III. Military Commissions and the Laws of War

Refusal to obey a clear congressional command against deciding *Hamdan* was not the only example of the Court's rush to judgment and rejection of settled practice. The *Hamdan* majority held that Bush's military commissions did not meet the procedural standards set out in the UCMJ. The justices found that while the UCMJ recognizes the president's ability to create military commissions, it also requires the president to make a finding explaining why a deviation from courts-martial is needed. In issuing his November, 2001, order establishing military commissions, President Bush had found that the rules for district courts and courts-martial were impracticable, tracking the language in article 36 of the UCMJ.[97] The Court held that "the 'practicability' determination the president has made is insufficient to justify variances from the procedures governing courts-martial."[98] The Court observed that "[n]othing in the record before us demonstrates that it would be impracticable to apply court-martial rules in this case. There is no suggestion, for example, of any logistical difficulty in securing properly sworn and authenticated evidence or in applying the usual principles of relevance and admissibility."[99] Justice Stevens was particularly disturbed by the rule permitting a military commission to exclude a defendant from a hearing involving classified information. The "jettisoning of so basic a right" as the right to be present, he wrote, "cannot lightly be excused as 'practicable.'"[100]

Hamdan's holding on this point is clearly in conflict with *Quirin* and *Yamashita*. In *Quirin*, the Court rejected challenges to the illegality of

---

[96] Landgraf, 511 U.S. at 274.

[97] See Bush Military Order, *supra* note 6, § 1(f); 10 U.S.C. § 836(a) (1990) (UCMJ art. 36(a)).

[98] Hamdan, 126 S. Ct. at 2791.

[99] *Id.* at 2792.

[100] *Id.*

the military commission used to try the Nazi saboteurs, and did not review FDR's procedures. It limited its review to whether the commission could properly exercise jurisdiction over the case, and went no farther. It certainly did not demand that FDR issue rules that were consistent with those for courts-martial, or make a sufficient showing of impracticability as to individual commission procedures. *Yamashita* also refused to exercise any review over military commission procedures, but instead limited its inquiry to whether the military commission had jurisdiction over the case.[101]

The Court's refusal to accept the president's determination of the need for military commission procedures points to a deeper refusal by the *Hamdan* majority to follow the Court's customary deference to the political branches in wartime. Justice Stevens put on display his intent to ignore the political branches' formal and functional superiority in setting war policy in his rejection of the government's claim that conspiracy in war crimes is a chargeable offense. The defects in Hamdan's charges "are indicative of a broader inability on the Executive's part here to satisfy the most basic precondition— at least in the absence of specific congressional authorization—for establishment of military commissions: military necessity."[102] The majority substituted its own view that the rights of an al Qaeda terrorist suspected of war crimes to see all the evidence should come first. It then decided for itself that the demands of the war on terrorism did not require the use of military commissions outside an active battlefield to try enemy combatants for crimes committed before 9/11.

This runs counter to long-held understandings of the allocation of the power to prosecute wars. The text, structure, and history of the Constitution establish that the Founders entrusted the president with the primary responsibility, and therefore the power, to use military force in situations of emergency. Article II, Section 2 states that the "President shall be Commander in Chief of the Army and Navy of the United States, and of the Militia of the several States, when called into the actual Service of the United States." He is further vested with all of "the executive Power" and the duty to

---

[101] See *supra* notes 57–59 and accompanying text.

[102] Hamdan, 126 S. Ct. at 2785.

execute the laws.[103] Those powers give the president broad constitutional authority to use military force in response to threats to the national security and foreign policy of the United States. The power of the president is at its zenith under the Constitution when directing military operations of the armed forces, because the power of commander-in-chief is assigned solely to the president.

Several significant Framers during the ratification period observed that one of the chief virtues of the presidency was its ability to effectively wage war. As Hamilton wrote in *The Federalist*, "[e]nergy in the executive is a leading character in the definition of good government. It is essential to the protection of the community against foreign attacks."[104] This point applies directly to the war context. Wrote Hamilton: "Of all the cares or concerns of government, the direction of war most peculiarly demands those qualities which distinguish the exercise of power by a single hand. The direction of war implies the direction of the common strength; and the power of directing and employing the common strength, forms an usual and essential part in the definition of the executive authority."[105] Future Supreme Court Justice James Iredell argued that "[f]rom the nature of the thing, the command of armies ought to be delegated to one person only. The secrecy, d[i]spatch, and decision, which are necessary in military operations, can only be expected from one person."[106] While the issue of whether the president or Congress can start a war remains controversial today, with both sides of the debate appealing to the original understanding, there does not seem to have been any dispute that once war had begun, the president as commander-in-chief was best suited to fight it.

Until *Hamdan*, it had been the consistent practice of the federal courts to stay out of disputes over wartime policy. In *The Prize Cases*, for example, the Court explained that, whether the president "in

---

[103] U.S. Const. art. II, §§ 1, 3.

[104] The Federalist No. 70, at 471 (Jacob E. Cooke ed., 1961) (Alexander Hamilton).

[105] The Federalist No. 74, at 501 (Alexander Hamilton).

[106] Jonathan Elliot, ed., 4 The Debates in the Several State Conventions on the Adoption of the Federal Constitution 107 (1836); see also 2 Joseph Story, Commentaries on the Constitution of the United States § 1491 (1833) (in military matters, "[u]nity of plan, promptitude, activity, and decision, are indispensable to success; and these can scarcely exist, except when a single magistrate is entrusted exclusively with the power").

fulfilling his duties as Commander-in-chief" was justified in treating the southern States as belligerents and instituting a blockade, was a question "to be decided *by him.*"[107] The Court could not question the merits of his decision, but must leave evaluation to "the political department of the Government to which this power was entrusted."[108] As the Court also observed, the president enjoys full discretion in determining what level of force to use. *Hamdan* rejects the traditional deference that courts have observed toward decisions of military necessity and threatens to make, as Justice Thomas observed, the Court "the ultimate arbiter of what is quintessentially a policy and military judgment, namely, the appropriate military measures to take against those who 'aided the terrorist attacks that occurred on September 11, 2001.'"[109]

The five justices in *Hamdan* compounded these mistakes by declaring that military commissions must comply with Common Article 3 of the Geneva Conventions. They rejected out of hand the usual judicial deference to presidential interpretation of treaties.[110] It does not appear that the Court has ever rejected an executive branch's interpretation of a law of war treaty, especially during wartime itself. Justice Stevens did not cite any examples to the contrary. The Court's substantive analysis of the conventions was, quite frankly, weak. It did not come to grips with the basic fact that al Qaeda has never signed the Geneva Conventions and therefore does not benefit from its protections. Rather, the Court simply declared that when Common Article 3 says it applies to conflicts "not of an international character," that means all wars not involving nations, rather than internal civil wars.[111] It did not examine the events surrounding the adoption of the 1949 conventions, the substantial commentary observing that the Geneva Conventions did not apply to international terrorist groups, or President Reagan's decision to reject the additional 1977 protocols to the conventions because they provided

---

[107] The Prize Cases, 67 U.S. (2 Black) 635, 670 (1862) (emphasis in original).

[108] *Id.*

[109] Hamdan v. Rumsfeld, 126 S. Ct. 2749, 2838 (2006) (Thomas, J., dissenting) (quoting AUMF, 115 Stat. 224).

[110] Sumitomo Shoji America, Inc. v. Avagliano, 457 U.S. 176, 184–85 (1982); United States v. Stuart, 489 U.S. 353, 369 (1989).

[111] Hamdan, 126 S. Ct. at 2795–96.

protections to terrorists.[112] Instead, the *Hamdan* majority cited Jeremy Bentham's use of the word "international" to mean effectively "between nations," rather than to refer to global issues distinct from domestic ones.[113] But there is no evidence, and the Court did not refer to any, that this understanding of the word was held by those American officials who signed or ratified the conventions. Interpreting "international" in this way is also at odds with common understandings of the word today. According to Stevens' logic, for example, "international" environmental law would encompass only environmental issues between nations, but not issues related to global commons. And "international" human rights would be an utter contradiction in terms.

Again, the Court trampled its own precedents to block military commissions. *Johnson v. Eisentrager* had found that the president and Senate had never intended the 1929 Geneva Conventions to provide benefits to enemy combatants in our own courts, but instead any violations would be cured by political and diplomatic means.[114] Even if the Geneva Conventions might provide protection to al Qaeda, the Court once believed that this was a question for the president and Congress, not the courts, to decide. The Supreme Court had never found the Geneva Conventions to be self-executing treaties.

To get around *Eisentrager*, the five justices in the *Hamdan* majority made some serious and basic errors. For the Court to decide that Common Article 3 of the conventions—which requires that the trials of a detainee are "pronounced by a regularly constituted court affording all the judicial guarantees which are recognized as indispensable by civilized peoples"—applies to military commissions, it must have concluded either that the Geneva Conventions themselves changed, or that the UCMJ changed the applicability of the conventions. The Court seemed to suggest that since Hamdan relied on the 1949 Geneva Conventions, rather than the 1929 Geneva Conventions, that *Eisentrager* did not control.[115] The 1949 Geneva Conventions, however, contain exclusive, non-judicial, enforceability provisions just as the 1929 conventions did, and do not require any mechanism

---

[112] *Id.* at 2795–98.

[113] *Id.* at 2796.

[114] *Id.* at 2794 (citing Johnson v. Eisentrager, 339 U.S. 763, 789 n.14 (1950)).

[115] *Id.* at 2794.

for domestic judicial enforcement.[116] The *Hamdan* Court claims that the Geneva Conventions are incorporated through section 821 of the UCMJ, which recognizes the jurisdiction of military commissions over "offenses that by statute or by the law of war may be tried by such commissions."[117] But this raises the question why the Geneva Conventions' reliance on political and diplomatic, and not judicial, remedies also is not considered part of the laws of war for purposes of section 821.

Perhaps because of this difficulty, the Court assumed for purposes of argument that the 1949 Geneva Conventions entailed the same remedial mechanisms as the 1929 Geneva Conventions.[118] But if the Geneva Conventions held constant, then any change in the application of Common Article 3 must have been the result of a difference in Congress' understanding when it enacted section 821. Neither *Quirin*, nor *Yamashita*, nor *Eisentrager* construed section 821's predecessor to impose any Geneva Convention standards upon the operation of military commissions. As the Court incorporated Common Article 3 through section 821, the key moment of decision on the part of Congress must have been when it enacted the UCMJ, which the Court must have inferred was a rejection of *Eisentrager*.

The problem with the Court's approach, however, is that events could not have happened that way. Congress enacted the UCMJ on May 5, 1950.[119] When it did so, it re-enacted section 821's recognition of military commissions unchanged from its text at the time of *Quirin*.[120] The Court presented no evidence *at all* that Congress understood in 1950 that the UCMJ overruled *Eisentrager* and applied Geneva Common Article 3 to non-state actors. This would have been impossible, because *Eisentrager* was decided on June 5, 1950.[121] In other words, Congress could not have understood the UCMJ to

---

[116] See generally Geneva Convention Relative to the Treatment of Prisoners of War, Aug. 12, 1949, 6 U.S.T. 3316, 75 U.N.T.S. 135; Convention Between the United States of America and Other Powers Relating to Prisoners of War, July 27, 1929, 47 Stat. 2021.

[117] See Hamdan, 126 S. Ct. at 2778–80.

[118] *Id.* at 2794.

[119] Uniform Code of Military Justice, Pub. L. No. 81-506, 64 Stat. 107 (May 5, 1950) (UCMJ).

[120] UCMJ ch. 169, § 1 (art. 21), 64 Stat. 115 (May 5, 1950).

[121] Johnson v. Eisentrager, 339 U.S. 763 (1950).

reject *Eisentrager*'s rule on the non-enforceability of the Geneva Conventions, because *Eisentrager* did not announce its rule until after Congress had acted. Further, Congress could not have intended to incorporate Common Article 3 because it had not yet become a treaty obligation of the United States by the time Congress had enacted the UCMJ. While the Geneva Conventions were signed in 1949, the United States did not ratify them until 1955.[122] This glaring mistake of simple chronology shows how far the five justices in *Hamdan* were willing to go to impose their preferred policies on the war on terrorism.

Hamdan itself is certainly not the broad *constitutional* defeat for the Bush administration's terrorism policies that many in the media claimed in its immediate aftermath. The Court was addressing only the use of military commissions. It did not hold them unconstitutional, nor did it revisit its *Hamdi* decision two years ago, which allows the government to hold terrorists until the end of fighting. Even if no military commissions were held, no al Qaeda terrorists at Guantanamo Bay would be back on the street. Justice Stevens' majority opinion carefully did not address the president's inherent constitutional authority. It limited itself to interpreting two provisions of the UCMJ, one that declared that passage of the UCMJ was not meant to deprive military commissions of their usual jurisdiction, and the second that required the use of courts-martial procedures except where not practical.[123] None of the justices doubted that Congress could restore the place of military commissions by passing a more explicit authorization than the one it passed on September 18, 2001.

The question, however, is why Congress should have to enact an enumerated law in the war powers area. The Court considered the AUMF's broad authorization to use all necessary and appropriate force sufficient to uphold the detention of enemy combatants without criminal charge, even though the law did not specifically grant the power of detention and the Anti-Detention Act appeared to prohibit

---

[122] The United States signed the Geneva Conventions on August 12, 1949 and ratified them on August 2, 1955. See 6 U.S.T. 3316.

[123] See generally Hamdan, 126 S. Ct at 2749–99 (limiting its analysis to executive authority under UCMJ art. 21 (10 U.S.C. § 821 (1956)) and UCMJ art. 36 (10 U.S.C. § 836 (1990))).

non-criminal detention.[124] Obviously, Congress cannot legislate in anticipation of every circumstance that may arise in the future. That is one of the reasons, along with the executive branch's advantages in expertise and structural organization, why Congress delegates authority in the first place. Those who consider themselves legal progressives generally support the administrative state and vigorously defend broad grants of authority from Congress to the agencies of the executive branch. Agencies such as the Federal Communications Commission or the Environmental Protection Agency exercise powers over broad sectors of the economy under the vague congressional mandate that they regulate to protect the public interest or "public health."[125] Those agencies make decisions with enormous effects, such as which parts of the radio spectrum to sell, or how much pollution to allow into the air, all with little formal guidance from Congress.

Yet, when Congress delegates broad authority to the president to defend the nation from attack, the defenders of the administrative state demand that Congress list every power it wishes to authorize. While the threats to individual liberty may be greater in this setting, it makes little sense to place Congress under a heavier burden to describe every conceivable future contingency that might arise when we are fighting war, perhaps the most unpredictable and certainly most dangerous of human endeavors. Rather, we would expect and want Congress to delegate power to that branch, the presidency, that is best able to act with speed to threats to our national security. War is too difficult to plan for with fixed, antecedent legislative rules. War also is better run by the executive, which is structurally designed to take quick, decisive action. If the AUMF authorized the president to detain and kill the enemy, it ought to include the power to try the enemy for war crimes as well. *Hamdan* shows an inconsistent approach to review of delegation from Congress to president, one that seems oddly inverted given the stakes at issue for the nation's security.

Hamdan portends much more than whether the administration can subject ten or twenty al Qaeda suspects to military commission trial. It clearly announces that the imperial judiciary respects few

---

[124]Hamdi v. Rumsfeld, 542 U.S. 507 (2004).

[125]See, e.g., Whitman v. American Trucking Association, 531 U.S. 457, 472 (2001).

limits on how far it is willing to extend its powers of judicial review. Justices used to understand the inherent uncertainties and dire circumstances of war, and the limits of their own abilities. No longer. But here, unlike with abortion or religion, the Supreme Court does not have the last word. Congress and the president can enact a simple law putting the Court back in its traditional place, and our war effort will probably go forward with its usual combination of presidential initiative and general congressional support. The Supreme Court may believe it is protecting the Constitution by requiring Congress to pass a law signaling its support for Bush's antiterrorism policies, but all it has done is interfered with the working arrangement that the president and Congress had already reached. As with the 2005 Detainee Treatment Act, the justices will have merely forced the president and Congress to expend significant political time and energy to overrule them—time and energy better spent on taking the fight to al Qaeda.

A False Dawn for Federalism: Clear Statement Rules after *Gonzales v. Raich*

*Ilya Somin**

Introduction

The Supreme Court's 2005 decision in *Gonzales v. Raich*[1] severely undermined hopes that the Court might enforce meaningful constitutional limits on congressional power.[2] In the aftermath of *Raich*, some observers hoped and others feared that judicial limits on federal power might be resuscitated in *Gonzales v. Oregon*[3] and *Rapanos v. United States*,[4] the two most significant federalism cases of the 2005–2006 term. The appointment of two new conservative justices— Chief Justice Roberts and Justice Alito—may have increased the chance of departing from precedent, though the justices these newcomers replaced had both dissented in *Raich*.

Oregon and *Rapanos* could potentially have constrained the virtually limitless Commerce Clause power that the Supreme Court allowed the federal government to claim in *Raich*. A less high-profile case, *Arlington Central School District v. Murphy*,[5] addressed the scope

---

*Assistant Professor of Law, George Mason University School of Law; B.A., Amherst College, 1995; J.D., Yale Law School, 2001; M.A., Harvard University Department of Government, 1997; Ph.D. expected. For helpful suggestions and comments, I would like to thank Jonathan Adler, Douglas Laycock, Marty Lederman, Mark Moller, John Copeland Nagle, and Maxwell Stearns.

[1] 125 S. Ct. 2195 (2005).

[2] For a detailed analysis of the ways in which *Raich* undermined judicial review of congressional Commerce Clause authority, see Ilya Somin, Gonzales v. Raich: Federalism as a Casualty of the War on Drugs, Cornell J.L. & Pub. Pol'y (forthcoming 2006) (Symposium on the War on Drugs), available at http://papers.ssrn.com/sol3/papers.cfm?abstract_id=916965 (visited July 24, 2006).

[3] 126 S. Ct. 904 (2006).

[4] 126 S. Ct. 2208 (2006).

[5] 126 S. Ct. 2455 (2006).

of Congress' power to set conditions on grants to state governments under the Spending Clause. Although the federal government suffered setbacks in all three cases, none of them actually imposes significant constitutional limitations on congressional power.

Oregon, Rapanos, and *Arlington* all involved challenges to assertions of federal regulatory authority that might run afoul of "clear statement rules." These doctrines require Congress to clearly indicate its intent in the text of a statute before courts can interpret it in a way that "raises constitutional problems," impinges on an area of traditional state authority, or imposes conditions on state governments that accept federal funds.

Part I briefly reviews the *Raich* decision and explains how it opened the door to virtually unlimited federal power under the Commerce Clause. I also briefly discuss a parallel precedent that gave Congress equally unconstrained power under the Spending Clause, *Sabri v. United States.*[6]

Part II shows that the major federalism cases of the 2005–2006 term fail to impose any constitutional limits on federal power, and also do not extend the reach of clear statement rules. Thus, the legacy of *Raich* remains intact. Indeed, all three decisions actually reinforce that legacy by emphasizing that Congress does not lack the power to regulate almost any activity, but merely failed to exert it to the utmost in these specific instances.

Part III argues that clear statement rules are neither a viable nor an adequate substitute for substantive judicial limits on federal power. *Raich* poses a serious threat to the longterm viability of federalism clear statement rules. If congressional Commerce Clause authority is virtually unlimited, it is difficult to see how any assertion of that power can trigger a clear statement requirement by raising constitutional problems or by impinging on a policy area reserved to the states.

The last section of Part III shows that clear statement rules are an inadequate substitute for judicial enforcement of substantive limits on federal power, even if the doctrinal difficulties created by *Raich* can be overcome. Clear statement rules sometimes protect the interests of state governments, but that is very different from protecting constitutional federalism. Indeed, state governments will often find

[6] 541 U.S. 600 (2004).

it in their interest to support the expansion of federal power; courts applying clear statement rules cannot prevent this.

Indeed, clear statement rules may actually facilitate the expansion of federal power rather than restrain it. By reducing the chance that state governments will be blindsided by unexpected assertions of federal regulatory authority, they may make it more likely that states will collaborate in the expansion of federal power. The argument that clear statement rules can replace substantive judicial protection of federalism rests on the mistaken assumption that constitutional federalism is ultimately about protecting the interests of state governments rather than those of the general population.

I. Judicial Endorsement of Unlimited Federal Power

The Supreme Court's recent federalism decisions have embraced a nearly unlimited conception of federal power. In the Commerce Clause field, this result arises from the Court's well-known decision in *Gonzales v. Raich*.[7] Less well-known is the Court's 2004 decision in *Sabri v. United States*, which produced a similar outcome with respect to the Spending Clause.

A. Gonzales v. Raich *and the Unlimited Commerce Clause Power*[8]

The Commerce Clause gives Congress the power to "regulate commerce . . . among the several States."[9] Until the New Deal constitutional revolution of the 1930s, the Supreme Court generally did not treat this grant of power as an unlimited license for Congress to regulate any activity with even a remote connection to interstate

---

[7] 125 S. Ct. 2195 (2005).

[8] The analysis of *Raich* in this section is a condensed version of that in Somin, Federalism as a Casualty of the War on Drugs, *supra* note 2, at 4–13. For other analyses reaching similar conclusions about *Raich*, see Jonathan H. Adler, Is Morrison Dead? Assessing a Supreme Drug (Law) Overdose, 9 Lewis & Clark L. Rev. 751, 753–54 (2005) (contending that *Raich* effectively repudiates *Lopez* and *Morrison*); and Glenn H. Reynolds & Brannon P. Denning, What Hath Raich Wrought? Five Takes, 9 Lewis & Clark L. Rev. 915 (2005) (same). For arguments that *Raich* leaves greater room for judicial limitation of federal power, see Randy E. Barnett, Foreword: Limiting Raich, 9 Lewis & Clark L. Rev. 743 (2005); and George D. Brown, Counterrevolution? National Criminal Law after Raich, 66 Ohio St. U. L.J. 947, 974–82 (2005) (arguing that *Raich* merely refuses to extend *Lopez* and *Morrison* rather than cutting back on them).

[9] U.S. Const. art. I, § 8, cl. 3.

commerce.[10] The Court's famous 1824 decision in *Gibbons v. Ogden*,[11] often described as a precursor to the modern conception of virtually unlimited federal power,[12] in fact defined congressional Commerce Clause authority in a relatively narrow way.[13] A series of decisions during the New Deal period expanded congressional power to encompass any activity that substantially affects interstate commerce, even if the regulated action did not itself involve interstate trade in goods or services. Most notably, the 1942 case of *Wickard v. Filburn*[14] upheld a federal law limiting wheat-growing even in a case where the wheat in question never entered interstate commerce, but was instead consumed on the same farm where it was grown.[15]

After *Wickard*, the Supreme Court virtually abandoned efforts to constrain Congress' Commerce Clause authority until the Rehnquist Court's decisions in *United States v. Lopez*[16] and *United States v. Morrison*.[17] The former struck down a provision of the Gun Free School Zones Act (GFSZA), which forbade gun possession in close proximity to schools, while the latter invalidated a section of the Violence Against Women Act (VAWA) that created a federal cause of action for victims of violent attacks motivated by gender bias. *Lopez* and *Morrison* rekindled debate over the proper scope of federal power, but left the actual extent of judicial review in this area unclear.

---

[10] See, e.g., United States v. E.C. Knight, 156 U.S. 1 (1895) (holding that the Commerce Clause does not give Congress the power to break up an alleged sugar producer cartel); Hammer v. Dagenhart, 247 U.S. 251 (1918) (holding that the clause does not give Congress the power to regulate child labor).

[11] Gibbons v. Ogden, 22 U.S. (9 Wheat.) 1 (1824).

[12] See, e.g., United States v. Lopez, 514 U.S. 549, 603 (1995) (Souter, J., dissenting) (citing the "the Court's recognition of a broad commerce power in *Gibbons v. Ogden*"); Wickard v Filburn, 317 U.S. 111, 120 (1942) (claiming that "Chief Justice Marshall's opinion [in *Gibbons*] described the Federal commerce power with a breadth never yet exceeded").

[13] See Somin, Federalism as a Casualty of the War on Drugs, *supra* note 2, at 30–32.

[14] Wickard v. Filburn, 317 U.S. 111 (1942).

[15] For a detailed history of the case, see Jim Chen, Filburn's Legacy, 52 Emory L.J. 1719 (2003); and Jim Chen, Filburn's Forgotten Footnote—Of Farm Team Federalism and Its Fate, 82 Minn. L. Rev. 249 (1997).

[16] 514 U.S. 549 (1995).

[17] 529 U.S. 598 (2000).

The two cases outlined three areas of congressional Commerce Clause authority:

1. Regulation of "the use of the channels of interstate commerce."

2. "Regulat[ion] and protect[ion] [of] the instrumentalities of interstate commerce, or persons or things in interstate commerce, even though the threat may come only from intrastate activities."

3. "[R]egulat[ion] [of] . . . those activities that substantially affect interstate commerce."[18]

The most expansive category—and the only one at issue in *Lopez, Morrison,* and *Raich*—is the third: congressional power over activities that "substantially affect interstate commerce." The *Lopez-Morrison* majority sought to confine this category by limiting the government's ability to use "aggregation" analysis in claiming that virtually any activity that affects interstate commerce is fair game if its impact is analyzed in conjunction with that of other similar actions. *Lopez* cabined the aggregation principle by focusing on the noncommercial aspects of the activity regulated by the GFSZA. Such gun possession had "nothing to do with 'commerce' or any sort of economic enterprise, however broadly one might define those terms."[19] Therefore, aggregation analysis could not be applied to it because doing so would inevitably lead to such a broad interpretation of federal power that the Court would be "hard pressed to posit any activity by an individual that Congress is without power to regulate."[20] Although the Court conceded that "noneconomic" activity could still be regulated as part of a broader "regulatory scheme," such inclusion would have to be "essential" to the broader program.[21]

The *Morrison* decision went farther than *Lopez* in suggesting that "noneconomic" activity cannot be subjected to aggregation analysis. It struck down the relevant provision in VAWA even in the face of considerable evidence mustered by Congress indicating that violence against women had a substantial aggregate effect on interstate

---

[18] Lopez, 514 U.S. at 558–59; see also Morrison, 529 U.S. at 609.
[19] Lopez, 514 U.S. at 560.
[20] *Id.* at 564.
[21] *Id.* at 561.

commerce.[22] Chief Justice Rehnquist's opinion for the Court emphasized its "reject[ion]" of "the argument that Congress may regulate noneconomic, violent criminal conduct based solely on that conduct's aggregate effect on interstate commerce."[23] While the Court indicated that it "need not adopt a categorical rule against aggregating the effects of any noneconomic activity in order to decide these cases,"[24] it emphasized that previous Supreme Court cases had only used aggregation to uphold "regulation of intrastate activity only where that activity is economic in nature."[25]

In 2005, the apparent limitations on federal authority established by *Lopez* and *Morrison* were virtually eviscerated in *Gonzales v. Raich*.[26] *Raich* upheld the application of the Controlled Substances Act's (CSA) ban on marijuana possession to cases where homegrown marijuana was used for medical purposes, as permitted by California law, and in a manner unconnected with any commercial activity.[27]

Raich undermined the *Lopez-Morrison* framework for limiting federal power in three separate ways. First, *Raich* adopts a definition of "economic" that is almost limitless, thereby ensuring that virtually any activity can be "aggregated" to produce the "substantial[] [e]ffect [on] interstate commerce" required to legitimate congressional regulation under *Lopez* and *Morrison*.[28] According to the *Raich* majority, the word "economic" "refers to 'the production, distribution, and consumption of commodities.'"[29] Almost any human activity involves the "distribution" or "consumption" of a commodity. Even having dinner at home surely involves the "consumption" of the commodity of food, while giving a birthday present to a friend entails commodity "distribution."

---

[22] See Morrison, 529 U.S. at 628–29 (Souter, J., dissenting) (describing the "mountain of data assembled by Congress . . . showing the effects of violence against women on interstate commerce").

[23] *Id.* at 617.

[24] *Id.* at 613.

[25] *Id.*

[26] 125 S. Ct. 2195 (2006).

[27] See *id.* at 2200 (describing the facts of the case).

[28] See Lopez, 514 U.S. at 558–59; see Morrison, 529 U.S. at 609.

[29] Raich, 125 S. Ct. at 2211 (quoting Webster's Third New International Dictionary 720 (1966)).

Raich also makes it easier for Congress to impose controls on even "noneconomic" activity by claiming that it is part of a broader "regulatory scheme."[30] Here the Court greatly expanded *Lopez's* statement that Congress can regulate noneconomic activity if it is an "essential part of a larger regulation of economic activity."[31] The *Raich* majority ignored the *Lopez* requirement that the regulation of the noneconomic activity must be an *"essential"* part of a *"regulatory scheme"* intended to control interstate *"economic activity."*[32] If "essentiality" is no longer required, the regulation of almost any activity can be claimed to be part of a broader regulatory scheme. Indeed, the government could satisfy the requirement by claiming that any new regulation of noneconomic activity is just an addition to one of the numerous regulatory programs already in existence.[33]

Finally, *Raich* reasserts the so-called "rational basis" test, holding that "[w]e need not determine whether [defendants'] activities, taken in the aggregate, substantially affect interstate commerce in fact, but only whether a 'rational basis' exists for so concluding."[34] This holding suggests that even in the rare case where an activity is considered "noneconomic" under *Raich's* expansive definition of "economic," the regulation is not part of a broader regulatory scheme, and there is no real substantial effect on interstate commerce, congressional regulation will likely *still* be upheld if Congress could "rationally" conclude that such an effect exists.

---

[30] *Id.* at 2208–10.

[31] Lopez, 514 U.S. at 561. This language is quoted in *Raich*. Raich, 125 S. Ct. at 2210. However, the Court does not engage in any discussion of the implications of the word "essential" and seems to assume that it is of no significance.

[32] Lopez, 514 U.S. at 561 (emphasis added).

[33] Somin, Federalism as a Casualty of the War on Drugs, *supra* note 2, at 12.

[34] Raich, 125 S. Ct. at 2208. The "rational basis" test had been applied in some pre-*Lopez* Commerce Clause cases. See, e.g., Hodel v. Virginia Surface Mining & Reclamation Assn., 452 U.S. 264, 276 (1981) ("The court must defer to a congressional finding that a regulated activity affects interstate commerce, if there is any rational basis for such finding."); Katzenbach v. McClung, 379 U.S. 294, 303–04 (1964) ("Where we find that the legislators, in light of the facts and testimony before them, have a rational basis for finding a chosen regulatory scheme necessary to the protection of commerce, our investigation is at an end."). But it had been implicitly set aside in *Lopez* and *Morrison*, which failed to apply it and instead closely scrutinized the government's rationale for the challenged statutes. See Somin, Federalism as a Casualty of the War on Drugs, *supra* note 2, at 12–13.

Taken in combination, these three elements of *Raich* place nearly insurmountable obstacles in the path of efforts to ensure meaningful judicial review of congressional exercise of the Commerce Clause power. After *Raich*, virtually any activity is considered "economic," virtually any noneconomic activity can still be regulated as part of a broader regulatory scheme, and any stray activity that does not fall within the first two categories can be swept up under the rational basis test.

B. Unlimited Federal Power under the Spending Clause

The Spending Clause gives Congress the power to spend tax revenue to "pay the Debts and provide for the common Defence and the general Welfare of the United States."[35] The modern Supreme Court has generally been highly deferential to congressional efforts to define "general Welfare" broadly. Nonetheless, *South Dakota v. Dole*,[36] the leading modern precedent on the subject, does set criteria that Congress must meet if it wishes to impose conditions on federal grants to state governments. Any such conditions must 1) serve the "general welfare" under a standard that "defer[s] substantially to the judgment of Congress," 2) state any conditions that the states must meet in order to acquire the funds "unambiguously," 3) ensure that conditions are not "unrelated to the federal interest in particular national projects or programs" for which the funds were provided to the state, and 4) not violate "other constitutional provisions."[37] Furthermore, the Court noted the possibility that federal grants might be invalidated if "the financial inducement offered by Congress [is] so coercive as to pass the point at which pressure turns into compulsion."[38]

Of the four *Dole* requirements, only Condition Three—"relatedness" to a federal interest—holds out the hope of substantive limits on the scope of federal power as opposed to purely procedural ones. In the aftermath of the Rehnquist Court's newfound interest in enforcing federalism-based limits on congressional power, some

[35] U.S. Const. art. I, § 8, cl. 1.
[36] 483 U.S. 203 (1987).
[37] *Id.* at 207–08.
[38] *Id.* at 211 (quotation omitted).

commentators expected that the Court might use the relatedness test to set meaningful limits on conditional federal spending.[39]

Basim Omar Sabri was a Minneapolis real estate developer who allegedly bribed a city official to ensure that the Minneapolis Community Development Agency (MCDA) would permit him to go forward with his plans to "build a hotel and retail structure."[40] Sabri was charged under 18 U.S.C. § 666(a)(2), which "imposes federal criminal penalties" on anyone who offers a bribe to a state or local official employed by an agency that receives more than $10,000 in federal funds during any one year period.[41] The Supreme Court upheld this application of § 666(a)(2) even under the assumption that Sabri's bribe had no connection to the use of the federal funds received by MCDA. The Court held that it could "readily dispose of [the] position that, to qualify as a valid exercise of Article I power, the statute must require proof of connection with federal money as an element of the offense."[42] Even if no such connection exists, Congress could still choose to impose conditions because of the fungibility of money:

> It is true, just as Sabri says, that not every bribe or kickback offered or paid to agents of governments covered by § 666(b) will be traceably skimmed from specific federal payments, or show up in the guise of a *quid pro quo* for some dereliction in spending a federal grant. . . . But this possibility portends no enforcement beyond the scope of federal interest, for the reason that corruption does not have to be that limited to affect the federal interest. Money is fungible, bribed officials are untrustworthy stewards of federal funds, and corrupt contractors do not deliver dollar-for-dollar value. Liquidity is not a financial term for nothing; money can be drained

---

[39] See, e.g., Lynn Baker, Conditional Federal Spending After Lopez, 95 Colum. L. Rev. 1911, 1962–77 (1995) (arguing that such limitations are a natural extension of the *Lopez* decision); Lynn Baker, The Revival of States' Rights: A Progress Report and a Proposal, 22 Harv. J.L. & Pub. Pol'y 95, 102–103 (1998) (compiling evidence indicating that a majority of the Supreme Court might have been willing to move in that direction). For my own argument for limiting federal grants to state governments, see Ilya Somin, Closing the Pandora's Box of Federalism: The Case for Judicial Restriction of Federal Subsidies to State Governments, 90 Geo. L.J. 461 (2002).

[40] Sabri v. United States, 541 U.S. 600, 602 (2004).

[41] *Id.* at 603 (quoting 18 U.S.C. § 666(a)(2)).

[42] *Id.* at 605.

> off here because a federal grant is pouring in there. And officials are not any the less threatening to the objects behind federal spending just because they may accept general retainers. . . . It is certainly enough that the statutes condition the offense on a threshold amount of federal dollars defining the federal interest, such as that provided here, and on a bribe that goes well beyond liquor and cigars.[43]

This fungibility argument seriously undermines any hope that *Dole's* third prong might lead to meaningful judicial limits on conditional federal spending. After all, virtually any condition can be justified on the ground that if state or local governments are permitted to do X, it could siphon off funds from purpose Y, which the federal grants are intended to promote. And this would be true even if there is no connection between X and Y whatsoever beyond the mere fact that both agendas are being pursued by a government agency receiving federal funds.[44]

Unlike *Raich*, which was a 6-3 decision with strong dissents by Justice O'Connor and Justice Thomas,[45] *Sabri* was unanimous, with only Justice Thomas authoring a concurrence attempting to devise a more limited rationale for allowing the federal criminal case against Sabri to proceed.[46] Thus, *Sabri* was, if anything, an even more decisive setback for judicial review of federalism than the better-known *Raich* decision.

II. Pyrrhic Defeats: Unlimited Federal Power in the 2005–2006 Term

In light of *Raich* and *Sabri*, the Supreme Court could potentially resuscitate judicial enforcement of limits on federal power by overruling one or both of these precedents, or at least restricting their

---

[43] *Id.* at 605–06.

[44] For a more detailed analysis of *Sabri* reaching similar conclusions, see Gary Lawson, Making a Federal Case of It: Sabri v. United States and the Constitution of Leviathan, 2003–2004 Cato Sup. Ct. Rev. 119 (2004). See also Richard W. Garnett, The New Federalism, The Spending Power and Federal Criminal Law, 89 Cornell L. Rev. 1 (2003) (making similar arguments prior to the *Sabri* decision).

[45] See Gonzales v. Raich, 125 S. Ct. 2195, 2220–29 (2005) (O'Connor, J., dissenting); *id.* at 2229–39 (Thomas, J., dissenting).

[46] See Sabri, 541 U.S. at 610–14 (Thomas, J., concurring) (questioning the Court's fungibility rationale and arguing that the application of the statute to Sabri should be upheld under the Commerce Clause)

impact. Alternatively, it could limit federal power through purely procedural rather than substantive restraints. In the 2005–2006 term, however, it failed to pursue either of these options.

A Pyrrhic victory is one that is so costly to the winning side that it might have done better to avoid the battle at all. The federal government lost all three of the major federalism cases of the 2005–2006 Supreme Court term, yet the Court's reasoning served to reaffirm more than constrain the virtually limitless nature of congressional power. Although the feds did not win even Pyrrhic victories, they achieved the much more valuable outcome of protecting their victory in the larger battle despite (and in part because of) losing three minor skirmishes. For advocates of federal power, *Oregon, Rapanos,* and possibly even *Arlington* were Pyrrhic defeats, setbacks that underscore their dominant position in the larger struggle.

A. Oregon, Rapanos, *and Limits on Congressional Commerce Clause Power*

In addition to cutting back on *Raich* directly by reimposing substantive limits on federal power, the Court in *Oregon* and *Rapanos* could have constrained federal authority by relying on restrictive rules of statutory interpretation. There are two rules of construction by which the Court majority could have constrained congressional power. The "constitutional avoidance" canon requires courts to reject interpretations of a statute that "raise serious constitutional problems" unless there is a clear statement in the law that Congress intended it to be interpreted in that way.[47] The "federalism canon" requires a similar "unmistakably clear" statement of congressional intent in statutes that "alter the usual constitutional balance between the States and the Federal Government."[48] In the final analysis, neither substantive nor procedural limits on federal power were imposed by either decision.

---

[47] See, e.g., Edward J. DeBartolo Corp. v. Florida Gulf Coast Bldg. & Const. Trades Council, 485 U.S. 568, 574 (1988); NLRB v. Catholic Bishop of Chicago, 440 U.S. 490, 504 (1979) (requiring a clear expression of an affirmative intention of Congress before a statutory interpretation that raises serious constitutional questions can be accepted).

[48] Gregory v. Ashcroft, 501 U.S. 452, 460 (1991).

1. Gonzales v. Oregon

Some perceive *Gonzales v. Oregon*[49] as a partial repudiation of *Raich* or at least as a reassertion of state autonomy.[50] *Oregon* rejected the Bush administration's attempt to interpret the CSA in a way that would have permitted it to punish Oregon doctors who use prescription drugs to facilitate assisted suicide, as they are permitted to do under the state's Death with Dignity Act.[51] The CSA, of course, is the same statute as the one at issue in *Raich*.

In reality, *Oregon* does not in any way undercut *Raich*'s constitutional holding. Both the majority and dissenting justices took pains to point out that the decision was a purely statutory one and did not conclude that Congress lacked constitutional authority to forbid assisted suicide using its powers under the Commerce Clause. Justice Kennedy's majority opinion emphasized that "there is no question that the Federal Government can set uniform national standards" for the "regulation of health and safety" despite the fact that "these areas" have traditionally been "a matter of local concern."[52] Justice Scalia's dissent, joined by Justice Thomas and Chief Justice Roberts, similarly noted that "using the federal commerce power to prevent assisted suicide is unquestionably permissible" under the Court's precedents, and that the only question addressed by *Oregon* is "not whether Congress *can* do this, or even whether Congress *should* do this; but simply whether Congress *has* done so in the CSA."[53]

The majority did make a small bow to federalism by stating that part of the basis of its decision was a lack of proof that, in enacting the CSA, Congress had "the farreaching intent to alter the federal-state balance" by overriding the states' traditional authority to regulate the practice of medicine.[54] This holding might be welcomed

[49] 126 S. Ct. 904 (2006).

[50] See, e.g., Linda Greenhouse, Justices Reject U.S. Bid to Block Assisted Suicide, N.Y. Times, Jan. 18, 2006, at A1 ("While the court's decision was based on standard principles of administrative law, and not on the Constitution, it was clearly influenced by the majority's view that the regulation of medical practice belonged, as a general matter, to the states."); Tony Mauro, Court Sides with Oregon Over Assisted Suicide Law, Legal Times, Jan. 23, 2006, at 10 (suggesting that the Court had "sid[ed] with states' rights").

[51] Oregon, 126 S. Ct. at 911–26.

[52] *Id.* at 923 (quotation omitted).

[53] *Id.* at 939 (Scalia, J., dissenting).

[54] *Id.* at 925.

by those who would like to replace substantive judicial review of Commerce Clause cases with "clear statement" rules that require Congress to plainly indicate its intent in cases where a statute is intended to infringe on a particularly sensitive area of state authority.[55] Previous Supreme Court precedents already require Congress to make its intentions "unmistakably clear in the language of the statute" whenever it seeks to "alter the usual constitutional balance between the States and the Federal Government."[56]

However, the *Oregon* Court specifically disclaimed reliance on any such principle, claiming that "[i]t is unnecessary even to consider the application of clear statement requirements" because the correct interpretation of the CSA could so easily be determined through the use of ordinary statutory analysis and "commonsense."[57]

Only Justice Thomas, in a solitary dissent, suggested that there was a possible tension between the Court's reasoning in *Oregon* and its recent holding in *Raich*.[58] Thomas emphasized that the majority had "beat[en] a hasty retreat" from *Raich's* characterization of the CSA as "'a comprehensive regulatory scheme specifically designed to regulate which controlled substances can be utilized for medicinal purposes *and in what manner*.'"[59] He went on to note that he found the Bush administration's assertion of federal authority over assisted suicide to be both "sweeping" and "perhaps troubling."[60] Justice Thomas even implied that the government's position might be inconsistent with "principles of federalism and our constitutional structure."[61] But, after *Raich*, such concerns are "now water under the dam."[62] The administration stance in *Oregon* was, according to Thomas, "merely the inevitable and inexorable consequence of" *Raich*.[63] In any event, Thomas, like the other justices, emphasized

---

[55] See, e.g., Thomas M. Merrill, Rescuing Federalism after Raich: The Case for Clear Statement Rules, 9 Lewis & Clark L. Rev. 823 (2005).

[56] Gregory v. Ashcroft, 501 U.S. 452, 460 (1991).

[57] Oregon, 126 S. Ct. at 925.

[58] *Id.* at 939–42 (Thomas, J., dissenting).

[59] *Id.* at 939 (quoting Gonzales v. Raich, 125 S. Ct. 2195, 2211 (2006)) (emphasis added by Justice Thomas).

[60] *Id.* at 940.

[61] *Id.* at 941.

[62] *Id.*

[63] *Id.*

that *Oregon* was merely a case about "statutory interpretation, and not [about] the extent of constitutionally permissible federal power."[64] In a footnote, Thomas points out that Oregon had "not seriously pressed a constitutional claim" and had accepted the validity of *Raich*, thereby "foreclose[ing]" any possible "constitutional challenge."[65] Thomas' argument aside, the other eight justices, especially those in the majority, did all they could to foreclose any possibility that *Oregon* might undercut *Raich* in a meaningful way.

2. Rapanos v. United States[66]

Rapanos v. United States[67] involved the scope of federal authority to regulate "wetlands" under the Clean Water Act of 1972 (CWA), which gives the Army Corps of Engineers the power to regulate discharges into "navigable waters,"[68] a term defined as encompassing "the waters of the United States."[69] Two property owners claimed that the Corps lacked both statutory and constitutional authority to regulate land they owned that was "11 to 20 miles away from the nearest navigable water" and connected to it only by man-made drains.[70] In a split 4-1-4 decision, the Court refused to endorse the government's claim that the CWA gives the Corps the power to regulate virtually any wetland area, regardless of the degree of connection to "navigable" waterways and instead remanded the case to the district court for further factfinding.[71] *Rapanos* is in some respects a sequel to *SWANCC v. United States Army Corps of Engineers,*[72] a 2001 decision in which the Court held that the CWA does not authorize the Corps to regulate isolated, nonnavigable intrastate waters merely because they are occasionally utilized by migratory birds.[73]

---

[64] *Id.*

[65] *Id.* at 945 n.2.

[66] Some of the material in this section is a revised version of a post produced for the *Volokh Conspiracy Blog*. See Ilya Somin, Preliminary Thoughts On Rapanos And Federalism—Much Ado About Very Little, The Volokh Conspiracy (June 19, 2006), available at http://volokh.com/posts/1150751435.shtml (visited June 28, 2006).

[67] 126 S. Ct. 2208 (2006).

[68] 33 U.S.C. §§ 1311(a), 1344(a).

[69] 33 U.S.C. § 1362(7).

[70] Rapanos, 126 S. Ct. at 2214, 2219.

[71] *Id.* at 2235.

[72] SWANCC v. United States Army Corps of Engineers, 531 U.S. 159 (2001).

[73] *Id.* at 172–74.

Some observers hoped and others feared that *Rapanos* might rein in the impact of *Raich* on judicial review of federalism.[74] Such hopes and fears have turned out to be groundless. *Rapanos* does not enforce any constitutional limits on federal power. Nor does it increase the protection for federalism provided by rules of statutory interpretation.

Neither Justice Scalia's opinion nor Justice Kennedy's concurrence addresses the constitutional issues raised by the property owners.[75] Both rely exclusively on statutory interpretation arguments about the meaning of the Clean Water Act (CWA).[76] They hold that Congress in the CWA *didn't* give the Army Corps of Engineers the power to regulate any and all bodies of water, no matter how small or non-navigable. But that does not mean that it *couldn't* do so if it wanted to. Indeed, it is striking that Scalia's opinion does not even mention *Raich*, while Kennedy's does so only briefly, using it to justify interpreting the CWA to give the Corps greater regulatory authority than the plurality would allow.[77]

Rapanos also does little or nothing to limit congressional power through rules of statutory interpretation. The *Rapanos* majority largely eschews both the constitutional avoidance and federalism canons, despite the fact that the Court previously relied on both in

---

[74]See, e.g., Sara Beardsley, The End of the Everglades? Supreme Court Case Jeopardizes 90 percent of U.S. Wetlands, Sci. Am., May 22, 2006, available at http://www.sciam.com/article.cfm?chanID=sa006&colID=5&articleID=000997CF-938F-146C-91AE83414B7F0000 (visited June 28, 2006) (claiming that *Rapanos* might radically reduce federal regulatory authority over wetlands and noting that "federalist watchdogs cling to *Rapanos* . . . as an opportunity to curb Washington's power").

[75]In their brief, the owners claimed that the Army Corps of Engineers' interpretation of the CWA expands federal power beyond the limits of the Commerce Clause, even after *Raich*. See Brief for Petitioner at i, 23–28, Rapanos v. United States, 126 S. Ct. 2208 (2006) (No. 04-1034) (Dec. 2, 2005), available at 2005 WL 3294932.

[76]Rapanos, 126 S. Ct. at 2220–25 (interpreting CWA reference to "waters of the United States" to cover only "relatively permanent, standing or continuously flowing bodies of water forming geographic features that are described in ordinary parlance as streams[,] . . . oceans, rivers, [and] lakes") (citations and quotation marks omitted); *id.* at 2248 (Kennedy, J., concurring) (interpreting it to require "the existence of a significant nexus between the wetlands in question and navigable waters in the traditional sense").

[77]*Id.* at 2250 (Kennedy, J., concurring) (citing Gonzales v. Raich, 125 S. Ct. 2195, 2206 (2005)).

rejecting the Army Corps of Engineers' "migratory bird rule" in the *SWANCC* case. [78]

Justice Scalia's plurality opinion briefly cites the two canons to buttress its interpretation of the CWA.[79] However, Scalia mostly relies on a detailed textual analysis of the statute.[80] His opinion does not hold that either canon would require rejection of the government's interpretation of the CWA even if the latter were otherwise the most persuasive available option. This is a significant omission, since previous avoidance canon cases specifically note that clear statement rules require courts to reject even "an otherwise acceptable construction of a statute" if endorsing it "would raise serious constitutional problems."[81]

According to Scalia, "[e]ven if the phrase 'the waters of the United States' were ambiguous as applied to intermittent flows," the federalism and constitutional avoidance canons would compel rejection of the Corps of Engineers' interpretation of the CWA.[82] He notes that, under the federalism clear statement rule, "[w]e ordinarily expect a 'clear and manifest' statement from Congress to authorize an unprecedented intrusion into traditional state authority."[83] However, Scalia's discussion of the canon assumes that they apply only when a statute is "ambiguous" on the issue at hand,[84] and fails to reiterate earlier precedents that require Congress to make its intention to upset the "usual" federal-state balance "unmistakably clear in the language of the statute."[85] Instead, Scalia contends that such an intention requires a "clear and manifest statement from Congress," a potentially less demanding standard.[86]

With respect to the constitutional avoidance canon, Scalia concludes only that "we would expect a clearer statement from Congress

---

[78] SWANCC, 531 U.S. at 172–74.

[79] Rapanos, 126 S. Ct. at 2224.

[80] *Id.* at 2220–23, 2225–34.

[81] Edward J. DeBartolo Corp. v. Florida Gulf Coast Bldg. & Const. Trades Council, 485 U.S. 568, 574 (1988).

[82] *Id.*

[83] Rapanos, 126 S. Ct. at 2224.

[84] *Id.*

[85] Gregory v. Ashcroft, 501 U.S. 452, 460 (1991).

[86] Rapanos, 126 S. Ct. at 2224.

to authorize an agency theory of jurisdiction that presses the envelope of constitutional validity."[87] This is a weaker requirement than the traditional formulation of the canon, which holds that "when an otherwise acceptable construction of a statute would raise serious constitutional problems, the Court will construe the statute to avoid such problems unless such construction is clearly contrary to the intent of Congress."[88]

Justice Scalia may not actually intend to weaken the standards required by the two avoidance canons. His departure from previous, stronger formulations of these rules may simply constitute loose use of language. Even so, there is no indication that he and the other justices who signed on to his opinion intend to strengthen the two canons in order to offset some of the impact of *Raich.*

In any event, Scalia's treatment of the canons probably lacks precedential significance and does not bind lower courts because Justice Kennedy specifically rejected it in his concurring opinion. Because *Rapanos* is a 4-1-4 decision, Kennedy's vote was decisive to the result. As Chief Justice Roberts (who signed on to Scalia's interpretation of the CWA) points out in a concurring opinion, cases where there is no one opinion endorsed by a majority of the Court are governed by *Marks v. United States.*[89] According to *Marks*:

> When a fragmented Court decides a case and no single rationale explaining the result enjoys the assent of five justices, the holding of the Court may be viewed as that position taken by those Members who concurred in the judgments on the narrowest grounds.[90]

In this case, Kennedy is probably the justice who concurred on the "narrowest grounds," since his opinion places fewer restrictions

[87] *Id.*

[88] DeBartolo, 485 U.S. at 574. See also NLRB v. Catholic Bishop of Chicago, 440 U.S. 490, 504 (1979) (requiring a "clear expression of an affirmative intention of Congress" before a statutory interpretation that raises serious constitutional questions can be upheld). Scalia cites *DeBartolo* (Rapanos, 126 S. Ct. at 2224), but does not refer to the language quoted here.

[89] See 126 S. Ct. at 2236 (Roberts, C.J., concurring) (citing Marks v. United States, 430 U.S. 188, 193 (1977)).

[90] Marks, 430 U.S. at 193.

on the Corps than Scalia's, and also provides a less sweeping and more ambiguous interpretation of the CWA. Even if Justice Scalia's plurality opinion is binding instead of Justice Kennedy's concurrence, the implications for clear statement rules are little different. Thus, *Rapanos* is unlikely to expand the application of the two avoidance canons to statutes that rely on Congress' Commerce Clause authority.

Even as a matter of pure statutory interpretation, *Rapanos* probably does not impose significant limits on the scope of federal authority under the CWA. The full impact of *Rapanos* will not become clear until lower courts (starting with the district court that will consider the remanded *Rapanos* case itself) go through the process of applying Justice Kennedy's "significant nexus" test to particular cases. As this article goes to press, the U.S. Court of Appeals for the Ninth Circuit has just decided *Northern California River Watch v. City of Healdsburg*, the first lower court appellate decision to apply *Rapanos*. Unfortunately, *River Watch* sheds little light on the broader implications of *Rapanos*, with the important exception of confirming that Justice Kennedy's concurring opinion is the controlling one under *Marks v. United States*.[91] It is also worth noting that preliminary assessments by environmental scholars on both sides of the political spectrum conclude that the decision is likely to impose only minor limitations on the Army Corps of Engineers.[92]

[91] Northern Calif. River Watch v. City of Healdsburg, 2006 WL 2299115, at *1, 6 (9th Cir. Aug. 10, 2006) (holding that "the controlling opinion [in *Rapanos*] is that of Justice Kennedy"). *River Watch's* broader significance for interpretations of the "significant nexus" test is very limited because if was not a close case under that standard. See *id.* at *6–7 (noting extensive "hydrological," "physical," and "ecological" connections between the body of water at issue in the case and "navigable waters"). One possible noteworthy aspect of *River Watch* is the court's holding that "mere adjacency" to navigable waters is not sufficient to justify federal regulatory jurisdiction under *Rapanos*. *Id.* at *6.

[92] See, e.g., Jonathan Adler, All Wet: Landowners May Have Won The Battle Against Federal Wetlands Regulations, But Lost The War, National Review Online, June 27, 2006, available at http://article.nationalreview.com/?q = NDExM2MxYmY3OGE1Z-WRjOTYwMDkxZDM1M2NlZmJmYzY = (visited Aug. 9, 2006) (op ed by leading libertarian environmental law expert concluding that *Rapanos* "will do little to limit the scope of federal regulation"); Richard Lazarus, Discussion: Rapanos and Carabell, SCOTUS blog, June 19, 2006, available at http://www.scotusblog.com/movabletype/archives/2006/06/discussion_boar_1.html (visited Aug. 9, 2006) (prominent liberal environmental law scholar suggesting that "Kennedy['s concurrence] plus the Stevens dissent provides lots of regulatory space for the government and for environmental protection").

B. Arlington Central School District v. Murphy *and the* Spending Power

Arlington Central School District v. Murphy[93] received far less publicity than either *Oregon* or *Rapanos*. Nonetheless, *Arlington* raises the same issues in the Spending Clause context after *Sabri* as the other two cases do with respect to the post-*Raich* Commerce Clause.

The *Arlington* case involved competing interpretations of a provision of the Individuals with Disabilities Education Act (IDEA), which allows courts to "award reasonable attorneys' fees as part of the costs" to parents who win a case against their public school under the act.[94] The point in dispute was whether or not "this fee-shifting provision authorizes prevailing parents to recover fees for services rendered by experts in IDEA actions" in addition to traditional attorneys' fees.[95]

The IDEA cause of action is a condition of state governments' receipt of federal education funds.[96] For that reason, it is subject to one of the Court's strongest federalism clear statement rules. Because federal grants to state governments are "much in the nature of a contract," any conditions attached to the funds must be stated "unambiguously" in order to ensure that they are accepted "voluntarily and knowingly."[97]

The Supreme Court has not always applied this requirement rigorously. For example, in its 1999 decision in *Davis v. Monroe County Board of Education*,[98] the Court upheld the imposition of Title IX liability for student-to-student sexual harassment on schools receiving federal funds, despite the fact that such liability is not specifically mentioned in the text of Title IX and cannot easily be inferred from the structure or legislative history of the statute.[99]

---

[93] Arlington Central School Dist. Board of Education v. Murphy, 126 S. Ct. 2455 (2006).

[94] 20 U.S.C. § 1415(i)(3)(B).

[95] Arlington, 126 S. Ct. at 2457.

[96] *Id.* at 2458–59.

[97] Pennhurst State School & Hospital v. Halderman, 451 U.S. 1, 17 (1981).

[98] Davis v. Monroe County Board of Education, 526 U.S. 629 (1999).

[99] *Id.* at 643–49; see also *id.* at 657–64 (Kennedy, J., dissenting) (explaining why liability for student-to-student sexual harassment cannot be inferred from the text of Title IX).

In *Arlington,* however, the Court refused to interpret IDEA to allow courts to award funds for payment of experts. Justice Alito's majority opinion emphasized that the text of the IDEA, which permits only "the award of reasonable attorneys' fees," does not "even hint that acceptance of IDEA funds makes a State responsible for reimbursing prevailing parents for services rendered by experts."[100] Even Justice Breyer's dissenting opinion, joined by Justices Stevens and Souter, accepts that compensation for expenditures on experts cannot be inferred from the text alone.[101] Breyer in fact concedes that "the statute on its face does not *clearly* tell the States that they must pay expert fees to prevailing parents."[102] The dissenters claim that such a rule can nonetheless be justified by reference to IDEA's legislative history and purpose.[103] But if we concede that the text is unclear at best, it becomes impossible to prove that IDEA *"unambiguously"* permits courts to award expert fees to victorious plaintiffs.[104]

Arlington therefore maintains the rule that states must have clear notice of any conditions imposed on the receipt of federal funds. At the same time, it is telling that three justices dissented despite admitting that the text of the statute was unclear. Their view, in effect, constitutes a rejection of the clear statement rule. A fourth, Justice Ginsburg, concurred in the result, but emphasized that a "clear notice" requirement should not apply to cases involving remedies for violations as opposed to those involving the substance of the conditions themselves.[105] Ginsburg also argues that clear statement requirements should not be imposed on conditional grants enacted "pursuant to § 5 of the Fourteenth Amendment," as she believes IDEA was.[106]

Thus, *Arlington* reveals that the Spending Clause clear statement rule is far from irrevocably established. Three justices largely reject the requirement and a fourth (Ginsburg) would apply it only to a limited range of grants. And even the majority justices did not

---

[100] Arlington, 126 S. Ct. at 2459.

[101] *Id.* at 2466 (Breyer, J., dissenting).

[102] *Id.* at 2470 (emphasis in original).

[103] *Id.* at 2466–70.

[104] Pennhurst, 451 U.S. at 17 (emphasis added).

[105] Arlington, 126 S. Ct. at 2464 (Ginsburg, J., concurring).

[106] *Id.*

attempt to strengthen the rule relative to previous cases in order to offset the impact of *Sabri*. Moreover, they carefully noted that they do not intend to limit the substantive reach of Congress' Spending Clause power, emphasizing that "Congress has broad power to set the terms on which it disburses federal money to the States."[107]

Arlington reaffirms a longstanding, seemingly pro-federalism clear statement rule. But it also reveals that the rule commands only a narrow majority on the Court.

III. The Limits of Clear Statement Rules

In the aftermath of *Raich*, Thomas Merrill has argued that a federalism clear statement rule is a superior alternative to substantive limitations on congressional Commerce Clause authority, and Justice Breyer advances a similar argument in a recent book.[108] Other scholars defend clear statement rules as a useful supplement to substantive judicial review of federalism.[109] Unfortunately, clear statement rules are unlikely to be an adequate substitute for substantive judicial review, and it is not even clear that they make the situation better at the margin.

After *Raich*, it is far from clear that clear statement rules can still be applied in the Commerce Clause field, though they remain viable with respect to the Spending Clause, as *Arlington* demonstrates. Even if the post-*Raich* doctrinal challenges to clear statement rules can be overcome, these canons are unlikely to provide adequate protection for constitutional federalism. In some cases, they may even contribute to the growth of federal power.

A. The Uncertain Future of Federalism Clear Statement Rules

Neither academic advocates nor any of the justices who authored opinions in *Oregon* and *Rapanos* have so far considered the implications of *Raich* for the future of clear statement rules. It is far from

[107] *Id.* at 2459.

[108] See generally Merrill, *supra* note 55; Stephen E. Breyer, Active Liberty: Interpreting our Democratic Constitution 64–65 (2005).

[109] See, e.g., Ernest A. Young, Two Cheers for Process Federalism, 46 Vill. L. Rev. 1349, 1385–92 (2001) (arguing for clear statement rules, but also emphasizing the need for a "substantive backstop"); Larry J. Obhof, Federalism, I Presume? A Look at the Enforcement of Federalism Principles through Presumptions and Clear Statement Rules, 2004 Mich. St. L. Rev. 123, 150–64 (defending clear statement rules without taking a position on the merits of substantive judicial review of federalism).

clear that either the constitutional avoidance canon or the federalism canon remains viable after *Raich.*

1. The Constitutional Avoidance Canon

If *Raich* is correct and congressional Commerce Clause power is essentially unlimited, a statute that relies on a broad interpretation of that power cannot "raise serious constitutional problems."[110] After *Raich,* there can be no "problem" because there are no constitutional limits for Congress to infringe. To be sure, the avoidance canon might be resuscitated if federalism is viewed as an "underenforced constitutional norm."[111] Under this approach, the Court could explicitly admit that meaningful limits on federal power, though required by the Constitution, cannot be enforced because of political considerations or because of inadequate judicial competence. Clear statement rules might be viewed as a sort of second best strategy, providing a measure of protection for federalism without placing substantive judicial limits on congressional authority.[112] Even this relatively modest agenda, however, would require the Court to retreat from the vision of virtually unlimited federal power articulated in *Raich.*[113] A new Supreme Court decision would have to repudiate the reasoning of *Raich* and instead conclude that there are meaningful limits to congressional Commerce Clause authority after all—even if those limits can only be "enforced" through clear statement requirements.

2. The Federalism Canon

Raich poses a similar dilemma for the federalism canon. If federal regulatory authority is virtually unlimited, it becomes almost impossible for Congress to write a statute that "alter[s] the usual constitutional balance between the States and the Federal Government."[114] Under *Raich,* the "usual constitutional balance" is one where there are no structural limits to congressional authority. The only "usual constitutional balance" that can exist is whatever Congress decides on.

[110]Edward J. DeBartolo Corp. v. Florida Gulf Coast Bldg. & Const. Trades Council, 485 U.S. 568, 574 (1988).

[111]See generally Lawrence Sager, Fair Measure: The Legal Status of Underenforced Constitutional Norms, 91 Harv. L. Rev. 1212 (1978).

[112]This approach is similar to that defended in Merrill, *supra* note 55.

[113]See Somin, Federalism as a Casualty of the War on Drugs, *supra* note 2, at 4–13; see *supra* Part I.A.

[114]Gregory v. Ashcroft, 501 U.S. 452, 460 (1991).

As with the avoidance canon, it is possible to get around this problem by envisioning federalism as an "underenforced" constitutional norm. But, as already noted, this solution would require a major rollback of the reasoning adopted in *Raich*.

An alternative approach would be to unmoor the canon from the Constitution entirely and define the state-federal "balance" by reference to tradition and status quo practices. If Congress seeks to intervene in a field previously left to the states, it has to enact a statute that meets the terms of the clear statement rule. However, in the modern regulatory state there are few if any policy areas that remain free of federal involvement. Such traditional areas of state authority as education, criminal law, and local land use regulation are all now subject to extensive federal intervention. Indeed, *Arlington* (education), *Raich* (criminal law), and *Rapanos* (land use) addressed federal regulations in precisely these three fields.

Even if the specific assertions of federal authority considered in these three cases can be viewed as novel, it is undeniable that statutes such as the Clean Water Act, the CSA, and a variety of federal education statutes including IDEA and the No Child Left Behind Act,[115] have led to the entrenchment of federal power over policy issues that were once under more or less exclusive state control. Using the status quo as a baseline is therefore a nonstarter unless new federal regulations are considered in an arbitrarily narrow light. If, for example, the federal government has had a longstanding role in setting education policy, it is not clear why federal restrictions on gun possession in school zones (*Lopez*) should be viewed as altering the "usual" state-federal balance rather than applying it. [116]

This difficulty underscores the crucial point that defenders of the federalism clear statement rule lack a coherent theory that can determine where the rule should apply. Professor Merrill, the leading recent advocate of the canon, concedes that "no set formula is possible" and urges courts to make their decisions by drawing "on

---

[115] Indeed, the NCLBA expands federal control of education so much that liberal Democratic critics of the act have attacked it for undermining states' rights. See Sam Dillon, President's Initiative to Shake up Education is Facing Protests in Many State Capitols, N.Y. Times, Mar. 8, 2004, at 12 (noting liberal Democratic criticisms of the act for excessive intrusion on state control of education policy).

[116] Gregory, 501 U.S. at 460.

historical experience in implementing the Commerce Clause, leavened with some common sense."[117] It is certainly desirable to take advantage of both experience and common sense. However, judges with differing ideologies and backgrounds are likely to draw very different lessons from "historical experience." And that which appears to be "common sense" to liberal jurists may well be viewed as folly by conservatives or libertarians, and vice versa. If we want a post-*Raich* federalism clear statement rule to be applied at least somewhat consistently, courts will need some kind of theory to guide them in determining what factors are relevant to the rule's application and how to weigh them against each other in cases where they conflict.

3. Conditional Federal Spending

As the *Arlington* case demonstrates, the clear statement canon requiring Congress to unambiguously identify the conditions attached to federal grants to state governments remains intact—at least for the moment.[118] It is not threatened by *Raich* because it applies to all conditions attached to federal grants, apparently irrespective of their impact on the state-federal balance or even their impact on other constitutional values. Although this canon therefore escapes some of the problems bedeviling its two cousins, it is still far from clear that it is an adequate substitute for substantive limits on federal power.

B. Clear Statement Rules and the Fallacy of Equating Federalism and the Interests of State Governments

1. Why Clear Statement Rules Are Not Enough

Even if the doctrinal and conceptual problems bedeviling clear statement rules can be overcome, they are still an inadequate substitute for judicial enforcement of substantive limits on federal power. The key flaw in the case for clear statement rules is the implicit assumption that constitutional federalism is reducible to the protection of state government interests. For example, Professor Merrill contends that a federalism clear statement rule will be effective "to the extent [that] we think that state and local governments have at least some influence with Congress, and to the extent we wish to harness these political safeguards as part of a larger strategy of

---

[117] Merrill, *supra* note 55, at 845.
[118] See *supra* Part I.B.

accommodating stability and change in intergovernmental rela-tions."[119] The focus on state government interests is also evident in *Arlington*, where the Court emphasizes that the Spending Clause clear statement rule requires it to "view the IDEA from the perspec-tive of a state official who is engaged in the process of deciding whether the State should accept IDEA funds and the obligations that go with those funds."[120]

In theory, clear statement rules help activate the political power of state governments by alerting them to any overextension of federal power embedded in pending legislation.[121] The states can then "mobilize in opposition to such regulation," potentially obviating the need for substantive judicial review.[122] The flaw in this reliance on the political power of state governments is that state politicians often have incentives to undermine federalism rather than promote it, by acquiescing in the extension of federal power.

For example, state officials sometimes lobby for federal interven-tion to help form a cartel to prevent interstate competition for resi-dents and businesses.[123] State governments may also fall under the influence of interest groups that seek to impose their preferred poli-cies nationwide and, as a result, use their political leverage to lobby for uniform federal regulation.[124] Elsewhere, John McGinnis and I have explained in more detail the numerous incentives state govern-ments have to support the expansion of federal power, even at the expense of constitutional federalism.[125] Whether one has an original-ist/textualist or structural theory of federalism,[126] clear statement

[119] Merrill, *supra* note 55, at 834.

[120] Arlington Central School Dist. Board of Education v. Murphy, 126 S. Ct. 2455, 2459 (2006).

[121] Merrill, *supra* note 55, at 833.

[122] *Id.*

[123] Somin, Closing the Pandora's Box of Federalism, *supra* note 39, at 470; John O. McGinnis & Ilya Somin, Federalism vs. States' Rights: A Defense of Judicial Review in a Federal System, 99 Nw. U.L. Rev. 89, 117–18 (2004).

[124] See Lynn A. Baker & Ernest Young, Federalism and the Double Standard of Judicial Review, 51 Duke L.J. 75, 117–28 (2001).

[125] McGinnis & Somin, *supra* note 123, at 112–13, 114–15, 118, 119–20.

[126] For structural arguments in favor of judicial review of federalism, see, e.g., *id.*, and Baker & Young, *supra* note 124. For a textualist critique of unlimited federal power, see Somin, Federalism as a Casualty of the War on Drugs, *supra* note 2. For an originalist case for judicial enforcement of federalism, see, e.g., Randy E. Barnett, Restoring the Lost Constitution chs. 7, 11 (2004); and Saikrishna B. Prakash & John

rules are unlikely to be effective methods of implementing it because state governments will often have incentives to use their power in ways that undermine it. As Justice O'Connor notes in her majority opinion in *New York v. United States*, "powerful incentives might lead both federal and state officials to view departures from the federal structure to be in their personal interests."[127]

In theory, clear statement rules could empower ordinary voters to police the boundaries of federalism instead of state government officials. However, it is unlikely that very many voters have the time and expertise needed to carefully study thousands of pages of statutory text in order to identify potential infringements on federalism. Indeed, decades of survey evidence indicate that most citizens have very low levels of political knowledge and that many are ignorant of even very basic political facts.[128] Thus, it is highly improbable that voters can make effective use of the products of clear statement rules.

Of course, one could simply reject judicial enforcement of federalism entirely, as do scholars such as Herbert Wechsler, Jesse Choper, and Larry Kramer.[129] But then it is not clear why there is any need for judicially created clear statement rules. If, as critics of judicially enforced federalism claim, the political process is the best way to determine the appropriate balance of power between Washington and the states, then it is difficult to see why judges should enforce clear statement rules any more than they should enforce substantive limits on federal power.

C. Yoo, The Puzzling Persistence of Process-Based Federalism Theories, 79 Tex. L. Rev. 1459 (2001).

[127] New York v. United States, 505 U.S. 144, 182 (1992).

[128] For analysis of the evidence and its implications for judicial review, see Ilya Somin, Political Ignorance and the Countermajoritarian Difficulty: A New Perspective on the "Central Obsession of Constitutional Theory," 89 Iowa L. Rev. 1287 (2004).

[129] See Jesse Choper, Judicial Review and the National Political Process, ch. 4 (1980) (rejecting judicial review of federalism); Jesse Choper, The Scope of National Power Vis-à-vis the States: The Dispensability of Judicial Review, 86 Yale L.J. 1552 (1977); Herbert F. Wechsler, The Political Safeguards of Federalism: The Role of the States in the Composition and Selection of the Federal Government, 54 Colum. L. Rev. 543 (1954); and Larry D. Kramer, Putting the Politics Back into the Safeguards of Federalism, 100 Colum. L. Rev. 215 (2000).

2. Clear Statement Rules and the Expansion of Federal Power

Even if clear statement rules are an inadequate substitute for substantive judicial review, they could still serve a useful function by giving Congress an incentive to draft clearer and less ambiguous laws. And it is certainly possible that they do restrict the growth of federal power slightly. These benefits might be sufficient to justify the continued use of federalism clear statement rules. Even if such rules have relatively few benefits, they also do not seem to impose significant costs.

This calculation may turn out to be correct. But there is at least one potentially substantial cost of federalism clear statement rules that the existing literature on the subject fails to consider. If clear statement rules function as intended, they reduce the chance that a new federal program will inflict unwelcome surprises on state governments. For example, the Spending Clause clear statement requirement ensures that states that accept federal funds are only subject to those obligations that they agree to "voluntarily and knowingly."[130] Similarly, the requirement that statues that raise constitutional problems or upset the state-federal balance clearly state this result in the statutory text helps ensure that new statutes do not expand federal regulatory authority in ways that state officials find unacceptable.

By reducing the probability of unwelcome surprises from new federal legislation, clear statement rules increase the incentive of state governments to support expansion of federal power and accept federal funds. If clear statement rules are effective in protecting states against legislative surprises, they help to eliminate a potential reason for some state governments to oppose new extensions of federal power. For supporters of the expanding federal role in American public policy, this may be a beneficial result. But it certainly should not be welcomed by advocates of federalism and decentralization.

The magnitude of this effect depends in large part on the degree to which clear statement rules really do reduce perceived uncertainty about the impact of new federal statutes, an empirical issue on which we have no systematic evidence. If states have effective methods to minimize uncertainty even in the absence of clear statement rules,

---

[130] Pennhurst State School & Hospital v. Halderman, 451 U.S. 1, 17 (1981).

then the latter are unlikely to increase support for the expansion of federal power. But if clear statement rules do not serve to reduce uncertainty about the meaning of statutes, it is difficult to see why judges should bother to enforce them at all. The more effective clear statement rules are in achieving their intended purpose of decreasing legal uncertainty, the more likely they are to strengthen state government support for expanded federal power.

Conclusion

Although the federal government suffered three notable defeats during the 2005–2006 Supreme Court term, these setbacks do not herald a revival of judicially enforced limits on federal power. Two of the three decisions—*Oregon* and *Rapanos*—do not even restrict federal power through the use of clear statement rules, while the third does not expand the relevant rule beyond its preexisting scope.

The future viability of federalism clear statement rules remains in serious doubt. And even if the courts choose to keep the rules alive in the face of doctrinal conundrums created by *Gonzales v. Raich*, there is little reason to believe that they can ever be an adequate substitute for judicially enforced limits on federal power.

Dabit, Preemption, and Choice of Law

Larry E. Ribstein*

I. Introduction

Merrill Lynch, Pierce, Fenner & Smith, Inc. v. Dabit[1] finds Congress and the Supreme Court caught in the conflict between three significant policy goals. The first is the need to rein in litigation that increasingly threatens to swamp every type of business in liability and precaution costs. The second is a perceived need to control securities fraud, particularly in the wake of the stock market collapse and revelations of fraud at Enron and other companies. The third policy goal is the need to preserve our federal system by appropriately limiting the federal government's power. The conflict arises because Congress seemingly must expand federal power to control state courts and legislatures that seek to encourage local litigation. At the same time, controlling state fraud litigation seemingly increases the need for more federal antifraud law, further expanding federal power and shrinking the states' role in making corporate and securities laws.

By broadly interpreting Congress' preemption of state securities fraud remedies and extending the dominance of federal law, *Dabit* missed an opportunity to encourage Congress to consider how to reconcile these conflicting policy goals. This article shows that there is, in fact, a way out of the dilemma by which Congress can control abusive state and federal litigation without either unduly expanding federal power or sacrificing the states' role in remedying fraud: Congress can preserve the states' power to remedy securities fraud under their *corporation laws*. This would activate the corporate law

---

*Mildred Van Vorhees Jones Chair, University of Illinois College of Law. Thanks to Rich Booth, Jim Cox, David Hyman, and Richard Painter for valuable comments, and for comments at a University of Illinois College of Law workshop.

[1]126 S. Ct. 1503 (2006).

choice of law rule that enables firms to choose the applicable state law. States then would have an incentive to develop reasonable remedies rather than to invite abusive litigation. The availability of viable state fraud remedies law would, in turn, encourage Congress and the courts to address excessive private remedies under federal law.

Part II briefly summarizes the background of the case. Parts III–V discuss the three conflicting goals identified above. Part VI shows how the *Dabit* case forced the Court to make tradeoffs among these goals. Part VII discusses the choice-of-law path out of the thicket of these policy conflicts. Part VIII concludes.

II. Background

The Securities and Exchange Act of 1934 ("1934 Act") provides for comprehensive regulation of the trading of securities. One provision in particular has given rise to much of the litigation under the act. Section 10(b) makes it unlawful for any person

> To use or employ, in connection with the purchase or sale of any security . . . , any manipulative or deceptive device or contrivance in contravention of such rules and regulations as the Commission may prescribe as necessary or appropriate for the protection of investors . . .[2]

In 1942, the SEC promulgated rule 10b-5, which makes it unlawful for any person

> directly or indirectly, . . . , (a) To employ any device, scheme, or artifice to defraud, . . . or (c) To engage in act, practice or course of dealing which operates or would operate as a fraud or deceit upon any person, in connection with the purchase or sale of any security.[3]

The act does not provide for an express private remedy for injuries caused by violations of these provisions. However, *Kardon v. National Gypsum Co.*[4] held that there was an implied private remedy in the absence of any congressional intent to deny a remedy.[5] The Supreme

[2] 15 U.S.C. § 78j(b) (2000).
[3] 17 C.F.R. § 240.10b-5 (2000).
[4] 69 F. Supp. 512 (E.D. Pa. 1946).
[5] *Id.* at 514.

Court implicitly recognized the existence of the private remedy twenty-five years later in *Superintendent of Insurance v. Bankers Life & Casualty Co.*,[6] and explicitly endorsed the remedy twelve years after that in *Herman & MacLean v. Huddleston*.[7]

Having created a private action, the courts were left to define its boundaries. The logical starting place was the common law of fraud. But this body of law, developed largely in face-to-face transactions, proved unsuited to providing remedies for statements by firms to impersonal securities markets, which were the focus of the 1934 Act. Since section 10(b) and rule 10b-5 were part of that act, courts faced the quandary of how far they should venture beyond the confines of the common law to accomplish the act's purposes without usurping Congress' role.

Two cases have proved particularly important to the development of the 10(b) and 10b-5 private remedy. One fueled the expansion of the private cause of action into a powerful tool for plaintiffs' lawyers, while the other provided a judicial rationale for constraining that expansion.

The first case concerns the reliance issue. An action for common law fraud requires proof that the plaintiff relied on the misstatement. This requirement impeded actions for fraud on public securities markets brought by purchasers or sellers who allege that they bought or sold during defendant's fraud. Federal Rule of Civil Procedure 23 bars a class action unless questions common to the class predominate over those concerning individual class members. This may not be the case if the plaintiff had to prove reliance as to each class member. Moreover, proof of reliance is arguably an unnecessary technicality in light of a version of the Efficient Capital Markets Hypothesis (ECMH) that holds that public disclosures are quickly reflected in market prices.[8] Under this theory, defendant's misrepresentation may affect securities prices, and therefore injure even traders who were completely unaware of the misrepresentation. The logistics of class actions and the ECMH provided the impetus and rationale for

[6]404 U.S. 6, 13 n.9 (1971).

[7]459 U.S. 375, 387 (1983).

[8]This has been referred to as the "semi-strong" version of the ECMH in an early article on the theory. See Eugene Fama, Efficient Capital Markets: A Review of Theory and Empirical Work, 25 J. Fin. 383 (1970).

the "fraud-on-the-market" theory adopted in *Basic, Inc. v. Levinson*.[9] There the Supreme Court held that a plaintiff could recover without proof of reliance based solely on proof that the plaintiff traded after the defendant made material public misrepresentations to an efficient market,[10] but before the truth was revealed.

The other important case is *Blue Chip Stamps v. Manor Drug Stores*,[11] which denied recovery under section 10(b) by one who neither purchased nor sold stock—in this case, retailers who failed to exercise a right to buy stock given them under an antitrust decree allegedly because of misleadingly pessimistic statements in the prospectus that were intended to deter such purchases.[12] The common law permitted recovery by non-purchaser/sellers under some circumstances.[13] But the Court was concerned about the danger of vexatious litigation that might arise in open-market cases if plaintiffs could sue even without the verification of injury provided by an actual purchase or sale.[14] This concern for vexatious litigation has acquired increasing importance in the light of the class action litigation boom inspired by *Basic*.

Spiked by the fraud-on-the-market theory, the private class action remedy under 10(b) and 10b-5 grew into what some see as a major threat to firms trading in public securities markets. Congress heard evidence that firms were being sued whenever their shares dropped; that defendants were settling rather than paying the huge expense for discovery and trial; that "professional plaintiffs" who owned only a few shares were lending their names to complaints; that litigation represented a "litigation tax" on business, particularly for smaller companies; that the risk of litigation was undermining firms' disclosure of information; and that the huge costs of the lawsuits ultimately were paid by long-term investors.[15]

---

[9] 485 U.S. 224, 243–49 (1988).

[10] See Bradford Cornell & James Rutten, Market Efficiency, Crashes and Securities Litigation 1–2 (December 2005), available at http://ssrn.com/abstract=871106 (surveying various tests of market efficiency under the fraud-on-the-market theory).

[11] 421 U.S. 723 (1975).

[12] See *id.* at 752.

[13] See Restatement (Second) Torts § 525 (1976).

[14] 421 U.S. at 740–46.

[15] See, e.g., S. Rep. No. 104-98, at 9–10 (1995).

Congress responded to these problems with the Private Securities Litigation Reform Act of 1995 ("PSLRA").[16] This act included several provisions intended to curb abusive securities litigation, including higher pleading standards for federal securities fraud claims;[17] a stay of discovery while a court adjudicates a motion to dismiss;[18] a provision for selecting as lead plaintiff a shareholder with a significant stake in the action who presumably could monitor the lawyer for the class;[19] sanctions for frivolous litigation;[20] and a safe harbor for forward-looking statements, so issuers could disclose this information without fear of draconian liability.[21]

After the PSLRA was adopted, however, there was evidence that plaintiffs' lawyers were escaping the restrictions of the act by taking the weaker claims that the PSLRA deterred into state court,[22] sparking a boom in state securities litigation.[23] As a result, Congress passed the Securities Litigation Uniform Standards Act ("SLUSA"), which explicitly prohibited a private party from maintaining under state law any "covered class action" alleging

> (1) an untrue statement or omission of a material fact in connection with the purchase or sale of a covered security;

[16]Pub. L. No. 104-67, 109 Stat. 737 (codified in part at 15 U.S.C. §§ 77z-1, 78u-4).

[17]See 15 U.S.C. § 78u-4(b)(1), (2) (2000) (requiring that securities fraud complaints "specify" misleading statements and the facts on which plaintiff bases her belief is misleading, and "state with particularity facts giving rise to a strong inference that the defendant acted with the required state of mind"); *id.* § 78u-4(b)(4) (requiring allegation that the misconduct "caused the loss for which the plaintiff seeks to recover").

[18]*Id.* §§ 77z-1(b), 78u-4(b)(3) (2000).

[19]*Id.* §§ 77z-1(a)(3), 78u-4(a)(3) (2000).

[20]*Id.* §§ 77z-1(c), 78u-4(c) (2000).

[21]*Id.* §§ 77z-2(c), 78u-5(c) (2000).

[22]See, e.g., Small v. Fritz Companies, Inc., 65 P.3d 1255, 1261, 1263–65 (Cal. 2003) (holding that California law permitted action by non-seller and that SLUSA did not apply to such actions).

[23]See Michael A. Perino, Fraud and Federalism: Preempting Private State Securities Fraud Causes of Action, 50 Stan. L. Rev. 273, 315 (1998) (showing that "[t]he available data suggest that the most reasonable explanation for the increase in state court litigation is plaintiffs' desire to evade the Reform Act's procedural hurdles"). As it turned out, the concern may have been premature, since state actions declined even prior to passage of SLUSA. See *infra* note 49. On the other hand, abusive state actions might have increased without SLUSA because of a post-SLUSA California decision clarifying the right to bring class actions on behalf of non-California plaintiffs. See *infra* note 50.

> or (2) that the defendant used or employed any manipulative
> or deceptive device or contrivance in connection with the
> purchase or sale of a covered security.[24]

Congress thought it had closed the state law escape from the PSLRA. By using the same "in connection with" language used in § 10(b) and rule 10b-5, Congress seemed to be barring the actions under state law by which plaintiffs' lawyers had sought all of the benefits of the broad federal remedy without the PSLRA burdens.

But clever plaintiffs' lawyers were undaunted. Following SLUSA, they started bringing actions under state law based on allegations that plaintiffs *held* securities. Although these cases technically involved misstatements or omissions "in connection with the purchase or sale of a covered security," the lawyers counted on courts to hold that these actions were not preempted under SLUSA's language because the Court in *Blue Chip Stamps* had relied on the same "in connection with" language to bar actions by holders of securities under section 10(b).

In *Dabit*, the Supreme Court disagreed. The Court unanimously held that SLUSA preempted actions by those who did not purchase or sell.[25] It reasoned that *Blue Chip Stamps* relied on policy considerations specifically applicable to the private remedy context and had not intended to define the phrase "in connection with the purchase or sale." When Congress enacted SLUSA, it was aware of and therefore presumptively used the broad judicial construction given the "in connection with" language in certain other cases.[26]

The case seems straightforward, as indicated by the unanimous decision. As Judge Frank Easterbrook said in a case reaching the same result, "[i]t would be more than a little strange if the Supreme Court's decision to block private litigation by non-traders became the opening by which that very litigation could be pursued under state law, despite the judgment of Congress (reflected in SLUSA) that securities class actions must proceed under federal securities law or not at all."[27] Nevertheless, as the Second Circuit noted in

---

[24] 15 U.S.C. § 77p(b); *id.* § 78bb(f)(1) (2000).

[25] 126 S. Ct. 1503, 1515 (2006).

[26] *Id.* at 1513.

[27] Kircher v. Putnam Funds Trust, 403 F.3d 478, 484 (7th Cir. 2005), rev'd on other grounds, 126 S. Ct. 2145 (2006).

Dabit,[28] every federal appellate court that had considered the issue had refused to preempt holder actions as of the time of that decision.[29] Apparently only Judge Easterbrook thought the argument "strange."

This article shows that the *Dabit* result is not as obvious as it might appear and that the case has significant policy ramifications for the future of federal and state roles in securities litigation, and for business regulation generally.

III. Constraining Abusive Litigation

The private right of action under 10(b) and 10b-5 started in *Kardon* as a seemingly logical way of furthering the congressional purpose to increase disclosure and combat fraud. But throughout the history of private remedies neither the courts nor Congress have been able to deal adequately with the ants that keep arriving at the private rights picnic—the trial lawyers.

Plaintiffs' lawyers theoretically can serve as important monitors of corporate disclosure. Most of the other potential monitors, including independent directors, government regulators, securities analysts employed by investment banking firms, and corporate executives, either lack strong economic incentives to monitor, or have incentives to hide information about their company or their clients. Insiders and their tippees face legal barriers to capitalizing on their information, while outside investors find it difficult to recoup their research costs because they lack strong property rights in information. By contrast, class action trial lawyers earn significant fees from successfully prosecuting securities fraud cases. Although these lawyers rarely uncover fraud, since they usually appear on the scene when at least some of the true facts have been discovered, they are experts at uncovering the facts relating to the wrongdoing of particular

---

[28]Dabit v. Merrill Lynch, Pierce, Fenner & Smith, Inc. 395 F.3d 25, 43–44 (2d Cir. 2005).

[29]See Riley v. Merrill Lynch, Pierce, Fenner & Smith, 292 F.3d 1334, 1345 (11th Cir. 2002) (holding that SLUSA does not apply to claims dealing solely with the retention of securities); Falkowski v. Imation Corp., 309 F.3d 1123, 1130 (9th Cir. 2002) (holding that purchaser-seller rule satisfied by options transactions); Green v. Ameritrade, Inc., 279 F.3d 590, 598 (8th Cir. 2002) (holding that "nonsellers and nonpurchasers of securities are not covered by SLUSA's preemption provision").

parties and constructing legal theories that support liability.[30] In other words, while critics condemn class action lawyers' fees, those fees provide the high-powered incentives other corporate monitors lack.

In practice, however, class action suits are not an ideal device for disciplining fraud. To begin with, there is what might be called the extortion problem—that a class action lawyer can squeeze a settlement out of the defendants even if the plaintiff has little likelihood of pressing the case to a successful conclusion.[31] When defendants cannot get the suit dismissed, or perhaps even while the dismissal motion is pending, they face burdensome discovery involving the production of thousands of documents and depositions that can consume hours of busy executives' time. The company and its executives are potentially exposed to many millions of dollars of damages for losses to thousands of shareholders who traded before disclosure. Those who participated in the misrepresentations face personal liability and may not be entitled to indemnification or insurance against fraud. All of this makes managers highly susceptible to a "their money or your life" offer to settle in which they buy peace with the company's (that is, current shareholders') money. Not surprisingly, evidence pre-dating the PSLRA's passage indicated that a significant number of securities class action settlements were for nuisance value[32] and that settlement amounts did not depend on the merits of the claims.[33]

Even if the suit has significant *legal* merit, it may involve damages in excess of the harm defendants caused. To understand this problem

---

[30]See generally Bruce H. Kobayashi & Larry E. Ribstein, Class Action Lawyers as Lawmakers, 46 Ariz. L. Rev. 733 (2004) (discussing role of class action lawyers in drafting pleadings).

[31]Even prior to the PSLRA, it is unlikely that plaintiffs were filing many suits that were completely worthless in the sense that they had no chance of success. See John C. Coffee, Jr., Reforming the Securities Class Action: An Essay on Deterrence and its Implementation (Columbia Law and Economics Working Paper No. 293), at 3 n.5 (2006), available at http://ssrn.com/abstract=893833. The problem, at least prior to the PSLRA, was that the cases had enough nuisance value that they were earning millions of dollars for plaintiffs' lawyers even though everybody understood that the cases were either too weak or too small to justify the effort to take them to trial.

[32]See Joseph Grundfest, Why Disimply?, 108 Harv. L. Rev. 727, 742–43 (1995) (twenty-three percent of settlements in sample were for less than $2 million).

[33]See Janet Cooper Alexander, Do the Merits Matter? A Study of Settlements in Securities Class Actions, 43 Stan. L. Rev. 497, 513–14 (1991).

it is necessary first to quickly review how market damages are computed in securities fraud cases. Courts award each trading investor the difference between his trade price and the price at which the securities would have traded in the absence of fraud.[34] The non-fraud price is established by showing the market price of the security after disclosure of the true facts and then working back from that price to show how the company's stock price would have fluctuated during the fraud period if there had been no fraud. These hypothetical price movements are based on how the general market moved and how the individual stock would have moved in relation to the market based on its risk compared to that of the market as a whole.[35]

There are several inherent problems with this damage theory. First, investors' damages only very roughly measure the defendants' distortion of their trade prices. It is obviously impossible to know what the stock's price would have been at any time without defendant's fraud. The court can determine only how the stock reacted to disclosure of *some facts,* which may differ from the same facts that defendants did not disclose. Yet the court has to construct an entire fictional history of stock prices based on this speculation about the undistorted price plus additional speculation about how the company's stock price moved during the entire fraud period.

Second, the alleged damages necessarily are far greater than the aggregate damage defendants actually caused to the market. The losses of those who bought too high or sold too low because of the fraud are exactly balanced by the gains of those who bought too low.[36] Moreover, damages are often inflated by investors' short-term overreaction to the corrective disclosure,[37] and by the market's reaction to the likelihood that the corporation itself will have to pay damages for the fraud.[38] Given these inherent problems with the

[34]See Green v. Occidental Petroleum Corp., 541 F.2d 1335, 1344 (9th Cir. 1976) (Sneed, J., concurring in part).

[35]See Bradford Cornell & R. Gregory Morgan, Using Finance Theory to Measure Damages in Fraud on the Market Cases, 37 UCLA L. Rev. 883, 886 (1990).

[36]See Frank Easterbrook & Daniel Fischel, Optimal Damages in Securities Cases, 52 U. Chi. L. Rev. 611, 638–39 (1985).

[37]See Larry E. Ribstein, Fraud on a Noisy Market, 10 Lewis & Clark L. Rev. 137, 146 (2006).

[38]See Richard A. Booth, Who Should Recover What in a Securities Fraud Class Action? (Univ. of Md. Legal Studies Research Paper No. 2005-32), at 26 (2005), available at http://ssrn.com/abstract=683197. But see Cornell & Rutten, *supra* note 10, at 26

149

basic damage calculation, even the much lower settlements,[39] further discounted by amounts institutional investors fail to claim,[40] may be significantly more than aggregate damage to the market.

Third, most shareholders who recover damages in securities fraud cases are already, in effect, "insured" against fraud. Reasonable shareholders buy and hold diversified portfolios of shares, usually through mutual funds, rather than trying to outguess the market.[41] This means that the vast majority of reasonable shareholders are as likely over time to be gaining from fraud as losing from it. In other words, not only are the damages significantly more than the aggregate damage to the market from defendant's fraud, as discussed above, but many of the individual plaintiffs arguably do not deserve compensation.

Even if the damages in securities class actions were appropriate, there is the additional problem that the wrong party bears the burden—that is, the corporation itself rather than the individuals who were actually responsible for the misrepresentations or nondisclosures.[42] Damage suits against the corporation reduce the value of the company's shares because of the prospect of monetary liability,

(noting that this multiplier is limited by the fact that the market will discount for the probability that the recovery will be for only a small part of the alleged damages).

[39]See Coffee, *supra* note 31, at 14–15 (discussing studies showing that settlements over the last three years average less than three percent of investor market losses); Randall S. Thomas & James D. Cox, An Empirical Analysis of Institutional Investors' Impact as Lead Plaintiffs in Securities Fraud Class Actions (Vanderbilt Law and Economics Research Paper No. 06-09), at 6 (March 7, 2006), available at http://ssrn.com/abstract=898640 (finding that ratio of settlement amounts to estimated provable losses was statistically significantly lower following the PSLRA).

[40]See James D. Cox & Randall S. Thomas, Letting Billions Slip Through Your Fingers: Empirical Evidence and Legal Implications of the Failure of Financial Institutions to Participate in Securities Class Action Settlements, 58 Stan. L. Rev. 411, 413 (2005) (finding that less than thirty percent of institutional investors with provable losses perfect their claims in securities class action settlements).

[41]See Booth, *supra* note 38, at 6.

[42]See Janet Cooper Alexander, Rethinking Damages in Securities Class Actions, 48 Stan. L. Rev. 1487, 1497 (1996). The executives may technically have personal liability for directly participating in the fraud, for which they are not entitled to indemnification. See Globus v. Law Research Service, 418 F.2d 1276, 1278 (2d Cir. 1969) (barring indemnification under the federal securities laws for statements made with actual knowledge of fraud). However, this rule does not apply to settlements, and the insiders are usually able to arrange a settlement within the company's insurance limits that protects them from personal liability. See Coffee, *supra* note 31, at 33.

defense costs, and future insurance costs.[43] The shareholders therefore usually are victims rather than beneficiaries of the insiders' self-interested conduct.[44] Nevertheless, most reasonable shareholders who buy and hold diversified portfolios have no securities fraud claims of their own because they are not purchasers or sellers under *Blue Chip Stamps*. In short, securities fraud class actions involve significant wealth transfers from long-term investors to frequent traders and securities class action lawyers.[45]

Securities class actions involve not only perverse wealth transfers, but also potential social costs by deterring socially valuable activities. First, securities litigation may be especially burdensome for relatively innovative firms. These firms have more news to disclose, and their shares react more sharply to this news, than more seasoned companies. This litigation tax may deter the innovation and entrepreneurial activity that generate economic growth. Second, the risk of fraud liability may reduce the amount of information firms voluntarily disclose. This particularly affects forward-looking statements, which courts may evaluate in light of later information rather than the information the defendants had at the time of disclosure.[46] Investors would highly value management's assessment of the firm's prospects even if this involves some risk they may prove to be wrong. The litigation tax therefore may deter disclosures investors want.

The PSLRA fixed some of the problems with securities class actions, particularly by deterring weak lawsuits and suits based on forward-looking statements.[47] But the PSLRA did not address the

---

[43]These costs attributed to the suit are, of course, in addition to the fraud's effect on the firm's value. See *infra* note 53 and accompanying text.

[44]See Coffee, *supra* note 31, at 28–29.

[45]See Alexander, *supra* note 42, at 1503 (noting that "payments by the corporation to settle a class action amount to transferring money from one pocket to the other, with about half of it dropping on the floor for lawyers to pick up").

[46]See G. Mitu Gulati, Jeffrey Rachlinksi & Donald Langevoort, Fraud by Hindsight, 98 Nw. U. L. Rev. 773 (2004) (showing that while courts have acknowledged this risk, they have failed adequately to guard against it).

[47]See Adam C. Pritchard, Karen Nelson & Marilyn Johnson, Do the Merits Matter More? The Impact of the Private Securities Litigation Reform Act of 1995 (Michigan Legal Studies Research Paper No. 02-011) (2006) (J.L. Econ. & Org forthcoming), available at http://ssrn.com/abstract = 883684 (showing shift away from suits based on forward-looking statements and greater correlation between the incidence of litigation and earnings restatements and abnormal insider selling, with a higher likelihood of settlement for cases involving earnings restatements).

inherent problem of assessing excessive damages against the victims of the fraud.[48]

Whatever the dangers of federal securities cases addressed by the PSLRA, the specter of state litigation addressed by SLUSA seems worse.[49] State actions expose firms to the risk of litigation, potentially including class actions,[50] in the courts of every state where they sell their securities. These actions are not constrained either by the PSLRA or by other restrictions on federal recovery, such as the purchaser-seller limitation.[51]

The above analysis strongly suggests that securities class actions involve costs in excess of their benefits. If that were all there was to the problem, securities fraud class actions could be comfortably abolished. However, as discussed in the next section, some fraud liability may be an efficient way to deter fraud and ensure that firms disclose an optimal amount of information.[52] Thus, the proper policy response may be to appropriately structure fraud liability rather than simply abolishing it. This response may demand the efforts of both federal and state lawmakers, rather than banishing state lawmakers from the scene as SLUSA does.

IV. Controlling Fraud

The above discussion focuses on the mitigating effect of investors' ability to "insure" against fraud by diversifying. But fraud nevertheless is obviously a negative event for both affected firms and the market as a whole. Fraud clearly may increase a firm's cost of capital. It casts doubt on the quality of the firm's management, thereby

---

[48]For problems with the PSLRA damage rules apart from who pays the damages, see Richard A. Booth, Windfall Awards under PSLRA, 59 Bus. Law. 1043 (2004).

[49]Note that the danger may have been less than Congress supposed when it enacted SLUSA. Although state court actions rose after the PSLRA, they began falling a year later, even before SLUSA was passed. See Richard W. Painter, Responding To a False Alarm: Federal Preemption of State Securities Fraud Causes Of Action, 84 Cornell L. Rev. 1, 42–46 (1998) (discussing data on state class actions).

[50]See Diamond Multimedia Systems Inc. v. Superior Court, 968 P.2d 539, 557 (1999) (approving California class action on behalf of non-California buyers). *Diamond* came only after the adoption of SLUSA, within its exemption for pending actions. It is not clear whether trial lawyers would have won this victory in California had the stakes been higher.

[51]See *supra* notes 22–23 and accompanying text.

[52]See generally Easterbrook & Fischel, *supra* note 36.

reducing expected returns. Fraud at least theoretically may cause the market to question the accuracy of other information the firm releases to the market, thereby increasing the firm's risk. Moreover, revelations of fraud in a company may infect other companies that the market suspects might have similar problems.[53] Indeed, the infection may spread to whole industries and the entire market by raising the general cost of capital, particularly for relatively new or innovative companies that will have the most difficulty reassuring investors, and causing general misallocation of resources.[54] It follows that private securities litigation, despite its defects, should not necessarily be abolished because it is a potentially effective way to deter securities fraud. Indeed, damages and settlements in securities cases dwarf the penalties imposed by other means.[55] In other words, the efficiency of private litigation can be assessed only in the context of all of the tools for fighting fraud.

Congress, however, has never done such a global assessment. Rather, Congress and the courts applying implied remedies have backed into a series of sometimes contradictory moves. The Court first implied broad civil remedies under 10(b) and 10b-5 without any explicit congressional approval or detailed assessment of the costs and benefits of these remedies. Congress' first move was to enact the PSLRA and SLUSA during a stock market boom when fraud was not a major concern and litigation abuses were perceived to be the biggest problem facing securities markets. The revelation of Enron and other frauds in 2001 and 2002 convinced Congress to take some kind of action. Congress considered reversing the PSLRA limits on securities fraud cases, on the supposition that the reduced deterrent effect of securities fraud suits might have been responsible for the frauds.[56] But Congress chose instead to increase disclosure

---

[53]See Amar Gande & Craig M. Lewis, Shareholder Initiated Class Action Lawsuits: Shareholder Wealth Effects and Industry Spillovers (March 2006), available at http://ssrn.com/abstract=891028 (finding evidence that the share prices of firms are affected by lawsuits against other firms in the same industry).

[54]See Coffee, *supra* note 31, at 32.

[55]See *id.* at 10–11.

[56]See Richard Painter, Megan Farrell & Scott Adkins, Private Securities Litigation Reform Act: A Post-Enron Analysis 17–28 (2002), available at http://www.fedsoc.org/pdf/PSLRAFINALII.PDF (critically analyzing one pending bill). This study indicated that the supposition underlying the proposal was unfounded, as it showed that federal securities class action litigation had not actually declined in the wake of the PSLRA. For more recent data, see Securities Litigation Watch, State of the (Securities

regulation and passed the Sarbanes-Oxley Act.[57] Meanwhile, the concern with litigation abuse remains, figuring not only in *Dabit*, but also in *Dura Pharmaceuticals, Inc. v. Broudo*,[58] which limited the fraud-on-the-market theory by tightening the loss causation requirement.[59]

This chain of actions has created a system in which huge penalties are assessed against the victims, large bounties are paid to trial lawyers, innocent firms face burdensome new regulation under the Sarbanes-Oxley Act,[60] and most fraudsters escape civil liability. The PSLRA not only did not fix the basic problem with burdensome securities class actions, but bolstered the argument for additional regulation when the market crashed. The only thing everybody seems to know about the scope and direction of securities regulation is that the federal government should remain in charge, as SLUSA made clear by blocking most state securities litigation. Yet federal law's lurching policy shifts argue against a single set of answers provided by a single federal regulator and for preserving a role for the laboratory of state laws, as discussed in the next Part.

V. Bolstering Federalism

Dabit gave the Supreme Court a much needed opportunity to define state and federal roles in securities regulation. Courts implying a section 10(b) remedy assumed that Congress thought a federal remedy was necessary to combat securities fraud despite the long history of the state common law fraud action and state securities,

---

Litigation) Union (July 5, 2006), available at http://slw.issproxy.com/securities_litigation_blo/2006/07/state_of_the_se.html (summarizing data showing that securities class actions filings have fluctuated in a narrow range since the PSLRA, but that the average settlement size has significantly increased).

[57] See Public Company Accounting Reform and Investor Protection (Sarbanes-Oxley) Act, Pub. L. No. 107-204 (2002) (codified as amended in scattered sections of titles 15 and 18 of the U.S. Code (2000)). Title VII of the act is the Corporate and Criminal Fraud Accountability Act of 2002. See § 801, 116 Stat. 800 (2002). Title IX is White Collar Crime Penalty Enhancements Act of 2002. See § 901, 116 Stat., 804 (2002). Title XI is the Corporate Fraud and Accountability Act of 2002. See § 1101, 116 Stat. 807–10 (2002).

[58] 125 S. Ct. 1627 (2005).

[59] See Ribstein, *supra* note 37, at 153–54 (discussing Court's reasoning in *Dura*).

[60] See generally Henry N. Butler & Larry E. Ribstein, The Sarbanes-Oxley Debacle: What We Have Learned; How to Fix It (AEI Press 2006) (discussing the significant costs, including the added risk of litigation of Sarbanes-Oxley).

or "blue sky," laws that the federal statutes had explicitly declined to preempt.[61] Moreover, implied remedies inevitably encroach on the law of internal corporate governance, which is predominantly a matter of state law.

In the last forty years, the Court has taken varying approaches to the relationship between federal and state law. *J.I. Case Co.v. Borak*[62] recognized a private remedy under the proxy provision of the 1934 Act based on the need for some enforcement mechanism, ignoring the fact that state corporate law had long dealt with shareholders' role in corporate governance. In first applying the implied remedy in *Superintendent of Ins. v. Bankers Life & Cas. Co.*,[63] the Court seemed prepared to let federal law obliterate state law. The Court upheld the application of 10b-5 to an ordinary theft that was covered up through a securities transaction, reasoning that the "in connection with" language in 10(b) and 10b-5 reached any "deceptive practices touching" the sale of securities.[64]

The Court began to change course shortly after *Bankers Life*. The shift began in 1975 with recognition of the purchaser-seller standing rule in *Blue Chip Stamps*. Two years later, the Court held in *Santa Fe Indus., Inc. v. Green*[65] that section 10(b)'s prohibition of "any manipulative or deceptive device or contrivance" "in connection with the purchase or sale of any security" did not reach a controlled merger that was no more than a state law breach of fiduciary duty without misrepresentation or nondisclosure. Two other cases decided around the same time, *Cort v. Ash*[66] and *Piper v. Chris-Craft Indus., Inc.*,[67] held that the existence of a private remedy depended at least in part on state law's role in regulating the relevant area. In *CTS Corporation*

---

[61]See 1933 Act § 16, 48 Stat. 74, 84 (1933); 1934 Act § 28, 48 Stat. 881, 903 (1934).

[62]377 U.S. 426 (1964).

[63]404 U.S. 6 (1971).

[64]*Id.* at 12–13.

[65]430 U.S. 462, 478–80 (1977).

[66]422 U.S. 66, 78 (1975) (holding that one of four criteria for implying a remedy is whether the "cause of action [is] one traditionally relegated to state law, in an area basically the concern of the States, so that it would be inappropriate to infer a cause of action based solely on federal law").

[67]430 U.S. 1, 38–41 (1977) (holding, based on *Cort*, that plaintiff lacked standing under federal tender offer legislation, noting the existence of a state remedy for interference with prospective economic advantage).

155

v. Dynamics Corporation of America,[68] the Court declined to invalidate a state anti-takeover statute under either the Commerce Clause or the Supremacy Clause, reasoning that:

> It thus is an accepted part of the business landscape in this country for States to create corporations, to prescribe their powers, and to define the rights that are acquired by purchasing their shares. A State has an interest in promoting stable relationships among parties involved in the corporations it charters, as well as in ensuring that investors in such corporations have an effective voice in corporate affairs.[69]

This concern for existing state law is also evident in preemption cases outside the corporate area. For example, in *Medtronic, Inc. v. Lohr,*[70] the Court, in an opinion by Justice Stevens, said that "[i]n all pre-emption cases . . . we 'start with the assumption that the historic police powers of the States were not to be superseded by the Federal Act unless that was the clear and manifest purpose of Congress.'"[71] In *Bates v. Dow AgroSciences LLC,*[72] the Court, again by Justice Stevens, said that, "because the States are independent sovereigns in our federal system, we have long presumed that Congress does not cavalierly pre-empt state-law causes of action."[73]

The Court, however, has not been consistent in its respect for state law. The Court's initial securities cases did not consider state law,[74] and paid scant attention to congressional intent beyond assuming that Congress would want some enforcement mechanism. For example, *U.S. v. O'Hagan*[75] recognized a cause of action for misappropriation of information to trade, and *SEC v. Zandford*[76] allowed 10(b) recovery for simple theft of the proceeds of the securities sales, in

---

[68]481 U.S. 69 (1987).

[69]*Id.* at 91.

[70]518 U.S. 470 (1996).

[71]*Id.* at 485 (quoting Rice v. Santa Fe Elevator Corp., 331 U.S. 218, 230 (1947)).

[72]544 U.S. 431 (2005).

[73]*Id.* at 449.

[74]This disregard of state law runs through the Court's 10b-5 jurisprudence. See generally Mark J. Loewenstein, The Supreme Court, Rule 10b-5 and the Federalization of Corporate Law, 39 Ind. L. Rev. 17 (2006).

[75]521 U.S. 642, 653 (1997).

[76]535 U.S. 813 (2002).

both cases despite the long availability of remedies for theft and breach of fiduciary duty under state law.[77]

Rather than applying a general presumption against preemption of state law, the corporate cases are better rationalized under a narrower principle of respecting state law relating to internal corporate governance. As discussed above, the Court explicitly singled that area out for protection both in the scope of the implied 10(b) remedy in *Santa Fe* and in *CTS* regarding state and federal power to regulate takeovers.

This focus on internal governance can be explained on political grounds. As Jonathan Macey has argued, federal legislators normally hesitate to spend political capital to take over an area in which interest groups acting on the state level have made heavy investments.[78] Conversely, where interest groups have only a minimal investment in state law, legislators may be willing to respond to interest groups that are seeking federal regulation. Accordingly, when cases squarely deal with corporate governance, this theory suggests that the interest groups favoring state law, including lawyers, are too strong to make federal interference politically worthwhile. On the other hand, in securities fraud and other corporate cases that do not relate to internal corporate governance, federal securities law has become dominant and strong interest groups have invested in those laws.

This distinction between internal governance and other corporate cases also can be explained on policy grounds. The advantages of state competition are evident with regard to internal corporate governance.[79] This area of the law is heavily influenced by the state-of-incorporation choice of law rule, which promotes state competition by permitting firms easily to choose the law that applies to their corporate governance. Corporations have an incentive to choose the

[77] *Id.* at 820 (describing facts). See also Larry E. Ribstein, Federalism and Insider Trading, 6 S. Ct. Econ. Rev. 123 (1998) (discussing the links between the misappropriation theory and state law).

[78] See Jonathan R. Macey, Federal Deference to Local Regulators and the Economic Theory of Regulation: Toward a Public Choice Explanation of Federalism, 76 Va. L. Rev. 265, 276–81 (1990). See also Jonathan R. Macey, State and Federal Regulation of Takeovers: A View from the Demand Side, 69 Wash. U. L. Q. 383 (1991).

[79] See generally Roberta Romano, The Genius of American Corporate Law (AEI Press 1993).

state law that minimizes their cost of capital given both the costs of regulation and litigation and the need to protect investors from mismanagement and fraud. In securities fraud and other corporate cases, by contrast, corporations cannot easily choose the applicable law, but are subject to suit wherever shares are sold or shareholders live. Here the dominant interest group is plaintiffs' lawyers, and they have little interest in anything other than expanding the scope of liability.

The special respect for state law dealing with internal corporate governance was evident in SLUSA. SLUSA not only limits troublesome state securities class actions, but also embraces the corporate-securities distinction by providing for an exception to the preemption of actions under state corporate law, often referred to as the "Delaware carve-out:"

> (A) .... a covered class action described in subparagraph (B) of this paragraph that is based upon the statutory or common law of the State in which the issuer is incorporated . . . may be maintained in a State or Federal court by a private party. (B) . . . A covered class action is described in this clause if it involves—(I) the purchase or sale of securities by the issuer or an affiliate of the issuer exclusively from or to holders of equity securities of the issuer; or (II) any recommendation, position, or other communication with respect to the sale of securities of an issuer that—(aa) is made by or on behalf of the issuer or an affiliate of the issuer to holders of equity securities of the issuer; and (bb) concerns decisions of such equity holders with respect to voting their securities, acting in response to a tender or exchange offer, or exercising dissenters' or appraisal rights.[80]

The legislative history of this exception indicates that Congress was reluctant to invade the states' realm of regulating corporate governance and fiduciary duties of directors and wanted to preserve the expertise and efficiency of Delaware courts and case law.[81] The exception was crafted to track existing Delaware law, including its distinction between statements made to the securities markets

[80]15 U.S.C. § 77p(d)(1) (2000); 15 U.S.C. § 78bb(f)(3)(a) (2000).

[81]See Jennifer O'Hare, Director Communications and the Uneasy Relationship Between the Fiduciary Duty of Disclosure and the Anti-Fraud Provisions of the Federal Securities Laws, 70 U. Cinn. L. Rev. 475, 501–04 (2002).

generally and those specifically relating to disclosures connected with shareholder action.[82]

It is important to emphasize that the corporate/securities distinction is not necessarily the optimal place to draw the line between the federal and state roles.[83] One problem is that the distinction impedes coherent resolution of closely related corporate disclosure and governance issues.[84] Congress broadly, and sometimes exclusively, regulates issues that are intimately related to corporate governance just by finding a securities law "hook." For example, the federal government broadly regulates takeovers in the Williams Act.[85] It also regulates insider trading under 10(b) and 10b-5 even though the Supreme Court emphasized in *O'Hagan* that the basis of the regulation is theft, which is extensively regulated by state law.[86] Although federal regulation does not necessarily preempt state law, at least where application of that law is limited by the internal affairs doctrine as in *CTS*, there is a danger that the heavy hand of federal law will prevent full development of state law, as it has in the case of insider trading.[87]

Additionally, just as federal securities law may invade state corporate governance regulation, so may state corporate law intersect with federal securities regulation. Disclosure is obviously relevant to shareholders' ability to perform their traditional state law monitoring function, both in directly eliciting shareholder votes or transactions, and in enabling shareholders to decide when to pro-actively move to correct the managers' governance failure. It therefore makes little sense to regulate disclosure and substantive governance powers under two separate bodies of law.

These problems with separating "corporate" and "securities" law are manifest in the Sarbanes-Oxley Act, which moves beyond the

---

[82]*Id.* at 504. However, following the PSLRA, in a case to which the act did not apply, Delaware expanded its disclosure duty beyond the statements the "carve-out" covers. See *infra* notes 116–17 and accompanying text.

[83]See Robert B. Ahdieh, From "Federalization" to "Mixed Governance" in Corporate Law: A Defense of Sarbanes-Oxley, 53 Buff. L. Rev. 721 (2005).

[84]See generally Painter, *supra* note 56.

[85]Pub. L. No. 90-439, 82 Stat. 454 (1968).

[86]See, e.g., Ribstein, *supra* note 77, at 128.

[87]See *infra* note 121 and accompanying text (noting Delaware court's reluctance to challenge federal insider trading law).

typical federal role of regulating disclosure to covering matters like those usually covered by state corporate law. These include provisions mandating complete independence of audit committee directors, including a new federal definition of director independence; controlling executive compensation by requiring executives to return bonuses to the company and by prohibiting certain executive loans; defining the power of a board committee by requiring that the board's audit committee control the hiring and firing of accountants and the non-audit work accountants do for the corporation; and providing for SEC rules on off-balance-sheet transactions and special-purpose vehicles.[88]

Sarbanes-Oxley illustrates how federal law can encroach on the states in the absence of clear and easy to defend boundaries. A strong federal presence in corporate governance can discourage further development of state law, similar to the federal bankruptcy law's "vestigialization" of state-debtor creditor law that David Skeel has analyzed.[89] When Congress decides, as in SLUSA, to preempt state law, courts, in turn, consider the fact that state law is no longer "entrenched" or dominant relevant to the scope of preemption. Thus, while the degree of entrenchment of state law is arguably relevant to preemption as a policy and political matter, courts' inclusion of this factor in preemption analysis can promote creeping federalization of state law.

The current line separating federal and state law therefore has significant policy flaws. Part VII, below, suggests that there is a way to protect against both abusive litigation and fraud while preserving clear roles for federal and state law—that is, by making securities claims effectively part of the state's corporation law. However, Congress needs to be spurred into considering the appropriate roles of federal and state law. That is where the Supreme Court's holding in *Dabit* regarding the preemptive effect of SLUSA enters the picture.

VI. The *Dabit* Opinion

The question in *Dabit* seems quite simple. Did Congress, when it enacted SLUSA, mean to preempt class actions brought by plaintiffs

[88]See Public Company Accounting Reform and Investor Protection (Sarbanes-Oxley) Act, Pub. L. No. 107-204 (2002) (codified as amended in scattered sections of titles 15 and 18 of the U.S. Code (2000)).

[89]See David A. Skeel, Rethinking the Line Between Corporate Law and Corporate Bankruptcy, 72 Tex. L. Rev. 471, 489–512 (1994).

who merely held the security, but had not sold it at a loss? The answer depends on what Congress intended when it preempted class actions alleging "an untrue statement or omission of a material fact in connection with the purchase or sale of a covered security." As Justice Stevens, who wrote the opinion, asked in the oral argument: "[T]he question is whether we should construe the word 'the' to be the functional equivalent of 'his or her.'"[90] And, of course, Congress referred to "*the* purchase or sale . . . " rather than "his or her."

The issue in *Dabit* is complicated somewhat by the argument that (1) the Court's decision in *Blue Chip Stamps* interpreted the phrase "in connection with" to limit rights of action to purchasers and sellers, as opposed to holders, and (2) that Congress implicitly accepted this interpretation when it used the same language in SLUSA. However, the Court easily dispensed with that argument, holding that

> this Court in *Blue Chip Stamps* relied chiefly, and candidly, on "policy considerations" in adopting th[e] [purchaser-seller] limitation. The *Blue Chip Stamps* Court purported to define the scope of a private right of action under Rule 10b-5— not to define the words "in connection with the purchase or sale."[91]

The Court also noted the broad interpretation of "in connection with" in cases like *Bankers Life, Zandford,* and *O'Hagan,* noting that these interpretations had become "settled" in the meaning of the language.[92]

The Court acknowledged the presumption against preemption,[93] but held that it "carries less force here than in other contexts" because SLUSA merely denies the right to use the class action device rather than wholly preempting a state cause of action.[94] The Court also reasoned that the "tailored exceptions to SLUSA's pre-emptive command demonstrate that Congress did not by any means act 'cavalierly' here,"[95] and that "federal law, not state law, has long been

[90]Transcript of Oral Argument at 6, Merrill Lynch, Pierce, Fenner & Smith, Inc. v. Dabit, 126 S. Ct. 1503 (2006) (No. 04-1371).

[91]126 S. Ct. at 1512.

[92]*Id.* at 1513.

[93]See *supra* notes 70–73 and accompanying text.

[94]Dabit, 126 S. Ct. at 1514.

[95]*Id.*

the principal vehicle for asserting class-action securities fraud claims."[96] The Court noted that, since state law holder actions were hardly ever asserted until after SLUSA, "[t]his is hardly a situation ... in which a federal statute has eliminated a historically entrenched state-law remedy."[97] Although *Blue Chip Stamps* indicated a concern with preserving state remedies, the Court said that "we are concerned instead with Congress' intent in adopting a pre-emption provision, the evident purpose of which is to limit the availability of remedies under state law."[98]

Not only did the Court view its interpretation as only modestly interfering with state law, but it also believed that it furthered the significant federal interest evident in SLUSA to control abusive litigation. The Court noted the "particular concerns that culminated in SLUSA's enactment" to prevent state actions from frustrating the purpose of the PSLRA[99] and, echoing Judge Easterbrook's language in *Kircher*, said "[i]t would be odd, to say the least, if SLUSA exempted that particularly troublesome subset of class actions from its pre-emptive sweep."[100]

The oral argument indicates that the Court was troubled by other elements of the case. Justice Breyer was concerned about whether clever plaintiffs could manipulate all purchaser-seller claims into holder claims, as the plaintiff had done in this case.[101] Chief Justice Roberts observed that "what [plaintiffs] want to do is cash in on the fraud ... their claim is that they didn't get to sell the stock at an inflated price to somebody who didn't know about the fraud. That's the damages that they want to collect. And that seems to be an odd claim to recognize."[102] And, indeed, disclosure of the truth would only have subjected the holders to the same harm as everybody else.

The *Dabit* result was, however, less straightforward than it might seem. To begin with, because the relevant statutory language was

[96] *Id.*

[97] *Id.* at 1515.

[98] *Id.* at 1515 n.13.

[99] *Id.* at 1513.

[100] *Id.* at 1514 (citing *Kircher*).

[101] Transcript of Oral Argument at 31–32, Merrill Lynch, Pierce, Fenner & Smith, Inc. v. Dabit, 126 S. Ct. 1503 (2006) (No. 04-1371).

[102] *Id.* at 29.

not clear, the presumption against preemption the Court applied in previous cases may not have been rebutted. The Court easily could have held that its purchaser-seller rule in *Blue Chip Stamps* was based at least partly on the "in connection with" language. The Court's suggestion that only the class action remedy rather than the plaintiff's right of action was being preempted[103] seems rather technical given the significance of the remedy to the enforcement of the right.[104] Although non-class actions might *allege* significant market damages, their actual value may be too low to attract much interest from plaintiffs or plaintiffs' lawyers.[105]

The Court's suggestion that the presumption against preemption should not apply because the state remedies were insufficiently "entrenched"[106] is also suspect. In fact, the state blue sky and fraud laws antedated the federal securities laws, and the 1933 and 1934 Acts explicitly preserve these remedies.[107] To be sure, the federal securities class action, particularly as developed after *Basic*, overshadowed state litigation, at least until adoption of the PSLRA. But there would not be much left of the presumption against preemption if it applied only where states make the same judgments as the federal government, such as to adopt rules conducive to nationwide securities class actions. Moreover, it is questionable whether the state remedy should be ousted as a result of *judicial* expansion of federal remedies without any political decision by Congress. Indeed, Congress' main role regarding the federal remedy has been to narrow it in the PSLRA.

The Court was arguably on firmer ground in stressing that the prior role of state law is less important where Congress expressly wants to preempt it than in a context like *Blue Chip Stamps* where the Congress has not expressed its intent. The preemption purpose here suggests that Congress wanted close questions to be decided

---

[103]See *supra* note 94 and accompanying text.

[104]This holding in *Dabit* might be interpreted as indicating the Court's retreat from the class action remedy. The retreat is further supported by the Court's holding in *Dura* limiting the fraud-on-the-market remedy.

[105]See *supra* notes 39–40 (noting that settlements and claims in securities class actions are much less than investor losses).

[106]See *supra* note 97 and accompanying text.

[107]See 15 U.S.C. § 77p(a) (2000); 15 U.S.C. § 78bb(a) (2000).

for federal law. However, Congress was preempting only a particular type of state action—that is, a state action filed to circumvent federal restrictions in the PSLRA. Thus, the argument actually cuts the other way for *holder* actions that could not be brought in federal court even before the PSLRA. In other words, applying SLUSA to holder actions effectively extends the act from an anti-circumvention statute to a broad restriction on all kinds of state actions. Although Congress evinced an intent to impose *"uniform"* standards, this still begs the question of the universe of actions that are to be treated uniformly. Thus, an ambiguity remains that arguably should be settled by the presumption against preemption.

To the extent that the Court's decision might have been driven by practical concerns with holder remedies, these problems are not as serious as they might seem at first glance. Justice Breyer's concern at oral argument that holder actions could swallow purchaser-seller actions is mitigated by the Second Circuit's insistence that the class include *only* those who were induced to hold, rather than to purchase or sell.[108] Nor were Judge Easterbrook and Justice Stevens necessarily correct in believing that holder claims are especially vexatious and therefore clearly the sort of action Congress sought to preempt in SLUSA. *Blue Chip Stamps* involved plaintiffs who had not bought the stock at all, in contrast to the plaintiffs in *Dabit*, who had clearly bought and then held. Although they are relying on a state of mind as to whether they would have sold if they had the true facts, the same might be said of typical fraud-on-the-market plaintiffs who are presumed to have relied merely from the fact of having bought into an efficient market after defendant's material misrepresentations. This reasoning could support a holding claim based on material misrepresentations and nondisclosures. Finally, although the vexatious nature of non-purchaser/seller claims applies to the *federal* remedy for trading losses, it does not necessarily apply to the sort of holder claims that the states might develop under the state-of-incorporation approach discussed below in Part VII.

Reduced to its essence, *Dabit* rests on the primacy of federal over state securities law. As Justice Stevens emphasized at the beginning

---

[108]Dabit, 395 F.2d at 47 ("[w]e therefore hold that when the class definition includes persons with SLUSA-preempted claims and does not permit the court to distinguish any non-preempted subclass, SLUSA requires that the claim be dismissed").

of his opinion, "[t]he magnitude of the federal interest in protecting the integrity and efficient operation of the market for nationally traded securities cannot be overstated."[109] Thus, *Dabit* gives Congress a green light to regulate under the securities laws. This power may extend even to matters like those covered in Sarbanes-Oxley that arguably relate closely to internal corporate governance. There will accordingly be fewer areas in which state corporate law can be regarded as "entrenched" and therefore protected from preemption under the reasoning in *Dabit*. In short, *Dabit* gives momentum to the federalization of corporate law.

VII. Toward a State Role in Securites Regulation

Part VI suggests that there were strong arguments for deciding *Dabit* the other way—that is, refusing to preempt holder actions in the absence of explicit congressional direction. A significant benefit of this result is that it would have forced Congress to decide what the state role should be in securities regulation. Even given *Dabit*, this issue is still potentially on the table. Moreover, the policy options available in the *Dabit* situation indicate the options that might be available in other contexts where preemption is at issue.

This Part shows that there is a way to avoid both the risk of abusive state litigation and the danger of over-federalization while preserving a state role for disciplining fraud: Congress could amend SLUSA to, in effect, extend the "Delaware carve-out" to provide that federal law does not preempt disclosure regulation enacted as a part of a state's business organization law and applicable to firms organized under that state's law.[110]

Specifically, I propose exempting from preemption *any* "covered class action that is based upon the statutory or common law of the State in which the issuer is incorporated and brought in the courts of that State . . . [and that] may be maintained in a State or Federal court

---

[109]Merrill Lynch, Pierce, Fenner & Smith, Inc. v. Dabit, 126 S. Ct. 1503, 1509 (2006).

[110]Jennifer O'Hare proposes a similar rule. See O'Hare, *supra* note 81, at 508–25. O'Hare's suggestion is limited to liability based on the fiduciary duty of disclosure rather than, as I suggest, extended to any provision adopted as part of a state's corporation law.

by a private party."[111] This tracks the current provision except that it deletes the qualification on exempted class actions in subsection (B) of the statutory carve-out.[112] This rule would effectively ensure adoption of a state-of-corporation choice-of-law rule for securities litigation—which otherwise might be opposed by trial lawyers and other interest groups—by federally preempting state law that is applied on any other basis.[113]

This broad exception for actions brought under state-of-incorporation law would address all three of the relevant considerations discussed in this paper—that is, abusive litigation, fraud, and federalism. First, with respect to abusive litigation, the risk that states would become havens for costly corporate litigation is significantly mitigated if corporations can easily escape these states simply by reincorporating. The states would have incentives to consider litigation costs imposed on firms and their shareholders based out of state because they would lose incorporation business by adopting excessively burdensome laws. For the same reason, states also would have an incentive to clarify application of their laws and earn a reputation for legal stability. State legislators might be reluctant to support a corporate-type choice of law rule for state securities regulation over trial lawyers' opposition. My proposal would effectively impose such a rule by linking preemption with state-of-incorporation choice of law rule.

---

[111]The exemption would cover *any* action based on the law of the incorporating state of the issuer of shares that are the subject of the action. This would extend not only to the issuer and its agents, but also, for example, to parties like Merrill Lynch in the *Dabit* case that made recommendations concerning the issuer's shares. Thus, firms would have to take into account in selecting their incorporating state whether that state's law would unreasonably burden third parties like Merrill Lynch.

[112]See *supra* note 80 and accompanying text.

[113]The proposed rule also has the virtue of clarifying the application of the carve-out, since under the current version there are questions as to what sorts of statements it applies to. See, e.g., Greaves v. McAuley, 264 F. Supp. 2d 1078, 1083 (N.D. Ga. 2005) (holding that claims based on press releases and Form S-4 disclosures in connection with a merger are "to holders of equity securities of the issuer" and therefore are covered by the carve-out); Alessi v. Baracha, 244 F. Supp. 2d 354, 358 (D. Del. 2003) (holding that a recommendation to the shareholders deemed to concern "decisions of . . . equity holders with respect to . . . acting in response to a tender or exchange offer" even if it was in connection with a buyout program that was not technically a tender or exchange offer). These ambiguities are exacerbated by the Supreme Court's holding that decisions to remand to state court are not reviewable even if they are contrary to SLUSA. See Kircher v. Putnam Funds Trust, 126 S. Ct. 2145, 2157 (2006).

Second, while reducing abusive state litigation, my proposal would preserve a viable state role in regulating fraud. To be sure, some may be concerned that the restriction to state-of-incorporation laws would spur a competition for laxity in fraud rules. Just as states may externalize costs of excessively burdensome securities laws on out-of-state firms and their managers in order to attract litigation, so might they externalize costs of excessively lax corporate laws on out-of-state investors in order to attract corporate managers, who instigate firms' incorporation decisions. However, corporations and their managers have incentives to "bond" their disclosures by incorporating in states that offer reasonable protection against fraud. Firms choosing lax states risk increasing their costs of attracting capital from investors. For this reason, firms based in countries with lax securities regulation and enforcement have voluntarily listed their securities in the U.S. and other countries with stronger laws.[114] Thus, state-of-corporation fraud laws can provide an efficient backup to federal antifraud law.

Third, with respect to the federalism consideration, my proposal would preserve a state role in disclosure regulation. This is significant because letting the federal government monopolize securities litigation removes any chance the states might have to experiment with different liability regimes. An example of the role the states might play in regulating securities disclosure and fraud is provided by *Malone v. Brincat*,[115] in which the Delaware Supreme Court let shareholders sue directors for breach of fiduciary duty based on false financial statements in SEC reports and shareholder communications.[116] Since the plaintiffs were holders rather than trading shareholders, the theory of recovery potentially supplements federal liability. However, the court's theory was also narrower than federal law in that the court did not apply the fraud-on-the-market presumption of reliance, imposed a higher scienter requirement than under

---

[114]See Larry E. Ribstein, Cross-Listing and Regulatory Competition, 1 Rev. of L. & Econ. 1, 139 (2005), available at http://www.bepress.com/rle/vol1/iss1/art7 (2005) (discussing evidence of the bonding theory of cross-listing).

[115]722 A.2d 5 (Del. 1998). Like *Diamond*, the case arose after passage of SLUSA but before its effective date.

[116]This action would be preempted under SLUSA as interpreted in *Dabit* because it alleged fraud other than in connection with issuer communications regarding specific shareholder votes or other actions.

federal law, applied the business judgment rule to director judgments about disclosure, and allowed for the possibility of a duty of care opt out. *Malone* upheld the lower court's dismissal on the basis that plaintiff had not alleged exactly how the fraud had injured the shareholders, but allowed the plaintiff to plead a specific damage theory, without suggesting what that theory might be. The Delaware courts and other states might have explored several alternatives in subsequent cases. They also might choose to relax one or more of these limitations, or impose other restrictions on recovery. But SLUSA effectively prevented state courts from developing the *Malone* theory of recovery. The proposed expanded carve-out would rectify this problem.

The claims the proposed carve-out authorizes would be in addition to potential corporate derivative actions that SLUSA already permits because they are not "covered class actions."[117] Shareholders might be able to show that the defendants' fraud damaged the corporation by, for example, reducing the credibility of its management and future disclosures, and thereby reducing expected returns and increasing risk.[118] These types of state law claims would have important advantages over the fraud-on-the-market claim that is the focus of federal law and market-based actions under state law because they would seek recovery against wrongdoing insiders on behalf of, rather than against, the corporation. Moreover, the liability's deterrent effect would depend more on the structure of the settlement—that is, whether it requires personal contributions from wrongdoing insiders—than on the total amount of the damages.[119]

It is unclear that Delaware would, in fact, have developed the *Malone* theory, in particular by articulating the basis for measuring

---

[117]A "covered class action" is defined as a lawsuit in which "damages are sought on behalf of more than 50 persons or prospective class members." Securities Act of 1933, § 16(f), 15 U.S.C. § 77p(f)(2)(A) (2000), Securities Exchange Act of 1934, § 28(f), 15 U.S.C. § 78bb(f)(2)(A), (5)(B) (2000). By contrast, a derivative action is sought on behalf of a single party, the corporation.

[118]See *supra* note 53 and accompanying text.

[119]In this respect these state actions would reach the result, suggested by Professor Coffee, of restructuring settlements in federal fraud-on-the-market cases to ensure a greater contribution by the wrongdoers. See Coffee, *supra* note 31, at 39–50. At the same time, these actions, unlike Coffee's solution, would preclude recovery of excessive fraud-on-the-market damages, with all of the problems these suits entail, as discussed above in Part II.

damages, even if SLUSA let it do so. Chief Justice Steele of the Delaware Supreme Court was quite skeptical of the plaintiff's theory when he was vice chancellor, noting that

> When a shareholder is damaged merely as a result of the release of inaccurate information into the marketplace, unconnected with any Delaware corporate governance issue, that shareholder must seek a remedy under federal law. . . . Congress has articulated a standard of disclosure to protect the national securities market. It makes little sense for Delaware courts to impose either a duplicative or stricter standard on directors of Delaware corporations. Neither the Delaware corporation code nor the common law suggests that Delaware can or should pick up the perceived regulatory slack when federal scrutiny may not include review of every actionable theory divinable by a dogged plaintiff.[120]

Vice Chancellor Strine was similarly dubious about plaintiff's argument for state law insider trading liability, noting that "[i]t might . . . fuel further legislative developments, as what was understood by Congress to be a narrow and fixed 'Delaware carve-out' for traditional fiduciary duty claims turns out to be an expanding excavation site that unsettles the structure of federal securities law."[121]

While Delaware courts now may resist expanding securities fraud remedies, this does not indicate that permitting a state corporation law remedy would be empty or futile. First, other states, particularly including California, might take a different approach. Indeed, the California Supreme Court showed none of Vice Chancellor Strine's reticence about colliding with federal law when it permitted securities class actions by out-of-state buyers even after SLUSA.[122] Second, even Delaware might be bolder if federal law clearly authorized state-of-corporation regulation, rather than the more qualified signal Congress gave in SLUSA.[123] Third, it is not clear what any states,

---

[120]Malone v. Brincat, No. 15510, 1997 WL 697940, at *2 (Del. Ch. October 30, 1997), rev'd, 722 A.2d 5 (Del. 1998).

[121]In re Oracle Corporation Derivative Litigation, No. Civ. A18751, 2004 WL 2756278, at *24 (Del. Ch. December 2, 2004) (footnotes omitted).

[122]See *supra* note 50.

[123]Delaware's reluctance to push the envelope of state liability given the PSLRA and SLUSA is consistent with Mark Roe's theory about the constraints federal law imposes on state competition. See Mark J. Roe, Delaware's Competition, 117 Harv. L. Rev. 588 (2003).

including Delaware, might do if Congress or the U.S. Supreme Court were to significantly shrink the federal remedy. To be sure, the states generally have shown little appetite to regulate substantive disclosure requirements since the advent of the federal securities laws. But this could reflect transactional lawyers' preference for a single federal law. On the other hand, it would not be surprising to see litigators press for state fraud law, though under a state-of-incorporation approach they would have to contend with corporate lawyers who want their states to continue to attract incorporations.

Finally, even if states do not authorize a significant remedy, this does not mean that they are acting inefficiently. The states' decision not to act once the choice-of-law rule forces them to internalize the costs as well as the benefits of litigation may instead mean that no state remedy is justified. In other words, the state "laboratory" may be providing useful guidance as to the appropriate scope of securities fraud liability.

To be sure, my proposal is not a perfect solution. Unlike Roberta Romano's proposal that federal law should permit firms to choose the jurisdiction that provides its securities laws,[124] my suggestion does not let firms opt out of federal law or select a securities law jurisdiction that is different from the state of incorporation.[125] However, while Romano's proposal is probably the right endpoint for securities law, it is not realistic to expect a spontaneous realignment of the political interests that support the current equilibrium. My proposal would facilitate an incremental approach through which full-fledged jurisdictional competition could evolve. One possible scenario would be for Congress and the federal courts to use the survival of a viable state remedy as a justification for shrinking the federal remedy. The Supreme Court in *Dura*[126] notably appeared headed in this direction, but stopped short of clarifying the precise

[124]See Roberta Romano, Empowering Investors: A Market Approach to Securities Regulation, 107 Yale L.J. 2359 (1998).

[125]However, as with state actions after the PSLRA and holder suits after SLUSA, plaintiffs would probably use the state remedies only for cases not covered by the federal remedy. It is conceivable that plaintiffs would choose to sue in state court in order to try to take advantage of the ability to obtain a global settlement there under *Matsushita Electric Industrial Co. v. Epstein*, 516 U.S. 367 (1996). For an analysis of the relevant issues, see Painter, *supra* note 56, at 95–99.

[126]See *supra* notes 58–59.

contours of the fraud-on-the-market remedy.[127] The Court or Congress might be emboldened to confront the manifest problems of the federal remedy if SLUSA left a clear state fallback rather than the existing statute's more limited exception to preemption.[128]

VIII. Conclusion

This article has shown that the basic problem facing the Court and Congress in securities regulation is how to address the tripartite concerns of abusive litigation, the need to constrain fraud, and the need to preserve a role for state corporate law. The problem is that these considerations seem mutually exclusive. Federal law therefore has been buffeted in multiple directions, first toward broad judicial remedies, then toward restricting federal remedies in the PSLRA and state remedies in SLUSA, then broadening federal regulation in the Sarbanes-Oxley Act.

Dabit presented an opportunity to encourage Congress to consider another alternative—the laboratory of state law. Although the Court treated the issue as straightforward, in fact it was far from clear that SLUSA preempted holder suits. If the Court had held that state holder suits were allowed under SLUSA in the absence of explicit preemption, Congress would have been forced to consider whether to allow supplemental state securities regulation. This article suggests an alternative path Congress could have taken in the wake of such a holding—that is, expand SLUSA's Delaware carve-out to allow the states to get back into the securities business through their corporate statutes. This could lead to a much better reconciliation of the three objectives mentioned above.

Although *Dabit* went the other way, this article's analysis is still relevant in showing what may be lost by excessive willingness to expand federal power, at least in the corporate and securities area. There are unexplored state options that could provide a path to a more rational and coherent approach to regulation. The Court should consider what might be gained by forcing Congress to reconsider

---

[127]See Ribstein, *supra* note 37, at 154–65 (discussing the potential implications of *Dura*).

[128]This sort of evolution toward a choice-of-law regime also could result from firms' cross-listing their securities in foreign markets, as cross-listing jurisdictions provide exemptions from their laws first to foreign firms and then to domestic firms. See, e.g., Ribstein, *supra* note 114, at 99.

the states' role through more rigorous application of a presumption against preemption.

Whatever the Court were to decide in *Dabit*, the relative roles of federal and state corporate and securities regulation raise important questions for both Congress and the courts. We could hardly do worse than the current situation.

DaimlerChrysler Corp. v. Cuno, State Investment Incentives, and the Future of the Dormant Commerce Clause Doctrine

*Brannon P. Denning**

Introduction

In *DaimlerChrysler Corp. v. Cuno*,[1] one of the 2005 term's closely-watched cases, the Supreme Court declined to decide whether tax incentives commonly used by states and municipalities to attract corporate investment violated the dormant Commerce Clause doctrine (DCCD). In a unanimous opinion by Chief Justice Roberts, the Court held that the state taxpayer plaintiffs in the case did not have standing to challenge the franchise tax credit offered by Ohio to manufacturers who made certain capital investments in the state.[2] The decision means that the case will be returned to the Ohio state courts, where it was initially brought by the plaintiffs. Thus, U.S. Supreme Court review of the merits of the case—if any—will have to await further litigation.

The outcome was anticipated,[3] even welcomed,[4] by legal scholars. But *Cuno*, along with another closely-watched case from North

---

*Associate Professor of Law and Director of Faculty Development, Cumberland School of Law at Samford University.

[1] 126 S. Ct. 1854 (2006).

[2] *Id.* at 1865.

[3] See, e.g., Kristin E. Hickman, How Did We Get Here Anyway?: Considering the Standing Question in DaimlerChrysler v. Cuno, 4 Geo. J.L. & Pub. Pol'y 47 (2006); Kristin E. Hickman & Donald B. Tobin, Taxpayer Standing and DaimlerChrysler v. Cuno: Where Do We Go From Here?, Tax Notes, Feb. 20, 2006, at 863.

[4] See, e.g., Brannon P. Denning, Cuno and the Court: The Case for Minimalism, 4 Geo. J.L. & Pub. Pol'y 33 (2006) (urging the Court to write a "minimalist" opinion; suggesting that a decision disposing of the case on standing would be one option open to the Court).

Carolina that was dismissed on standing grounds,[5] still leaves the constitutional status of state tax incentives in doubt. *Cuno* was a difficult case, I argue here, because the case exposed the difficulty the Court has had defining "discrimination" in DCCD cases. Cases like *Cuno* will continue to bedevil courts unless the Supreme Court clarifies what it means when it says that the DCCD is primarily concerned with eliminating state laws that discriminate against out-of-state goods or out-of-state economic actors.

In the pages that follow, I will summarize the litigation that led to the Court's decision and offer predictions as to what the future holds for DCCD challenges to state tax incentives. In particular, I will sketch some possibilities for clarifying the concept of discrimination in DCCD cases. There is much at stake. The DCCD has provided a measure of economic and political union among the states since its inception. The prohibition against discrimination is the most important doctrinal branch of the DCCD. But courts must clearly distinguish between discrimination of the sort that the Framers sought to eliminate and healthy competition among states. If they do not—if every effort states make to structure their tax code in ways that make them attractive to out-of-state businesses is subject to judicial review by federal courts, then the more persuasive arguments for the DCCD's abandonment will seem.[6]

I. *Cuno*: The Court's Holding

Ohio offered a franchise tax credit for taxpayers purchasing manufacturing machinery and equipment and installing it in the state.[7] Cities were also authorized to offer property tax waivers to businesses that invest in particular areas of the state.[8] DaimlerChrysler

---

[5]See Patrick Hogan, Judge Dismisses Dell Incentive Case, Austin Bus. J., May 10, 2006, available at http://www.bizjournals.com/austin/stories/2006/05/08/daily34.html.

[6]See, e.g., Edward A. Zelinsky, Cuno v. DaimlerChrysler: A Critique, 34 St. Tax Notes 37 (Oct. 4, 2004); Edward A. Zelinsky, Restoring Politics to the Commerce Clause: The Case for Abandoning the Dormant Commerce Clause Prohibition on Discriminatory Taxation, 29 Ohio N.U.L. Rev. 29 (2002).

[7]Ohio Rev. Code Ann. § 5733.33(B)(1) (1999).

[8]*Id.* §§ 5709.62(C), (D)(1). The Court noted, however, that Ohio has begun phasing out its franchise tax and has begun discontinuing the credits like that given to DaimlerChrysler. DaimlerChrysler Corp. v. Cuno, 126 S. Ct. 1854, 1859 n.1 (2006).

received the benefit of both when, in 1998, the company agreed to expand a Jeep assembly plant located in Toledo.[9] A group of Toledo taxpayers represented by Northeastern law professor Peter Enrich[10] sued in state court, claiming that the incentives violated the DCCD. DaimlerChrysler removed the case to federal district court and won.[11] On appeal, the Sixth Circuit agreed that the property tax exemption was constitutional, but struck the franchise tax exemption on the ground that it "coerced" DaimlerChrysler into locating its manufacturing equipment in the state.[12]

The plaintiffs had opposed removal to federal court, fearing an inability to satisfy standing requirements.[13] The district court disagreed,[14] holding that the taxpayers had standing to object to the property tax exemption and the franchise tax credit based on *Massachusetts v. Mellon*.[15] The Sixth Circuit's opinion did not even mention the standing issue. Even so, many observers thought that plaintiffs still faced considerable hurdles on the standing question, and when the Supreme Court requested briefing on the issue when it granted cert.,[16] it seemed the Court was setting the stage for dismissal on those grounds. In an opinion by Chief Justice John Roberts,[17] the Court did just that, unanimously concluding that the plaintiffs had no standing to challenge the franchise tax credit.[18]

[9]Cuno, 126 S. Ct. at 1859.

[10]Professor Enrich had written an article laying out the argument for challenging tax credits like those offered by Ohio. See Peter Enrich, Saving the States from Themselves, 110 Harv. L. Rev. 377 (1996).

[11]See Cuno v. DaimlerChrysler, 154 F. Supp. 2d 1196 (N.D. Ohio 2001).

[12]Cuno v. DaimlerChrysler Corp., 386 F.3d 738, 745–46 (6th Cir. 2004).

[13]126 S. Ct. at 1860.

[14]*Id.*

[15]262 U.S. 447 (1923).

[16]DaimlerChrysler Corp. v. Cuno, 126 S. Ct. 36 (2005).

[17]Justice Ginsburg concurred in the result and in part of the rationale. She explained that the decision "is solidly grounded in longstanding precedent . . . decisions that antedate current jurisprudence on standing to sue. . . . One can accept . . . the nonjusticiability of . . . federal and state taxpayer suits in federal court without endorsing as well the limitations on standing later declared in" the Court's later cases. 126 S. Ct. at 1868–69 (Ginsburg, J., concurring) (citations omitted).

[18]The Court granted cert. only on the franchise tax exemption. The plaintiffs abandoned arguments that they were injured because they were displaced by DaimlerChrysler's expansion and also abandoned arguments by Michigan residents that, but for the Ohio incentives, DaimlerChrysler would have expanded in Michigan, bringing attendant benefits. *Id.* at 1859.

The opinion began with testimony to the importance of standing and its relation to Article III's limitation of the federal judiciary's jurisdiction to decide "Cases and Controversies."[19] That limitation, the Court explained, ensured that the federal judiciary did not trespass on the domain of the other branches; standing doctrine reinforces the case-or-controversy requirement by requiring litigants to allege concrete injuries traceable to the defendant's conduct and likely to be redressed by the relief requested.[20]

In general, the Court has held that federal and state taxpayers challenging governmental action they allege to be unconstitutional *do not* have the kind of injury necessary to confer standing.[21] Taxpayers, the Court has held, do not have a "concrete and particularized" injury, but rather a "generalized" injury common among all taxpayers.[22] The only exception the Court has recognized to this general rule involves the taxing and spending decisions allegedly made in violation of the Establishment Clause.[23]

The *Cuno* plaintiffs alleged that tax credits depleted funds available to the state, funds to which the plaintiffs as taxpayers contributed, and imposed additional burdens on taxpayers since they would likely have to pick up the tab.[24] But the Court noted that this alleged injury was not "concrete and particularized," and, furthermore, it was not even clear that there would actually *be* any injury. "The very point of the tax benefits is to spur economic activity, which in turn *increases* revenue."[25]

Moreover, the alleged injury was pure conjecture, because it depended "on how legislators respond[ed] to a reduction in revenue, if that is the consequence of the credit. Establishing injury requires

[19]U.S. Const. art. III; Cuno, 126 S. Ct. at 1860–61.

[20]126 S. Ct. at 1861 (citing Allen v. Wright, 468 U.S. 737, 751 (1984)).

[21]See Doremus v. Board of Education, 342 U.S. 429 (1952) (standing of state taxpayers); Frothingham v. Mellon, 262 U.S. 447 (1923); see also Cuno, 126 S. Ct. at 1861–63 (discussing cases). See generally Hickman, *supra* note 3, at 54–56 (summarizing the doctrine).

[22]Cuno, 126 S. Ct. at 1862 (internal quotation marks omitted).

[23]Flast v. Cohen, 392 U.S. 83 (1968).

[24]126 S. Ct. at 1862.

[25]*Id.* The Court noted that the out-of-state plaintiffs "claimed they were injured because they lost out on the added revenues that would have accompanied Daimler-Chrysler's decision to expand facilities in Michigan." *Id.*

speculating that elected officials will increase a taxpayer-plaintiff's tax bill to make up a deficit . . . ."[26] Likewise, "establishing redressability requires speculating that abolishing the challenged credit will redound to the benefit of the taxpayer because the legislators will pass along the supposed increased revenue in the form of tax reductions."[27] Both, the Court continued, are fundamental policy matters over which the Court may have no say.[28] "Under such circumstances," Chief Justice Roberts continued, "we have no assurance that the asserted injury is 'imminent'—that it is 'certainly impending.'"[29]

The Court held that the concerns militating against granting standing to federal taxpayers applied to state taxpayers as well, reiterating the Court's holding in *Doremus v. Board of Education*.[30] Like the federal government, "[s]tate policymakers . . . retain broad discretion to make 'policy decisions' concerning state spending" and "[f]ederal courts may not assume a particular exercise of this state fiscal discretion in establishing standing . . . ."[31] To hold otherwise would commit to the federal courts broad supervisory powers over a vast array of state taxing and spending decisions "contrary to the more modest role Article III envisions for federal courts."[32]

The Court further rejected plaintiffs' arguments that the Establishment Clause exception to the taxpayer standing rule recognized in *Flast v. Cohen*[33] be expanded to cover DCCD challenges.[34] "[A] finding that the Commerce Clause satisfies the *Flast* test would leave no principled way of distinguishing those other constitutional provisions that we have recognized constrain government's taxing and spending decisions."[35] This, in turn, would open federal courts up

---

[26] *Id.* at 1862–63.

[27] *Id.* at 1863.

[28] *Id.*

[29] *Id.*

[30] 342 U.S. 429 (1952).

[31] 126 S. Ct. at 1863–64.

[32] *Id.* at 1864.

[33] 392 U.S. 83 (1968).

[34] 126 S. Ct. at 1864–65.

[35] *Id.* at 1865.

to the sorts of generalized grievances prohibited by the case-or-controversy requirement.

Finally, the Court refused to allow the plaintiffs to invoke their status as *municipal* taxpayers to challenge a state action. The plaintiffs claimed that since Ohio law required the franchise tax revenue to be distributed to municipalities, the credits reduced those amounts and, again, depleted the municipal funds to which taxpayers contributed.[36] The plaintiffs also argued that federal courts could hear their DCCD challenges, despite standing problems, because they had standing to challenge the property tax exemption for businesses that invest in particular areas of the state.[37] Plaintiffs relied on *United Mine Workers v. Gibbs*,[38] which authorizes supplemental jurisdiction over certain claims that arise from a "common nucleus of operative facts."[39]

As to the first, the Court noted that the plaintiffs' challenge "is still to the state law and state decision, not those of their municipality."[40] In any event, the problems of immediacy of the injury and its redressability were still present: Ohio had, since 2001, suspended the distribution of franchise tax revenues to local governments. "Any effect that enjoining DaimlerChrysler's credit will have on municipal funds . . . will not result from automatic operation of a statutory formula, but from a hypothesis that the state government will choose to direct the supposed revenue from the restored franchise tax to municipalities."[41]

Nor was the Court inclined to subscribe to the plaintiffs' capacious reading of *Gibbs*.[42] The Court stressed it had "never . . . [applied] the rationale of *Gibbs* to permit a federal court to exercise supplemental jurisdiction over a claim that does not satisfy those elements of the

---

[36] *Id.*

[37] See *supra* note 8 and accompanying text.

[38] 383 U.S. 715 (1966).

[39] *Id.* at 725; 126 S. Ct. at 1866–68.

[40] 126 S. Ct. at 1866.

[41] *Id.*

[42] *Id.* ("Plaintiffs assume that *Gibbs* stands for the proposition that federal jurisdiction extends to all claims sufficiently related to a claim within Article III to be part of the same case, regardless of the nature of the deficiency that would keep the former claims out of federal court if presented on their own.").

Article III inquiry" like standing.[43] Were it to adopt the plaintiffs' view of *Gibbs*, the Court warned, nearly all of the Court's case-or-controversy doctrines would be eroded.[44] Since Article III was designed to maintain the judicial power within its proper boundaries, any interpretation of *Gibbs* that would undermine those limits cannot be the correct one.[45]

"Plaintiffs failed to establish Article III injury with respect to their *state* taxes," the Court concluded, and "even if they did so with respect to their *municipal* taxes, that remedy does not entitle them to seek a remedy as to the state taxes."[46]

II. The Dormant Commerce Clause Doctrine and Investment Incentives

In the short run, the Court was able to put off an extremely vexing question with its decision on standing. The disposition on standing was not, as mentioned, unexpected. In fact, just a few days before the Court announced its decision in *Cuno*, a North Carolina state court judge threw out a similar case brought by taxpayers challenging that state's provision of tax incentives to Dell Computer. According to the judge, the taxpayers had not proven injury sufficient to maintain standing.[47]

But the Supreme Court has, in all likelihood, simply postponed a decision on the merits, assuming that no congressional legislation is forthcoming. The Ohio plaintiffs are now free to pursue their case in Ohio's state courts where they originally brought it, and the U.S. Supreme Court is always free to review the decision of that state's high court. In this Part, I canvass the options that the Ohio courts have open to them when considering the constitutionality of the Ohio program under the DCCD. The next Part, however, suggests that *Cuno* seemed so difficult because the particular investment scheme highlighted difficulties with the entire concept of "discrimination" under the DCCD. Reframing that concept might clarify not

---

[43]*Id.* at 1867.

[44]*Id*

[45]*Id.* at 1868.

[46]*Id.*

[47]See Hogan, Judge Dismisses Dell Incentive Case, *supra* note 5.

only the underlying case in *Cuno*, but also aid in clearing up some doctrinal anomalies that persist in the DCCD generally.

A. A DCCD Primer

Courts apply the DCCD using a two-tier standard of review. For state and local laws or regulations that "discriminate" against interstate commerce on their face, or, if facially-neutral, in their purposes or effects, a form of strict scrutiny applies (hereinafter the "anti-discrimination principle"). While a slightly different test obtains when the DCCD is applied to state and local taxes on interstate commerce, the anti-discrimination principle applies equally to both taxes and non-tax regulations. To survive judicial scrutiny, the government must prove that it is pursuing a legitimate (*i.e.*, non-protectionist) interest and that no less discriminatory means exist that allow it to pursue that interest. Few regulations survive this scrutiny. For those laws that are truly non-discriminatory, a more deferential test is applied—plaintiffs must prove that the burdens on interstate commerce "clearly exceed" the "putative local benefits." [48]

There are a few exceptions that bear mentioning. First, the Court has not, to date, applied the rules of the DCCD to discriminatory *cash* subsidies of in-state industries. If Alabama wishes to ladle cash out to preferred local industries, to the exclusion of their out-of-state competitors, it may do so. A second, related, exception—the *market-participant* exception—permits a state *acting as an ordinary buyer or seller in a particular market* (as opposed to a "market regulator") to favor local businesses. For example, if Alabama spent state funds to build a plant that manufactured widgets and, because of a national widget shortage, restricted sales to in-state widget consumers, the market-participant exception would allow it to do so. Conversely, Alabama may, by law, decide to spend state funds to purchase only in-state widgets. Finally, Congress may legislate affirmatively to permit states to pass laws that would otherwise be invalid under the DCCD—*e.g.*, permitting states to ban the import or sale of out-of-state widgets.[49]

---

[48]For a succinct introduction to the DCCD, see Dan T. Coenen, The Commerce Clause 216–223 (2004).

[49]See *id.* at 287–314 (discussing the exceptions to the DCCD in greater detail).

B. The DCCD and State Economic Incentives

Cuno is not the first DCCD challenge to state schemes designed to benefit the local economy. Many of the previous cases, though, involved rather clear facial discrimination between in-state and out-of-state economic activity. For example, in *Boston Stock Exchange v. State Tax Commission*,[50] the Court invalidated a New York law taxing out-of-state securities transactions more than those occurring in state.[51] "The obvious effect of the tax," the Court wrote, was "to extend a financial advantage to sales on the New York exchanges at the expense of the regional exchanges."[52]

A few years later, in *Maryland v. Louisiana*,[53] the Court invalidated a "first-use" tax equal to the state's severance tax on natural gas extracted offshore and pumped into Louisiana for processing.[54] The tax was designed both to mitigate damage to Louisiana's "waterbottoms barrier islands, and coastal areas resulting from the introduction of natural gas into Louisiana from areas not subject to state taxation" as well as "to equalize competition between gas produced in Louisiana and subject to the state severance tax . . . and gas produced elsewhere not subject to a severance tax . . . ."[55] Because of the exemptions and credits provided for in the state act, however, "Louisiana consumers of [Outer Continental Shelf] gas for the most part are not burdened by the Tax, but it does uniformly apply to gas moving out of the State."[56] As a result of these exemptions and credits, "the Louisiana First-Use Tax unquestionably discriminate[d] against interstate commerce in favor of the local interests . . . ."[57]

In a third case, *Westinghouse Electric Corp. v. Tully*,[58] the Court struck down a New York tax credit available to special entities

[50]429 U.S. 318 (1977).

[51]*Id.* at 319–20.

[52]*Id.* at 331.

[53]451 U.S. 725 (1981).

[54]*Id.* at 731 ("Since most States impose their own severance tax, it is acknowledged that the primary effect of the First-Use Tax will be on gas produced in the federal [Outer Continental Shelf] area and then piped to processing plants located within Louisiana.").

[55]*Id.* at 732.

[56]*Id.* at 733, 756–57.

[57]*Id.* at 756.

[58]466 U.S. 388 (1984).

(DISCs[59]) recognized under the Internal Revenue Code and accorded special tax treatment under the Code. In order to avoid the loss of state tax revenue *and* to avoid a tax policy that would create a disincentive for DISCs to form in and export from New York, the state enacted a franchise tax credit, which "lowered the effective tax rate on the accumulated DISC income reflected in the consolidated return to 30% of the otherwise applicable franchise tax rate" as long as the income was derived "from export products 'shipped from a regular place of business of the taxpayer within [New York].'"[60]

The effect of the credit, found the Court, was to treat differently otherwise similarly situated parent corporations whose only difference was "the percentage of their DISCs' shipping activities conducted from New York. This adjustment," the Court continued, "has the effect of allowing a parent a greater tax credit on its accumulated DISC income as its subsidiary DISC moves a greater percentage of its shipping activities into the State of New York."[61] Not only did the law provide an incentive to move activities to New York, it also "penalize[d] increases in the DISC's shipping activities in other states."[62]

Like the laws in *Boston Stock Exchange* and *Maryland v. Louisiana*, the Court found that the credit and its effects "encouraged the development of local industry by means of taxing measures that imposed greater burdens on economic activities taking place outside the state than were placed on similar activities within the State."[63] The Court also rejected New York's argument that the disallowance of tax credit, as opposed to imposing a higher tax, held any constitutional significance. "The discriminatory economic effect of these two measures would be identical."[64]

Other cases offer an important gloss on the exceptions to the general DCCD rules described above. For example, the Court has differentiated between provision of cash subsidies to local industries and subsidies effected through the tax codes—for example through

---

[59]DISC is an acronym for "Domestic International Sales Corporation." *Id.* at 390.

[60]*Id.* at 393 (alteration in the original).

[61]*Id.* at 400.

[62]*Id.* at 401.

[63]*Id.* at 404.

[64]*Id.*

exemptions or credits offered to local, but not out-of-state businesses or products.[65] As Justice Scalia put it in *New Energy Co. of Indiana v. Limbach*, "[d]irect subsidization of domestic industry does not ordinarily run afoul of [the anti-discrimination principle]; discriminatory taxation of out-of-state manufacturers does" because "[t]he Commerce Clause does not prohibit all state action designed to give its residents an advantage in the marketplace," but rather only that favoritism *"in connection with the State's regulation of interstate commerce."*[66]

In *Limbach*, though, the Court rejected arguments that the market-participant exception immunized the tax credit from strict scrutiny. While conceding that "the tax credit scheme has the purpose and effect of subsidizing a particular industry, as do many dispositions of the tax laws," that did not "transform it into a form of state participation in the free market."[67] The Ohio law involved "neither its purchase nor its sale of ethanol, but its assessment and computation of taxes—a primeval governmental activity."[68]

Limbach and later decisions thus stand for the proposition that activity economists would consider identical is treated differently for DCCD purposes. A tax credit or exemption of $100 is the same to an entity as a direct payment of $100 from the state treasury. Similarly, even indirect subsidization, such as occurs under the market-participant exception when the state makes a decision to favor in-state interests in the purchase or sale of goods, is held to be impermissible when effected through a state's tax code.

C. Business Incentives and the DCCD: The View from the Academy

The Ohio tax credit challenged in *Cuno* "grant[ed] a taxpayer a non-refundable credit against the state's corporate franchise tax if the taxpayer 'purchses new manufacturing machinery and equipment . . . [and] the new manufacturing machinery and equipment

[65]New Energy Co. v. Limbach, 486 U.S. 269, 278 (1988) (invalidating sales tax credit for ethanol produced in Ohio or in states offering reciprocal treatment for Ohio-produced ethanol).

[66]*Id.* (emphasis in original). See also Bacchus Imports, Ltd. v. Dias, 468 U.S. 263 (1984) (invalidating tax exemption for locally-produced alcoholic beverage).

[67]New Energy Co., 486 U.S. at 277.

[68]*Id.* See also Camps Newfound/Owatonna v. Harrison, 520 U.S. 564 (1997) (rejecting similar argument).

are installed in [Ohio].'"[69] While the tax credit was available on a non-discriminatory basis to in-state and out-of-state firms, the Sixth Circuit concluded that it "discriminate[d] against interstate economic activity by coercing businesses already subject to the Ohio franchise tax to expand locally rather than out-of-state."[70] Though businesses locating machinery elsewhere will not face an *increase* in their tax burden, "a competitor that invests out-of-state," plaintiffs pointed out, "will face a comparatively higher tax burden because it will be ineligible for any credit against its Ohio tax."[71] Apparently finding the case on all fours with prior Court cases, and rejecting the narrower reading of those cases offered by the defendants, the Sixth Circuit struck down the Ohio tax credit.[72] The question that arises, though, is whether the Court cases described above led ineluctably to the Sixth Circuit's decision invalidating the tax credit.

Not surprisingly, two contending views of the Court's cases were offered in *Cuno*. The plaintiffs' attorney, Peter Enrich, took the position that not only were specific cases sufficient to invalidate the Ohio tax credit, but further that the anti-discrimination principle articulated and applied in those cases should be broadly construed to prohibit "the distorting effects of state policies on the national economy, rather than on their disparate impacts on competing businesses."[73] Broadening the principle in this way would, argued Enrich, take account of "the vital Commerce Clause concerns—the threat to the economic vitality of other states, the prospect of inefficient allocation of economic resources, and the specter of rising interstate hostility" that "have . . . received less attention" in the Court's decisions.[74] Applying the anti-discrimination principle in that way could result in the invalidation of a wide variety of heretofore unquestioned means by which state and local governments encourage businesses to locate, expand, or remain in a given area. This raises the specter of giving federal judges veto power over state

---

[69]Cuno v. DaimlerChrysler Corp., 386 F.3d 738, 741 (6th Cir. 2004) (quoting Ohio Rev. Code Ann. § 5733.33(B)(1) (alteration in the original)).

[70]*Id.* at 743.

[71]*Id.*

[72]*Id.* at 746.

[73]Enrich, *supra* note 10, at 454.

[74]*Id.* at 449.

and local taxing and spending programs.[75] It would seem to doom the distinction the Court currently maintains between taxes and direct subsidies. It might even call into question the validity of the market-participant doctrine, if buying or selling by state and local governments would result in "economic distortion."

That said, there is language in the Court's opinions that hints at such a broad conception of the anti-discrimination principle. In *Boston Stock Exchange*, for example, Justice White's opinion mentioned, as an objection to the New York tax, that it "foreclose[d] tax-neutral decisions" about where the securities transfers should take place.[76] He noted that the Court "'has viewed with particular suspicion state statues requiring business operations to be performed in the home State that could be more efficiently performed elsewhere.'"[77] Later he referred to the effect as having caused "the flow of securities sales [to be] diverted from the most economically efficient channels and directed to New York," resulting in "diversion of interstate commerce and diminution of free competition in securities sales . . . ."[78]

The opposite view, taken by the defendants in *Cuno*, is that a narrower reading of the Court's cases is possible—and desirable. Drawing on the arguments of two state and local tax practitioners,[79] DaimlerChrysler argued that only those taxes that "penalize" interstate commercial activity should fall under the DCCD.[80] Under this approach, a tax incentive that distinguishes "between in-state and out-of-state activities" and "rewards in-state activities without similarly rewarding the same out-of-state activities" would not violate the DCCD as long as it doesn't have a "negative impact" on protected commerce.[81] However, as Walter Hellerstein and Dan Coenen have astutely pointed out, the Court itself has rejected arguments that the DCCD should make a distinction between benefits to in-state

[75]A good deal of Professor Enrich's article makes the normative case against state investment incentives. See *id.* at 378–405.

[76]429 U.S. 318, 332 (1977).

[77]*Id.* at 336 (quoting Pike v. Bruce Church, Inc., 397 U.S. 137, 145 (1970)).

[78]*Id.*

[79]Philip M. Tatarowicz & Rebecca F. Mims-Velarde, An Analytical Approach to State Tax Discrimination Under the Commerce Clause, 39 Vand. L. Rev. 879 (1986).

[80]Cuno v. DaimlerChrysler Corp., 386 F.3d 738, 745 (6th Cir. 2004).

[81]Tatarowicz & Mims-Velarde, *supra* note 79, at 928–29.

activity and burdens on out-of-state activity.[82] More important in their opinion is the penalty analysis's failure "to draw a meaningful line between a tax incentive that penalizes out-of-state activity and one that merely rewards in-state activity."[83] Perhaps the reward/ penalty distinction could be refined by resort to extrinsic aids, like evidence regarding the likely purpose of the statute—the purpose of both New York's securities transfer tax and Louisiana's first-use tax seemed aimed at penalizing specific out-of-state commerce, or at least protecting in-state industries, rather than rewarding in-state activity—though a purpose-based inquiry is not without its own difficulties.

Hellerstein and Coenen proposed yet another approach, one ultimately adopted by the lower court in *Cuno*. Conscious of the need to avoid giving free rein to some of the Court's more expansive language noted above, Hellerstein and Coenen proposed the following analytical framework for tax incentive decisions. "First, the provision must favor in-state over out-of-state activities; second, the provision must implicate the coercive power of the state. If, but only if, both of these conditions are met, courts should declare the tax incentive unconstitutional."[84] Specifically, tax incentives that provide relief to *existing* taxpayers within the state implicate the "coercive power of the state" in ways that Hellerstein and Coenen find constitutionally unacceptable.[85] If, however, the incentives involve "exemptions from or reductions of *additional* state tax liability to which the taxpayer would be subjected only if the taxpayer were to engage in the targeted activity in the state," the constitutional values of the DCCD are not implicated.[86] In addition, Hellerstein and Coenen would largely preserve the Court's disparate treatment of taxes and subsidies.[87]

---

[82]Walter Hellerstein & Dan T. Coenen, Commerce Clause Restraints on State Business Development Incentives, 81 Cornell L. Rev. 789, 814 (1996).

[83]*Id.*

[84]*Id.* at 806.

[85]*Id.* at 807.

[86]*Id.*

[87]*Id.* at 838–48; see also Dan T. Coenen, Business Subsidies and the Dormant Commerce Clause, 107 Yale L.J. 965 (1997). There is a fourth take on *Cuno*. Edward Zelinsky has written that *Cuno* represents the *reductio ad absurdum* of an anti-discrimination principle that distinguishes between economically identical activities, like taxes and subsidies. His solution is to junk the anti-discrimination principle, at least in tax cases, and to leave other doctrines and the political processes to police state abuses.

III. Rethinking "Discrimination" in the DCCD

Cuno has always struck me as a difficult case for two reasons. First, it was somewhat different than the ordinary facial discrimination case in which in-state economic actors were favored over competitors from out-of-state. The tax credit, for example, did not depend on the geographic origin of the firm seeking it, though it did make a geographical distinction regarding the economic activity at issue. Even so, the Ohio credit simply *felt* different than the tax incentives in the cases discussed above. The actions of Ohio in *Limbach*, New York in *Westinghouse* and *Boston Stock Exchange*, and Louisiana in enacting its first-use tax seemed to conform more readily to the paradigm of "protectionism," at which the DCCD's anti-discrimination principle is said to be primarily directed.

These difficulties lead to a series of deeper questions. What *is* discrimination? Why has it emerged as a central concern of the DCCD? Upon close reading, the Court has not been particularly helpful at answering either of these questions in its opinions. As to the first, labeling a law as "discriminatory" is really a conclusion rather than an explanation. The Court usually defines "discrimination" under the DCCD as differential treatment of in-state and out-of-state activity or economic actors that benefits the former and burdens the latter.[88] But this seems both over- and underinclusive, since the Court has consistently refused to consider the *amount* of burden to out-of-state actors[89] and because the Court doesn't require a showing of any actual benefit to particular in-state competitors.

As for the second question, the Court (along with many scholars) has tended to assume the Framers' interest was in creating and supporting a national common market, the better to facilitate free

See, e.g., Zelinsky, Restoring Politics to the Commerce Clause, *supra* note 6, at 29–32 (summarizing argument). A current work-in-progress responds to Professor Zelinsky's arguments. Brannon P. Denning, The Indispensibility of the Anti-Discrimination Principle to the Dormant Commerce Clause Doctrine: A Response to Edward Zelinsky (July 4, 2006) (copy on file with author).

[88] See, e.g., Granholm v. Heald, 544 U.S. 460, 472 (2005); Oregon Waste Systems, Inc. v. Dept. Environmental Quality, 511 U.S. 93, 99 (1994).

[89] See, e.g., Boston Stock Exchange v. State Tax Commission, 429 U.S. 318, 333 (1997) (rejecting a de minimis argument).

trade.[90] With free trade as the constitutional value the DCCD protects, it follows for anyone holding that view that the doctrine should evolve to eliminate as many state obstacles to free trade as possible. This view finds particular expression in Justice White's opinions in *Bacchus Imports* and *Boston Stock Exchange*. But as Professor Enrich's writings suggest, adopting a strong version of this view converts the DCCD into a form of economic substantive due process, empowering federal courts to invalidate portions of state and local regulatory schemes based on an amorphous conclusion that the effects "distort" the national economy.

My evolving view of the DCCD is that this focus is misplaced.[91] I have argued elsewhere that the Framers seemed anxious to centralize power over interstate commerce to prevent the cycles of disfavored treatment and retaliation among states not uncommon during the Confederation era.[92] Ensuring the elimination of interstate trade barriers was not driven by ideological attachment to free trade itself, but was rather a means to the end of interstate harmony and national political unity, both of which were threatened by the trade conflicts of the mid-1780s.

Thus, there is much to Thomas Reed Powell's quip that one writing the Restatement of Constitutional Law would include, as part of the black-letter text, the sentence: "'Congress may regulate interstate commerce.' A Comment would add: 'The states may also regulate interstate commerce, but not too much.' And then there would follow a Caveat: 'How much is too much is beyond the scope of this Restatement.'"[93] The Framers, I have concluded, thought that the Commerce Clause, along with other specific provisions, operated to restrain the

[90]This rationale is especially pronounced in the cases described above. See, e.g., *id.* at 334–35, 336–37 (discussing the "free trade purpose" of the Commerce Clause); see also Maryland v. Louisiana, 451 U.S. 725, 754 (1981).

[91]See, e.g., Denning, Indispensibility of the Anti-Discrimination Principle, *supra* note 87 (forthcoming). This position is not completely unique to me. See also Richard B. Collins, Economic Union as a Constitutional Value, 63 N.Y.U. L. Rev. 43 (1988); Maxwell L. Stearns, A Beautiful Mend: A Game Theoretical Analysis of the Dormant Commerce Clause Doctrine, 45 Wm. & Mary L. Rev. 1 (2003).

[92]See generally Brannon P. Denning, Confederation-Era Discrimination against Interstate Commerce and the Legitimacy of the Dormant Commerce Clause Doctrine, 94 Ky. L.J. 37 (2005–2006).

[93]Paul A. Freund, Foreword, in Thomas Reed Powell, Vagaries and Varieties in Constitutional Interpretation ix (1956) (Lawbook Exchange reprint 2002).

states, but the extent of that restraint was not thought through.[94] The whole history of the DCCD has been a working out of Powell's Caveat.[95] How much *is* too much?

All of the doctrinal tests that have emerged from the Court's DCCD jurisprudence—Chief Justice Marshall's distinction between police powers regulations and regulations of interstate commerce *qua* commerce; *Cooley's* national/local distinction; the direct/indirect test; balancing; the anti-discrimination principle—have been attempts to implement[96] the constitutional principle that states can't regulate interstate commerce "too much." The Court's entire DCCD project has been a temporally extended attempt to craft "decision rules" to implement the "constitutional operative proposition" the Constitution compels.[97]

The failure to clearly distinguish the implementing or decision rules from what, exactly, the Constitution requires has led to the confusion that plagues not only *Cuno*, but also discussion of the DCCD generally. Clarifying what Mitchell Berman calls the "constitutional operative proposition" and distinguishing it from the decision rules intended to implement the proposition—as well as defending those rules themselves—holds the possibility of clarifying the DCCD in ways that the efforts of scholars to work from the bottom up, synthesizing and reconciling conflicting DCCD decisions, has not.

As suggested above, I think that the Framers worried more about preservation of interstate harmony in the service of political union—sometimes expressed in the Court's opinions as the prevention of economic Balkanization—than about free trade itself. However, as Thomas Powell's restatement demonstrates, saying that "States may not regulate interstate commerce in a way that endangers national political union" will not decide concrete cases. Therefore, the Court has to create tools that will.

[94]Denning, Confederation-Era Discrimination, *supra* note 92, at 90.

[95]For a too-brief summary of that doctrinal history, see *id.* at 91 n.308.

[96]I use this term in the sense that Richard Fallon does—the creation of doctrinal tools to operationalize otherwise vague constitutional principles. See Richard H. Fallon, Jr., Implementing the Constitution (2001).

[97]See generally Mitchell Berman, Constitutional Decision Rules, 90 Va. L. Rev. 1 (2004); Kermit Roosevelt, III, Constitutional Calcification: How the Law Becomes What the Court Does, 91 Va. L. Rev. 1649 (2005).

The Court used to apply the DCCD through the creation of conceptual categories of state regulation—regulation of navigation and carriers, inspection laws, regulation of intrastate sales of goods, for example—each with its own set of rules.[98] Since the early 1970s, however, the Court has tended to approach DCCD questions through the two-tier standard of review, whose level of scrutiny turns on whether or not "discrimination" exists.

As a defining concept in the DCCD, one that very nearly determines the validity or invalidity of state regulations, discrimination has won out, I would argue, because it is the better proxy for the reasons states had their commercial regulatory powers limited in the first place. In many of the examples of Confederation-era commercial friction, states sought competitive advantages for their products or sought to benefit their citizens and wanted someone else, i.e., out-of-state commercial actors, to bear the cost. *Those* producers' or traders' states would then retaliate, sometimes setting off a cycle of protectionism and retaliation that inhibited amicable relations and frustrated efforts to forge any type of national identity.[99]

What emerged as the DCCD's anti-discrimination principle could be regarded as a prophylactic rule, willing to tolerate more false positives rather than risking false negatives in the service of national unity. Thus, as states got the message that facially discriminatory laws would not survive judicial scrutiny, and passed facially-neutral statutes that burdened out-of-state commerce the same as facially-discriminatory laws did, the Court adapted the doctrine in response.[100]

But in the press of refining the doctrinal tests for discrimination, the purpose the anti-discrimination principle served was lost. The result is what Kim Roosevelt terms "constitutional calcification."[101]

---

[98]See Michael S. Greve, The Dormant Commerce Clause as an Ex Ante Rule 10 ("The history of the dormant Commerce Clause over the past seven decades can be understood as a sustained effort to move from subject-matter limitation to procedure (for lack of a better word), from exclusivity to antidiscrimination.") (unpublished manuscript on file with author).

[99]For examples, see Denning, Confederation-Era Discrimination, *supra* note 92, at 40–48, 59–66, 70–73.

[100]See, e.g., Hunt v. Washington Apple Advertisers Commission, 432 U.S. 333 (1977); Dean Milk v. Madison, 340 U.S. 349 (1951); H.P. Hood & Sons, Inc. v. DuMond, 336 U.S. 525 (1949).

[101]Roosevelt, *supra* note 97, at 1692–93.

Three major problems result from calcification, according to Roosevelt: (1) "doctrinal deformation" in which good decision rules are mistakenly discarded or are accepted as the operative propositions, while other doctrinal changes are made to maintain consistency;[102] (2) treatment of decision rules as operative propositions whereby the Court "announces as constitutional truths rules that should neither be followed by nonjudicial actors nor internalized by the general public";[103] and (3) inflation of the judicial role, as calcification calls into question the notion the Court is but one of many bodies with responsibility for constitutional interpretation.[104]

The current DCCD shares at least some of each of these aspects of calcification. First, while overstated, it is widely perceived (even by members of the Court) that the doctrine is inconsistent, if not incoherent.[105] This means, of course, we only know what the DCCD will or will not permit when the Court tells us. Moreover, as I have been emphasizing in this section, there has been a growing tendency to focus on the elimination of discrimination either as an end in and of itself, or in the service of an assumed free-trade orientation of the Constitution. This both conflates the rules and operative proposition, and has resulted in the deformation of the DCCD itself. Expansion of the doctrine to invalidate "economically distorting" or "inefficient" state laws would merely push the DCCD further afield.[106]

* * *

What then is to be done? In my view, the anti-discrimination principle needs to be re-tethered to the constitutional operative proposition it was supposed to implement. While a complete reconceptu-

---

[102]*Id.* at 1693.

[103]*Id.* at 1713.

[104]*Id.* at 1716–17.

[105]See, e.g., Camps Newfound/Owatonna v. Harrison, 520 U.S. 564, 611 & n.3 (1997) (Thomas, J., dissenting). For three ready examples of cases with similar facts but different outcomes, compare West Lynn Creamery v. Healy, 513 U.S. 168 (1994), with Pharmaceutical Research and Manufacturers Association v. Walsh, 538 U.S. 644 (2003); and Hunt v. Washington Apple Advertisers Association, 432 U.S. 333 (1977), with Exxon v. Maryland, 437 U.S. 117 (1978); and Maine v. Taylor, 477 U.S. 131 (1986), with Hughes v. Oklahoma, 441 U.S. 322 (1979).

[106]Cf. Michael J. Graetz & Alvin C. Warren, Jr., Income Tax Discrimination and the Political and Economic Integration of Europe, 115 Yale L.J. 1186 (2006) (arguing that the decisions of the European Court of Justice regarding taxation suffer from a similar drift).

alization of the principle must await another article,[107] I here offer the following as a first cut at the direction such a rethinking might take. First, political union and preventing of interstate friction must replace "free trade" as the constitutional value that lies at the heart of the DCCD. Second, the anti-discrimination principle itself must be recognized as a mere tool used to refine and implement that value, not as an end itself.

Therefore, I propose that courts ask the following questions when deciding whether a law is "discriminatory," and thus presumed unconstitutional under the DCCD. First, does the law favor in-state over out-of-state economic interests, either by benefiting the former or burdening or penalizing the latter? Second, is the means by which the in-state interest is benefited or the out-of-state interest penalized likely to produce retaliatory action on the part of other states or local governments? Only if the answer to both questions is "yes," would a reviewing court apply strict scrutiny, which would still give the state or local government the opportunity to prove that the end was legitimate and that there was no less discriminatory means to achieve that end.

The obvious question is whether it is possible for courts to perform Step Two of my analysis with any degree of certainty.[108] I think that it is possible, and that judges might approach this second step in a variety of ways. First, as the Court does now, judges might create presumptions that certain categories of laws, if they favor in-staters or burden out-of-staters, are likely to encourage replication or retaliation. Tariffs and embargoes are the historic paradigms here.

Second, for laws that do not neatly fit within these categories, courts might rely on other states themselves to sound "fire alarms" over state and local laws, alerting the Court to state abuses. In a fascinating recent article, Professor Chris Drahozal found that since 1970 "the Court has struck down state statutes more often when a state or local government challenged the statute, either as a party or as an amicus curiae, than when no government entity challenged

---

[107]I offer some more details in Denning, Indispensibility of the Anti-Discrimination Principle, *supra* note 87.

[108]See generally Adrian Vermeule, Judging Under Uncertainty (2006) (arguing that few interpretive theories pay sufficient attention to the institutional capacities of courts and the judges that staff them).

the statute."[109] The two cases in which the Court upheld state laws despite opposition by other state governments, Drahozal argues, confirm "the wisdom of heeding fire alarms," since the cases "have been soundly criticized . . . ."[110]

A third possibility is for the Court to perform a sort of thought experiment, asking what would happen if all or most states adopted a particular tax or regulation. Would widespread adoption tend to undermine or inhibit political union, including the economic ties that bind states to one another? Such an inquiry would be similar to the "internal consistency" test the Court uses as part of its DCCD analysis in tax cases. For a tax to be internally consistent, the Court asks whether a similar tax, imposed by all states, would place interstate commerce at a disadvantage relative to intrastate commerce.[111] If it would, then the tax is unconstitutional.

This is, of course, meant to be neither a comprehensive list, nor an in-depth discussion of the possibilities I did mention. Such a discussion will require a separate article, which I hope to write. I merely intended to show that there is no reason to assume that attempts to tie the concept of discrimination more closely to the specific evils the Framers likely had in mind when they decided to limit state power over interstate commerce will tax judicial competence.

And what about the tax incentive offered in *Cuno*? Here we come full-circle. If one applies the two-step test I articulate above, I think that the Ohio tax incentive would pass muster. While the law certainly favored in-state activity over that occurring outside the state, it was not restricted to *Ohio* corporations agreeing to locate in Ohio. Nevertheless, let's assume that it would fail the first part of the test. The tax incentive does not seem like the kind of measure that would inaugurate a cycle of retaliation among states that would undermine political or economic unity. Subsidies ("bounties") were not

---

[109]Christopher R. Drahozal, Preserving the American Common Market: State and Local Governments in the United States Supreme Court, 7 S. Ct. Econ. Rev. 233, 253 (1999).

[110]*Id.* at 270.

[111]See Oklahoma Tax Commission v. Jefferson Lines, Inc., 514 U.S. 175, 185 (1995); see generally 1 Jerome Hellerstein & Walter Hellerstein, State Taxation ¶ 4.15[1][a] at 4-132 (3d ed. 1993 & 2006 Supp.).

unknown at the time of the Framing—states often sought to stimulate the production of goods with cash payments—but no one seemed to complain about them. Presumably if they worked, other states would emulate them, perhaps offering larger bounties to compete for producers to locate in their state.

This appears to be precisely what states, in fact, do with business tax incentives. While some might term this a "race to the bottom," because the tax revenues foregone in the quest for business tend to be made up out of spending for public goods like education, the harm, to the extent it exists, is visited on state citizens themselves. It may be bad public policy for states to engage in this kind of competition for business, but that does not make it unconstitutional. Nor do I think that kind of competition *is* unconstitutional, given the unlikelihood that it will bring states and local governments into conflict with one another.

Conclusion

To one hoping for a definitive resolution of the constitutional questions surrounding subsidies and tax incentives, *Cuno* was bound to have been a disappointment. By deciding the case on standing grounds, the Court clearly signaled a desire to leave the merits for another day. And, as I expressed elsewhere,[112] there are reasons to celebrate the Court's minimalist resolution of the case. I argued in the second half of this essay that *Cuno's* difficulty lies in the imprecision infecting the Court's use of the term "discrimination." This is unfortunate, since concluding that a state or local law is discriminatory vis-à-vis interstate commerce virtually decides whether the law stands or falls under the DCCD. Those of us interested in the DCCD should take the lull provided by *Cuno* to examine the concept more closely in light of the reasons the DCCD evolved in the first place. If, as I have argued, the DCCD was intended to prevent political disharmony caused by economic competition during the Confederation era, then the rules the Court has developed, which proceed on the assumption that an ideological affinity for free trade drove the Framers, should be rethought. Even if the specific reworkings of the antidiscrimination principle I have lightly sketched here are unconvincing, I do hope that they spark a conversation that informs future academic discussion and judicial application of the DCCD.

[112]See Denning, Cuno and the Court, *supra* note 4.

The Per Curiam Opinion of Steel: *Buckley v. Valeo* as Superprecedent? Clues from Wisconsin and Vermont

*Allison R. Hayward**

I. Introduction

> [W]e are talking about speech, money is speech, and speech is money, whether it be buying television or radio time or newspaper advertising, or even buying pencils and paper and microphones. That's the—that's certainly clear, isn't it?

Comments of Justice Potter Stewart during oral argument in *Buckley v. Valeo*, November 14, 1975.[1]

> I think it was Holmes who said, once you admit the necessity of drawing a line, you can always find something on one side or the other. It's quite different between $1,000 and $2,000 or 100 feet and 75 feet and advocacy with respect to an election and advocacy with respect to an issue. It's an entirely different quality of a distinction. . . .

Comments of Chief Justice Roberts during oral argument in *Wisconsin Right to Life v. FEC*, January 17, 2006.[2]

> I thought what [*Buckley*] said and what many of our other cases say, with regard to expenditures in particular, is that you're not talking about money here. You're talking about speech. So long as all that money is going to campaigning, you're talking about speech. And when you say you don't need any more speech than this, that's a very odd thing for a United States government to say. Enough speech. You don't

*Assistant Professor of Law, George Mason University School of Law. I would like to acknowledge generous summer 2006 support from George Mason University School of Law.

[1] Transcript of Oral Argument at 67, Buckley v. Valeo, 424 U.S. 1 (1976) (No. 75-436).

[2] Transcript of Oral Argument at 49, Wisconsin Right to Life v. FEC, 126 S. Ct. 1016 (2006) (No. 04-1581).

need any more than this. . . . We, the State, will tell you how
much campaigning is enough. That's extraordinary.
Comments of Justice Scalia during oral argument in *Randall v. Sorrell*, February 28, 2006.[3]

The rich tapestry of American campaign finance law continued to accumulate threads with the Court's decisions this term in *Randall v. Sorrell*[4] and *Wisconsin Right to Life v. FEC*.[5] Those two cases brought before the Court a variety of campaign finance regulations, from contribution limits and expenditure limits to restrictions on incorporated entities. Despite expressions of discomfort by many justices with the way modern campaign finance is regulated, the Court declined to rework *Buckley v. Valeo's*[6] holding to relieve that discomfort. Nor did it sanction a more lenient constitutional test to satisfy those other justices who would prefer to give legislatures and Congress leeway to regulate politics.

Since some scene-setting background may be useful for many readers, here is a brief, not comprehensive, but accurate description of what political activity can be regulated, and what activity is protected by the Constitution: For most individual donors,[7] contributions *to* candidates and other political committees may be limited, but not (as we learned this term in *Randall*, of which more later) if those limits are too extreme. For most individuals, making independent expenditures *about* candidates, parties, and politics may not be limited in amount, but the spender may be required to disclose his or her identity on any communications, and may also be required to file publicly available reports with the government. Groups of individuals may combine to engage in politics, but if they pass certain financial thresholds they too may be required to report.

---

[3] Transcript of Oral Argument at 50–52, Randall v. Sorrell, 126 S. Ct. 2479 (2006) (04-1528).

[4] 126 S. Ct. 2479 (2006).

[5] 126 S. Ct. 1016 (2006).

[6] 424 U.S. 1 (1976).

[7] Foreign nationals are barred by federal law from making contributions or expenditures at any level. Government contractors are also restricted at the federal level, as are certain governmental employees, and a multifaceted array of state and local laws may restrict donors who contract with the government, or are lobbyists, or are licensees of various types.

Contributions to groups can be limited, as may the contributions groups make to other recipients like candidates or political parties.

Not all spending activity is sufficiently "political" to be regulated. What any particular spender can do outside the federal restrictions, for example, varies with the status of the spender (a party? a federal officeholder or candidate? the press?), whether the activity is coordinated with a candidate or party, and what the spender wants to say (for example, expressly advocate the election or defeat of a clearly identified candidate?).

For corporations and labor organizations, the rules are a bit more straightforward, as least at the federal level, because contributions and expenditures are prohibited. And yet this seemingly flat ban on activity is porous for those prohibited sources in a position to take advantage of certain statutory allowances—i.e., groups that can establish a political action committee (PAC); have "members" or executives and shareholders to whom they can direct political communications without limit; are exempt nonprofits that take no corporate funding; are a press entity engaged in its "press function"; or find it useful to communicate while avoiding "express advocacy" or "electioneering communications."[8]

Much of the design of this tapestry of limits, prohibitions, and reporting requirements arises from the peculiarities of the Court's *Buckley v. Valeo* decision, which held constitutional certain aspects of the Federal Election Campaign Act[9] and rejected others. The Court in both *Wisconsin Right to Life* and *Randall* kept within the *Buckley* framework, and in *Randall* took great pains to explain why this was necessary. The Court had the opportunity to revisit *Buckley* but did not. Has *Buckley* now become unassailable—what some might call a superprecedent?

This essay argues that, even were one to grant the existence of a class of decisions that are "superprecedents," *Buckley v. Valeo* is a

---

[8] The open question to be answered in the remand of *Wisconsin Right to Life* is whether the Constitution requires exemption from the "electioneering communications" ban for an incorporated issue group to run grassroots lobbying advertisements that mention, among other officeholders, someone who is a candidate for reelection during the thirty days before that candidate's primary.

[9] Federal Election Campaign Act of 1971, 86 Stat. 3, as amended by the Federal Election Campaign Act Amendments of 1974, 88 Stat. 1263 (1974) (current version at 2 U.S.C. §§ 431 et seq.).

poor candidate for that classification. To set the stage, the essay first reviews the *Randall* and *Wisconsin* decisions from this term and how they use the Court's campaign finance precedents. It then discusses what might be meant by "superprecedent" and how a superprecedent might be identified. Then, looking at *Buckley*'s history, analysis, and application, it discusses whether *Buckley* should be classified as a superprecedent, and answers that question "no." Finally, it revisits what *Buckley*-type thinking has done to campaign finance regulation, and makes some preliminary suggestions for how, if the opportunity presents itself again, the Court might rework its analysis.

II. The *Wisconsin Right to Life v. FEC* and *Randall v. Sorrell* Decisions

The Court's consideration of both *Randall v. Sorrell* and *Wisconsin Right to Life v. FEC* in the same term presented the justices with a broad array of campaign finance issues, and the opportunity to rethink significant portions of the law. In *Wisconsin Right to Life*, a state nonprofit corporation made an as-applied challenge to those portions of the Bipartisan Campaign Reform Act (BCRA) designed to restrict the ability of corporations to engage in political activity.[10] The regulation of corporations in politics has been a part of federal law since the passage of the Federal Corrupt Practices Act in 1907, and many states enacted similar laws dating to that time.[11] These laws initially prohibited corporations from making campaign contributions, later extending the ban to labor unions and to campaign expenditures by either form of organization.[12]

In more recent times, corporate (and labor union) funding in federal politics has avoided legal prohibitions by, among other things, focusing on "issues" advertising rather than on contributions or expenditures. Perceiving those moves as exploiting a "loophole" in the law, Congress enacted an electioneering communications ban.[13]

---

[10] Bipartisan Campaign Reform Act of 2002 (BCRA) § 203, 116 Stat. 91, codified at 2 U.S.C. § 441b(b)(2).

[11] Robert Mutch, Before and After Bellotti: The Corporate Political Contributions Cases, 5 Election L.J. 293, 294–96 (2006).

[12] See history as set forth in United States v. International Union United Auto. Workers, 352 U.S. 567, 570–84 (1957), and in McConnell v. FEC, 540 U.S. 93, 115–18 (2003).

[13] McConnell, 540 U.S. at 127–32.

Under BCRA, broadcast, cable, or satellite advertising referring to a candidate for federal office, targeted to that candidate's district and running within thirty days of the candidate's primary or sixty days of the general election, may not be funded using general treasury funds of either corporations or labor unions.[14] That ban was designed to survive constitutional scrutiny by presenting the Court with a clear, unambiguous rule, backed up with research demonstrating its necessity as well as its tailoring.[15] The law's supporters hoped the Supreme Court would conclude that the electioneering communications law was constitutional under *Buckley v. Valeo*. It did so in 2003, in *McConnell v. FEC*.[16]

In *McConnell*, the Court also noted that Congress had provided a "backup" definition of "electioneering communication" in the event the primary definition was found unconstitutional. The Court then said: "We uphold all applications of the primary definition and accordingly have no occasion to discuss the backup definition."[17] The Federal Election Commission argued in *Wisconsin Right to Life* that that sentence demonstrated that the Court had foreclosed the possibility of making *any* "as applied" challenge to the electioneering communications ban. In January 2006, the Court rejected that ambitious reading. It sent the case back so that the district court could consider the merits of the Wisconsin group's claim.

As of this writing, the government has engaged in broad discovery of the group's activities far beyond the advertisements. If the constitutionality of regulating electioneering communications rests on the clarity and precision of the statute, then it seems inappropriate, and time consuming, to permit the government to compel the production of extraneous facts useful only in building some broader argument about the "purpose" of the group's advertising.[18] This would seem especially true where publicity can chill political activity, not to mention inflate the legal bills of the group resisting the encroachment. Nevertheless, those questions were being debated almost two

---

[14]2 U.S.C.§ 441b(c)(3)(A).

[15]540 U.S. at 193–95.

[16]*Id.* at 194.

[17]*Id.* at 190 n.73.

[18]Memorandum in Support of Plaintiff's Summary Judgment Motion at 41–47, Wisconsin Right to Life v. FEC, No. 04-1260 (D.D.C. June 23, 2006) (on file with author).

full years after the group initially asked for a preliminary injunction to insulate their advertisement. Whatever the fate of subsequent litigants, as-applied challenges to the electioneering ban have not yet offered a timely way to delineate the rights of grassroots lobbying groups.

In *Randall v. Sorrell*,[19] the Court reviewed Vermont's laws setting limits on contributions and expenditures, aspects of the regulatory regime under *Buckley v. Valeo* not considered in (or disrupted by) *McConnell*. Here, the legislature of Vermont had enacted Act 64 in 1997, containing contribution limits and spending limits as an explicit challenge to the holding in *Buckley v. Valeo* striking down expenditure limits as unconstitutional.[20] Under Act 64, expenditures were capped at $300,000 in a two-year cycle for candidates for governor, ranging down to $2,000 for state representatives in single-member districts in that period.[21] Incumbents seeking reelection were subjected to even lower limits; and political party expenditures benefiting six or fewer candidates were presumed to be coordinated with those candidates and were counted within those expenditure limits.[22] Act 64 also limited contributions to candidates for governor to $400 per two-year cycle, down to $200 for state representative.[23] Act 64 adjusted expenditure limits, but not contribution limits, for inflation.[24] All affiliated committees of a political party were aggregated and subject to a single contribution limit, and individuals were limited to contributing $2,000 to a party in a two-year cycle.[25] Here, too, political party expenditures benefiting six or fewer candidates would presumptively count against the contribution limit.[26]

The Court found both the expenditure limits and the contribution limits unconstitutional. Justice Breyer's plurality opinion, joined in

---

[19] 126 S. Ct. 2479 (2006).

[20] 17 Vt. Stat. Ann. §§ 2801 et seq. (2002); Andrew B. Kratenstein, Recent Legislation; Campaign Finance Reform, 36 Harv. J. on Legis. 219, 220 (1999).

[21] 126 S. Ct. at 2486.

[22] *Id.*

[23] *Id.*

[24] *Id.*

[25] *Id.*

[26] *Id.* at 2486–87. The act also contained disclosure requirements not at issue in this litigation and a limit on out-of-state contributions found unconstitutional below and not challenged in this case. *Id.* at 2487.

full only by Chief Justice Roberts, contained a ringing endorsement
for the continued vitality of the Court's holdings in *Buckley v. Valeo*.
It interpreted the *Randall* litigation as a direct challenge to *Buckley's*
conclusion that expenditure limits are unconstitutional, rejecting
that challenge. Precedents should be observed, wrote Justice Breyer,
especially where "the principle has become settled through iteration
and reiteration over a long period of time."[27] Moreover, the litigants
had failed to demonstrate that the times had changed sufficiently
to undermine the "critical factual assumptions" in *Buckley*.[28]

The opinion drew a contrast between the claimed necessity for
expenditure limits argued in *Randall* and the more extensive record
supporting BCRA in *McConnell*.[29] It also rejected Vermont's argument that its statute served a state interest in preserving officeholders' time, an interest the state contended was not considered in
Buckley and formed a basis for distinguishing *Buckley*. Breyer rejected
that argument, stating that the *Buckley* Court had that interest before
it, and in any event "the connection between high campaign expenditures and increased fundraising demands seems perfectly
obvious."[30] Justice Alito concurred with the result, but described
Vermont's invitation to revisit the *Buckley* precedent as "a backup
argument" and "an afterthought" it would be best not to address.[31]

III. The Notion of Superprecedents

The plurality opinion in *Randall* emphasized respect for precedent
and stare decisis. "Stare decisis . . . avoids the instability and unfair-
ness that accompany disruption of settled legal expectations. For
this reason, the rule of law demands that adhering to our prior case
law be the norm."[32] The Court's respect for precedent, however, is
selective: it is accorded to *Buckley v. Valeo* and its bifurcated analysis
of campaign finance restrictions, not to its more recent analysis in

[27] *Id*. at 2489.

[28] *Id*.

[29] *Id*. at 2490.

[30] *Id*.

[31] *Id*. at 2500 (Alito, J., concurring). Justice Alito did not acknowledge any awareness
that the Vermont statute had been designed specifically to challenge *Buckley*. See
Editorial, . . . And Go To High Court, Boston Herald, Sept. 29, 2005, at 36; Editorial,
Vermont the Model?, Burlington Free Press, Aug. 9, 2002, at 10A.

[32] 126 S. Ct. at 2489.

Nixon v. Shrink Missouri Government PAC.[33] In attempting to explain this fealty to *Buckley*, some have suggested that, like a few other select decisions, the Court is looking to *Buckley* as a "superprecedent."[34]

"Superprecedents" gained attention recently during the confirmation hearings for then-Judge John Roberts. Senator Arlen Specter asked Judge Roberts whether he agreed that certain decisions—*Roe v. Wade*, for instance—had become so deeply embedded in constitutional law that they necessarily survive reassessment.[35]

The expression "superprecedent" is not new, but its meaning has changed over the years. The initial use of the term appears to be in a 1976 article in which William Landes and Richard Posner speculate about the existence of such precedents. A superprecedent, as they saw it, was "so effective in defining the requirements of the law that it prevents legal disputes from arising in the first place or, if they do arise, induces them to be settled without litigation."[36] They do not provide examples, but one thinks of *Marbury v. Madison*,[37] the Legal Tender Cases,[38] or *Humphrey's Executor*[39] in this light.

Decisions like *Roe v. Wade* and *Buckley v. Valeo* do not seem to fit the Landes-Posner model. Both decisions are cited frequently. Neither has prevented legal disputes from arising nor encouraged them to be settled without litigation.[40] Yet both serve as "foundations for subsequent lines of judicial decisions,"[41] however much debate accompanies those applications. If *Buckley* is an ordinary case, it is due the respect of an ordinary case. What "superprecedence" seems

[33] 528 U.S. 377 (2000).

[34] See, e.g., Exchange on the Election Law Listserv (June 26, 2006), archived at http://majordomo.lls.edu/cgi-bin/lwgate/ELECTION-LAW_GL/archives/election-law_gl.archive.0606/date/ (on file with author).

[35] See Jeffrey Rosen, So Do You Believe in "Superprecedent"?, N.Y. Times (Week in Review), Oct. 30, 2005, § 4, 1.

[36] William M. Landes & Richard A. Posner, Legal Precedent, A Theoretical and Empirical Analysis, 19 J.L. & Econ. 249, 251 (1976).

[37] 5 U.S. (1 Cranch) 137 (1803).

[38] 79 U.S. (12 Wall.) 457 (1871).

[39] 295 U.S. 602 (1935).

[40] Westlaw lists 10,763 "citing references" for *Buckley v. Valeo*, 16,140 for *Roe v. Wade*, but 1425 for *Humphrey's Executor*.

[41] Michael J. Gerhardt, Super Precedent, 90 Minn. L Rev. 1204, 1205 (2006). Gerhardt divides "superprecedents" into three categories: "foundational institutional practices," "foundational doctrine," and "foundational decisions." *Id.* at 1207–20.

to connote is a precedent the Court must follow, whether or not it has otherwise sound reasons for moving away from it in the case at hand.[42]

The *Buckley* framework forms the basis for a line of campaign finance decisions because nothing like it had been articulated previously. As the *Randall* plurality noted, "Congress and state legislatures have used *Buckley* when drafting campaign finance laws. And, as we have said, this Court has followed *Buckley*, upholding and applying its reasoning in later cases. Overruling *Buckley* now would dramatically undermine this reliance on our settled precedent."[43]

Is "reliance" on a novel formulation sufficient to insulate a precedent like *Buckley* from reconsideration? If so, how much reliance? Settled expectations are important, but they cannot provide the final answer. Otherwise, what justification had the Court for reconsidering separate-but-equal accommodations for people of different races? That holding was articulated in 1896 in *Plessy v. Ferguson*[44] and was a standard upon which governments relied until *Brown v. Board of Education*[45] "disrupted" those expectations in 1954. *Plessy* had provided a rule—invidious and distasteful though it may have been—for twenty-eight years longer than *Buckley* has.[46]

Perhaps currency is relevant—that is, a watershed decision that makes a break from the past should be honored at least for a decent interval, but as times change its power could diminish. Looked at that way, reliance is not as relevant as timeliness. Even if that approach doesn't have much to say for it as a matter of principle, one might expect the Court to be more respectful of more recent precedent simply because the individual justices, in subsequent cases, would want to apply a precedent they themselves had crafted.

That has not happened with the campaign finance cases, however. Returning to *Randall*, the plurality is devoted to *Buckley* with respect to Vermont's expenditure limits; but it distinguished the more recent *Shrink Missouri* decision to conclude that Vermont's contribution

---

[42] See Randy E. Barnett, It's a Bird, It's a Plane, No It's Super Precedent: A Response to Farber and Gerhardt, 90 Minn. L. Rev. 1232, 1240–41 (2006).

[43] 126 S. Ct. 2479, 2490 (2006).

[44] 163 U.S. 537 (1896).

[45] 347 U.S. 483 (1954).

[46] Barnett, *supra* note 42, at 1243–44.

limits were constitutionally deficient. The contribution-limits aspect of the decision expresses loyalty yet again to *Buckley*, repeating the rule provided there that the Court could (hypothetically) find that contribution limits that "prevented candidates . . . from amassing the resources necessary for effective advocacy" would run afoul of the First Amendment.[47] "[W]e see no alternative to the exercise of independent judicial judgment as a statute reaches those outer limits."[48]

The plurality then musters two reasons why the Vermont statute is in danger of reaching those outer limits—the statute's limits apply per election cycle, not to separate primary and general elections; and they are very low (the lowest in the nation), less than one-sixth the level of the Missouri Auditor limit upheld in *Shrink Missouri*.[49] Examining the record, the plurality then found five factors indicating that the limits were not closely drawn to meet an anticorruption objective: the limits would hurt challengers in competitive races;[50] they were overly burdensome on political parties;[51] their low level was aggravated by including volunteer expenses;[52] they were not adjusted for inflation; and they lacked any special evidence supporting an extreme state regulation.[53] Throughout the discussion, Justice Breyer expresses dismay at the burdens the limits place on associational activity, especially among political parties and campaign volunteers.

While it is heartening that the Court took the burdens imposed by contribution limits seriously, that is not the approach taken in recent precedent, particularly the Court's 2000 decision in *Shrink Missouri*—which Breyer joined while providing a concurrence that resembles *Randall* in many respects.[54]

---

[47] 126 S. Ct at 2491 (quoting Buckley v. Valeo, 424 U.S. 1, 21 (1976)).

[48] *Id.* at 2492.

[49] *Id.* at 2493–94 (citing Nixon v. Shrink Missouri Government PAC, 528 U.S. 377 (2000)). Justice Souter, in dissent, disputed the plurality's reading of the record, arguing that once population-adjusted, the limits are not unusually low. *Id.* at 2512–13 (Souter, J., dissenting).

[50] *Id.* at 2495.

[51] *Id.* at 2496.

[52] *Id.* at 2498.

[53] *Id.* at 2499.

[54] Shrink Missouri , 528 U.S. at 399–405 (Breyer, J., concurring).

Justice Souter, who wrote the majority opinion in *Shrink Missouri*, takes issue in his *Randall* dissent with Breyer's willingness to second-guess the Vermont legislature, imploring the Court instead to follow *Shrink Missouri* and defer to legislative judgment. "To place Vermont's contribution limits beyond the constitutional pale, therefore, is to forget not only the facts of *Shrink* but also our self-admonition against second-guessing legislative judgments about the risk of corruption. . . ."[55] For Souter in *Randall*—as for the Court's majority in *Shrink*—the test is whether the limits are "depressed to the level of political inaudibility."[56] That test leaves plenty of space for legislatures to regulate. Souter's dissent in *Randall*, like Breyer's plurality opinion, also clothes itself in *Buckley*.[57]

If it makes sense to segregate certain decisions as superprecedents, *Buckley* seems to be a poor contender, at least for the conventional reasons. *Buckley* lives on because it provides a new rule in a contentious area, and nobody yet seems able to come up with something more agreeable. It also lives on by being sufficiently vague and general to support a range of results. If *Buckley* is to be considered a superprecedent, then perhaps the true test of a superprecedent is not whether there has been substantial reliance on it, or whether it is recent, or whether it settles a question for all time, but whether it can be cited in support of *conflicting conclusions*.[58] Perhaps that is why *Buckley* is a "superprecedent" and *Shrink Missouri*, apparently, is not.

IV. Making Sausage and Superprecedents

Buckley is a flexible source of authority partially because it is an odd and analytically incomplete opinion. One characteristic we might expect from a superprecedent is a synthesis of authorities into

---

[55] Randall, 126 S. Ct. at 2513 (Souter, J., dissenting).

[56] *Id.* at 2516. Justice Ginsburg joined Breyer's concurrence in *Shrink*, but joined Souter's dissent in *Randall*.

[57] *Id.* at 2511–12.

[58] See Richard L. Hasen, Buckley is Dead, Long Live Buckley: The New Campaign Finance Incoherence of McConnell v. Federal Election Commission, 153 U. Pa. L. Rev. 31 (2004). Hasen describes two periods of Supreme Court campaign finance jurisprudence since *Buckley*, an earlier period of skepticism, see *id.* at 36–41, and a later period of deference, *id.* at 42–46. Whatever their differences, both sets of decisions *claim* faithfulness to *Buckley v. Valeo*.

a coherent whole. That is, a superprecedent would bring together strands of legal analysis in a manner that rendered the resulting opinion clear and "obvious" in a way other decisions had been unable to do. *Buckley v. Valeo's* history and analysis show deficiencies precisely there.

When one reads the archived materials produced during the drafting of the per curiam *Buckley* decision,[59] one observes a team of justices struggling with the constitutionality of a complicated piece of legislation—and left seemingly rudderless by precedent. The justices also assigned the opinion among several chambers, which may have generated some of the per curiam opinion's incoherence.[60]

Justice Powell's bench memo for *Buckley* is preserved in his papers. It is a thoughtful piece focusing on justiciability.[61] On the merits of the claim, Powell and his clerk struggled with how to evaluate regulations of contributions and expenditures, whether different standards were justified, and whether the law was unconstitutionally vague. But there just wasn't much law in the discussion. Neither Marshall's nor Brennan's papers appear to contain a similar memorandum, perhaps because they were not preserved for the archives, or perhaps because they never had one written.

A week after conference, portions of the opinion were assigned to various justices.[62] After returning from winter holiday, memoranda circulated among the justices with edits and concerns about the

[59] The papers of Justice Thurgood Marshall are available in the Library of Congress Reading Room. Justice William Brennan's papers are also housed there and can be accessed by permission of the estate's designees. Justice Lewis Powell's papers are held at Washington and Lee University and are available to researchers by appointment. Justice Potter Stewart's papers are held by the Manuscripts and Archives Department at Yale University and will be open to research on the retirement of Justice Stevens, the last of the justices to serve with Justice Stewart.

[60] Richard L. Hasen, The Untold Drafting History of Buckley v. Valeo, 2 Election L J. 241, 245 (2003). See also Richard L. Hasen, Buckley is Dead, *supra* note 58, at 36.

[61] Memorandum from Chris Whitman to Justice Powell (September 18, 1975) (on file with author) [hereinafter Powell Bench Memorandum].

[62] Hasen, Drafting History, *supra* note 60, at 245. Chief Justice Burger took the introduction, Justice Powell the disclosure section, Justice Brennan public financing, Justice Stewart the contribution and expenditure limitations, and Justice Rehnquist the portion dealing with the composition of the Federal Election Commission. Justice Stewart circulated his draft permitting contribution limits but not expenditure limits on Christmas Eve, 1975. *Id.* at 245–46.

emerging opinion. Justice Brennan worried about the vagueness of the definition of "expenditure." He apparently succeeded in persuading Justice Stewart to add a footnote delineating the specific phrases that would be labeled "express advocacy"—the now derisively named "magic words" footnote in *Buckley*.[63] By mid-January the draft was essentially complete. The Court delivered its decision on January 30, 1976.[64]

Buckley v. Valeo was heard, discussed in conference, assigned, written in bits and pieces, revised, and delivered in about two and one-half months. Was that sufficient time for producing so momentous a decision? That is similar to the time taken between argument and decision in *McConnell v. FEC* (three months),[65] and *Massachusetts Citizens for Life v. FEC* (about two and one-half months).[66] But other, narrower decisions have taken longer. *FEC v. National Conservative PAC*, which found expenditure limits unconstitutional in the presidential public funding system, took almost four months, as did the second consideration of *FEC v. Colorado Republican*.[67] *Austin v. Michigan Chamber of Commerce* took five months, as did *First National*

---

[63] Hasen, Drafting History, *supra* note 60, at 247; see Buckley v. Valeo, 424 U.S. 1, 44 n.52 (1976). Justice Marshall also apparently succeeded in having Justice Stewart eliminate a passage explaining why the expenditure limits were overbroad. Hasen, Drafting History, *supra* note 60, at 248. Further evidence is found in an undated memorandum titled "Disclosure Provisions," from Justice Marshall's clerks to the justice, on file with the author. Similar to the Powell bench memorandum, see *supra* note 61, this memorandum between Justice Marshall and his clerks shows each grappling with how to treat the new law, but without citation to any precedent. One exception is that the clerks do not "think it fruitful to discuss whether the expenditure of money involved in this case is akin to the destruction of a draft card in *O'Brien*. We think the speech-conduct distinction is a tenuous one." See Memorandum from Law Clerks to Justice Marshall, Disclosure Provisions at 5 (undated) (on file with author).

[64] Hasen, Drafting History, *supra* note 60, at 248.

[65] 540 U.S. 93 (2003), argued September 8, 2003, decided December 10, 2003. One expects that, in time, the jointly authored Stevens/O'Connor opinion in *McConnell* will yield its own intriguing drafting history.

[66] 479 U.S. 238 (1986), argued October 7, 1986, decided December 15, 1986.

[67] FEC v. National Conservative Political Action Committee, 470 U.S. 480 (1985), argued November 28, 1984, decided March 18, 1985; FEC v. Colorado Republican Federal Campaign Committee, 533 U.S. 431 (2001), argued February 28, 2001, decided June 25, 2001.

Bank of Boston v. Bellotti.[68] *McIntyre v. Ohio Elections Commission,* which considered whether a state law could require a pamphleteer to disclose her identity on her handbills, took six months from argument to decision.[69] Another case often invoked when discussing "superprecedents," *Roe v. Wade,* took a little over three months, but was argued twice so that newly appointed Justices Powell and Rehnquist could participate.[70]

Randall v. Sorrell took four months from argument to decision.[71] While *Wisconsin Right to Life* was vacated and remanded a mere six days after oral argument, the core issue in that case is still being contested by the parties. We should expect that, if the Court agrees to hear the "grassroots lobbying" challenge to the electioneering communications prohibition, either in *Wisconsin Right to Life* or in a similar case, *Christian Civic League of Maine v. FEC,*[72] the final decision will take *more* than six days to draft. Perhaps *Buckley v. Valeo* would have improved from additional time spent on drafting, although it is not clear what clarifying principle the Court might have discovered even with additional time.

Without such a principle, the final opinion itself is inconsistent and analytically weak. *Buckley* comes out initially as very protective of money spent in politics, insisting that contributions and expenditures "operate in an area of the most fundamental First Amendment activities."[73] It rejects the position taken in the court of appeals[74] that campaign finance restrictions could be upheld under *United States v. O'Brien* on the theory that the expenditure of money is a non-speech element that could be restricted, like the burning of a draft card was restricted in *O'Brien.*[75]

---

[68] Austin v. Michigan State Chamber of Commerce, 494 U.S. 652 (1990), argued October 31, 1989, decided March 27, 1990; First National Bank of Boston v. Bellotti, 435 U.S. 765 (1978), argued November 9, 1977, decided April 26, 1978.

[69] 514 U.S. 334 (1995), argued October 12, 1994, decided April 19, 1995.

[70] 410 U.S. 113 (1973), argued December 13, 1971, reargued October 11, 1972, decided January 22, 1973.

[71] 126 S. Ct. 2479 (2006), argued February 28, 2006, decided June 26, 2006.

[72] No. 05-1447 (Notice of Appeal filed May 11, 2006).

[73] Buckley v. Valeo, 424 U.S. 1, 14 (1976).

[74] Buckley v. Valeo, 519 F.2d 821, 840–41 (D.C. Cir. 1975).

[75] Buckley, 424 U.S. at 15–16.

The Court applied strict scrutiny to provisions limiting expenditures, but applied an unclear lower level of scrutiny to provisions burdening contributions.[76] In subsequent decisions, the Court has been compelled to acknowledge *Buckley's* lack of a clear standard of review for contributions.[77] The Court also failed to explain how it could factor in the elements that apparently make contributions inferior—they are more attenuated, or symbolic, or contingent—without calculating into the equation "nonspeech" conduct and implicitly using the reasoning of the rejected *O'Brien* decision. Notably, where *Buckley* discusses the standard of review explicitly, there are not citations to precedent.[78] In the later discussion of contribution limits, the one precedent cited is *United States Civil Service Commission v. National Association of Letter Carriers*,[79] a distantly relevant authority in which the Court upheld Hatch Act limits on partisan political activity by federal employees.[80]

Buckley upheld the $1,000 contribution limit to candidates without much discussion about how that figure could be justified. All the *Buckley* Court said is that if "'some limit on contributions is necessary, a court has no scalpel to probe, whether, say, a $2,000 ceiling might not serve as well as $1,000.' Such distinctions in degree become significant only when they can be said to amount to differences in kind."[81] When might that be? Can limits be too low? How low is too low, and why? The two citations the Court provides,[82] which involve party primaries and whether state laws can restrict participation, are not illuminating.

Buckley also had to assess the scope of the campaign finance laws and address what kinds of groups would be regulated. It articulated a "major purpose" test without much elaboration.[83] The "major purpose" test protected from regulation groups that might make contri-

---

[76] *Id.* at 25.

[77] Nixon v. Shrink Missouri Gov't PAC, 528 U.S. 377, 386 (2000).

[78] *Id.* at 20–21.

[79] 413 U.S. 548 (1973).

[80] *Id.*, cited at 424 U.S. at 29.

[81] Buckley, 424 U.S. at 30 (quoting 519 F.2d at 842).

[82] Kusper v. Pontikes, 414 U.S. 51 (1973); Rosario v. Rockefeller, 410 U.S. 752 (1973).

[83] A federal appeals court had articulated a similar standard to narrow the scope of the 1971 campaign finance law, while explicitly avoiding ruling on that law's constitutionality. United States v. National Committee for Impeachment, 469 F.2d 1135, 1140–41 (2d Cir. 1972).

butions or expenditures in addition to other activities.[84] So long as they did not have the "major purpose" of electing a candidate, they would be free from the reporting requirements and limitations federal political committees faced. That standard has vexed courts, agency enforcement, and regulated entities for thirty years.[85]

Buckley's narrowing construction of expenditures to "express advocacy," and that standard's scope and legal effect, has been a topic of hot dispute from the outset. For many years it was interpreted by many to be of constitutional dimension, which would have been good news for groups like Wisconsin Right to Life.[86] In *McConnell*, however, the Court concluded that "express advocacy" was a statutory construction, not a constitutional standard, and in the process upheld the electioneering communications portion of BCRA.[87]

How to explain the dearth of authority for *Buckley's* scrutiny of limits, the "major purpose" concept, and the "express advocacy" content test for expenditures? Federal law had, after all, contained expenditure and contribution limits for much of the preceding century. One would think the Court would have synthesized the wisdom of the ages when articulating those rules.

But the lack of foundation wasn't a symptom of poor research. As historian Robert Mutch has noted in his history of corporate campaign finance regulation, "Congress has sought financial equality among candidates, or at least the lessening of inequality, since

---

[84] Buckley, 424 U.S. at 79 ("To fulfill the purposes of the Act they need only encompass organizations that are under the control of a candidate or the major purpose of which is the nomination or election of a candidate. Expenditures of candidates and of 'political committees' so construed can be assumed to fall within the core area sought to be addressed by Congress. They are, by definition, campaign related.")

[85] Allison R. Hayward & Bradley A. Smith, Don't Shoot the Messenger: The FEC, 527 Groups, and the Scope of Administrative Authority, 3 Election L.J. 82, 85–86, 99–100 (2005).

[86] See Brice Clagett & John R. Bolton, Buckley v. Valeo, Its Aftermath, and Its Prospects: The Constitutionality of Government Restraints on Political Campaign Financing, 20 Vand. L. Rev. 1327, 1333 (1976) (concluding that *Buckley* held that only communications containing express advocacy could constitutionally be regulated); Hearings on the Constitution and Campaign Reform Before the Senate Committee on Rules and Administration, 106th Cong. (2000) (statement of Joel Gora) ("The funding of any speech that falls short of such 'express advocacy' is wholly immune from regulation."); see also Citizens for Responsible Government State PAC v. Davidson, 236 F.3d 1174, 1187 (10th Cir. 2000) (citing cases).

[87] McConnell v. FEC, 540 U.S. 93, 190–91 (2003).

1911, and for sixty years thereafter philosophical objection to this goal was as rare as adherence to the limits intended to achieve it."[88] So, without enforcement (and injury), it was not necessary to contest the constitutionality of the various types of expenditure and contribution limits enacted over the years. Moreover, when cases prosecuted against unions under the same general ban came before the Court, the justices avoided deciding the constitutional issues.[89] *Buckley*, while grabbing bits and pieces from other kinds of cases, could not synthesize precedent into an intelligible principled decision, even if a majority could have aligned behind one, because there wasn't much to use.

Buckley also left some of the most intractable questions unanswered, and subsequent decisions have not always been helpful.[90] What is the constitutional standard of review protecting contributions to political committees and associations, as opposed to candidates? What justification could there be for a standard inferior to strict scrutiny, especially where the political committee does not make contributions to candidates or parties, so there is no possible claim of circumvention of those limits? What groups can constitutionally be restricted as political committees? What spending can be treated as a contribution or expenditure, anyway? If an *expenditure* is being regulated because the state has an interest in preventing "circumvention" of a *contribution* limit (or prohibition), should the law be subjected to strict scrutiny, or something less?

Instead of deeming *Buckley* a "superprecedent," we may want to adopt a different category—a "provisional precedent"—for decisions that articulate broad standards based on the judgment and intuition of justices possessing the same human limitations we all share.[91] Justices will face hard cases where a decision and a reasoned explanation will require saying something new. The Court should

[88] Robert E. Mutch, Campaigns, Congress, and Courts: The Making of Federal Campaign Finance Law 54 (1988).

[89] United States v. CIO, 335 U.S. 106, 110 (1948); United States v. International Union United Auto. Workers, 352 U.S. 567, 591–92 (1957).

[90] Clagett & Bolton, *supra* note 86, at 1360–65 (discussing outstanding issues).

[91] Rarely, the Court admits that a decision may only articulate a rule of constitutional law for a limited time. See Grutter v. Bollinger, 539 U.S. 306, 343 (2003) ("We expect that 25 years from now, the use of racial preferences will no longer be necessary to further the interest approved today.").

exercise restraint and humility in those contexts, to be sure, but it also needs to decide the case. Part of the exercise of restraint should come later by showing a willingness to review critically such decisions as the years unfold. Given its history, scope, and analytical gaps, *Buckley* is a good candidate for that classification.

V. Beyond *Buckley*

As campaign finance caselaw has grown over time, the Court has continued to apply the bifurcated *Buckley* analysis to limits and prohibitions at the federal and state levels. With each decision, the Court explains, distinguishes, and balances, adding complexity to the field. Real life continues to confound the *Buckley* standards by presenting situations where justices need to redefine scope or complicate the analysis with new exceptions.[92] The quotes from the justices at the outset of this essay are on the mark—campaign finance regulation is about "speech," but it is about a lot of other arcane detail, too.

With every opinion that attempts to square the First Amendment with the regulation of politics, the complexity only increases. To see how this works in practice, look at either the exemption for "qualified nonprofits" or the definition of "member." Because of Court precedents following *Buckley*, a corporate speaker might be entitled to a narrow court-crafted exemption for "qualified" nonprofits articulated in *Massachusetts Citizens for Life v. FEC.*[93] That test itself is complicated, and it is not self-evident that the characteristics the Court listed in the decision, such as whether a group took corporate funding, were meant to be illustrative and based on the facts in that case, or were to be a rule applied to all other groups. Corporations with members determine the bona fides of membership under another court-crafted rule, articulated in *National Right to Work v. FEC.*[94] There, the Court concluded that "member communications" could not be made to just anyone a group claimed as its member. After the Federal Election Commission promulgated a very narrow

[92] Daniel Hays Lowenstein, A Patternless Mosaic: Campaign Finance and the First Amendment After Austin, 21 Cap. U. L. Rev. 381 (1992) (describing inflexible campaign finance analysis and problems the Court has when new cases don't fit easily into existing categories).

[93] 479 U.S. 238, 263–64 (1986).

[94] 459 U.S. 197, 205–06 (1982).

"member" definition, the issue was relitigated, but has not reached the Supreme Court again.[95]

At least in those contexts there has been some subsequent clarification (if also complication) of the Court-created standards. With the "major purpose" test, however, subsequent litigation has done little to clarify how the test might determine political committee status, and the Court has not stepped in to help explain its rule.[96]

The spawn of *Buckley* will continue to multiply. In the corporate and labor context, incorporation or union status practically dictates a result that will be deferential to regulators. The one exception to that general rule is corporate-funded independent advertising about ballot measures.[97] *Wisconsin Right to Life* will test how broad the corporate "issues speech" protection reaches by offering the Court a sympathetic grassroots lobbying campaign that nevertheless identifies a federal candidate running for election. The Court will have to choose a category: Is the Wisconsin group more like a "corporation" whose candidate-specific electioneering can be barred by federal law? Or, regardless of its status, is the activity the kind of "issues speech" that deserves protection and an audience? *Buckley*, its express advocacy standard stripped of any constitutional dimension by *McConnell*, could probably be cited to support either result.

In the contribution limits context, the Court will be presented with new cases where contribution limits are low, or arguably burden the associational rights of parties or volunteers, but the other facts differ from those present in the unconstitutional Vermont law. If the Court follows *Randall*, it will apply something more deferential than strict scrutiny and will be obliged to mine the case record for reasons why the restriction is or is not permissible. The canny litigant will play upon the associational burden of the challenged law, since it would appear Justice Breyer is especially concerned about those kinds of restrictions. We will see whether the Court and enforcement agencies treat Breyer's factors in *Randall* as illustrative, or as a rule to be applied mechanically to other claims, much as the factors

[95] Chamber of Commerce v. FEC, 76 F.3d 1234 (D.C. Cir. 1996). The FEC did not petition the Court for a writ of certiorari.

[96] Hayward & Smith, *supra* note 85, at 99–100 (citing FEC v. Massachusetts Citizens for Life, Inc., 479 U.S. 238 (1986)); FEC v. GOPAC, 917 F. Supp. 851 (D.D.C. 1996); and Akins v. FEC, 101 F.3d 731 (D.C. Cir. 1997)).

[97] First National Bank of Boston v. Bellotti, 435 U.S. 765 (1978).

articulated in *Massachusetts Citizens for Life* and *National Right to Work* have been used.

If the Court were to reconsider its precedents in the campaign finance cases, it would be useful to politicians, donors, and the public for it to articulate a principled rule. One such rule is regularly expressed in dissent by Justices Thomas and Scalia. They would focus on the speech elements in campaign finance activity and apply strict scrutiny to contributions and expenditures, as well as corporate activity.[98] That would discard the confusing rationales used to differentiate between similar activities and would make other rules devoted to deciding whether something is a "contribution" or an "expenditure"—like the much contested question of coordination— less important. It would protect the political activity of incorporated and non-incorporated groups equally.

That choice would also unsettle campaign finance laws, to be sure. But as the system adjusted, we would be left with a simpler, clearer, and more consistent playbook. Strict scrutiny would also result in less burdensome regulations. It would seem that only relatively high contribution limits could be found constitutional. Yet at some high level, a regulator might persuasively argue that a contribution would so likely be corrupting that a specified, lower limit could withstand even strict scrutiny. Regulators might also persuasively argue that limits (or prohibitions) in certain more "corrupting" contexts (those involving government contractors and lobbyists spring to mind) are appropriate. It may not be the case that strict scrutiny would operate as a per se rule abolishing all limits or prohibitions.

Of the six justices joining the judgment in *Randall,* at least three and possibly five believe the bifurcated *Buckley* legacy is illegitimate.[99] With the right opportunity, the day when the Court applies strict scrutiny to both contributions and expenditures may not be far away. It seems less evident that a Court majority would embrace a rule protecting corporate, labor, and potentially other prohibited

---

[98] 126 S. Ct. 2479, 2502 (2006) (Thomas J., dissenting); FEC v. Beaumont, 539 U.S. 146, 164–65 (2003) (Thomas, J., dissenting).

[99] It is presumptuous to conclude that simply because Roberts and Alito joined the *Randall v. Sorrell* plurality and its embrace of *Buckley* in that situation, they would otherwise defer to limits on contributions. Cf. Editorial, Campaign Finance Bellwether: The Supreme Court's Vermont Ruling Seems Like a Defeat for Reformers. In the Long Run It May Not Be, Wash. Post, July 3, 2006, at A20.

sources who want to make contributions and expenditures in campaigns. Vestiges of Progressive-era thinking about the pernicious social effects of corporations, and the tit-for-tat logic that treats unions like corporations, will probably live on.

The Court's legacy with regard to these actors is to defer to legislative restrictions in the context of candidate campaigns and elections, now generously construed in *McConnell* to reach beyond express advocacy. Yet it isn't always clear whether that deference to regulation is because the spender is entitled to fewer speech rights, or belongs to a class that exhibits a higher propensity for corruption, or has an unfair advantage in a capitalist economy, or something else.[100] If the reason for deference is that the entity itself has reduced First Amendment rights, the Court should explain why, and account for how such a categorical approach is appropriate in all instances. The Court would have to explain why independent expenditures by "associations"—corporate, labor, political club, group blog, or knitting circle—could constitutionally be restricted or prohibited.

Another way to resolve the contradictions in the *Buckley* legacy would be for the Court to drift the other way. It might conclude that campaign finance activity, like ordinary economic activity, can be regulated under a very deferential standard of review. Although he describes it as a rejection of the "money is speech" formulation, Justice Stevens essentially argues that approach in his various dissents in campaign finance cases, and a deferential attitude runs throughout the Stevens/O'Connor-authored opinion in *McConnell*.[101] That would leave to the rough-and-tumble of politics—and the self-interested calculations of incumbent officeholders—the question of how strenuously legislation should regulate contributions, expenditures, independent spending, and the like, and what purposes legislatures can pursue when they write such laws. If lawmakers saw fit to pursue egalitarian or "democracy enhancing" goals with limits and prohibitions, they could do so openly. The public, for its part, could pray that those avowed goals weren't mere pretext.

---

[100] Mutch, Before and After Bellotti, *supra* note 11, at 323 ("More than eighty years after the First Amendment challenge was first raised, we still do not have definitive answers to the central questions: What exactly are corporations, and what is their role, if any, in a democracy?").

[101] Randall, 126 S. Ct. at 2508 (Stevens, J., dissenting); McConnell v. FEC, 540 U.S. 93, 137–38 (2003).

Buckley attempted to find a middle road between two alternatives—regulating campaign finance activity like ordinary economic activity, and protecting it as core First Amendment speech. Unfortunately, there is no coherent middle road. Neither *Buckley* nor the Court's more recent decisions can reason a path absent some ad hoc balancing based on the justices' individual experience, biases, and what may appear "perfectly obvious"[102] to them.

The Court's recent debate on these questions hasn't moved far beyond the debate the Court had in 1975. Justice Breyer might be Justice Brennan. Justice Thomas might be Chief Justice Burger. *Buckley*, like a bad treaty, settled nothing to anyone's satisfaction. Perhaps the time will come soon for the Court to seriously reconsider its effort. Professor Laurence Tribe, in explaining why a new version of his famous treatise on constitutional law would not be forthcoming, seems to think that we are entering an era of change in many constitutional doctrines.[103] If *Buckley* is truly a "provisional precedent," perhaps its time has come and gone as well.

---

[102] Randall, 126 S. Ct. at 2490.

[103] Laurence H. Tribe, The Treatise Power, 8 Green Bag 2d 291, 297 (2005) ("There is an emerging realization that the very working materials of American constitutional law may be in the process of changing.").

Unanimously Wrong

Dale Carpenter*

The Supreme Court was unanimously wrong in *Rumsfeld v. FAIR*.[1] Though rare, it is not the first time the Court has been unanimously wrong. Its most notorious such decisions have come, like *FAIR*, in cases where the Court conspicuously failed even to appreciate the importance of the constitutional freedoms under attack from legislative majorities.[2] In these cases, the Court's very rhetoric exposed its myopic vision in ways that now seem embarrassing. Does *FAIR*, so obviously correct to so many people right now, await the same ignominy decades away?

FAIR was wrong in tone, a dismissive *vox populi*, adopted by a Court seeming to reflect and reinforce popular reactions to the case. But most importantly, *FAIR* was wrong in rationale, which is worse than getting a single result wrong. Not very much of practical significance for the whole country ordinarily hinges on the result in a single case settling the claim of a single litigant or group of litigants.

*Julius E. Davis Professor of Law, University of Minnesota Law School. I thank Jordan Reilly for research assistance.

[1]126 S. Ct. 1297 (2006).

[2]For examples of decisions that were unanimous but have since been widely criticized either for their results or their rationales, see Bradwell v. State, 83 U.S. (16 Wall.) 130 (1873) (unanimously upholding state law excluding women from the practice of law); Minor v. Happersett, 88 U.S. (21 Wall.) 162 (1874) (unanimously upholding state law denying women the right to vote); Schenck v. United States, 249 U.S. 47 (1919) (unanimously upholding convictions for anti-war speech under the Espionage Act of 1917); Debs v. United States, 249 U.S. 211 (1919) (unanimously upholding conviction of Eugene Debs for political-convention speech praising draft resisters); Hirabayashi v. United States, 320 U.S. 81 (1943) (unanimously upholding conviction for violating curfew order applicable only to persons of Japanese ancestry). I emphasize that not all of these decisions were necessarily wrong in result. See, for example, Jim Chen's excellent discussion of why *Minor v. Happersett* was correctly decided on his blog at *Jurisdynamics*, Totally Mistaken, Never in Doubt, at http: jurisdynamics.blogspot.com/2006/07/totally-mistaken-never-in-doubt.html (last visited July 19, 2006).

Whether law schools may exclude military recruiters who, following federal "Don't Ask, Don't Tell" (DADT) policy, discriminate against gay law students does not matter that much to most people. The decision may even have the paradoxical effect of advancing the antidiscrimination cause by forcing conscientious law schools to make plain their opposition to anti-gay discrimination in the military; a decision in the law schools' favor would have allowed them to relax on the issue.[3]

But the rationale justifying the result in a single case can have significant consequences because it can affect decisions in the future. In *FAIR*, the Supreme Court botched several doctrines in its ordinarily libertarian free-speech jurisprudence, including the foundational question of what counts as protected speech, and it botched them all in a way that could constrict liberty. Whether *FAIR* has harmful long-term effects for speech awaits future decisions, but Chief Justice John Roberts' first major constitutional decision gives us some reason to worry.

The fact of unanimity—it was 8-0 and likely would have been 9-0 if Justice Samuel Alito had participated[4]—does not make the decision less wrong. If it is indeed wrong, unanimity only makes its wrongness more egregious, putting in very stark relief the failure of even a single justice on the current Court to overcome the passions of the moment in order to safeguard constitutional freedoms.[5] Instead of defending liberty, the Court's conservatives apparently saw a chance to defend military honor against law-school elites. Its liberals apparently saw a chance to defend government power while proving they can be cold-eyed realists on matters of national security.

---

[3]Amy Kapczynski, Queer Brinkmanship: Citizenship and the Solomon Wars, 112 Yale L.J. 673, 674 (2002) ("The military also may have done universities a favor by returning them to their heritage of dissent: Forced to relinquish the accommodations upon which they relied to manage the conflict, universities and law schools now have little choice but simply to confront it.").

[4]Justice Alito was not confirmed until after oral argument in *FAIR*.

[5]For those who approve the decision, unanimity makes the result more obviously right. "The decision was so obviously right," observed Professor Tom McCoy, "that it had to be unanimous unless some member of the Court was incapable of reasoning through the well-established doctrines that controlled the case." David L. Hudson, Jr., Law Schools Told to Allow Military Recruiters, 5 ABA Journal Report 10 (Mar. 10, 2006). Whether *FAIR* was really the product of "well-established doctrines," or an amendment to them, is the subject of this article.

Chief Justice Roberts prides himself on striving for "unanimity or near unanimity" in order to "promote clarity and guidance" to the legal community and to decide cases "on the narrowest possible ground."[6] *FAIR* seems clear in at least one sense: Congress clearly may force schools to admit military recruiters if it chooses to do so. Whether deciding the case on this basis was the "narrowest possible ground" for decision is a different matter. Neither clarity nor narrowness, furthermore, can salvage error.

FAIR was not necessarily wrong in its ultimate result, upholding the constitutionality of the Solomon Amendment.[7] Perhaps, for example, the government really could show a close connection between recruitment needs and a policy of withdrawing federal funds from entire universities whose law schools defend their anti-discrimination principles by excluding military recruiters. That is a possibility I do not explore here, as the courts in this litigation did not explore it, and Congress has never held a single hearing regarding the alleged recruitment need for the Solomon Amendment.

Let me get one other preliminary issue out of the way. My grandfather served in the Pacific in World War II and lived with the wounds of that conflict for the rest of his life. My father served in the U.S. Army in Germany at the height of Cold War tensions over the building of the Berlin Wall. I have nothing but respect for this country's armed forces and especially for those who serve. Much as I disagree with DADT as a matter of policy, and much as I abhor its needless cruelty to gay Americans who want to serve their country, I probably could not have voted as a law school faculty member to bar military recruiters from our premises. Nevertheless, I support law schools' efforts to protest and call attention to DADT, and I believe that law schools should have the option to bar recruiters if they choose to do so. They should have this option free of either direct federal coercion enforced by criminal penalty or indirect coercion enforced by loss of almost all federal funding.

In Part I, I briefly describe some relevant background about the Solomon Amendment and the litigation challenging it. The Solomon Amendment began modestly, involving only Defense Department

---

[6]James Taranto, Getting to Yes, Wall St. J., July 1, 2006, at A11 (quoting Chief Justice Roberts).

[7]10 U.S.C. § 983 (2005).

219

funds, but quickly metastasized. In Part II, I discuss the unconstitutional-conditions doctrine, an important issue raised by the Solomon Amendment and likely to figure prominently in the future of liberty and federalism but one that is left mostly untouched by *FAIR*. In Part III, I analyze the Court's treatment of free speech and the freedom of association. On free speech, the Court unsuccessfully distinguished its compelled-speech cases and seemingly narrowed the reach of its third-party speech cases. It also minted a test for expressive conduct based on "inherent expressiveness" that is either completely unworkable or extremely narrow. On the freedom of association, the Court narrowed its jurisprudence largely to concerns about membership and seemingly dropped any deference to an association's own judgment about whether compliance with state regulation would significantly impair its message. Both of these holdings are a break with the Court's precedents. There was an abundance of commentary on the Solomon Amendment and its constitutionality before *FAIR*.[8] It is not my purpose to rehash all of the constitutional arguments here. Instead, my focus is on the decision itself and its possible implications.

I. Background

A. *The Solomon Amendment*

In the 1970s, educational institutions began adding "sexual orientation" to policies prohibiting various forms of discrimination. As

[8]See, e.g., Diane H. Mazur, A Blueprint for Law School Engagement With the Military, 1 J. Nat'l Security L. & Pol'y 473 (2005) (noting the symbolic nature of the arguments for the law and criticizing judicial deference to military judgment); John C. Eastman, Is the Solomon Amendment "F.A.I.R."? Some Thoughts on Congress's Power to Impose this Condition on Federal Spending, 50 Vill. L. Rev. 1171 (2005) (arguing that the Solomon Amendment is within congressional power); Gerald Walpin, The Solomon Amendment is Constitutional and Does Not Violate Academic Freedom, 2 Seton Hall Circuit Rev. 1 (2005) (arguing that the law serves the expressive purpose of getting the military's message to law students); Abigail K. Holland, The High Price of Equality: The Effect of the Solomon Amendment on Law Schools' First Amendment Rights, 38 Suffolk U. L. Rev. 855 (2005) (arguing that the Solomon Amendment is unconstitutional under the First Amendment); Andrew P. Morriss, The Market for Legal Education & Freedom of Association: Why the "Solomon Amendment" is Constitutional and Law Schools Are Not Expressive Associations, 14 Wm. & Mary Bill Rts. J. 415 (2005) (arguing that law schools operate primarily as economic cartels, not as expressive associations); Clay Calvert & Robert D. Richards, Challenging the Wisdom of Solomon: The First Amendment and Military Recruitment

part of this expansion of antidiscrimination policies, law schools required prospective employers recruiting students in their facilities to agree not to discriminate on the basis of several criteria, including sexual orientation. They did this both on their own initiative and in compliance with the guidelines of the American Association of Law Schools. The new on-campus recruitment policies meant excluding recruiters from the military, which by longstanding policy barred homosexual servicemembers.

In response to these developments, in 1994 Congress passed the Solomon Amendment, named after its primary sponsor, U.S. Representative Gerald Solomon (R-NY). The legislation arose during a period of heightened attention to the role of gays in the military prompted by President Bill Clinton's proposal to let openly gay people serve. (Congress ultimately codified the ban on gays in the military under DADT that same year.) Congress held no hearings on the need for the Solomon Amendment and the Department of Defense initially opposed it as "unnecessary."[9]

The Solomon Amendment originally mandated only that "[n]o funds available to the Department of Defense may be provided by grant or contract to any institution of higher education that has a policy of denying, or which effectively prevents, the Secretary of Defense from obtaining for military recruiting purposes ... entry to campuses or access to students on campuses."[10]

From that narrow beginning, the Solomon Amendment metastasized. In subsequent years, the funding condition was expanded to include funds available to universities from the Departments of Homeland Security, Health and Human Services, Labor, Education, and Transportation, as well as the National Security Agency and the Central Intelligence Agency. Congress also clarified that the condition applied to an entire university even if only a "subelement" within the university (e.g., a university's law school) denied access

on Campus, 13 Wm. & Mary Bill Rts. J. 205 (2004) (arguing that the speech interests of the law schools outweigh those of the military); Francisco Valdes, Solomon's Shames: Law as Might and Inequality, 23 T. Marshall L. Rev. 351 (1998) (suggesting strategies for law schools to ameliorate the presence of military recruiters before the "equal access" requirement was added to the law).

[9]140 Cong. Rec. 11,440 (1994) (statement of Rep. Underwood).

[10]National Defense Authorization Act for Fiscal Year 1995, Pub. L. No. 103-337, § 558, 108 Stat. 2663, 2776 (1994).

to military recruiters. Finally, in 2004, Congress further required that, under the funding condition, military recruiters must be given access to the institution "that is at least equal in quality and scope to the access to campuses and to students that is provided to any other employer."[11] At no point during this metastasizing process did Congress or anyone else show an actual recruitment need for the law.

As it now stands, the Solomon Amendment puts at risk tens of billions of dollars in funding annually to universities.[12] The money goes to many causes, like important scientific and medical research. Under the current version of the law, even law schools that do not themselves receive federal funds from any of the agencies and departments covered by the Solomon Amendment have reluctantly agreed to allow military recruiters in their facilities.

B. The Litigation

In September 2003, a group of law schools and faculties organized as the Forum for Academic and Institutional Rights (FAIR) brought suit in a New Jersey federal district court against Secretary of Defense Donald Rumsfeld and other department heads whose departmental funding to universities is subject to the recruitment condition. FAIR argued that the Solomon Amendment violated their First Amendment rights. The district court denied FAIR's request for a preliminary injunction against enforcement.

On appeal, a divided panel of the Third Circuit held that FAIR was likely to prevail on its First Amendment claims, and directed the district court to enjoin enforcement of the Solomon Amendment. However, on January 20, 2005, the Third Circuit granted the government's request to stay its decision pending appeal to the Supreme Court. The Supreme Court granted the government's petition for

---

[11]Ronald W. Reagan National Defense Authorization Act for Fiscal Year 2005, Pub. L. No. 108-375, § 552, 118 Stat. 1811, 1911 (2004).

[12]In fiscal year 2003, the amount of federal funding to universities covered by the Solomon Amendment was almost $35 billion. See Brief for Amicus Curiae the American Association of University Professors in Support of Respondents at 23, Rumsfeld v. FAIR, 126 S. Ct. 1297 (2006) (No. 04-1152) (hereinafter AAUP Amicus Brief) (calculating amount based on total federal funding for universities ($57.5 billion) minus non-covered student aid ($23 billion)). In 2004, the law jeopardized $351 million in research funding for the University of Minnesota alone.

writ of certiorari on May 2, 2005, and heard oral argument in December 2005.

C. The Arguments

Before the Supreme Court, FAIR argued that an educational institution's decision to bar military recruiters is constitutionally protected, both as an expression of moral and professional disapproval of anti-gay discrimination and as an exercise of associational freedom. These constitutional interests are especially important in a setting, like a university, where academic freedom is paramount.

Central to the arguments was the Court's 2000 decision in *Boy Scouts of America v. Dale*,[13] in which the Court held that the Boy Scouts had an associational right to exclude an openly gay scoutmaster despite a state law barring discrimination against gays.

The government distinguished *Dale* by noting that the Solomon Amendment does not affect the composition of the schools' membership; the recruiters' presence is only temporary and episodic. Further, the government argued that unlike *Dale*, the case did not involve an attempt by the state to convey any message about service by gays in the military. Everyone understands that recruiters speak only for their employers and not for the schools in which they recruit, argued the government.[14]

FAIR responded that the freedom of association recognized in *Dale* was indeed implicated. The Solomon Amendment, FAIR claimed, violates the schools' freedom of association by infringing their "right to choose for themselves which causes to assist or resist." The freedom of association is not limited to the ability to control membership in an organization, FAIR argued, but extends to the full range of associational activities by which a group aids or refuses to aid a cause.[15]

The parties also disagreed over whether the Solomon Amendment unconstitutionally compelled speech by the universities. The government argued that it did not, since it simply does not force schools to send the message that they agree with the military's exclusion of

[13]530 U.S. 640 (2000).

[14]Brief for Petitioners at 12, Rumsfeld v. FAIR, 126 S. Ct. 1297 (2006) (No. 04-1152) (hereinafter Petitioners' Brief).

[15]Brief for the Respondents at 30–35, Rumsfeld v. FAIR, 126 S. Ct. 1297 (2006) (No. 04-1152) (hereinafter "Respondents' Brief").

gays.[16] FAIR countered that the Solomon Amendment does compel speech. It requires the schools to serve military recruiters affirmatively through quintessential "speech" activities, like distributing, posting, and printing literature announcing the presence of the recruiters; introducing students to the government; and sponsoring private fora for the exchange of information (the recruiting interview sessions themselves). This, argued FAIR, requires a school "to disseminate, carry, or host a message against its will."[17]

The parties also disagreed over whether the law schools' prohibition on military recruiters could be considered "speech." The government argued that the schools' action is not a form of "expressive conduct" protected under the intermediate scrutiny standard of *United States v. O'Brien*.[18] Refusing to give recruiters equal access to facilities, argued the government, is not inherently expressive. It is merely conduct, and as such does not enjoy any First Amendment speech protection.

FAIR responded that, on the contrary, the schools' refusal to allow employers who discriminate to recruit is part of their overall message that such discrimination is immoral and unprofessional. Barring recruiters who discriminate is a way to "punctuate" a school's message by refusing to assist discrimination, FAIR asserted.[19]

Finally, the parties disagreed at length over whether the Solomon Amendment violates the "unconstitutional conditions" doctrine, under which the government generally may not condition the receipt of a government benefit on the relinquishment of a constitutional right. FAIR emphasized that the Solomon Amendment places a "penalty" on the exercise of First Amendment rights and thus violates the unconstitutional-conditions doctrine. This is not a case, noted FAIR, where the government has simply required that certain funds be used only for the purpose for which they are provided (e.g., the government may require that education funds be spent on education). Instead, the Solomon Amendment attempts a sweeping denial of almost all federal assistance to an entire educational institution merely because one part of it—a part that might itself receive

---

[16]See Petitioners' Brief, *supra* note 14, at 20–22.

[17]See Respondents' Brief, *supra* note 15, at 21–28.

[18]391 U.S. 367 (1968).

[19]See Respondents' Brief, *supra* note 15, at 28–30.

no federal money—refuses to allow the military to recruit.[20] The government maintained that since it would be free to compel the schools to admit military recruiters, and that such a requirement would not itself violate the First Amendment, it could take the less drastic step of simply encouraging compliance through a funding condition.[21]

II. Unconstitutional Conditions After *FAIR*

Before the decision in *FAIR* was announced, constitutional law professors might have been a bit anxious. Law school faculties wanting to enforce their antidiscrimination policies by barring military recruiters had been prominently and widely denounced as out-of-touch and unpatriotic,[22] practically mocking the soldiers who guard them while they sleep.[23] A decision against the law schools might be taken as partial vindication of this view. But for myself, I was not anxious because the Court might uphold the law. It always seemed likely that the Court would do so in a time of high national stress and real danger. Even if the Supreme Court ruled unanimously against the law schools challenging the law, that was no cause for anxiety by itself.

No, the fear was that the Supreme Court might actually decide the hardest and most interesting question in the litigation: whether the Solomon Amendment violated the notoriously under-theorized unconstitutional conditions doctrine. The most succinct formulation of the doctrine holds that the "government may not grant a benefit on the condition that the beneficiary surrender a constitutional right,

---

[20]*Id.* at 37–38.

[21]See Petitioners' Brief, *supra* note 14, at 40–43.

[22]"While Americans in uniform are engaged around the world in the global war on terror, the idea that academic elites would bar military recruiters from campus runs against the very ethos of patriotism." Statement of House Armed Services Committee Chairman Duncan Hunter, R-Cal., on U.S. Supreme Court Ruling Allowing Military Recruiters Access to College Campuses, available at http://www. house.gov/hasc/pressreleases/13-6-06HunterStatementMilitaryRecruiters.pdf (last visited Aug. 29, 2006).

[23]The phrase comes from Rudyard Kipling, via George Orwell: "It would be difficult to hit off the one-eyed pacifism of the English in fewer words than in the phrase, 'making mock of uniforms that guard you while you sleep.'" George Orwell, The Orwell Reader 274 (Harcourt Brace 1984).

even if the government may withhold that benefit altogether."[24] This simple statement of the doctrine masks huge complexities that have vexed our brightest constitutional theorists.[25]

Much of the popular reaction to *Rumsfeld v. FAIR* prior to the decision suggested that this part of the case was easy: "If you don't want to let military recruiters on your campus, don't take the money. If you want the money, let the military recruit. There can be no constitutional problem putting schools to that choice." But this part of the case was never as easy as that reaction suggested. I will not, here, offer a theory of unconstitutional conditions. Instead, I will point out some of the difficulties in the doctrine, discuss the Court's brief treatment of it, and point to some problems it presents for constitutional law in the future.

A. Some Problems in the Unconstitutional Conditions Doctrine

In 1958, the Court held in *Speiser v. Randall* that a state could not require veterans otherwise eligible for property tax exemptions to swear that they did not advocate forcible overthrow of the government.[26] Threatening the veterans with this economic loss—to which they had no independent constitutional entitlement—amounted to an unconstitutional "penalty" on the exercise of their First Amendment right not to swear loyalty to the government. The unconstitutional conditions doctrine was born. A tangle of other precedents ensued, with no clear analytical framework emerging.[27]

In this unstable environment, it is not difficult to imagine cases that test the constitutional line. If the government may deny an

[24]Kathleen M. Sullivan, Unconstitutional Conditions, 102 Harv. L. Rev. 1415, 1415 (1989).

[25]See, e.g., Richard A. Epstein, The Supreme Court 1987 Term: Unconstitutional Conditions, State Power, and the Limits of Consent, 102 Harv. L. Rev. 5 (1988); Sullivan, *supra* note 24; David Cole, Beyond Unconstitutional Conditions: Charting Spheres of Neutrality in Government-Funded Speech, 67 N.Y.U. L. Rev. 675 (1992).

[26]Speiser v. Randall, 357 U.S. 513, 529 (1958).

[27]Regan v. Taxation with Representation of Wash., 461 U.S. 540 (1983) (Congress may deny tax deductions for contributions to a lobbying organization); FCC v. League of Women Voters of Cal., 468 U.S. 364 (1984) (Congress may not cut off funding to broadcasting station that engages in on-air editorializing); Rust v. Sullivan, 500 U.S. 173 (1991) (Congress may require federal health funding recipients not to counsel patients about abortion); Legal Servs. Corp. v. Velazquez, 531 U.S. 533 (2001) (Congress may not deny funding to lawyers in federal legal aid program who counsel clients to challenge existing welfare laws).

entire university all funding (e.g., cancer research funding) because one part of the university exercises a constitutional right to bar military recruiters, could it similarly leverage its economic power to require the university to allow a military officer on campus to deliver the government's message about the need for high defense spending? Could it threaten to withdraw all university funding unless the university agreed to forgo its right to "ameliorate" the recruiters' presence on campus (e.g., by posting written notices outside the interview room indicating the school's disagreement with the military's exclusion of gays)?

On the one hand, under the Court's precedents the federal government could not decide to distribute food stamps (an elective government benefit) only to people who agree not to criticize the war in Iraq (which they have a constitutional right to do). On the other hand, the government can decide to give money to people to send their children to public schools (an elective government benefit) but not to private schools (which they have a constitutional right to send their children to). Surely this is not unconstitutionally conditioning funds. How would the Court draw the line in a way that did not seem result-oriented and ad hoc?

The problems get thornier the more one thinks about them. If the government cannot condition funding to universities to encourage them to admit military recruiters, as FAIR argued, could it continue to condition funding on a school's agreement not to discriminate against students or employees on the basis of race or sex (as it now does through civil rights laws)? Or is there some way to distinguish the conditional funding embedded in civil rights law from the Solomon Amendment?

This latter issue worried a great many liberal legal commentators who ordinarily oppose state-sponsored anti-gay discrimination, like DADT and the Solomon Amendment, but were afraid that a ruling in FAIR's favor on the unconstitutional conditions issue might endanger civil rights laws involving funding conditions.[28] Amicus

---

[28]See, e.g., Tobias Barrington Wolff, "Don't Ask, Don't Tell" Harms the Constitution, but So Does This Cure, L.A. Times, May 15, 2005, at M5 (decrying DADT as "irrational" and the Solomon Amendment as "outrageous" but suggesting the case "could undermine decades of progressive legislation" protecting women and minorities from discrimination).

briefs on FAIR's side labored to distinguish the Solomon Amendment from antidiscrimination laws like Titles VI and IX.[29] My purpose here is not to suggest a resolution of these difficulties, but to call attention to them. Their very complexity may lead the Court to avoid the doctrine in ways inhospitable to underlying liberty claims, as I suggest below.

B. The Step Not Taken in FAIR

Every unconstitutional-conditions claim, where the government conditions economic benefit x on forgoing or engaging in activity y, involves two steps.

> STEP 1: The litigant must establish that the government could not directly require (e.g., through a criminal penalty) the litigant to forgo or engage in activity y.

> STEP 2: The litigant must establish that it is unconstitutional to condition the availability of economic benefit x on the litigant's forgoing or engaging in activity y.

The unconstitutional conditions litigant must win on both steps in order to prevail; the government need only win on one.

In *Rumsfeld v. FAIR*, activity y was prohibiting the military to recruit on campus. Economic benefit x was a vast array of government funds and aid otherwise available to every part of a university. Because FAIR lost on step one of the analysis—the government could directly require the schools to allow the military to recruit on campus—the Court did not address step two.

That does not quite mean that the Court said absolutely nothing about the unconstitutional conditions issue. After noting Congress' broad authority on matters of military recruiting, the Court laid out what it evidently regarded as the relevant unconstitutional conditions precedents:

> Congress' power to regulate military recruiting under the Solomon Amendment is arguably greater because universities are free to decline the federal funds. In *Grove City College*

---

[29]See, e.g., AAUP Amicus Brief, *supra* note 12, at 19, 29–30 (arguing that, unlike the Solomon Amendment, the antidiscrimination conditions of Titles VI and IX are not imposed for the purpose of suppressing expression and academic freedom; that there is a nexus between the condition and the funding; and that there is a compelling interest in antidiscrimination that is actually served by the Civil Rights Act).

v. Bell, 465 U.S. 555, 575–76 (1984), we rejected a private college's claim that conditioning federal funds on its compliance with Title IX of the Education Amendments of 1972 violated the First Amendment. We thought this argument "warrant[ed] only brief consideration" because "Congress is free to attach reasonable and unambiguous conditions to federal financial assistance that educational institutions are not obligated to accept." Id., at 575. We concluded that no First Amendment violation had occurred—without reviewing the substance of the First Amendment claims—because Grove City could decline the Government's funds. Id., at 575–576.

Other decisions, however, recognize a limit on Congress' ability to place conditions on the receipt of funds. We recently held that "'the government may not deny a benefit to a person on a basis that infringes his constitutionally protected . . . freedom of speech even if he has no entitlement to that benefit.'" United States v. Am. Library Ass'n, 539 U.S. 194, 210 (2003) (quoting Bd. of County Comm'rs, Wabaunsee County v. Umbehr, 518 U.S. 668, 674 (1996)).[30]

This is a revealing choice of background precedents. One, *Grove City*, is a case in which the Court did not mention the unconstitutional conditions doctrine and subjected the funding condition to a mere "reasonableness" requirement. The other, *American Library Association*, is a case in which the Court rejected a claim that it was unconstitutional for Congress to require public libraries receiving federal funds to install anti-pornography filters on computers with Internet access. It is an inauspicious discussion for those concerned about Congress' use of its economic power to curtail the exercise of rights.

However, this part of the Court's opinion at least acknowledges the possibility of a constitutional problem when Congress conditions funds, something which much of the popular commentary on the case and even a few law professors doubted pre-*FAIR*. It seems there *is* an unconstitutional conditions doctrine, after all.

The very next sentence in the opinion offers a tantalizing hint at what might have been: "Under this principle, known as the unconstitutional conditions doctrine, the Solomon Amendment would be unconstitutional if Congress could not directly require universities

---

[30]Rumsfeld v. FAIR, 126 S. Ct. 1297, 1306–07 (2006).

to provide military recruiters equal access to their students."[31] Is the Court saying that FAIR would have won had it been able to establish an underlying constitutional right to exclude military recruiters? This seems the implication of the sentence, though we are not told how the Court would have reasoned to that result in the teeth of decisions like *Grove City*.

What the Court almost gives in one sentence, however, it takes away in the very next: "This case does not require us to determine when a condition placed on university funding goes beyond the 'reasonable' choice offered in *Grove City* and becomes an unconstitutional condition."[32] Thus, while acknowledging the existence of the unconstitutional conditions beast, the Court extracts its teeth. Where Congress is conditioning funds to achieve what it could not mandate, the Constitution requires only that the condition be "reasonable." We all know what that means.

C. A Future for Unconstitutional Conditions

This entire part of the Court's opinion, however, is dicta since the Court decided the case on the basis of step one of the unconstitutional conditions analysis.[33] The opinion has nothing really valuable to say about this huge area of potential constitutional litigation, an area that has special significance in an era of annual federal budgets approaching *$3 trillion* and a Congress eager to use this enormous economic leverage to get individuals, associations, and states to do its bidding.

To see why conditional funding is important, consider the very context in which *FAIR* was decided. By any measure, an economic actor with $3 trillion to spend every year is a powerhouse. Its decisions shape the whole economy and affect the lives of everyone in the nation. Its power can be used to mold both the marketplace of goods and the marketplace of ideas.

Some industries and some fields of inquiry depend for their existence on the largesse of this powerhouse. Much research in modern universities could not proceed without federal funding. Universities cannot afford to forgo this funding if they are to remain competitive

[31] *Id.* at 1307.
[32] *Id.*
[33] *Id.*

with their peer institutions.[34] Thus, universities will do everything they can to keep the money flowing. Congress knows this and can impose almost any condition it wants on the funds. An example is the recently added requirement that universities spend time and resources hosting an annual "Constitution Day" designed to teach students about the Constitution—the very document that protects the academic freedom not to teach about the Constitution.[35] Another example is the Solomon Amendment. By themselves, these sorts of restrictions may not threaten First Amendment values like free speech, association, and academic freedom. But cumulatively, they do.

Congress' economic might combined with its growing willingness to use that might endangers two structural postulates of the Constitution: limited government and federalism. Congress is using its power to coerce private citizens and associations to relinquish or limit the exercise of important constitutional rights, including the right to criticize the policies of the government itself. This is not a hallmark of limited government. In addition, when Congress uses its leverage against state institutions, like state universities, it is forcing them to relinquish large areas of control to its central authority. This growth of the federal government is something the Framers could not have imagined. Translating the Framers' vision of limited power and federalism into the modern age of a federal behemoth is a challenge for constitutionalism in this century.

Those of us concerned about federalism and liberty in the face of Congress' willingness to use its economic might to curtail both have perhaps three options. First, we could argue that much of what Congress does to condition funding is unconstitutional as being beyond its spending power. This is almost certainly a losing argument until the Court modifies or reverses the broad congressional spending authority recognized in *South Dakota v. Dole*,[36] an unlikely event.

---

[34]In fiscal year 2003, almost ten percent of universities' expenditures were at risk under the Solomon Amendment. See AAUP Amicus Brief, *supra* note 12, at 23.

[35]For analysis suggesting that Constitution Day may be unconstitutional, see Heidi Kitrosser, Is Constitution Day Constitutional? (Sept. 10, 2005), at http://www.law.umn-edu/upleads/images/2085/IsConstitutionDayConstitutional-draft2.pdf.

[36]483 U.S. 203 (1987) (upholding conditional funding for highways).

Second, we could argue for a dramatic reduction in taxes, which would shrink the size of the federal government and thus reduce both the dependence on federal funds and the opportunity for mischievous funding conditions. If the first option was unlikely, this second one is impossible. The largest tax reductions in the last fifty years—under Presidents Ronald Reagan and George W. Bush—have not succeeded in reducing the size of the federal budget.

The third option is to accept reality: the federal government will remain a large, growing, and omnipresent force in our lives. We need a realistic understanding of how government power operates today. This power can be reined in, perhaps slightly, through robust substantive protection for speech and association, and through an unconstitutional conditions doctrine that fetters Congress' ability to eat away at federalism and liberty through funding conditions. A constitutional theory unable to account for and deal with this threat cannot be considered very protective of either federalism or liberty in the 21st century.

Two other issues bearing on the unconstitutional conditions issue warrant some mention. First, while Chief Justice Roberts believes that unanimity encourages narrow opinions, it is not clear that the Court's choice was the narrowest ground available for decision. If the Court had decided the case on the basis of step two—the way it did in *Grove City*—it could have avoided any discussion of the substantive First Amendment issues. If one believes that *FAIR* ended up making no new substantive law in the First Amendment area, the Court's opinion does seem a minimalist one. However, if one believes that the Court's opinion actually contracted First Amendment liberties, or at least made them more uncertain,[37] it is hardly clear that the Court's decision to resolve the issue on step one was the narrowest one available.

Second, it could be that the Court's reluctance to engage in serious and difficult step two analysis about unconstitutional conditions will increasingly lead it to resolve cases in step one by denying the underlying liberty claims. If that is right, *FAIR* is just one manifestation of a larger problem in future constitutional litigation.

---

[37]See discussion *infra* Part III.

III. The Errors of *FAIR*

I have suggested that *FAIR* may not have been wrong in result but that both its tone and rationale are wrong. Let me explain what I mean.

A. *The Cultural Backdrop and the Court's Tone*

Powerful legal, cultural, and political issues tugged at the justices in *FAIR*. The litigation over the Solomon Amendment lay at the intersection of three great controversies in modern American law and life.

First, there are the needs of the military to recruit the best and brightest in a time of war and uncertainty about national security. The schools' decisions to exclude military recruiters would never be a very popular one—less so in present circumstances. To many, universities' exclusion of the military looks like the action of an elite cast completely disconnected from the needs and ethos of the nation in which they live.

Second, the case was set in the context of the ongoing cultural struggle over whether discrimination against gays is ever acceptable and, if so, under what circumstances. To the schools, the exclusion of the military recruiters is a way to defend their moral view that discrimination against gays in the military is wrong and allowing recruitment by those who discriminate on this basis is contrary to their professional standards. FAIR's reliance on *Dale*, which held that gays could be excluded from an association, to justify *excluding those who exclude gays* was an especially ironic note in the litigation.

Third, the case raised questions about the extent of government power over the lives of its citizens and of the continuing vitality of federalism—the relationship between the states and the federal government—both of which I have already discussed. Government power to suppress constitutional rights has historically taken the form of old-fashioned compulsion: for example, a threat of jail for failure to abide by the government's command. However, in an age of vast federal spending, government power to compel conduct is more likely to take the form of conditions placed on that spending. When that form of compulsion affects state institutions, like a state university, the central question ceases to be simply about the relationship between the federal government and the individual citizen (or associations) and begins to be about the relationship between

233

the federal government and the states. Not surprisingly, the Cato Institute filed an amicus brief on the side of the law schools.[38]

With such momentous cultural and legal issues at stake, we needed something more than an opinion that treats the liberty claims almost with contempt. The problems with the Court's tone start with its recitation of the facts. In the course of describing the litigation below and the evolution of the Solomon Amendment, the Court included this sentence:

> Although the statute required only "entry to campuses," the Government—*after the terrorist attacks on September 11, 2001*—adopted an informal policy of "'requir[ing] universities to provide military recruiters access to students equal in quality and scope to that provided to other recruiters.'"[39]

This passage might lead the uninformed reader, not familiar with the case, to conclude that the terrorist attacks of September 11, 2001, actually had something to do with the decision of "the Government" to expand the scope of the Solomon Amendment to add an "equal treatment" requirement to the preexisting statutory access requirement. Perhaps, one might speculate, the government foresaw increased personnel needs after 9/11 and, to protect the nation from future attacks, decided it needed to step up its recruitment in law schools. That sounds plausible, but there is one large problem with it. There is no evidence whatsoever that the Solomon Amendment actually addressed any recruitment problem or that it was really intended to do so. There is similarly no evidence that the government was addressing any problem arising from 9/11 when it decided to expand the reach of the Solomon Amendment.

Why does the Court slip this non sequitur about 9/11 into the opinion? It is not simply a factual claim that the new equal-treatment policy chronologically followed 9/11, although it did. It is meant to suggest a causal relationship between the expanded Solomon Amendment and 9/11, a relationship *for which there is no evidence.* References like this to 9/11 are a modern echo of the old World War II quip, "Don't you know there's a war on?" On the one hand, these sorts of statements try to silence serious critics of government

[38]Amicus Curiae Brief of the Cato Institute in Support of Respondents, Rumsfeld v. FAIR, 126 S. Ct. 1297 (2006) (No. 04-1152).

[39]FAIR, 126 S. Ct. at 1303 (emphasis added) (citation omitted).

policy by suggesting ever so lightly that they are either unpatriotic or foolishly oblivious to security needs. On the other hand, they reflect the Court's unthinking acceptance of almost any security claim made by the government. While the Court has always been deferential to Congress' judgment about military needs, this deference in cases like *FAIR* becomes almost complete submission.

By contrast, the Court nowhere discusses the enormous financial stakes for universities that bar military recruiters. Instead, the Court adopts the government's misleading description of the money as "specified federal funding."[40] Yes, specific federal money for research and other things is lost if part of a university bars military recruiters: almost all of it.

The Court also fails to recognize the importance of antidiscrimination norms and policies in universities. The Court believes nothing very important is lost when these norms and policies are eroded, that is, when law students, faculty, and administrators must accept the presence of anti-gay discrimination in their midst. The law schools must make their facilities available to an employer—a representative of the state, no less—that refuses even to consider the merits of some of their students on a ground that the law schools believe is invidious and purposeless.

Yet this affront to the dignity of their students and erosion of their policies barely registers with a Court swooning before the wholly unsubstantiated needs of post-9/11 national security. The Court variously describes the interests and liberty at stake as "minimal,"[41] a "far cry" from recognized interests,[42] "incidental,"[43] "trivializ[ing]" important freedoms,[44] "plainly overstat[ed],"[45] and "exaggerat[ed]."[46] The Court's opinion is an exercise in single-entry bookkeeping. The only interests that count are the government's unsupported ones. On both the insubstantiality of the schools' interests and on

---

[40] *Id.*
[41] *Id.* at 1307 n.4.
[42] *Id.* at 1308.
[43] *Id.*
[44] *Id.*
[45] *Id.* at 1313.
[46] *Id.*

the substantiality of the governments', the Court's tone echoes the popular reaction to the case.

B. Minimizing Free Speech

On the substantive question of whether the schools enjoyed a constitutional right to exclude military recruiters, the Court rejected three different speech claims raised by FAIR. According to the Court, schools are not "compelled" by the law to say anything very important,[47] are not objectionably required to host the speech of the government within their own forum,[48] and are not denied their right to engage in expressive conduct.[49] In each case, the Court arguably narrowed its precedents, limiting the reach of free-speech rights.

1. Compelled Speech

The First Amendment forbids the government to make citizens its mouthpiece. The most famous case announcing this idea is *West Virginia State Board of Education v. Barnette*,[50] which upheld the right of schoolchildren to refuse to salute the flag or to recite the Pledge of Allegiance. *Barnette*, it should be remembered, is one of the few cases where the Court actually held its ground in defending liberty, in the middle of World War II no less, against the state's claims that the needs of national unity are paramount. Canonical now, *Barnette* was controversial in 1943, requiring the Court to overrule one of its own precedents from just three years earlier.[51] A *FAIR*-minded court might have noted that "West Virginia defends its policy—in the aftermath of the Japanese sneak attack of December 7, 1941—as a way to promote the war effort."

Next to the forced recitation of a statement of principles drafted by the government, it must be admitted that the degree of compelled speech required by the Solomon Amendment is fairly light. Under it, law schools are required to include in emails and other notices factual statements about the presence and location of military recruiters on campus, just as they do for other recruiters. Here, as elsewhere,

---

[47]*Id.* at 1308.
[48]*Id.* at 1309–10.
[49]*Id.* at 1310–11.
[50]319 U.S. 624 (1943).
[51]Minersville Sch. Dist. v. Gobitis, 310 U.S. 586 (1940).

law schools are a lot less sympathetic than Jehovah's Witnesses schoolchildren.

But *Barnette* was extended in *Wooley v. Maynard*[52] to allow motorists to cover up a state motto on their license plates. The license plates did not literally compel motorists to "say" anything at all. And no reasonable person would understand that a motorist was endorsing the state's message ("Live Free or Die") simply because it appeared on a standard state-issued license plate. But the Court concluded that even this amounted to compelled speech since the law "in effect requires that appellees use their private property as a 'mobile billboard' for the State's ideological message—or suffer a penalty . . . ."[53] The same appears to be the case in *FAIR*. The Solomon Amendment in effect requires the law schools to use their private property for the state's message—or suffer a penalty. And it does not matter, as the Court acknowledges, that the statements required of the law school are factual rather than ideological.[54]

The Court tries to get around these uncomfortable precedents in a couple of ways. First, it argues that the Solomon Amendment does not dictate the content of the compelled speech, and certainly requires nothing akin to a state-prescribed pledge or state motto. The schools must only communicate for the military the type of matters, if any, that they communicate for other employers.[55] If a school announces by school-wide email that the law firm of Scrooge & Marley will interview interested students in Room 1 at noon, it must also announce in a school-wide email where and when the military will interview interested students. If the law school makes no such announcement for other employers, it need say nothing for the benefit of military recruiters. The Solomon Amendment thus employs a triggering mechanism for compelled speech, where *Barnette* and *Wooley* actually dictated specific content.

This is a distinction, yes, but one that has previously made no difference in the Court's precedents. In *Miami Herald Publishing Co.*

---

[52]430 U.S. 705 (1977).

[53]*Id.* at 715.

[54]FAIR, 126 S. Ct. at 1308 ("[T]hese compelled statements of fact . . ., like compelled statements of opinion, are subject to First Amendment scrutiny.")

[55]*Id.*

v. Tornillo,[56] the state similarly employed a triggering mechanism that required newspapers to publish replies to criticism that appeared in the newspaper. Like the Solomon Amendment, nothing in Florida's right-of-reply law mandated that newspapers engage in any speech at all (absent the trigger), and nothing in the statute required specific content in the compelled speech once triggered. Like the Solomon Amendment, nothing in the Florida law prohibited the newspapers from expressing their own views on any subject. They could "ameliorate" the presence of the unwanted reply from aggrieved politicians. Nevertheless, the *Tornillo* Court held that the law was unconstitutional because it "exacts a penalty on the basis of the content of [the] newspaper."[57] Applying this principle to *Wooley*, does anyone believe that the case would have come out differently had New Hampshire required motorists' license plates to bear the state motto only if they affixed other messages to their car bumpers?

The Court is not obliged to stand by its precedents, and it can of course limit them. *Wooley*, in particular, may be a stretch of the compelled speech doctrine to cover a truly trivial intrusion on private conscience and speech. Perhaps the Court should overrule it. But the logistical and informational speech compelled by the Solomon Amendment is hardly a "far cry" from the appearance of four words on a standard state-issued license plate.

The Court also distinguished *Barnette* and *Wooley* by arguing that "[t]he compelled speech to which the law schools point is plainly incidental to the Solomon Amendment's regulation of conduct[, the admission of military recruiters] . . . ."[58] The Court gives the example of Title VII, which forbids private employers to discriminate on the basis of race and would, therefore, require an employer to remove a "White Applicants Only" sign from its premises.[59] In both the Solomon Amendment and Title VII, argues the Court, the limitation of speech is incidental to the conduct regulation. But this analogy does not work.

It is true that speech facilitating illegality is not protected simply because it is speech. A perjurer's perjury may be admitted against

---

[56]418 U.S. 241 (1974).

[57]*Id*. at 256.

[58]FAIR, 126 S. Ct. at 1308.

[59]*Id*.

him as evidence of his crime. But it is equally true that the government cannot suppress protected speech simply because the underlying or accompanying conduct can be made illegal. Advocating law violation cannot be made criminal simply because law violation itself can be. Much more is required before speech advocating law violation may be punished[60]

The key distinction between these two truisms of First Amendment law, I think, is whether the suppression of speech really is incidental to the larger purpose and impact of the law. Whether *that* is so depends on (1) what we think of the substantiality of the expressive component of the conduct being regulated—the ban on recruiters who discriminate—and on (2) whether we think the government's real interest in regulating the conduct is speech-related, that is, an attempt to suppress some message being sent by the conduct. For reasons I explain below, I think both of these considerations cut in favor of the law schools. For now, it is enough to say that these are hard questions not answered by a quick analogy to Title VII.

2. Third-Party Speech

Closer than *Barnette* or *Wooley* to the actual facts of *FAIR* are a series of cases in which the Court has "limited the government's ability to force one speaker to host or accommodate another speaker's message."[61] The Solomon Amendment requires law schools to host government speakers—military recruiters—who use space for interviews in the law school to promote the government's own messages about the desirability of military service, to defend DADT, and to object to the law schools' views. The interviews themselves are quintessential speech activities in which ideas and information are exchanged.[62]

---

[60]Brandenburg v. Ohio, 395 U.S. 444, 447–48 (1969).

[61]126 S. Ct. at 1309.

[62]Prior to *FAIR*, some commentators argued that the Solomon Amendment served First Amendment values by exposing students to views opposing the law schools' own. See Walpin, *supra* note 8 (arguing that the law serves expressive purpose of getting military's message to law students). It has never been accepted First Amendment doctrine that the government may compel the presence of speakers contrary to the speakers' or associations' own views as a way to encourage debate or diversity. See Miami Herald Pub. Co. v. Tornillo, 418 U.S. 241, 256 (1974). It is for the speaker or association, not the government, to decide what messages it will convey or host.

The Court distinguishes the third-party compelled-speech cases in a couple of ways. First, it argues that a constitutional violation has previously been recognized only where "the complaining speaker's own message was affected by the speech it was forced to accommodate."[63] But this is not a fair way to distinguish the cases. *Tornillo*, involving the politicians' right-of-reply in newspapers, "affected" the newspapers only because they could have used the space for some other speech purpose.[64] The same is true of the law schools, whose interview and other spaces are taken up by military recruiters whose messages they object to.

The Court further argues that the law schools' speech is not affected by the presence of military recruiters because "the schools are not speaking when they host interviews and recruiting receptions."[65] These activities, argues the Court, are not "inherently expressive," unlike a parade, a newsletter, or a newspaper.[66] This conclusion is parasitic on the Court's discussion of expressive conduct, which I address below.[67] It is enough here to say that the Court's conclusion betrays how little it appreciates the important expressive nature of antidiscrimination policies that embody a school's commitment to its vision of morality, ethical conduct, and professionalism. Perhaps the government has non-speech-related interests sufficient to override these expressive interests, but to deny that the expressive interests are even present is blindness.

Finally, the Court rejects FAIR's argument that the law schools might be perceived as endorsing the government's message if military recruiters are allowed into their buildings.[68] The perception of endorsement is indeed unlikely since the law schools have loudly and consistently objected to the presence of recruiters who discriminate. Reasonably informed observers, like law students, will surely understand that the schools are simply complying with the law. This endorsement argument gives the Court the opportunity to make fun of the law schools. High school students can tell the difference

---

[63]FAIR, 126 S. Ct. at 1309.

[64]Tornillo, 418 U.S. at 256.

[65]FAIR, 126 S. Ct. at 1309.

[66]*Id.* at 1309–10.

[67]See discussion *infra* Part III.B.3.

[68]FAIR, 126 S. Ct. at 1310.

between messages the schools endorse and those they are required to carry, notes the Court. "Surely students have not lost that ability by the time they get to law school," the Court quips in a passage greeted with much mirth by opponents of FAIR.[69]

No knowledgeable observer will think law schools endorse anti-gay discrimination simply because they must permit military recruiters on campus or even include announcements of their presence in emails and other notices. The confusion will be even less likely if the law schools engage in the sort of ameliorative counter-speech the Court reassures us they are free to engage in.

But this fact should make no difference to the compelled-speech claim. Nobody would understand the motorist in *Wooley* necessarily to endorse any message that appears on his and everybody else's license plate. Nobody would confuse the politician's right-of-reply op-ed with a newspaper's own viewpoint in *Tornillo*. Under the compelled-speech doctrine, the vice of the law is in the requirement that the speaker host a third party's objectionable message, not necessarily in any confusion this might create about whether the complaining speaker endorses the third party's message. It is *always* true, even in the context of a parade, that the complaining speaker may distance itself from the third party's message in various ways. The law schools thus correctly lost what should have been an irrelevant point.

3. Expressive Conduct

Most disconcerting for free speech is the Court's mistreatment of the "expressive conduct" doctrine. The Court has never had a satisfying theory of what conduct should get free-speech protection. Conduct can be engaged in for essentially expressive purposes; when it does, speech interests are present. At the same time, when the government regulates conduct it is unusually likely to have interests unrelated to the suppression of ideas.

Some conduct, like flag-burning[70] and nude dancing,[71] does get some level of constitutional protection. Some conduct, like sexual

---

[69]*Id.*

[70]Texas v. Johnson, 491 U.S. 397, 414–20 (1989); United States v. Eichman, 496 U.S. 310, 314–15 (1990).

[71]Barnes v. Glen Theatre, Inc., 501 U.S. 560, 565–66 (1991).

activity in an adult bookstore,[72] does not. Obviously some conduct, like burning a flag in protest, is such a potent way to express a view that its First Amendment significance cannot be missed. Even words could not adequately convey the power of publicly burning a flag in protest. Yet we would not want to subject all criminal laws to First Amendment scrutiny simply because the defendant claims that he was trying to communicate something by his conduct.

a. From Context-Specific to Context-Free

Different verbal formulations have been offered to explain the distinction between conduct that gets some protection from conduct that gets none, but these attempts have always been indeterminate. In *Arcara v. Cloud Books, Inc.*, the Court suggested that conduct would get some First Amendment protection where it contained "a significant expressive element."[73] In *Spence v. Washington*, which reversed a conviction for affixing a peace symbol to the flag under a state law prohibiting "improper use" of the flag, the Court suggested that expressive conduct would be protected where there was "[a]n intent to convey a particularized message" and "in the surrounding circumstances the likelihood was great that the message would be understood by those who viewed it."[74] The Court relied on the *Spence* formulation in *Texas v. Johnson*, in which it reversed a conviction under state law for burning a flag in protest during the Republican National Convention.[75] However, the Court seemed to disavow part of the *Spence* formulation in *Hurley v. Irish-American Gay, Lesbian and Bisexual Group of Boston*, saying that: "[A] narrow, succinctly articulable message is not a condition of constitutional protection, which if confined to expressions conveying a 'particularized message' would never reach the unquestionably shielded painting of Jackson Pollock, music of Arnold Schoenberg, or Jabberwocky verse of Lewis Carroll."[76]

Now, says the Court: "[W]e have extended First Amendment protection *only to conduct that is inherently expressive.*"[77] The Court

---

[72]Arcara v. Cloud Books, Inc., 478 U.S. 697, 707 (1986).

[73]*Id.* at 706.

[74]418 U.S. 405, 410–11 (1974).

[75]491 U.S. at 404 (quoting Spence, 418 U.S. at 414 n.8).

[76]515 U.S. 557, 569 (1995).

[77]Rumsfeld v. FAIR, 126 S. Ct. 1297, 1310 (2006) (emphasis added).

cites no precedent for this conclusion or for the phrase "inherently expressive." No prior majority opinion on the subject has suggested that in deciding whether conduct is expressive we should look *only* at the conduct itself, rather than at both the conduct and the context in which it occurs. It is notable that in its discussion of expressive conduct, the *FAIR* decision makes no reference to the *Spence/Johnson* or *Arcara* tests for what conduct could count as expressive.

While the words "inherently expressive" appeared in the plurality opinion in a nude dancing case, *City of Erie v. Pap's A.M.*,[78] the plurality used it there in a sense opposite what the *FAIR* Court uses it for. In *Pap's A.M.*, the Court explained that "[b]eing 'in a state of nudity' is not an inherently expressive condition" but that, nevertheless, "nude dancing of the type at issue here is expressive conduct ...."[79] The *Pap's A.M.* plurality thought that nude dancing could be protected by the First Amendment as expressive conduct despite the fact that it is *not* inherently expressive. Now we have a unanimous Supreme Court endorsing the opposite and far more restrictive view.

Certainly *Johnson* and *Hurley* considered the context in which conduct occurs. In *Johnson*, the Court observed that the act occurred "as part—indeed, as the culmination—of a political demonstration that coincided with the convening of the Republican Party and its renomination of Ronald Reagan for President."[80] In *Hurley*, the Court found a parade expressive in part because it involves actual speech (e.g., slogans on banners), but also because it involves spectators lining the streets, people marching in costumes and uniforms, marching bands, pipers, and floats.[81]

---

[78]529 U.S. 277 (2000). A search has turned up the term "inherently expressive" and similar phrases in a few concurring and dissenting opinions in First Amendment cases, see, for example, Barnes v. Glen Theatre, Inc., 501 U.S. 560, 581 (1991) (Souter, J., concurring); *id.* at 578 n.4 (Scalia, J., concurring); *id.* at 587 n.1 (White, J., dissenting), and in a couple of majority opinions where the Court obviously did not intend the restrictive sense of the *FAIR* Court, see, for example, Hurley v. Irish-American Gay, Lesbian & Bisexual Group of Boston, 515 U.S. 557, 568 (1995); Lehnert v. Ferris Faculty Ass'n, 500 U.S. 507, 518 (1991); Ellis v. Bd. of Ry., Airline & S.S. Clerks, Freight Handlers, Express & Station Employees, 466 U.S. 435, 456 (1984).

[79]Pap's A.M., 529 U.S. at 289.

[80]Johnson, 491 U.S. at 406.

[81]Hurley, 515 U.S. at 569.

b. What Is "Inherently Expressive" Conduct?

Beyond the unprecedented nature of the Court's restrictive view, it is difficult to predict what conduct will count as "inherently expressive," and thus get First Amendment protection, and what conduct will not be deemed "inherently expressive," and thus get no First Amendment protection. I am not sure the distinction amounts to much more than the old informal obscenity standard, "I know it when I see it," in which case it has further unsettled an already uncertain area of First Amendment law.

The Court appears to mean that inherently expressive conduct is that conduct for which the expressive component is "'overwhelmingly apparent,'"[82] and thus needs no further accompanying speech or consideration of circumstances in which it occurs to signal that it is expressive. Barring military recruiters is "expressive only because the law schools accompanied their conduct with speech explaining it" and thus fails the newly created "inherently expressive" test. The test, the Court thinks, helps us separate flag burning (inherently expressive) from the exclusion of the military from law school recruiting (not inherently expressive). As the Court puts it:

> An observer who sees military recruiters interviewing away from the law school has no way of knowing whether the law school is expressing its disapproval of the military, all the law school's interview rooms are full, or the military recruiters decided for reasons of their own that they would rather interview someplace else.[83]

The Court here mishandles existing doctrine and does so in a way that narrows First Amendment freedom. We do not know much about the message *any* conduct conveys, or whether it conveys any message at all, unless we know the context in which it occurs. Yes, as the Court suggests, a law school's exclusion of the military could signal disagreement with some governmental or military policy, like DADT (expressive), or it could merely reflect that the law school ran out of space for interviews (not expressive).

[82]FAIR, 126 S. Ct. at 1311 (quoting Johnson, 491 U.S. at 406).
[83]126 S. Ct. at 1311.

Yet applying this context-free methodology to *Johnson*, an observer who sees someone burning a flag might think the flag-burner is expressing disagreement with the nation's foreign policy (expressive), or that he accidentally set it on fire (not expressive), or that he was attempting to generate heat in the cold (not expressive), or that he was simply disposing of a tattered flag in the manner prescribed by the government (not expressive?). Applying the *FAIR* methodology to *Hurley*, the observer might think this group of people walking in the street are doing so because the sidewalks are under repair (not expressive), or because they are from Mars and do not know any better (not expressive), or because they are part of a group celebrating Irish pride on St. Patrick's Day (expressive).

Context, including what the actor says about his conduct, matters. The uninformed observer, unaware of context, could not tell whether *any* particular act was expressive. So it should not matter that a few "listeners" or "observers," who might as well be living on a different planet, cannot appreciate why the law schools want to exclude military recruiters until they are told why. In fact, in the current environment of heightened sensitivity to law school recruitment policies, the reasonably informed observer has a good idea why a law school might want to exclude the military. Even if in principle we could draw a line between protected conduct and unprotected conduct that would leave schools' recruitment policies outside the protected realm, the Court's discussion of this question is troubling.

If Chief Justice Roberts had used the *Spence* two-pronged test (repeated in *Johnson*), for example, he would have asked whether there had been "an intent to convey a message" and whether that message "*in the surrounding circumstances*" would have been understood by those who viewed it. The answer in the context of the law schools' recruitment policies should have been "yes" to both questions. The law schools certainly intended their policies to convey a message to students, to faculty, to the community, and to the government, that they deeply disapprove of DADT. (That is a controversial moral view, but the law schools are entitled to hold and promote it.) Under the circumstances, in which the media, the courts, and numerous critics debated the law schools' policies, and the law schools themselves explained the need for their recruitment policies, this message-sending would be understood by those made aware of it. Using the *Spence/Johnson* test, the Solomon Amendment does

245

indeed "limit[] what law schools may say,"[84] contrary to the conclusion in *FAIR*, by prohibiting their expressive conduct.

c. The Government's Interest in the Solomon Amendment

Even if barring military recruiters is expressive conduct, this conclusion alone does not mean the Solomon Amendment is unconstitutional. In the past, in expressive conduct cases, the Court has asked whether the government's interest in regulating the expressive conduct is related to speech. If so, strict scrutiny applies; if not, a very relaxed form of intermediate scrutiny applies.[85] Unfortunately, the Court has not told us how to determine Congress' "interest" in legislation. The analysis surely does not call for an inquiry into legislators' subjective motives, of which there are undoubtedly many. But it also cannot mean simply taking the government's word for it when its lawyers identify an interest. Instead, it would seem to call for an objective inquiry based on the nature of the claimed interest, its plausibility, the circumstances in which the legislation was adopted, and the statutory text.

Using these considerations as a guide, is the government's interest in the Solomon Amendment related to expression? The government claimed in litigation that the Solomon Amendment was an exercise of Congress' power to raise and support the military, and the Court accordingly gave substantial deference to its "judgment" about military needs.[86] The problem with this claimed recruitment need is that it has no support. There is no evidence of the effect of law schools' antidiscrimination policies on recruitment. There is no evidence, for example, that the JAG Corps was having any difficulty finding excellent officers. Instead, there has been a glut of highly qualified applicants. In fact, the Department of Defense initially opposed the Solomon Amendment as "unnecessary" and "duplicative,"[87] although it later reversed its position. As the Solomon Amendment grew in later years, no evidence on actual recruitment needs was

[84]*Id.* at 1307 (arguing that the Solomon Amendment does not limit what law schools may say).

[85]Johnson, 491 U.S. at 403.

[86]126 S. Ct. at 1311 ("judgment" about the means to meet military recruitment needs is for Congress, not the courts). Elsewhere the Court describes Congress' power over military affairs as "broad and sweeping." *Id.* at 1306.

[87]140 Cong. Rec. 11,440 (1994) (statement of Rep. Underwood).

ever produced. The military has so many other methods of recruiting law students that forcing law schools to allow interviews to occur on campus, and forcing them to make announcements about military recruiting, has never been needed.

If not filling recruitment needs, what was the government's interest in the Solomon Amendment? It seems to have been entirely symbolic, arising out of a desire to punish the "starry-eyed idealism" of academic elites who think "they are too good—or too righteous—to treat our Nation's military with the respect it deserves."[88] Recall that almost two decades passed between the time schools began excluding military recruiters and the time Congress reacted, a fact that undermines (but by itself does not defeat) a claimed recruitment need. Recall also that the Solomon Amendment was passed in the immediate aftermath of the controversy over gays in the military, which brought fresh attention to the issue. In this charged atmosphere, in which Congress had just asserted itself forcefully to codify the gay ban, members of Congress perceived law school policies aimed at anti-gay discrimination by the military as a "backhanded slap at the honor and dignity of service in our Nation's Armed Forces."[89] Rep. Solomon himself wanted to "tell[] recipients of Federal money at colleges and universities that if you do not like the Armed Forces, if you do not like its policies . . . do not expect Federal dollars to support your interference with our military recruiters."[90] The Solomon Amendment would "send a message over the wall of the ivory tower of higher education."[91]

These statements and others, as well as the two-decade delay in reacting to the schools' policies and the context in which the law was adopted, provide objective evidence of an ideological interest in passage of the Solomon Amendment. It is an interest based on hostility toward universities and their faculties and a desire to punish

---

[88]*Id*. at 11,441 (1994) (statement of Rep. Pombo).

[89]*Id*.

[90]*Id*. at 11,439 (statement of Rep. Solomon). Ironically, Rep. Solomon thought universities had a "first-amendment right[]" to bar military recruiters, but that Congress could condition funds on their choosing not to do so. *Id*. In this, Rep. Solomon had a more expansive view of First Amendment freedom than does the current Supreme Court.

[91]*Id*. at 11,441 (statement of Rep. Pombo).

247

them for their views—an interest deeply at odds with First Amendment principles. Congress' interest was therefore speech-related and ought to draw strict scrutiny.

I am not asserting that Congress had a single motive in passing the Solomon Amendment or even that an inquiry into subjective motives is necessary. Some members of Congress undoubtedly genuinely believed that the law would aid recruiting. But in this case, where there is no objective evidence to support Congress' claimed recruitment interest, and there is objective evidence supporting a speech-related interest, the ideological interest is the one that ought to be attributed to Congress. Simply to give Congress a free pass, accepting any interest that its lawyers concoct without any further examination in a case where there is objective evidence of a speech-related interest, would be to seriously weaken the expressive-conduct doctrine. Yet that appears to be what the Court did.

C. Minimizing the Freedom of Association

The First Amendment protects a freedom of association that extends to expressive groups.[92] FAIR, relying heavily on *Dale*, argued that this freedom protects the right of law schools to exclude military recruiters. The government argued for a narrow interpretation of *Dale* and other freedom of association cases as applying only to government control over a group's membership.

There was much irony in the dispute over the meaning of *Dale* as it applied to the Solomon Amendment controversy. Some of the same people who criticized *Dale* as "anti-gay" six years before relied on it to make an aggressive claim about associational rights. Of course, the irony went both ways. Some conservatives who hailed *Dale* as a great victory for freedom six years before now argued for a very narrow interpretation of it.

---

[92]Explicit protection for the freedom of association came first in *NAACP v. Alabama*, 357 U.S. 449 (1958), which recognized a right of a civil rights group to keep its membership list confidential from the state of Alabama. The Court has subsequently described the freedom as extending to expressive associations in cases like *Roberts v. United States Jaycees*, 468 U.S. 609 (1984), and *Boy Scouts of America v. Dale*, 530 U.S. 640 (2000).

One reaction to FAIR's claim might have been to note that insofar as recruitment interviews facilitate commercial transactions—the meeting of employer and prospective employee—these activities are not strongly protected by the freedom of association.[93] The Court makes a nod to this possibility when it says that recruiting services lack "expressive quality" because the schools are merely "assist[ing] their students in obtaining jobs."[94] If the Court had rejected the freedom of association claim on the ground that recruiting is a commercial activity not protected by the freedom of association, it would have been a defensible interpretation and application of its precedents. Instead, the Court ventured into new territory.

1. The Freedom of Association and Membership

Does the freedom of association protect, as the government contended, only the membership decisions a group makes? Or does it encompass, as the schools contended, a broader right that protects many associational activities by which a group promotes its message? If it is the former, the freedom of association is not a very robust doctrine, since it leaves the state free to hobble a group's message in numerous indirect but nevertheless very effective ways. If it is the latter, the freedom of association risks giving expressive groups a broad right to refuse to comply with general regulations backed by important state interests. It would be the freedom that swallowed the law.

While one scholar pre-*FAIR* questioned whether law schools qualified as expressive associations,[95] the government did not contest this issue and the Court was not detained by it. Under *Dale*, a group is expressive even if disseminating ideas is not its primary purpose. It simply needs to engage in expressive activity in order to qualify for protection.[96] Law schools meet that threshold, even if they have

[93]Dale Carpenter, Expressive Association and Anti-Discrimination Law After Dale: A Tripartite Approach, 85 Minn. L. Rev. 1515, 1576–80 (2001) (quasi-expressive associations should be protected by the freedom of association in their expressive activities, but not in their commercial activities).

[94]Rumsfeld v. FAIR, 126 S. Ct. 1297, 1310 (2006).

[95]Morriss, *supra* note 8 (arguing that law schools operate primarily as economic cartels, not as expressive associations).

[96]Dale, 530 U.S. at 655 ("[A]ssociations do not have to associate for the 'purpose' of disseminating a certain message in order to be entitled to the protections of the First Amendment. An association must merely engage in expressive activity that could be impaired in order to be entitled to protection.").

other, economic purposes, and even if these other purposes are the dominant ones.

After deciding that a group is expressive, *Dale* instructs us to ask whether the law or regulation about which it complains would "significantly affect its expression."[97] One way to answer this question would be to take a hard-and-fast categorical approach: if the law regulates group membership, as did the antidiscrimination law in *Dale* by requiring the Boy Scouts to admit an openly gay scoutmaster, it "significantly affects" the group's expression. If the law does not regulate group membership, then it does not "significantly affect" group expression. The government took this categorical position in *FAIR*, arguing that the freedom of expressive association protects only a group's membership decisions, and that since the Solomon Amendment did not require the schools to admit military recruiters as "members" (presumably, as faculty, students, administrators, or staff) the law did not violate their freedom of association.

The *FAIR* Court correctly rejected that view, agreeing with the law schools that "the freedom of expressive association protects more than just a group's membership decisions."[98] This comports with the Court's cases, which have extended the freedom of association beyond control of group membership.[99]

A second way to answer whether a law significantly affects an association's expression would be case-by-case and contextualized, examining the particular ways a regulation might impair a group's ability to get its message across, no matter whether the law regulated or affected group membership. The Court appears to have eschewed that approach as well.

Instead of these two possible approaches, the *FAIR* decision opts for a third, giving us what we might call a hybrid *categorical-contextual approach*. Laws regulating membership—usually antidiscrimination laws that control the membership criteria a group might want to use—certainly may significantly affect an association's

---

[97]*Id.* at 655–59.

[98]126 S. Ct. at 1312.

[99]See, e.g., NAACP v. Alabama, 357 U.S. 449 (1958); Healy v. James, 408 U.S. 169 (1972); Brown v. Socialist Workers '74 Campaign Comm. (Ohio), 459 U.S. 87 (1982). In *Dale*, the Court observed that unconstitutional restrictions on the freedom of association "may take many forms," not simply control of a group's membership. 530 U.S. at 648.

expression.[100] But the Court adds that laws may also significantly affect an association's expression if they "mak[e] group membership less desirable."[101] Laws that impose penalties for group membership or that require the disclosure of secret membership lists are examples falling into this category. They make membership in the expressive association less attractive.

This synthesis of the Court's association jurisprudence has not previously appeared in its decisions. Prior to *FAIR*, the Court had worried primarily about the effect a regulation might have on the group's ability to get across its message, however that impediment operated. Now the focus of associational freedom seems to have been narrowed to concerns about membership or effects on membership that in turn may affect the group's message.

So while the *FAIR* decision states that associational freedom protects more than a group's membership, in substance it has announced a test for protecting associational freedom that is limited to membership concerns. Thus, the Court holds that the schools have failed to show that "the statute affects the composition of the group by making group membership less desirable."[102] The whole point of the schools' claim was that having to host a message they regard as repugnant would impair their own message that discrimination against gay Americans is wrong, regardless of whether compliance had any impact on their "membership." The Court rejects this claim by saying, in effect, "Show us how compliance would affect your message by affecting your group's membership." It concludes this by narrowly reading prior associational-freedom cases as involving laws that "did not directly interfere" with membership, but which "made group membership less attractive."[103] There is notably no citation or quotation supporting this narrower reading of the scope of associational freedom. Perhaps the Court's attempt to cabin the reach of associational freedom in *FAIR* is defensible, but it does seem a more restrictive view than it has taken in the past.

---

[100]Roberts v. U.S. Jaycees, 468 U.S 609 (1984) (state law forbidding sex discrimination); Dale, 530 U.S. 640 (state law forbidding sexual orientation discrimination).

[101]FAIR, 126 S. Ct. at 1312.

[102]*Id.*

[103]*Id.* at 1312.

Am I being unfair to *FAIR*? Perhaps this new description of the freedom of association is more expansive than I am suggesting. Any law or regulation that makes the group less attractive to potential members, much less a law that directly regulates group membership, will potentially infringe its freedom of association. A law school could argue in the next case, for example, that the presence of military recruiters interviewing in its building might make it less attractive to students, staff, administrators, and faculty who prefer a discrimination-free environment.

2. Deference No More

But even if that is factually correct and supportable, I expect the law schools would still lose their claim. The reason they would lose this hypothetical future claim tells us something else significant about *FAIR* that may not be obvious on a first reading. It is not obvious because what is important here is not what the decision says, but what it *does not* say.

Consider that the *Dale* Court explicitly deferred to the Boy Scouts on both the question of the content of the group's message *and the question of what would impair that message.* "As we give deference to an association's assertions regarding the nature of its expression, we must also give deference to an association's view of what would impair its expression," said the *Dale* Court.[104] That deferential posture is completely missing from the *FAIR* decision both in rhetoric and in substance. The omission seems deliberate, since the Court quotes parts of the *very next sentence* from *Dale* about how a group cannot "'erect a shield'" against the law "'simply by asserting'" their expression will be impaired by compliance with it.[105]

Rather than deferring to the law schools about what impairs their expression, the Court almost mocks their claims: "The law schools *say* that allowing military recruiters equal access impairs their own expression by requiring them to associate with the recruiters . . . ."[106] The emphasis on "say" is the Court's own, as if we would be foolish to trust a group's stated judgment about what would impair its expression (the way we trusted the Boy Scouts of America in *Dale*).

[104]Dale, 530 U.S. at 653.

[105]FAIR, 126 S. Ct. at 1312 (quoting Dale, 530 U.S. at 653).

[106]*Id.* (emphasis in original).

While a group must surely do more than *say* compliance with a law would significantly impair its message, the schools did do more than that here[107]—and still lost. Thus, deference is replaced by skepticism.

An alternative and more hopeful reading of *FAIR* might be this: Perhaps the Court is saying that where a law neither regulates group membership nor affects group composition by making membership less attractive, the Court will not defer to the association's judgment that compliance with the law will significantly affect its expression. Where a law either regulates membership or makes membership less attractive, the Court will continue to defer to the group's judgment that compliance will significantly affect its expression.

If that is the line the Court intends to draw, it is a sensible one. There is, after all, something especially sensitive about control over associational membership that goes directly to the group's ability to control its own message. Deference on the question of message impairment where membership is altered by the government may be the appropriate judicial mechanism by which this sensitivity is registered. Deference outside this especially sensitive question of membership control risks making the freedom of association an exemption from laws that any group simply does not like.

But I doubt this is the line the Court intended to draw. Instead, the opinion makes no reference to deference, mentions only effects on membership, and closes with the bare observation that a recruiter's "mere presence on campus does not violate a law school's right to associate, regardless of how repugnant the law school considers the recruiter's message."[108] The freedom of association, concludes the *FAIR* Court, is untroubled by the government's insistence that its representatives be present on the association's property while delivering a "message" contradicting the association's own.

Conclusion

One could support the Court's result in *FAIR*—that the Solomon Amendment is constitutional—while still being quite concerned about the decision's potential narrowing effects on First Amendment freedoms. The upshot of the Court's view about free speech and

---

[107]Respondents' Brief, *supra* note 15, at 14 (explaining effects of Solomon Amendment at law schools).

[108]FAIR, 126 S. Ct. at 1313.

associational rights is this: the government could *require* schools to admit military recruiters under threat of criminal sanction, not merely withdraw funds from schools that bar the recruiters. The state may mandate that its representatives be present, that they be allowed to deliver messages directly contrary to the association's own, and that the association must not only tolerate their presence but affirmatively assist in and facilitate the state's opposing speech. That Congress chose not to do so in the Solomon Amendment is now a matter of legislative grace, not constitutional freedom. Prior to the decision, even many supporters of the Solomon Amendment agreed that the government could not go so far.[109] On this basis alone, the *FAIR* decision should concern anyone devoted to First Amendment freedom.

As a practical matter, the ruling changes nothing in the steps many schools have taken to "ameliorate" the presence of military recruiters by, for example, hosting fora on the military's policy on the day military recruiters are present, or posting notices of opposition to the presence of discrimination on campus, even outside the door where military recruiters are interviewing. In fact, the decision appears to give a bright green light to these efforts that some schools may have avoided until now for fear they would lose funding. From the opinion:

> Law schools remain free under the statute to express what-ever views they may have on the military's congressionally mandated employment policy, all the while retaining eligibil-ity for federal funds. See Tr. of Oral Arg. 25 (Solicitor General acknowledging that law schools "could put signs on the bulletin board next to the door, they could engage in speech, they could help organize student protests").[110]

---

[109]In a debate with me on the constitutionality of the Solomon Amendment held at the University of Minnesota Law School on September 25, 2005, my renowned conservative colleague, Professor Michael Paulsen, agreed that the government could not directly mandate the admission of military recruiters in private universities because such a requirement would violate the First Amendment. Professor Paulsen maintained that the Solomon Amendment was nevertheless constitutional because it involved only conditional funding, not a direct mandate. Very little of the popular commentary supporting the constitutionality of the Solomon Amendment before *FAIR* did so on the ground that the government could enforce a direct mandate.

[110]126 S. Ct. at 1307.

There was some concern among law school faculties considering amelioration before *FAIR* that posting these notices and engaging in other ameliorative activities might be considered a violation of the Solomon Amendment because it denied military recruiters access to their facilities that was "equal" to the access given other employers (against whom they do not protest).[111] As a matter of statutory construction, that worry should be over.

On the other hand, while Congress probably could not directly prohibit these amelioration activities, the question remains after *FAIR* whether Congress could condition federal funds on a school's agreement not to ameliorate the presence of military recruiters while they are interviewing. After all, the schools are only losing money, and besides, don't they know there's a war on?

---

[111]"[T]he military has routinely threatened law schools for any gesture of protest that treats military recruiters differently, even if the difference could have no material effect on recruiting efforts." Respondents' Brief, *supra* note 15, at 8 (giving examples).

Taking Accommodation Seriously: Religious Freedom and the *O Centro* Case

Richard W. Garnett & Joshua D. Dunlap*

> The Government's argument echoes the classic rejoinder of bureaucrats throughout history:
> If I make an exception for you, I'll have to make one for everybody, so no exceptions.[1]

For church-state junkies, the Supreme Court's most recent term offered something of a break, even a welcome breather. After all, the Court's previous 2004–2005 session featured an exhausting cluster of closely watched and widely remarked Establishment Clause blockbusters.[2] In *Cutter v. Wilkinson,*[3] the Court rejected—unanimously—the argument that Congress had unconstitutionally established religion by passing legislation that specially accommodates the needs of religious believers in prisons.[4] In *McCreary County v. ACLU,*[5] a bare majority of the justices concluded that two particular displays of the Ten Commandments lacked the "secular" purpose required by the Court's precedents.[6] And, in *Van Orden v. Perry,*[7] a different,

---

*Richard W. Garnett is the Lilly Endowment Associate Professor of Law at the University of Notre Dame. Joshua D. Dunlap is a degree candidate (J.D. expected, May 2008) at the Notre Dame Law School. The authors are grateful to Tom Berg for his advice and assistance.

[1] Gonzales v. O Centro Espirita Beneficente Uniao do Vegetal, 126 S. Ct. 1211, 1223 (2006).

[2] See generally, e.g., Marci A. Hamilton, The Establishment Clause During the 2004 Term: Big Cases, Little Movement, 2004–2005 Cato Sup. Ct. Rev. 159 (2005).

[3] 544 U.S. 709 (2005).

[4] *Id.* at 714.

[5] 125 S. Ct. 2722 (2005).

[6] *Id.* at 2739–41.

[7] 125 S. Ct. 2854 (2005).

but still 5-4, majority decided that a large stone Ten Commandments monument, on the grounds of the Texas State Capitol, was a permissible recognition, not an illegal endorsement, of religion.[8] As it happened, *Van Orden* was the final opinion authored by Chief Justice Rehnquist during his long and distinguished service to the Constitution and to the country, a service whose highlights included a number of landmark opinions in Religion Clauses cases.[9]

This past term, however, the big Supreme Court stories were about military commissions and enemy combatants, political redistricting and campaign contributions, and the nomination and confirmation—the first in more than a decade—of two new justices. Largely overlooked in the crush of Court-related coverage was the term's lone church-state decision, *Gonzales v. O Centro Espirita Beneficente Uniao do Vegetal*, involving a small religious community from Brazil and their ritualized, but illegal, use of a hallucinogenic tea called "hoasca."

Strictly speaking, *O Centro* was not a Religion Clauses case at all. Instead, it involved the interpretation and application of a particular statute, the federal Religious Freedom Restoration Act (RFRA).[10] Congress enacted this measure in 1993, in response to the Court's controversial decision in *Employment Division v. Smith*.[11] In *Smith*, the justices concluded that, generally speaking, the First Amendment's Free Exercise Clause does not require governments to exempt religiously motivated conduct from the reach of neutral and generally applicable regulations.[12] If the use of a drug like peyote is unlawful, that use remains unlawful even when motivated by religious conviction or obligation. True, Justice Scalia wrote, the First Amendment does not allow governments to single out religiously motivated practices for penalty or disfavor;[13] and, he observed, a society that, like ours, is committed to respecting and protecting religious belief

---

[8] *Id.* at 2864.

[9] See generally, e.g., Richard W. Garnett, William H. Rehnquist: A Life Lived Greatly, and Well, 115 Yale L.J. 1847 (2006).

[10] 42 U.S.C. §§ 2000bb et seq.

[11] 494 U.S. 872 (1990).

[12] See, e.g., *id.* at 878–79 ("We have never held that an individual's religious beliefs excuse him from compliance with an otherwise valid law prohibiting conduct that the State is free to regulate.").

[13] *Id.* at 877–78.

is one we should expect to accommodate, in legislation, religiously motivated practice.[14] Still, as the Court once observed, the First Amendment does not require governments to permit the religious believer "to become a law unto himself."[15]

By enacting RFRA, however, Congress codified an apparently broad, bipartisan, and ecumenical consensus that the *Smith* rule does not adequately protect and respect religious liberty.[16] The act constrained governments more tightly: It outlawed the imposition by officials of substantial burdens on religious exercise—even through generally applicable laws—unless it is the "least restrictive means" of furthering a "compelling governmental interest."[17]

In one sense, then, the *O Centro* case is unremarkable and prosaic— a mid-term sleeper—and involves only the allocation of burdens of proof in cases arising under a specific federal statute. The justices agreed with the lower courts that the act required the government to demonstrate, in a particularized, more-than-conclusory way, that its refusal to exempt from the scope of the drug laws the otherwise-illegal religious use of hoasca was justified by a compelling state interest.

It would be a mistake, though, to move past the decision too quickly, for at least two reasons. First, it is no small thing that the new Roberts Court—unanimously—has made it clear that the tighter constraints imposed by Congress on the national government really do bind. The *Smith* case teaches clearly that the political process is the main arena, and politically accountable actors are the primary players, when it comes to accommodating the special needs of religious believers. *O Centro*—and RFRA—are entirely consistent with

---

[14] *Id.* at 890.

[15] *Id.* at 879 (quoting Reynolds v. United States, 98 U.S. 145, 167 (1879)).

[16] See William K. Kelley, The Primacy of Political Actors in Accommodation of Religion, 22 U. Haw. L. Rev. 403, 438 (2000) ("In the wake of *Smith*, a broad coalition— even a consensus—emerged that it would be appropriate to pass a statute to protect religious liberty more broadly than the Court had interpreted the Free Exercise Clause to require.").

[17] 42 U.S.C. §§ 2000bb-1(a), (b). In *City of Boerne v. Flores*, 521 U.S. 507 (1997), the justices ruled that Congress lacked the power under the Fourteenth Amendment to apply this more demanding standard to the actions of state and local governments.

this teaching.[18] However, it also underscores the point that when that process, and those actors, produce such an accommodation, courts and officials are to take it seriously. Second, it appears that the justices have, with one voice, rejected the notion that such accommodations amount to an unconstitutional privileging, endorsement, or establishment of religion. Again, the Constitution for the most part permits—for better or worse—governments to regulate in ways that, in effect, burden religious exercise. At the same time, and no less certainly, it allows—and even invites—governments to lift or ease the burdens on religion that even neutral official actions often impose. Notwithstanding our constitutional commitment to religious freedom through limited government and the separation of the institutions of religion and government, it is and remains in the best of our traditions to "single out" lived religious faith as deserving accommodation.[19]

I.

Before turning to the details and implications of the *O Centro* case, it makes sense to set out a brief and necessarily incomplete overview of the basic problem. In a nutshell: The First Amendment to our Constitution protects the "free exercise" of "religion" and prohibits

---

[18] This is not to deny, of course, that RFRA and similar state statutes confer substantial discretion on judges. The point is, the authorization for the exercise of this discretion has been conferred—and this exercise may be monitored and corrected—by politically accountable actors.

[19] As now-Chief Justice Roberts once wrote, in another context, "[A]ccommodation by the government of the religious beliefs of its citizens 'follows the best of our traditions.'" Brief for the United States as Amicus Curiae Supporting Petitioners at 35, Lee v. Weisman, 505 U.S. 577 (1992) (No. 90-1014) (quoting Zorach v. Clauson, 343 U.S. 306, 314 (1952)). See generally, e.g., Michael W. McConnell, The Problem of Singling Out Religion, 50 DePaul L. Rev. 1 (2000). Cf., e.g., Andrew Koppelman, Is It Fair to Give Religion Special Treatment?, 2006 U. Ill. L. Rev. 571, 574 ("Government may privilege religion, but the First Amendment requires that it do so at a very high level of abstraction. . . . Because religion is a distinctive human good, accommodation of religion as such is not unfair."). But see, e.g., Steven G. Gey, Why Is Religion Special? Reconsidering the Accommodation of Religion Under the Religion Clauses of the First Amendment, 52 U. Pitt. L. Rev. 75, 79 (1990) (arguing that "the accommodation principle is incompatible with a proper understanding of the religion clauses" and insisting that "[t]he establishment clause should be viewed as a reflection of the secular, relativist principles of the Enlightenment, which are incompatible with the fundamental nature of religious faith").

its "establishment."[20] So far, so good. But what do these two constitutional commands *mean*? What does the Constitution's requirement
that governments not "prohibit[] the free exercise" of "religion"
actually demand of officials, particularly in the contemporary context, where government actors and action are ubiquitous, and "religion" is an increasingly tailored-to-suit phenomenon?[21] What limits
does the First Amendment's ban on "establishment[s]" of religion
impose on the political community's ability to acknowledge, respect,
and even to support the role religious faith plays in the private
experiences of individuals and the common spaces of public life?
And, more specifically, what do these provisions mean for government's efforts, or obligation, to accommodate religious conviction by
lifting burdens from religious exercise? Does the protection afforded
"free exercise" require governments to exempt religiously motivated
conduct from the scope of generally applicable laws? If so, when?
If not, why not? Or, does the First Amendment's ban on "establishment[s]" of religion reflect a judicially enforceable commitment to
privatized religion, and to a bright line between the domains of
faith and law, such that even legislative decisions to accommodate
religious believers are suspect? If not, where is the line between
permissible accommodations and impermissible privileges? For
many years, these and related questions have been at the heart of
First Amendment conversations, litigation, and scholarship.[22]

So far as Supreme Court precedent and "black letter" law go, the
modern doctrine centers on and emerges from three principal cases:

[20] U.S. Const. amend. I.

[21] See generally, e.g., Alan Wolfe, The Transformation of American Religion: How
We Actually Live Our Faith (2003); Richard W. Garnett, Assimilation, Toleration,
and the State's Interest in the Development of Religious Doctrine, 51 UCLA L. Rev.
1645, 1662–66 (2004).

[22] See, e.g., Gerard V. Bradley, Beguiled: Free Exercise Exemptions and the Siren
Song of Liberalism, 20 Hofstra L. Rev. 245 (1991); Philip A. Hamburger, A Constitu-
tional Right of Religious Exemption: An Historical Perspective, 60 Geo. Wash. L.
Rev. 915 (1992); Michael W. McConnell, The Origins and Historical Understanding
of Free Exercise of Religion, 103 Harv. L. Rev. 1409 (1990); Michael W. McConnell,
Free Exercise Revisionism and the Smith Decision, 57 U. Chi. L. Rev. 1109 (1990);
Douglas Laycock, Formal, Substantive and Disaggregated Neutrality Toward Reli-
gion, 39 DePaul L. Rev. 993 (1990).

Sherbert v. Verner,[23] *Wisconsin v. Yoder*,[24] and *Smith*.[25] Mrs. Sherbert, a Seventh-Day Adventist, was fired for refusing to work on Saturday, the "Sabbath Day of her faith."[26] The South Carolina Employment Security Commission denied Mrs. Sherbert's claim for unemployment benefits because the "restriction upon her availability for Saturday work brought her within the provision disqualifying [her] for benefits."[27] Mrs. Sherbert challenged the commission's decision as a violation of her rights under the Free Exercise Clause. In the Supreme Court, Justice Brennan concluded for the majority that because Mrs. Sherbert's conduct—*i.e.,* refusing to work on her Sabbath—did not pose a threat to public safety, peace, or order, the First Amendment required the government to show that the burden on her free exercise imposed by the commission's decision was "justified by a compelling state interest."[28] The burden on Mrs. Sherbert was clear: Putting to her the choice between "following the precepts of her religion and forfeiting benefits," on the one hand, and "abandoning one of the precepts of her religion in order to accept work," on the other, imposed the "same kind of burden upon the free exercise of religion as would a fine imposed against appellant for her Saturday worship."[29] Nor was this burden justified by a compelling governmental interest. Justice Brennan insisted that "no showing merely of a rational relationship to some colorable state interest would suffice," but only "'the gravest abuses, endangering paramount interests'," would permit the government to limit an individual's free exercise of religion.[30]

In *Yoder*, the Court reviewed the convictions of members of the Old Older Amish who had violated Wisconsin's school-attendance law. Notwithstanding the state's requirement that young people attend school until the age of sixteen, the Yoders declined to send their children to public or private school after the eighth grade,

---

[23] 374 U.S. 398 (1963).
[24] 406 U.S. 205 (1972).
[25] See *supra* note 11.
[26] Sherbert, 374 U.S. at 399.
[27] *Id.* at 401.
[28] *Id.* at 403 (internal quotation marks and citation omitted).
[29] *Id.* at 404.
[30] *Id.* at 406 (quoting Thomas v. Collins, 323 U.S. 516, 530 (1945)).

opting instead for "informal vocational education" designed to pre-pare them for life in their community.[31] Writing for the Court, Chief Justice Burger agreed with the state that governments have a strong interest in regulating and requiring education. At the same time, he insisted that even such a weighty interest is "not totally free from a balancing process when it impinges on fundamental rights . . . such as those specifically protected by the Free Exercise Clause."[32] More specifically, the chief justice wrote that "in order for Wisconsin to compel school attendance . . . it must appear either that the State does not deny the free exercise of religious belief by its requirement, or that there is a state interest of sufficient magnitude to override the interest claiming protection under the Free Exercise Clause."[33] In *Yoder,* the Court was convinced that the application of the compul-sory-attendance law would "gravely endanger if not destroy the free exercise of respondents' religious beliefs."[34] And, it was not willing to accord decisive weight to the government's abstract claims about the importance of education, insisting instead that "it was incumbent on the State to show with more particularity how its admittedly strong interest in compulsory education would be adversely affected by granting an exemption to the Amish."[35]

Now, before turning to *Smith,* two points are worth noting about *Sherbert, Yoder,* and the line of religious-accommodation cases. First, the Court in both of these cases heard and rejected the suggestion that exemptions for religious believers from the burdens imposed by generally applicable laws amount to unconstitutional establish-ments of religion. In *Sherbert,* the Court said that "the extension of unemployment benefits to Sabbatarians in common with Sunday worshippers reflects nothing more than the governmental obligation of neutrality in the face of religious differences, and does not repre-sent that involvement of religious with secular institutions which it is the object of the Establishment Clause to forestall."[36] And in *Yoder,* the majority reasoned that accommodating the Amish religion "can

[31] Wisconsin v. Yoder, 406 U.S. 205, 222 (1972).

[32] *Id.* at 214.

[33] *Id.*

[34] *Id.* at 219.

[35] *Id.* at 236.

[36] Sherbert v. Verner, 374 U.S. 399, 409 (1963).

hardly be characterized as sponsorship or active involvement. The purpose and effect of such an exemption are not to support, favor, advance, or assist the Amish, but to allow their centuries-old religious society . . . to survive free from the heavy impediment" of the compulsory-attendance law.[37] Second, it is widely recognized that, in the years leading up to *Smith*, religious claimants' demands for free-exercise exemptions were usually rejected, notwithstanding the Court's professed adherence to the demanding *Sherbert* standard.[38] In some cases, the Court found ways to avoid applying the compelling interest test at all.[39]

The doctrinal landscape—if not the results for litigants in actual cases—changed markedly in 1990 with the decision in *Employment Division v. Smith*.[40] In something of a reprise of *Sherbert*, *Smith* involved two individuals who had been denied unemployment benefits after they were fired for using peyote—a hallucinogenic drug classified as a controlled substance under Oregon law—in a ceremony of the Native American Church. In *Smith*, however, the Court rejected the argument that this disqualification violated the Free Exercise Clause. Justice Scalia wrote, "[i]t is a permissible reading of the text . . . to say that if prohibiting the exercise of religion . . . is not the object of the [law] but merely the incidental effect of a generally applicable and otherwise valid provision, the First Amendment has not been offended."[41] Indeed, he continued, the Court had "never held that an individual's religious beliefs excuse him from compliance with an otherwise valid law prohibiting conduct that the State is free to regulate."[42] But what about *Sherbert* and *Yoder*? Justice Scalia distinguished the latter as a case involving "not the

[37] Yoder, 406 U.S. at 234 n.22.

[38] See, e.g., United States v. Lee, 455 U.S. 252 (1982); Bob Jones Univ. v. United States, 461 U.S. 574 (1983). See also Thomas C. Berg, What Hath Congress Wrought? An Interpretive Guide to the Religious Freedom Restoration Act, 39 Vill. L. Rev. 1, 9 (1994) ("After *Yoder*, the Court never again upheld a free exercise claim on the merits against a general law (except for three unemployment benefits cases that were virtual reruns of *Sherbert*).").

[39] See, e.g., Goldman v. Weinberger, 475 U.S. 503 (1986); Jimmy Swaggart Ministries v. Bd. of Equalization of Cal., 493 U.S. 378 (1990).

[40] 494 U.S. 872 (1990).

[41] *Id.* at 878.

[42] *Id.* at 878–79.

Free Exercise Clause alone, but the Free Exercise Clause in conjunction with other constitutional protections."[43] As for *Sherbert*, the Court emphasized that the case had involved a "system of individual exemptions" for secular reasons and purposes. The justices concluded that it stands for the rule that, in such a situation, an exemption that is available for other, non-religious reasons must also be extended in "cases of 'religious hardship,'" unless there is a compelling reason not to afford similar treatment.[44]

Prominent scholars have defended the *Smith* rule—if not, perhaps, the Court's creation of an inelegant "hybrid rights" claim—with reference to the practices at the founding and the original understanding of the relevant constitutional provision.[45] Justice Scalia's arguments, however, focused more on what the majority clearly regarded as the unattractive prospect of subjecting policy after policy to compelling-interest review whenever an individual could identify or imagine a burden on his or her sincere "religious" convictions. It was, for the majority, "horrible to contemplate that federal judges will regularly balance against the importance of general laws the significance of religious practice."[46] Far better, in the Court's view, to leave the matter of religious exemptions and accommodation to the politically accountable branches. True, the Court conceded, "leaving accommodation to the political process will place at a relative disadvantage those religious practices that are not widely engaged in."[47] Still, "that unavoidable consequence of democratic government must be preferred to a system in which each conscience is a law unto itself or in which judges weigh the social importance of all laws against the centrality of all religious beliefs."[48] What's

---

[43] *Id.* at 881.

[44] *Id.* at 884 (quoting Bowen v. Roy, 476 U.S. 693, 708 (1986)).

[45] See, e.g., Bradley, *supra* note 22; Hamburger, *supra* note 22. In *Smith*, Justice Scalia had characterized *Yoder* and other exemption cases as presenting "hybrid situation[]," rather than "a free exercise claim unconnected with any communicative activity or parental right." 494 U.S. at 882. The justices have done little to clarify how, exactly, a "hybrid rights" claim works or should be treated by courts. See generally, e.g., Stephen H. Aden & Lee J. Strang, When a "Rule" Doesn't Rule: The Failure of the Oregon Employment Div. v. Smith "Hybrid Rights" Exception, 108 Penn. St. L. Rev. 573 (2003).

[46] Smith, 494 U.S. at 889 n.5.

[47] *Id.* at 890.

[48] *Id.*

more, Justice Scalia insisted, "[v]alues that are protected against government interference through enshrinement in the Bill of Rights are not thereby banished from the political process."[49] And, of course, the "political process" quickly produced the Religious Freedom Restoration Act.

II.

Again, the *O Centro* case involved the use of a hallucinogenic tea called hoasca in the religious ceremonies of the O Centro Espirita Beneficiente Uniao do Vegetal (UDV), a religious community that originated in Brazil. Hoasca is made by brewing two indigenous Brazilian plants. It contains dimethyltryptamine (DMT) and—here's the difficulty—is categorized as a schedule I controlled substance under the federal Controlled Substances Act (CSA).[50] A small American group of UDV believers imported hoasca for use in religious ceremonies and, in 1999, the U.S. Customs Service seized three drums of the illegal tea. And although the government only threatened prosecution, that threat was enough to induce the UDV to stop the ritual use of hoasca in the United States.

However, the UDV then sought an injuction in federal court, contending, among other things, that the Religious Freedom Restoration Act's "compelling interest" standard requires the government to exempt believers' use of hoasca from the CSA's burdensome prohibitions. In the district court, the United States conceded that the "CSA imposes a substantial burden on [UDV believers'] sincere exercise of religion."[51] It insisted, though, that it has a compelling interest in "adhering to the 1971 Convention on psychotropic substances; . . . preventing the health and safety risks posed by hoasca; and . . . preventing the diversion of hoasca to non-religious use."[52] After hearing evidence regarding the potential health risks associated with hoasca use and the possible diversion of hoasca into the

---

[49] *Id.*

[50] Controlled Substances Act, 21 U.S.C. §§ 801 et seq. Under the CSA, it is a crime to knowingly or intentionally "manufacture, distribute, or dispense, or possess with intent to manufacture, distribute, or dispense, a controlled substance." 21 U.S.C. § 841(a)(1).

[51] O Centro Espirita Beneficiente Uniao do Vegetal v. Ashcroft, 282 F. Supp. 2d 1236, 1252 (D.N.M. 2002).

[52] *Id.* at 1252–53.

black market, the district court concluded that the evidence was "in equipoise"[53] and "virtually balanced."[54] And so, it ruled that the government had "failed to carry its heavy burden" of proving that its refusal to accommodate UDV's religiously motivated use cleared RFRA's high bar.[55] In the court's view, the government had not demonstrated "a compelling government interest in protecting the health of UDV members using hoasca or in preventing the diversion of hoasca to illicit use."[56] The United States Court of Appeals for the Tenth Circuit affirmed,[57] and the Supreme Court granted review.

Before the justices, the government pressed three arguments. First, it contended the district court's evidentiary "equipoise" was insufficient to authorize the injunction against the no-exemption enforcement of the CSA.[58] Next, it argued that the character of schedule I substances, and the government's strong interest in uniform application of the CSA, preclude individualized exemptions for particular religious groups.[59] Finally, the government insisted that its obligations under the 1971 Convention on Psychotropic Substances supply the compelling interest required by RFRA.[60] Writing for a unanimous Court, Chief Justice Roberts rejected each of these arguments.

First, with respect to the government's "equipoise" claim, the chief justice noted that "the UDV [had] effectively demonstrated"— indeed, the government had conceded—"that its sincere exercise of religion was substantially burdened."[61] Therefore, the burden of proof was "placed squarely on the Government by RFRA."[62] Indeed, the point of the act was precisely to protect religious exercise by

[53] *Id.* at 1262.

[54] *Id.* at 1266.

[55] *Id.* at 1269.

[56] *Id.*

[57] O Centro Espirita Beneficiente Uniao do Vegetal v. Ashcroft, 342 F.3d 1170 (10th Cir. 2003); O Centro Espirita Beneficiente Uniao do Vegetal v. Ashcroft, 389 F.3d 973 (10th Cir. 2004) (en banc).

[58] Gonzales v. O Centro Espirita Beneficiente Uniao do Vegetal, 126 S. Ct. 1211, 1218–19 (2006).

[59] *Id.* at 1220.

[60] *Id.* at 1224.

[61] *Id.* at 1219.

[62] *Id.* at 1220.

demanding more from the government than a tie-goes-to-the-regula-tor rule. Even if getting the district court to find the evidence in "equipoise" came close, it could not satisfy the standard imposed on the government by Congress. In the end, the government had failed to establish, as RFRA requires, that its refusal "would, more likely than not, be justified by the asserted compelling interests."[63]

Next, the justices were unmoved by the claim that the need for uniform application of the drug laws defeated UDV's claim for a religious exemption.[64] This claim, the Court seemed to believe, also missed the whole point of RFRA. After all, the law's purpose is to provide or prompt exemptions for religious believers and religiously motivated conduct in situations where officially imposed burdens on religion are not the "least restrictive" means of furthering compelling state interests.[65] To credit, let alone to accord conclusive weight to, a blanket assertion that there is "no need to assess the particulars of the UDV's use or weigh the impact of an exemption for that specific use, because the Controlled Substances Act serves a compel-ling purpose and simply admits of no exception,"[66] would severely hamstring RFRA's operation.

What's more, the chief justice observed that Congress had quite explicitly incorporated into RFRA the compelling-interest standard as it was understood and applied in the *Sherbert* and *Yoder* cases.[67] After reviewing these decisions, he concluded that "RFRA requires the Government to demonstrate that the compelling interest test is satisfied through application of the challenged law 'to the person'— the particular claimant whose sincere exercise of religion is being substantially burdened."[68] And, because RFRA requires such a par-ticularized inquiry, it is not enough for the government merely to "invok[e] the general characteristics of Schedule I substances" or

---

[63] *Id.* at 1219. It was irrelevant, the chief justice explained, that the "equipoise" determination was made at the preliminary injunction stage of the case. "Congress' express decision to legislate the compelling interest test indicates that RFRA challenges should be adjudicated in the same manner as constitutionally mandated applications of the test, including at the preliminary injunction stage." *Id.* at 1220.

[64] *Id.* at 1220–24.

[65] *Id.* at 1220.

[66] *Id.*

[67] *Id.* at 1220–21.

[68] *Id.* at 1220.

"Congress' determination that DMT should be listed under Schedule I."[69] The act requires consideration of "the harms posed by the particular use at issue[.]"[70]

Chief Justice Roberts also noted that the "Act itself contemplates ... exempting certain people from its requirements"; that is, "an exception has been made to the Schedule I ban for religious use" for the use of peyote in Native American religious ceremonies.[71] So, not only had the government failed to consider carefully, in a particularized way, whether any harm to a "compelling" government interest would result from an exemption for UDV believers from the hoasca ban, its insistence that no such exemption was possible flew in the face of its earlier decision to provide a religious exemption for thousands of Native Americans from a similar ban on peyote.[72]

The Court recognized that "the Government [could] demonstrate a compelling interest in uniform application of a particular program by offering evidence that granting the requested religious accommodations would seriously compromise its ability to administer the program."[73] In other words, the public interest in the efficient enforcement of a program or prohibition could conceivably outweigh an individual's free-exercise interests, but only if granting the requested exemption would actually endanger the regulatory scheme. In *O Centro*, "the Government's argument for uniformity ... rest[ed] not so much on the particular statutory program at issue as on slippery-slope concerns that could be invoked in response to *any* RFRA claim for an exception to a generally applicable law."[74] The government had failed to explain why an exception for religious use of hoasca would be any more disruptive to the Controlled Substance Act's regulatory system than an exception for peyote. In the justices' view, the peyote exception reflected Congress' determination that the government did not, in fact, have a compelling interest

[69] *Id.* at 1221.

[70] *Id.*

[71] *Id.*

[72] *Id.* at 1222 ("If such use is permitted in the face of the congressional findings ... it is difficult to see how those same findings alone can preclude any consideration of a similar exception [for the UDV] ....").

[73] *Id.* at 1223.

[74] *Id.* (emphasis added).

in unswerving adherence to a uniform, exceptionless prohibition on the religiously motivated use of controlled substances.[75]

Finally, the Court was unimpressed by the government's assertions relating to the 1971 Convention on Psychotropic Substances.[76] Although the justices agreed that the convention covers hoasca, they maintained that "[t]he fact that *hoasca* is covered by the Convention . . . does not automatically mean that the Government has demonstrated a compelling interest in applying the Controlled Substances Act [to the UDV's use of hoasca]."[77] Indeed, "[t]he Government did not even *submit* evidence addressing the international consequences of granting an exemption for the UDV."[78] Again, the bottom line under RFRA is that the "invocation of such general interests, standing alone, is not enough."[79] So far as the Court is concerned, "Congress has determined that courts should strike sensible balances, pursuant to a compelling interest test that requires the Government to address the particular practice at issue."[80]

III.

What is the significance of the *O Centro* decision and what are its implications, not only with respect to litigation under RFRA, but also more generally? As Professor Berg has observed, "RFRA and its background . . . raise some distinctive and bothersome problems of interpretation."[81] For thirteen years, though, the Supreme Court had little to say about them. From the beginning, some scholars wondered whether the act would, in application, have any real bite. Professor Paulsen, for example, wrote that he was willing to "wager that the courts will apply RFRA pretty much the way they applied the *Sherbert* test prior to *Smith*: inconsistently, insensitively, and incoherently."[82] *O Centro*, though, at the very least signals the Court's recognition that RFRA demands more of courts than a rubber-stamp

[75] *Id.* at 1224.

[76] *Id.* at 1224–25.

[77] *Id.* at 1225 (emphasis in original).

[78] *Id.* (emphasis in original).

[79] *Id.*

[80] *Id.*

[81] Berg, *supra* note 38, at 3.

[82] Michael Stokes Paulsen, A RFRA Runs Through It: Religious Freedom and the U.S. Code, 56 Mont. L. Rev. 249, 293 (1995).

endorsement of the government's stated reasons for refusing to exempt religious believers from regulatory burdens. At the same time, the opinion contains nothing to suggest that a repudiation of *Smith* is in the offing.

Again, it is clear that RFRA was designed to restore—in those contexts to which it applies—the compelling-interest standard that the Court at least purported to apply in the *Sherbert* and *Yoder* cases. At the same time, it is just as clear that the Court rarely applied that standard with the vigor it professed. It is one thing, after all, to invoke such a demanding standard and another to put it to work invalidating laws. The fact that the Court, during the years between *Sherbert* and *Smith,* had seemed to regard as "compelling" most of the asserted interests in free-exercise cases caused some to wonder whether, in practice, RFRA would "restore" much of anything.

The chief justice's opinion in *O Centro* could soothe, if not dispel, such concerns. He insisted, after all, that "RFRA, and the strict scrutiny test it adopted, contemplate an inquiry more focused than the . . . categorical approach"[83] that had often carried the day for the government in post-*Yoder* cases. In keeping with this "more focused" inquiry, it appears that, after *O Centro,* boilerplate findings and assertions by the government about a program's aims and importance are not enough to sustain its burden in RFRA cases. Instead, the Court's position and approach seem consonant with the approach offered more than a decade ago by Professor Laycock: "It is not enough that the government's regulation or program as a whole serves a compelling interest. . . . [I]t is not enough that the repeal of the law would defeat the government's compelling interest. Rather, government must make the much more difficult showing that an exception for religious claimants would defeat its compelling interest."[84] Indeed, Chief Justice Roberts echoed this interpretation in his opinion for the Court, reminding the government that it is not enough to "repeatedly invoke[] Congress' findings and purposes underlying the Controlled Substances Act"; after all, "Congress had a reason for enacting RFRA, too."[85]

---

[83] O Centro, 126 S. Ct. at 1220.

[84] Douglas Laycock & Oliver S. Thomas, Interpreting the Religious Freedom Restoration Act, 73 Tex. L. Rev. 209, 222 (1994).

[85] O Centro, 126 S. Ct. at 1225.

It is worth noting, though, that there is nothing glib or naïve in the chief justice's acceptance of the duty, assigned by Congress, of balancing the government's asserted interests in enforcement against those of religious believers in unburdened religious exercise. In *Smith*, remember, the difficulties, and even the dangers, associated with such balancing had, at the very least, confirmed the majority's view that, in most cases, the First Amendment neither requires nor authorizes it. There is no getting around the fact that these difficulties and dangers are real. As the Court acknowledged in *O Centro*, there was "no cause to pretend that the task assigned by Congress to the courts under RFRA is an easy one. Indeed, the very sort of difficulties highlighted by the Government here were cited by this Court in deciding that the approach later mandated by Congress under RFRA was not required as a matter of constitutional law under the Free Exercise Clause."[86] Nevertheless, the Court refused to allow the difficulty inherent in the compelling interest test deter them from striking the "sensible balances" called for by this duly enacted exercise of congressional power.[87]

In *Smith*, Justice Scalia had warned that "it is horrible to contemplate that federal judges will regularly balance against the importance of general laws the significance of religious practice."[88] At least with respect to the smaller sphere of "general laws" that RFRA affects, though, none of the justices in *O Centro* expressed similar horror. In fact, the confidence Chief Justice Roberts expressed in judges' ability to find "sensible balances" evokes Justice O'Connor's *Smith* concurrence, where she insisted that "courts have been quite capable of . . . strik[ing] sensible balances between religious liberty and competing state interests."[89] It should be emphasized, though, that *O Centro* is, in this respect, entirely consistent with the majority's conclusion and premises in *Smith*. That is, it is not that Chief Justice

---

[86] *Id.*

[87] *Id.* (quoting 42 U.S.C. § 2000bb(a)(5)).

[88] Employment Div. v. Smith, 494 U.S. 872, 889 n.5 (1990).

[89] *Id.* at 902 (O'Connor, J., concurring). Compare this language with Chief Justice Roberts in *O Centro*: "Congress determined that the legislated test 'is a workable test for striking sensible balances between religious liberty and competing prior governmental interests.' . . . This determination finds support in our cases; in *Sherbert*, for example, we rejected a slippery-slope argument similar to the one offered in this case." O Centro, 126 S. Ct. at 1223.

Roberts is more dashing and headstrong in the face of what Justice Scalia regarded as a horrible prospect. The point, instead, is that—consistent with Justice Scalia's invitation—the politically accountable legislative branch subjected itself to an exemption-friendly balancing regime and, of course, retains the power to change course, or bail itself out, should the need arise.[90] As Professor Berg has observed, under RFRA, "[t]he authorization for protecting religious freedom at the expense of other societal values now comes from legislation by the political branches, rather than interpretations of open-ended constitutional language by unelected judges."[91]

Besides affirming, in a general way, the "toothiness" of RFRA's compelling-interest standard, the *O Centro* case also suggests an important consideration for litigants and judges working out its application. It seems safe to say that the justices agree with Professor Paulsen's view that, under RFRA, a "lack of systematic pursuit [of an interest by the government] belies the [government's] assertion of [the interest's] compelling importance."[92] The chief justice wrote that "[t]he fact that the Act itself contemplates that exempting certain people from its requirements . . . indicates that congressional findings with respect to Schedule I substances should not carry the determinative weight, for RFRA purposes, that the Government would ascribe to them."[93] In addition, a refusal to provide relief from the burdens imposed by a general law on religious exercise is unlikely to be, as RFRA requires it to be, the "least restrictive means" to accomplish a compelling government objective when the legislature has already decided that *other* exemptions are consistent with its accomplishment.[94]

---

[90] Cf. Eugene Volokh, A Common Law Model for Religious Exemptions, 46 UCLA L. Rev. 1465 (1999) (describing and defending a "common-law exemption model" in which decisions about religious exemptions are initially made by courts but are revisable by legislatures).

[91] Berg, *supra* note 38, at 28.

[92] Paulsen, *supra* note 82, at 264.

[93] O Centro, 126 S. Ct. at 1221.

[94] Even in the free exercise context, as the Court in *Smith* recognized, it remains the case that when the government "has in place a system of individual exemptions, it may not refuse to extend that system to cases of 'religious hardship' without compelling reason." Smith, 494 U.S. at 884. For an interesting—and, perhaps, telling—decision applying this rule, see the opinion of now-Justice Alito in *Fraternal Order of Police Newark Lodge No. 12 v. City of Newark,* 170 F.3d 359 (3d Cir. 1999).

O Centro is instructive, and might provide something of a RFRA-roadmap, in another way, too. The decision indicates the justices' willingness to provide meaningful content to Congress' accommodation in the face of slippery-slope predictions. Responding colorfully to the government's contention that the Controlled Substances Act established a closed regulatory system that permits no RFRA-inspired exemptions, the chief justice observed that "[t]he Government's argument echoes the classic rejoinder of bureaucrats throughout history: If I make an exception for you, I'll have to make one for everybody, so no exceptions."[95] The chief justice's point was not, of course, that exemptions cannot have a cumulative effect, one that erodes or undermines the efficiency and efficacy of an important regulatory program. It was, instead, that the government's "general interest in uniformity," standing alone, is not enough under RFRA to excuse a "substantial burden on religious exercise."[96] As he emphasized, RFRA mandates "consideration, under the compelling-interest test, of exceptions to 'rule[s] of general applicability.'"[97] True, "there may be instances in which a need for uniformity precludes the recognition of exceptions to generally applicable laws under RFRA,"[98] but to see this possibility is not to give conclusive weight to those "slippery-slope concerns that could be invoked in response to any RFRA claim."[99]

The *O Centro* decision is noteworthy not only for the clues and guidance it provides concerning future litigation under RFRA and application of its compelling-interest standard.[100] Although, again, the case was not really an Establishment or Free Exercise Clause case, the Court's unanimous opinion nonetheless spoke—or did not speak—in important ways about the First Amendment's religious-freedom provisions. More than a few scholars[101]—and also one jus-

---

[95] O Centro, 126 S. Ct. at 1223.

[96] *Id.*

[97] *Id.* (quoting 42 U.S.C. § 2000bb-1(a)) (alteration in original).

[98] *Id.* at 1224.

[99] *Id.* at 1223.

[100] It is worth noting the possibility that *O Centro* will influence the understanding and application not only of the federal Religious Land Use and Institutionalized Persons Act, but also the states' own RFRA-type laws and even the states' own stricter-than-*Smith* constitutional standards.

[101] See, e.g., Marci A. Hamilton, The Religious Freedom Restoration Act Is Unconstitutional, Period, 1 U. Pa. J. Const. L. 1 (1998); Christopher L. Eisgruber & Lawrence

tice[102]—have suggested that RFRA crosses a line between permissible accommodation and unconstitutional establishment of religion. Or, as Professor Berg has put it, "some courts and commentators in the U.S. have not only rejected constitutionally mandated exemptions for religion; they have flirted with the idea that religious exemptions (or at least a fair number of them) are constitutionally forbidden."[103] In *O Centro*, though, it was enough for the chief justice to report, without dissent or recorded objection, that "[i]n *Cutter v. Wilkinson*, . . . we held that the Religious Land Use and Institutionalized Persons Act of 2000, which allows federal and state prisoners to seek religious accommodations *pursuant to the same standard as set forth in RFRA*, does not violate the Establishment Clause."[104]

Again, the compatibility of religious accommodations with the Establishment Clause was discussed in *Sherbert*,[105] *Smith*,[106] and *Boerne*.[107] In *Sherbert*, Justice Brennan wrote that religious exemptions do not violate the Establishment Clause because they reflect "nothing more than the governmental obligation of neutrality in the face of religious differences."[108] Similarly, although Justice Scalia concluded in *Smith* that religious accommodations are rarely mandated by the Free Exercise Clause, he indicated no unease the constitutionality of accommodations by the politically accountable branches.[109] Justice Stevens, on the other hand, contended in his *Boerne* concurrence that RFRA amounts to a "governmental preference for religion, as opposed to irreligion, . . . forbidden by the First Amendment."[110]

G. Sager, Why the Religious Freedom Restoration Act Is Unconstitutional, 69 N.Y.U. L. Rev. 437 (1994).

[102] City of Boerne v. Flores, 521 U.S. 507, 536 (1997) (Stevens, J., concurring) ("In my opinion, [RFRA] is a 'law respecting an establishment of religion' that violates the First Amendment to the Constitution.").

[103] Thomas C. Berg, The Permissible Scope of Legal Limitations on the Freedom of Religion or Belief in the United States, 19 Emory Int'l L. Rev. 1277, 1306 (2005).

[104] O Centro, 126 S. Ct. at 1223–24 (emphasis added).

[105] Sherbert v. Verner, 374 U.S. 398 (1963).

[106] Employment Div. v. Smith, 494 U.S. 872 (1990).

[107] City of Boerne v. Flores , 521 U.S. 507 (1997).

[108] Sherbert, 374 U.S. at 409.

[109] Smith, 494 U.S. at 890 (noting that the political community "can be expected to be solicitous of that value in its legislation").

[110] Boerne, 521 U.S. at 537 (Stevens, J., concurring).

O Centro rejects this view, and adopts instead the reasoning set out last year in Justice Ginsburg's opinion for the Court in *Cutter*.[111] In that case, as was noted earlier, the Court rejected an Establishment Clause challenge to another legislative accommodation, the Religious Land Use and Institutionalized Persons Act, which employs the same compelling-interest standard as does RFRA. The justices determined that "RLUIPA's institutionalized-persons provision [is] compatible with the Establishment Clause because it alleviates exceptional government-created burdens on private religious exercise."[112] That is, the Establishment Clause does not forbid Congress from choosing to remove the burdens that it imposes upon religious practitioners through generally-applicable laws. Furthermore, the Court noted that the compelling interest test of RLUIPA—and therefore RFRA—requires the courts to "take adequate account of the burdens a requested accommodation may impose on nonbeneficiaries" and satisfy themselves "that the Act's prescriptions are and will be administered neutrally among different faiths."[113] This aspect of the compelling-interest test ensures that accommodations will not violate the Establishment Clause by punishing non-religious individuals or endorsing a specific religion.

IV.

An important component of the legacy of the former chief justice, William H. Rehnquist, is the Court's move in Religion Clauses cases toward "neutrality" and equal treatment as the constitutional touchstones.[114] In the school-vouchers context, for example, Rehnquist gradually steered his colleagues away from a strict version of no-aid separationism to an approach that focuses on the religion-neutral criteria employed in school-voucher programs and the role of parents' private choices in directing public funds to religious schools.[115]

[111] Cutter v. Wilkinson, 544 U.S. 709 (2005).

[112] *Id.* at 720.

[113] *Id.*

[114] See generally, e.g., Daniel O. Conkle, Indirect Funding and the Establishment Clause: Rehnquist's Triumphant Vision of Neutrality and Private Choice, in The Rehnquist Legacy (Craig M. Bradley ed., 2006).

[115] See, e.g., Zelman v. Simmons-Harris, 536 U.S. 639 (2002). See generally, e.g., Nicole Stelle Garnett & Richard W. Garnett, School Choice, The First Amendment, and Social Justice, 4 Tex. Rev. L. & Pol. 301 (2000).

Public holiday displays or depictions of religious symbols may now be permitted, notwithstanding the Establishment Clause, if they do not communicate a message of "endorsement" of or favoritism toward religion.[116] According to the Court's line of public-forum cases, religious expression is permitted in the public square—indeed, it may not be singled out for exclusion—because and to the extent it represents a "viewpoint," or perspective, like any other, against which the government is not allowed to discriminate.[117] And, as has already been discussed, the rule in Free Exercise Clause cases, after *Smith*, is that exemptions for religious believers or religiously motivated conduct are rarely required when the allegedly burdensome law is generally applicable and religion-neutral. Under current doctrine, then, religion is not, for the most part, constitutionally entitled to privilege or special accommodation, nor must its expression be carefully policed or confined to private life.[118] Religion is protected, permitted, and welcome, it appears, because and to the extent of its same-ness.

A detailed analysis and evaluation of this thoroughgoing shift[119] in Religion Clauses cases' outcomes and animating premises is, as they say, well beyond the scope of this paper. Even if one believes— as we do—that an entirely wise commitment to the institutional separation of religion and government does not require judicially enforced public secularism,[120] or a "religion as a hobby"-style privatization of religious faith and activism,[121] one might still wonder about the merits, and even the coherence, of the Court's neutrality- and equality-centered approach to the freedom of religion.[122] And, even

[116] See, e.g., Van Orden v. Perry, 125 S. Ct. 2854 (2005).

[117] See, e.g., Rosenberger v. Rector & Visitors of the University of Virginia, 515 U.S. 819 (1995).

[118] For a very different understanding, see, e.g., Abner S. Greene, The Political Balance of the Religion Clauses, 102 Yale L.J. 1611 (1993).

[119] But see Locke v. Davey, 540 U.S. 712 (2004).

[120] On the other hand, Professor Sullivan has argued that "[t]he bar against an establishment of religion entails the establishment of a civil order—the culture of liberal democracy—for resolving public moral disputes." Kathleen M. Sullivan, Religion and Liberal Democracy, 59 U. Chi. L. Rev. 195, 198 (1992).

[121] See generally, e.g., Stephen L. Carter, The Culture of Disbelief: How American Law and Politics Trivialize Religious Devotion (1994).

[122] See generally, e.g., Steven D. Smith, Getting Over Equality: A Critical Diagnosis of Religious Freedom in America (2001); Alan Brownstein, Protecting Religious Liberty: The False Messiahs of Free Speech Doctrine and Formal Neutrality, 18 J.L. & Pol 119 (2002).

if one concludes, with Justice Scalia, that *Smith* represents the better understanding both of the relevant text's original public meaning and the nature and consequences of democratic government,[123] one might still insist that a meaningful commitment to religious liberty under law should translate into more than "religion blindness" as an overriding constitutional principle.[124]

Just last year, in one of the Ten Commandments cases, the Court re-affirmed what the justices have been saying for (at least) fifty years: When the government "respects the religious nature of our people and accommodates the public service to their needs," "it follows the best of our traditions."[125] True, religious believers and leaders are no less capable than others of venality and self-interest, and so not every exemption for religion that emerges from the political process will be a responsible accommodation rather than spoils for powerful interests.[126] True, just governments and worthy political leaders will use law's coercive and expressive powers to protect the vulnerable from serious harms, and should not turn a blind eye to such harms simply because they are inflicted in the name or because of religious faith. Nevertheless, it is a prominent and attractive theme in our political and constitutional traditions that governments not only may, but should, respect religious faith and protect religious freedom through legislative accommodations and by, at times, "singling out" religion.[127]

---

[123] Employment Div. v. Smith, 494 U.S. 872, 890 (1990) (stating that it is an "unavoidable consequence of democratic government" that "leaving accommodation to the process will place at a relative disadvantage those religious practices that are not widely engaged in").

[124] McConnell, The Problem of Singling Out Religion, *supra* note 19, at 3 (contending that "religion-blindness" "should not be treated as a general, or controlling, interpretation of the First Amendment.").

[125] Van Orden v. Perry, 125 S. Ct. 2854, 2859 (2005) (quoting Zorach v. Clauson, 343 U.S. 306, 314 (1952)).

[126] For a passionate critique of exemptions for religion from generally applicable laws, and an argument that religious institutions and believers are powerful, sometimes self-interested players in our political process, see, e.g., Marci A. Hamilton, God v. the Gavel: Religion and the Rule of Law (2005).

[127] The "singling out" of religion through exemptions is, according to prominent scholars, best regarded not as a "privilege" for religion but as a way of reducing government interference with religion or state-sponsored skewing of religion-related decisions. See generally, e.g., McConnell, *supra* note 19; Laycock, *supra* note 22.

But how "attractive," really, is this theme? Given that almost any regulation will burden or inconvenience someone, *why* should the political authorities in a pluralistic community take *particular* care that the measures they adopt in order to promote the common good, as they understand it, do not interfere with or constrain religiously motivated conduct?[128] Putting aside, for now, the question whether current constitutional doctrine permits religious accommodations—again, it does—and putting aside the fact the text of the First Amendment speaks specifically to "religion," how can such accommodations be justified? What good reasons do we have for worrying more about laws' effects on religious believers' practices and incentives than on those of others? Yes, religion is important to many people, but so are many other things. It has been argued that forcing people to violate *religious* norms and obligations imposes "special mental torment," given the way that religious believers perceive these norms and obligations and the results of violating them. In addition, it has been suggested that exemptions for religion reflect a recognition that people ought not to be put by the government in the position of having to violate a conflicting duty. And, perhaps it is enough to justify such exemptions that the civil-disobedience or political-stability costs of refusing them are particularly high.[129] In the end, though, none of these arguments or observations seems to mark "religion"—as opposed to autonomy, conscience, etc.—as unusually deserving of special solicitude by regulators.

Perhaps this is because, in fact, there *are no good reasons* for secular governments, accountable to communities that are diverse and divided, to single out religion for special accommodation? Perhaps, as Professor Leiter contends in a recent paper, there are no "credible principled argument[s] . . . that explain why, as a matter of moral

---

[128] See, e.g., Steven D. Smith, The Rise and Fall of Religious Freedom in Constitutional Discourse, 140 U. Pa. L. Rev. 149 (1991).

[129] These arguments have been presented and discussed by, for example, Dean John Garvey. See generally, e.g., John H. Garvey, Free Exercise and the Values of Religious Liberty, 18 Conn. L. Rev. 779 (1986). Garvey's own view is that what makes religious claimants distinct, and religion special, is, in the end, that "religion is a lot like insanity" and that "[w]e protect [religious believers'] freedom . . . because they are not free." *Id.* at 801.

or other principle, we ought to accord special legal and moral treatment to religious practices"?[130] If, as Leiter insists, the "distinctive features of religious belief" are, as Leiter argues, the "categoricity of its commands and its insulation from evidence," the case for specially accommodating religiously motivated practices would seem quite weak.[131] After all, why would we want the state to "carve out special protections that encourage individuals to structure their lives around categorical demands that are insulated from the standards of evidence and reasoning we everywhere else expect to constitute constraints on judgment and action"?[132]

Now, lawyers and judges probably can and will continue deploying and applying First Amendment doctrine, and litigating and deciding First Amendment cases, with or without the help (or hindrance) of a deep religious-freedom theory that justifies their enterprise. The Constitution's text—"Congress shall make no law respecting an establishment of religion, or prohibiting the free exercise thereof"—requires us to come up with a usable, if not principled, body of rules, presumptions, and tests, and so, of course, we will. That said, the questions remain, and remain important: Why is religion special? Why should government accommodate religious believers and practices, even if constitutional doctrines do not require it? Human freedom is a good, we can all agree, but what is distinctively good about *religious* freedom?

It was widely believed, before and at our Nation's founding, and for many years thereafter, that the reasons for protecting religious liberty were *religious* reasons.[133] It was, for example, James Madison's view that a legal right to religious freedom followed from a truth about human beings and the world, namely, that "religion or the duty which we owe to our Creator and the manner of discharging it, can be directed only by reason and conviction, not by force or violence."[134] Consistent with this view, we might say that religious freedom under and through law is best explained by the fact that

---

[130] Brian Leiter, Why Tolerate Religion?, at 1, available at http://ssrn.com/abstract=904640.

[131] *Id.* at 23, 24.

[132] *Id.* at 27.

[133] See generally, e.g., Smith, *supra* note 128, at 154–66.

[134] James Madison, Memorial and Remonstrance Against Religious Assessments (1785).

"the law thinks religion is a good thing"[135] and is correct in so thinking. We might affirm that human beings are made to seek the truth, are obligated to pursue truth and to cling to it when it is found, and that this obligation cannot meaningfully be discharged unless persons are protected against coercion in religious matters.[136] And, we might say that secular governments have a moral duty— even if, under *Smith*, it is not a legally enforceable duty—to promote the ability of persons to meet this obligation and flourish in the ordered enjoyment of religious freedom, and should therefore take affirmative steps to remove the obstacles to religion that even well meaning regulations can create. We could say this, but do we believe it?

[135] John H. Garvey, An Anti-Liberal Argument for Religious Freedom, 7 J. Contemp. Legal Issues 275, 291 (1996).

[136] See, e.g., Second Vatican Ecumenical Council, Declaration on Religious Freedom ¶¶ 2, 3.

The End of the Exclusionary Rule, Among Other Things: The Roberts Court Takes on the Fourth Amendment

*David A. Moran**

I. Introduction

I have found through experience that when one argues a case in the United States Supreme Court, it can be more than a bit difficult to put the resulting decision in perspective. Depending on whether one wins or loses (and I've had both experiences), it is all too easy to think of the case as either the most important breakthrough in years or the death of the law as we know it.

I hope the reader will apply the appropriate degree of skepticism, therefore, when I say that my 5-4 loss in *Hudson v. Michigan*[1] signals the end of the Fourth Amendment as we know it. In *Hudson*, the Court held that when the police violate the Fourth Amendment "knock and announce requirement" the normal Fourth Amendment remedy, exclusion of the evidence found after the violation, does not apply. While that result is remarkable enough given that the rule had been otherwise in every state except one[2] and in every

*Associate Dean, Wayne State University Law School. I gratefully acknowledge the help I received from Timothy O'Toole and Corinne Beckwith, both of the Public Defender Service of the District of Columbia, in clarifying my thinking throughout the *Hudson* litigation. I also thank the Cato Institute and the National Association of Criminal Defense Lawyers for filing a superb amicus brief on my side in *Hudson*, and I thank Professor Tracey Maclin of Boston University Law School for writing that brief. After receiving that help from Cato, agreeing to write this article was the least I could do.

[1] 126 S. Ct. 2159 (2006).

[2] See People v. Stevens, 597 N.W.2d 53 (Mich. 1999). The *Stevens* reasoning had been specifically rejected by appellate courts in at least nine states, see Brief for the Petitioner at 17, Hudson v. Michigan, 126 S. Ct. 2159 (2006) (No. 04-1360) (collecting cases from eight states) [hereinafter Petitioner's Brief]; Supplemental Brief for the Petitioner at 1, Hudson v. Michigan, 126 S. Ct. 2159 (2006) (No. 04-1360) (citing case from additional state), while courts in the remaining 40 states apparently suppressed evidence found following knock and announce violations without even entertaining

federal circuit except one,[3] what makes *Hudson* truly exceptional is the reasoning in Justice Antonin Scalia's opinion for the Court. As many observers have noted, that opinion calls into question the entire rationale of the exclusionary rule, not just in the knock-and-announce context, but for all types of Fourth Amendment violations.[4] Given that the Court had not seriously questioned the vitality of the exclusionary rule in federal court for nearly a century and had extended the rule to the states forty-five years ago, it is difficult to overstate the importance of *Hudson* and what it suggests the Court is likely to do to the Fourth Amendment in the next few years.

But enough about my case. In this article, I will survey all of the Court's 2005 term Fourth Amendment cases, of which *Hudson* was but one of five. I will begin by discussing the Court's four other Fourth Amendment decisions before turning back to *Hudson* and what it means for the right of the people to be free from unreasonable searches and seizures.

II. Consent, Anticipatory Warrants, Parolees, and a Truly Strange Exigency Case: The Term's Other Fourth Amendment Cases.

Of the Court's five Fourth Amendment cases this term, *Hudson* attracted by the far the most public attention, and rightly so because the result in *Hudson* portends a major shift in the Court's jurisprudence. By contrast, two of the other four cases, *United States v. Grubbs*[5] and *Brigham City v. Stuart*,[6] produced completely unsurprising unanimous opinions in favor of the government, while a third, *Georgia*

---

arguments such as those accepted in *Stevens*, see Petitioner's Brief, *supra*, at 17 (collecting cases from 12 states).

[3] See United States v. Langford, 314 F.3d 892, 894–95 (7th Cir. 2002). The reasoning in *Langford* had been specifically rejected by two other circuits. See United States v. Dice, 200 F.3d 978, 984–86 (6th Cir. 2000); United States v. Marts, 986 F.2d 1216, 1220 (8th Cir. 1993), while courts in all of the remaining circuits suppressed evidence found following knock and announce violations without considering the arguments accepted in *Langford*. See Petitioner's Brief, *supra* note 2, at 17 (collecting cases from two circuits.

[4] See, e.g., Akhil Reed Amar, The Battle of Hudson Heights: A Small Case Portends Big Changes for the Exclusionary Rule, Slate (June 19, 2006), at http://www.slate.com/id/2143983.

[5] 126 S. Ct. 1494 (2006).

[6] 126 S. Ct. 1943 (2006).

v. Randolph,[7] bitterly divided the Court but resulted in a holding so narrow as to make the case of almost no precedential value. The Court's final case of the term, *Samson v. California,*[8] was an important case that split the Court 6-3, but the result, a further restriction on the already severely limited rights of parolees, should not have been a shock to anyone. In this section, I will discuss each of these four cases in turn.

A. Grubbs: *Anticipatory Warrants and Some Fuzzy Math*

From a purely theoretical point of view, the most interesting of the term's other Fourth Amendment cases is *Grubbs.* The Warrants Clause of the Fourth Amendment provides, in relevant part, that "no Warrants shall issue, but upon probable cause." The phrasing seems to suggest that there must be probable cause *at the moment a magistrate issues a search warrant.* In other words, the plain language appears to require that at the moment the magistrate signs the warrant, there must be a "fair probability that contraband or evidence of crime will be found in a particular place."[9]

The problem in *Grubbs* was that there was no such fair probability of finding contraband or evidence in Grubbs' house at the moment the magistrate signed the warrant because the warrant was of the "anticipatory" variety. That is, the warrant was issued on the anticipation that there would be contraband or evidence found in Grubbs' home at some future time. In Grubbs' case, that anticipation was very well-founded since he had ordered a videotape containing child pornography from postal inspectors; as soon as the postal inspectors delivered the videotape, there would unquestionably be contraband in his home.[10] Nonetheless, Grubbs argued, the warrant was fatally defective because there was no probable cause that any contraband or evidence was in his home at the moment the magistrate signed the warrant.[11]

The Court thus had to squarely confront, for the first time, the issue of whether anticipatory warrants are per se violative of the Warrants Clause. The Court had never had occasion to answer the

---

[7]126 S. Ct. 1515 (2006).

[8]126 S. Ct. 2193 (2006).

[9]Illinois v. Gates, 462 U.S. 213, 238 (1983).

[10]126 S. Ct. at 1497.

[11]*Id.* at 1498.

question before because every circuit to consider the question (including the Ninth Circuit, which had ruled in Grubbs' favor on other grounds)[12] had held that anticipatory warrants are constitutional.[13]

Writing for all eight justices,[14] Justice Scalia made short work of Grubbs' argument. According to Scalia, *all* search warrants are anticipatory because the magistrate's probable cause determination in an ordinary case amounts to nothing more or less than a "prediction that the item will still be there when the warrant is executed."[15] When, for example, a warrant issues to tap a telephone, the magistrate is anticipating that the subject of the warrant will use the phone to discuss a crime, not that the subject is discussing a crime over the phone at the very moment the magistrate is signing the warrant. An anticipatory warrant, like ordinary warrants, simply requires the magistrate to determine that it is currently probable that contraband or criminal evidence will be present when the warrant is executed.[16]

The Court went on to reject Grubbs' claim that this theory would allow the government to obtain anticipatory warrants for every home in America by simply claiming that there will be probable cause if contraband or criminal evidence is delivered to that home at some time in the future. According to the Court, the magistrate may issue an anticipatory warrant only if he or she concludes both that there is probable cause that the triggering condition (in Grubbs' case, the controlled delivery of the videotape) will occur and that the fulfillment of this triggering condition will result in a fair probability that contraband or criminal evidence will be found at the specified place.[17] Since there was clearly probable cause that the controlled delivery to Grubbs' house would occur and that such a delivery would result in contraband being found in that house, the Court

[12]United States v. Grubbs, 377 F.3d 1072 (9th Cir. 2004), amended, 389 F.3d 1306 (9th Cir. 2004).

[13]126 S. Ct. at 1499. It also appears that no state appellate court has ever held that anticipatory warrants violate the Fourth Amendment.

[14]Justice Alito did not participate in *Grubbs* because it was argued before he was confirmed.

[15]*Id.*

[16]*Id.* at 1500.

[17]*Id.*

concluded that the magistrate properly issued the anticipatory warrant.[18] Finally, the Court reversed the Ninth Circuit's conclusion that the magistrate's failure to explicitly list the triggering condition in the warrant violated the particularity requirement.[19]

I find it difficult to argue with almost anything in Justice Scalia's opinion for the Court. My one minor quibble is purely mathematical. While the Court has always resisted quantifying the level of certainty required for probable cause, the term is widely understood to mean a quantum of proof approximately equal to "as likely as not."[20] By holding that the magistrate must find that "there is a fair probability that contraband or evidence of a crime will be found in a particular place [and] that there is probable cause to believe the triggering condition will occur,"[21] the Court has actually (and, almost certainly, unknowingly) reduced the level of proof required for probable cause. Applying this test to Grubbs' case, the Court concluded that the warrant was properly issued because "the occurrence of the triggering condition—successful delivery of the videotape to Grubbs' residence—would plainly establish probable cause for the search" and "the affidavit established probable cause to believe the triggering condition would be satisfied."[22]

To illustrate how this method of analysis actually reduces the proof required for probable cause, suppose a magistrate concludes that there is a 60% chance that the subject will accept delivery of a suspicious package and that there is a 60% chance that the package contains child pornography. The magistrate would then conclude, applying the Court's test, that there is probable cause to expect

---

[18]*Id.*

[19]*Id.* at 1500–01. Although the eight justices who participated in *Grubbs* unanimously rejected the Ninth Circuit's holding that an anticipatory warrant must explicitly state the triggering condition, Justice Souter, joined by Justices Stevens and Ginsburg, did not join Justice Scalia's opinion for the Court on this point and instead wrote a separate concurring opinion in which he argued that the failure to list the triggering condition could result in "untoward consequences with constitutional significance." *Id.* at 1502.

[20]See, e.g., 2 Wayne R. LaFave, Search and Seizure: A Treatise on the Fourth Amendment 66–91 (4th ed. 2004) (observing that question remains open whether probable cause is "more probable than not, or [if] something short of this suffice[s]").

[21]126 S. Ct. at 1500 (citing Illinois v. Gates, 462 U.S. 213, 238 (1983)) (internal citation, quotation marks, and emphasis omitted).

[22]*Id.*

the occurrence of the triggering condition and to believe that the occurrence would result in the presence of contraband in the home, even though the probability that *both* conditions would be met is a mere 36%, significantly less than the normal level of proof required for probable cause. The proper test should be whether, after considering the probability that the triggering condition will be met and the probability that the occurrence of this triggering condition will result in the physical presence of contraband or criminal evidence at the location, there is a fair probability that contraband or criminal evidence will be found at the location when the warrant is executed.

This error in the Court's opinion is, I concede, a minor one of mostly theoretical significance. In Grubbs' case, as in almost all controlled delivery cases, the Court's method of analysis and the correct test will produce the same result because the contents of the package are known to a very high degree of certainty. Therefore, even if the likelihood that Grubbs would accept delivery was only 60%, the likelihood that such acceptance would result in contraband in his home was essentially 100% (because the postal inspectors knew that the tape contained child pornography) and, therefore, the likelihood that the two conditions would result in contraband in his home would still be 60%, that is, more probable than not. Nevertheless, one might have hoped that someone on the Court with a more mathematical bent would have spotted this issue.

B. Brigham City: *A Wacky Little "Flyspeck" of a Case*

The Court's unanimous decision in *Brigham City* upholding a warrantless entry and search was nothing but an easy application of the well-settled doctrine that the existence of a genuine emergency excuses the need for a warrant. In fact, the law is so well-settled in this area and the lower courts' decision in this case was so obviously wrong that it is difficult to understand why the Court chose to take the case and perform an exercise in pure error-correction. As Justice Stevens aptly put it in his brief concurring opinion, "This is an odd flyspeck of a case."[23]

[23]Brigham City v. Stuart, 126 S. Ct. 1943, 1949 (2006) (Stevens, J., concurring). In his concurrence, Justice Stevens noted that the state courts' decision suppressing the evidence was so obviously wrong as a matter of Fourth Amendment law that he wondered whether those courts might actually have meant to suppress the evidence as a matter of Utah law (which grants citizens more protection against searches and seizure than the Fourth Amendment does), even though those courts never cited Utah law. *Id.* at 1950.

My hypothesis is that the Court took the case because the facts were entertaining.[24] Responding to a complaint about a loud party early one morning, police officers from the small town of Brigham City, Utah, watched through a screen door as five people, one of whom was a juvenile, engaged in a wild, bloody brawl inside the kitchen of the home.[25] The officers did exactly what one would expect them to do: they entered the kitchen, restored order, and arrested the brawlers.[26]

When the brawlers subsequently moved to suppress the evidence obtained from the home, the state courts did exactly the opposite of what one would expect them to do: they suppressed all of the evidence on the ground that the officers should have obtained a warrant before entering the kitchen.[27] The Court, of course, unanimously reversed, finding that the officers acted perfectly reasonably in immediately entering the kitchen given that one of the brawlers was spitting up blood and that the altercation was still ongoing.[28]

Perhaps the only noteworthy aspect of *Brigham City* is that it allowed Chief Justice Roberts one of his first opportunities to display his sense of humor in an opinion. In rejecting the defendants' claim that the officers should have waited for more serious injuries to be

[24]*Id.* at 1947. Chief Justice Roberts, in his unanimous opinion for the Court, claimed that the Court took the case "in light of differences among state courts and the Court of Appeals concerning the appropriate Fourth Amendment standard governing warrantless entry by law enforcement in an emergency situation." *Id.* (citing cases differing as to whether inquiry is purely objective or whether the court should consider officers' subjective motivations for warrantless entry). However, it is difficult to see how this case presented that issue at all since the Utah Supreme Court applied the same objective test that the Court has long endorsed for such inquiries and applied again here. Compare *id.* at 1946 (citing Utah Supreme Court's statement of test as whether "a reasonable person [would] believe that the entry was necessary to prevent physical harm to the officers or other persons") with *id.* at 1949 (concluding "officers had an objectively reasonable basis for believing both that the injured adult might need help and that the violence in the kitchen was just beginning").

[25]See *id.* at 1946 (describing juvenile punching one of the adult brawlers, causing him or her to spit up blood, before other combatants pushed juvenile against refrigerator with enough force to cause refrigerator to move across floor).

[26]*Id.* The defendants were charged with contributing to the delinquency of a minor, disorderly conduct, and intoxication. As Justice Stevens pointed out in his discussion of the petty nature of this case, the maximum sentence for the most serious of these charges was six months in jail. *Id.* at 1949–50 (Stevens, J. concurring).

[27]*Id.* at 1946–47.

[28]*Id.* at 1949.

inflicted before intervening, he wrote, "The role of a peace officer includes preventing violence and restoring order, not simply rendering first aid to casualties; an officer is not like a boxing (or hockey) referee, poised to stop a bout only if it becomes too one-sided."[29]

C. Randolph: *Consent and the Betraying Spouse*

Unlike *Brigham City, Georgia v. Randolph* clearly presented an unsettled Fourth Amendment question: whether the police could rely on the consent of one person with authority over premises to perform a warrantless entry and search when another person with equal authority over the premises objects. This question had been an open one ever since 1974 when the Court held that "the consent of one who possesses common authority over premises or effects is valid as against the *absent*, nonconsenting person with whom that authority is shared."[30] In *Randolph*, a sharply-divided Court held that such consent is not valid as against a *present*, nonconsenting person with whom authority is shared.

The person doing the consenting in *Randolph* was the defendant's estranged wife, Janet Randolph. After calling the police during a custody dispute with her husband, Mrs. Randolph volunteered to the responding officers that Mr. Randolph was a drug user and that there was evidence of his drug use in the marital home.[31] Mrs. Randolph, not surprisingly, "readily gave" her consent for a search of the home, but Mr. Randolph (an attorney) "unequivocally refused."[32] The officer, apparently preferring Mrs. Randolph's answer over Mr. Randolph's, accepted her invitation to search the home, where he found a straw with cocaine residue.[33] *Randolph* is thus the latest in a series of Fourth Amendment cases in which the police have used all-too-willing wives and girlfriends to gather incriminating evidence against husbands and boyfriends.[34]

---

[29] *Id.*

[30] United States v. Matlock, 415 U.S. 164, 170 (1974) (emphasis added).

[31] Georgia v. Randolph, 126 S. Ct. 1515, 1519 (2006).

[32] *Id.*

[33] *Id.* Mrs. Randolph subsequently withdrew her consent, but the officer used the straw to get a search warrant, which resulted in the discovery of more evidence of Mr. Randolph's drug use.

[34] See, e.g., Coolidge v. New Hampshire, 403 U.S. 443, 485–489 (1971) (upholding use of guns and other evidence retrieved from marital home by defendant's wife); Massachusetts v. Upton, 466 U.S. 727, 729 (1984) (upholding search warrant based on tip from defendant's ex-girlfriend, who admitted to detective that she "wanted to

Unlike the previous cases, however, the defendant in *Randolph* prevailed. Writing for five members of the Court, Justice David Souter concluded in a lengthy opinion that under "widely shared social expectations," reasonable people would not believe they have effective consent to enter a dwelling when one person who lives there is vocally objecting to that entry and that, therefore, the police also could not reasonably rely on such consent to perform a warrantless entry.[35] Chief Justice Roberts wrote a sharp dissent in which he ridiculed the majority's "social expectations" theory.[36] Justices Scalia and Thomas joined Chief Justice Roberts' dissent and filed additional dissenting opinions,[37] while Justices Breyer and Stevens joined Justice Souter's majority opinion and filed additional concurring opinions.[38]

One might think that *Randolph* marked a major expansion in Fourth Amendment rights, given that six of the eight participating justices felt compelled to write opinions. Such thinking would be bolstered by the expressions of mutual hostility contained in the majority opinion and Chief Justice Roberts' opinion.[39]

Such thinking would, however, be wrong. The holding of Justice Souter's majority opinion is so narrowly drawn that it will apply to only a tiny handful of cases every year: "a warrantless search of a shared *dwelling* for evidence over the *express* refusal of consent by a *physically present* resident cannot be justified as reasonable *as to him* on the basis of consent given to the police by another resident."[40] The emphasized words illustrate how rare such cases will be. Only a search of a *dwelling* will trigger the *Randolph* rule. Searches of

burn him"); Illinois v. Rodriguez, 497 U.S. 177 (1990) (upholding entry to defendant's apartment based on "consent" of girlfriend who called police to complain that defendant had assaulted her and who falsely claimed that she had common authority over apartment); Illinois v. McArthur, 531 U.S. 326, 328–29 (2001) (upholding evidence seized after defendant's wife, who was moving out of home, volunteered to police that defendant had "dope" hidden under couch).

[35]Randolph, 126 S. Ct. at 1521–28.

[36]*Id.* at 1531–39 (Roberts, C.J., dissenting).

[37]*Id.* at 1539 (Scalia, J., dissenting); *id.* at 1541 (Thomas, J., dissenting).

[38]*Id.* at 1528 (Stevens, J., concurring); *id.* at 1529 (Breyer, J., concurring).

[39]See, e.g., *id.* at 1524 n.4 (accusing dissenters of harboring "deliberate intent to devalue the importance of the privacy of a dwelling place"); *id.* at 1535 n.1 (Roberts, C.J., dissenting) (characterizing majority's accusation as "a bit overwrought").

[40]*Id.* at 1526 (emphasis added, footnote omitted).

businesses, cars, and other places might be allowed based on the consent of one person over the objection of someone else who would otherwise have the right to complain. Only an *express* refusal by a *physically present* resident will suffice to defeat the consent of another resident. Thus, officers may rely on the consent of a resident even if any reasonable person would assume that another resident would object if asked, unless that other resident is there and actually does object in clear terms.[41] If that other resident is there and does expressly object, that refusal is only effective *as to him*, not to the resident who did consent or a third resident who is not present.[42] Therefore, police officers faced with such a refusal might well decide that they should go ahead and search the dwelling in the hope of turning up evidence that can be used against the consenting resident and all of the absent residents.

The real-world impact of *Randolph* is exceedingly slight for two additional reasons. First, as the majority recognized, an officer can always enter over the objection of a resident in an emergency, as when the officer suspects that someone in the house is in danger.[43]

Second, an officer faced with an objecting co-resident will almost never be thwarted in his desire to obtain evidence from inside the home because two constitutional options remain open. In *Illinois v. McArthur*, on facts essentially identical to those in *Randolph* (an angry wife told the police that her husband had narcotics evidence hidden in the home), the Court held that the officer could keep the husband from entering the house while the police sought a search warrant.[44] Alternatively, the officer can simply ask the consenting resident to go inside, retrieve the evidence, and bring it back out for the officer,

---

[41]Thus, the Court in *Randolph* explained, the officers in *United States v. Matlock* could rely on the consent of the resident who authorized the search of the shared residence without having to consult with Matlock, who was handcuffed in a squad car parked in front of the house. Randolph, 126 S. Ct. at 1534 (Roberts, C.J., dissenting) (citing United States v. Matlock, 415 U.S. 164, 166 (1974)). Similarly, the officers in *Illinois v. Rodriguez*, 497 U.S. 177 (1990), could rely on the apparent consent of Rodriguez's girlfriend to enter the apartment without consulting Rodriguez, who was sleeping inside the apartment. See, e.g., Randolph, 126 S. Ct. at 1534 (Roberts, C.J., dissenting).

[42]The Court did not expressly decide whether such a third resident would be able to piggyback on the refusal of his or her co-tenant. 126 S. Ct. at 1526 n.8.

[43]*Id.* at 1526.

[44]531 U.S. 326, 331–37 (2001).

as the officers did in *Coolidge v. New Hampshire*.[45] Indeed, the majority in *Randolph* specifically noted that both alternatives will usually be open to officers in such situations.[46]

Randolph, then, is an interesting case primarily because it was the first case to reveal deep divisions among the justices in the Fourth Amendment context. Those deep divisions resurfaced in an even stronger fashion a few months later in *Hudson*. But *Randolph* is far too fact-bound and narrow to count as a truly important Fourth Amendment case.

D. Samson: *No Fourth Amendment Rights for Parolees*

Samson v. California, the Court's last Fourth Amendment case of the term did result in a very important, but utterly predictable, 6-3 decision that will soon result in the elimination, in *toto*, of the Fourth Amendment rights of those hundreds of thousands of Americans who are currently on parole.[47] Five years ago, in *United States v. Knights*,[48] the Court had held that a search of a probationer on reasonable suspicion (as opposed to probable cause) was a reasonable search within the meaning of the Fourth Amendment.[49] In *Samson*, the defendant was on parole, not probation, and the police officer who searched him on the street had no basis for any suspicion at all (aside from the fact that the officer knew that Samson was on parole), much less reasonable suspicion.[50] The question, then, in *Samson* was whether a completely suspicionless search of a parolee is reasonable given that a search on reasonable suspicion of a probationer is reasonable.

In an opinion by Justice Clarence Thomas, the Court answered that question in the affirmative. In reaching that conclusion, the Court applied a simple but obviously faulty syllogism. First, the Court pointed out, a parolee is subject to more restrictions on his

---

[45]403 U.S. 443, 487–89 (1971).

[46]Randolph, 126 S. Ct. at 1524–25 & n.6.

[47]According to the Department of Justice, there were approximately 765,400 adults on parole in the United States at the end of 2004. U.S. Department of Justice, Bureau of Justice Statistics: Probation and Parole Statistics (Dec. 22, 2005), available at http://www.ojp.usdoj.gov/bjs/pandp.htm.

[48]534 U.S. 112 (2001).

[49]*Id*. at 121–22.

[50]Samson v. California, 126 S. Ct. 2193, 2196 (2006).

or her freedom than a probationer.[51] Next, the Court reasoned, since *Knights* teaches that a probationer has a diminished expectation of privacy against police searches, a parolee must enjoy no expectation of privacy at all, at least in a state, such as California, that has set up a system permitting suspicionless searches of parolees.[52] Thus, the Court held that a parolee enjoys the same Fourth Amendment rights, none whatsoever, as a prisoner.[53]

The flaw in this reasoning is apparent, as Justice Stevens recognized for the three dissenters. Just because a parolee is subject to more restrictive conditions than a probationer, it does not follow that a parolee enjoys no expectation of privacy at all, as if he or she were still in prison.[54] The dissent also rejected as "entirely circular" the majority's reasoning that California's law requiring parolees to submit to suspicionless searches eliminates a parolee's expectation of privacy, comparing such reasoning to an argument that the government could eliminate the expectation of privacy in homes simply by "announc[ing] on nationwide television that all homes henceforth would be subject to warrantless entry."[55]

Justice Stevens assumed that it might well have been constitutional, under the "special needs" exception to the warrant requirement, to require Samson to submit to suspicionless searches conducted by his parole officer because such a search would have been for a purpose other than generalized crime control and because his parole officer would presumably know whether there were good

[51]See *id.* at 2198–99 (describing restrictive conditions imposed on parolees in general and in California in particular).

[52]See *id.* at 2199 (concluding that parole restrictions "clearly demonstrate that parolees like petitioner have severely diminished expectations of privacy by virtue of their status alone"); *id.* (observing that California law required petitioner to submit to suspicionless searches as condition of parole and concluding, because of his status as parolee and the parole condition, "petitioner did not have an expectation of privacy that society would recognize as legitimate") (footnote omitted).

[53]See Hudson v. Palmer, 468 U.S. 517 (1984) (holding that a prisoner enjoys no Fourth Amendment protection in his cell).

[54]See Samson, 126 S. Ct. at 2204–05 (Stevens, J., dissenting) (criticizing majority's "faulty syllogism" and arguing "that it is simply not true that a parolee's status . . . is tantamount to that of a prisoner or even materially distinct from that of a probationer").

[55]*Id.* at 2206 (Stevens, J., dissenting) (quoting Smith v. Maryland, 442 U.S. 735, 740–41 n.5 (1979)).

reasons to search Samson.[56] But the effect of the majority's holding, Justice Stevens pointed out, is to allow any police officer to search any parolee at any time without any suspicion, or even a reason, at all.[57]

The effect of *Samson* is indeed sweeping. We can expect every, or virtually every, state to soon pass California-type legislation requiring all parolees to submit to suspicionless searches at any time. Once that happens (and it surely will, just as sex offender registration swept across the country in only a few years), we will see as Justice Stevens put it, "an unprecedented curtailment of liberty"[58] for nearly a million of our fellow citizens. While this result is disturbing, it is hardly surprising given *Knights*.

III. *Hudson*: The Court Kills the Knock-and-Announce Rule and Puts the Exclusionary Rule on Life Support

I must confess that I really never saw it coming. When an attorney named Richard Korn telephoned me out of the blue in February 2005 to ask if I would take a look at a case, *People v. Hudson*,[59] that he had just lost in the Michigan courts and assess whether it would make a good vehicle for challenging the Michigan Supreme Court's 1999 decision in *People v. Stevens*,[60] I did not hesitate. After all, I had long been critical of *Stevens*, which had held that exclusion of evidence was not an appropriate remedy for a Fourth Amendment knock-and-announce violation.[61] *Stevens*, in effect, gave the Michigan

---

[56]*Id.* at 2207 (Stevens, J., dissenting). Compare Ferguson v. City of Charleston, 532 U.S. 67, 79 (2001) (holding "special needs" exception inapplicable to warrantless drug program because programmatic purpose of searches was not "divorced from the State's general interest in law enforcement"), with Griffin v. Wisconsin, 483 U.S. 868, 879 (1987) (upholding search of probationer under special needs exception since state's interest was in supervising probationer's rehabilitation, not in generalized crime control).

[57]Samson, 126 S. Ct. at 2207 (Stevens, J., dissenting).

[58]*Id.* at 2202 (Stevens, J., dissenting).

[59]No. 246403, 2004 WL 1366947 (Mich. Ct. App. June 17, 2004), lv. app. den., 692 N.W.2d 385 (Mich. 2006).

[60]597 N.W.2d 53 (Mich. 1999).

[61]In fact, whenever I was invited to speak to groups that included Michigan criminal defense attorneys, I always took the opportunity to criticize *Stevens* and to make a gratuitous offer to write a certiorari petition in an appropriate case. Mr. Korn called me because he had attended one of those talks four years earlier and had remembered my offer.

police carte blanche to violate the knock-and-announce rule, the ancient common law requirement that the police must knock and generally allow residents to open their doors, thereby sparing residents a forcible and terrifying police entry.[62] The Michigan Supreme Court's decision seemed especially vulnerable given that the United States Supreme Court had twice suppressed evidence seized after knock-and-announce violations,[63] and had, just eleven years ago, unanimously held that the knock-and-announce rule was part of the Fourth Amendment in *Wilson v. Arkansas*.[64]

Since the Michigan Supreme Court's refusal to suppress evidence seized after a knock-and-announce violation was out of step with the U.S. Supreme Court's ruling in *Wilson* and with the rule followed in every other state and federal circuit, except one,[65] I felt confident that the Court, if it granted certiorari, would pull Michigan back into line. My confidence was enhanced even further when the Court granted my certiorari petition just four days after it issued *Halbert v. Michigan*,[66] in which the Court reversed another Michigan Supreme Court decision that was radically out of line with the position taken by other state and federal courts. While I certainly realized that it was possible I could somehow lose *Hudson*, it never occurred to me that I could effectively kill an 800-year-old rule protecting personal privacy and simultaneously put the entire exclusionary rule at risk.

But that is exactly what happened. Now that I have recovered from the shock, it is time to do the post-mortem. I will begin by discussing the case itself and the opinions it produced. I will then

[62]See Semayne's Case, 77 Eng. Rep. 194, 195 (K.B. 1603). In *Wilson v. Arkansas*, 514 U.S. 927, 932 n.2 (1995), the Court observed that the rule actually may date to the era of the Magna Carta.

[63]See Miller v. United States, 357 U.S. 301 (1958); Sabbath v. United States, 391 U.S. 585 (1968). In both *Miller* and *Sabbath*, the Court suppressed evidence found after violations of 18 U.S.C. § 3109, the federal statute that codified the common-law knock-and-announce rule.

[64]Wilson, 514 U.S. at 934, 936.

[65]See *supra* notes 2–3.

[66]125 S. Ct. 2582 (2005). In *Halbert*, the Court overruled the Michigan Supreme Court's decision in *People v. Bulger*, 614 N.W.2d 103 (Mich. 2000), which held that Michigan need not appoint appellate counsel for indigent criminal defendants who plead guilty or nolo contendere and wish to file an application for leave to appeal from their pleas and/or sentences to the Michigan Court of Appeals. I represented Mr. Halbert in the United States Supreme Court.

turn to what the decision means for the knock-and-announce rule. Finally, I will discuss the implications for the exclusionary rule.

A. The Case and Justice Scalia's Majority Opinion

After reviewing the case file, I immediately recognized that *Hudson* was an ideal vehicle for challenging *Stevens*. First, there was never any dispute that a knock-and-announce violation had occurred when police officers with a search warrant raided the home that Booker T. Hudson, Jr., shared with his wife in Detroit. Indeed, the police officer in charge of the raid candidly testified at a suppression hearing that, despite having no grounds to dispense with the knock-and-announce requirement, he and the other six officers burst through the front door only three to five seconds after yelling, "Police, search warrant!"[67] This testimony clearly established a knock-and-announce violation because the Court had earlier held in *Richards v. Wisconsin*[68] that the police may force their way inside only after announcing their presence and waiting a reasonable amount of time, unless they have specific reasons to believe that the delay would frustrate the purpose of the search or endanger them. Faced with this testimony, the prosecutor at Hudson's suppression hearing conceded that the officers had violated the knock-and-announce rule.[69] That concession was justified because, even though it is not clear exactly how long the police are supposed to wait before performing a forcible entry, three to five seconds is clearly not enough.[70]

The second reason why *Hudson* struck me as a good vehicle to challenge *Stevens* was that Hudson had been convicted of a relatively minor crime. The police found some seven people in the house who had, between them, approximately twenty rocks of crack cocaine.[71] At his bench trial, the judge, finding no reason to believe that all, or even most, of the cocaine rocks belonged to Hudson, convicted him of possessing only the five rocks that the police found in his

---

[67]See Appendix to Cert. Pet. at 7–9, Hudson v. Michigan, 126 S. Ct. 2159 (2006) (No. 04-1360) (testimony of Officer Jamal Good) [hereinafter Pet. App.].

[68]520 U.S. 385, 394 (1997).

[69]Pet. App., *supra* note 67, at 10.

[70]Cf. United States v. Banks, 540 U.S. 31, 40–41 (2003) (holding that 15 to 20 seconds was enough time to wait before forcing entry to serve a narcotics search warrant).

[71]Remarkably, Justice Scalia's majority opinion characterizes this handful of rocks of cocaine as "[l]arge quantities of drugs." Hudson, 126 S. Ct. at 2162.

pants.[72] For this minor offense, the judge sentenced Hudson to probation.[73]

The legal issue in the case was straightforward, or so I thought. According to the Michigan Supreme Court, evidence found inside a home following a knock-and-announce violation should not be suppressed because such evidence should always be regarded as "inevitably discovered"; that is, the police still would have discovered the same evidence had they complied with the knock and announce requirement.[74] The Court had adopted the inevitable discovery doctrine as an exception to the exclusionary rule in *Nix v. Williams*,[75] but the Michigan Supreme Court's approach amounted to a massive expansion of the doctrine for two interrelated reasons. First, the Court had stressed that the inevitable discovery doctrine applies only when the prosecution can demonstrate that evidence would have been discovered by means "wholly independent" of the unconstitutional police conduct.[76] *Stevens*, however, did not require the existence of any independent means of discovery at all. Second, the Court in *Nix* specifically recognized that the inevitable discovery doctrine would not undermine the deterrence rationale of the exclusionary rule because the officer who engaged in the violation would not normally know whether the same evidence would inevitably be found by independent means.[77] By contrast, after *Stevens*, police in Michigan knew to a certainty that any evidence they found after knock-and-announce violations would always be regarded as "inevitably" discovered. For these reasons, every state and federal court to consider the argument that the inevitable discovery doctrine created a per se exception to the exclusionary rule for

[72]Joint Appendix at 22–23, Hudson v. Michigan, 126 S. Ct. 2159 (2006) (No. 04-1360). The judge also acquitted Hudson of a firearms charge because there was no evidence that he possessed the pistol found under a cushion in the chair on which he was sitting.

[73]*Id.* at 23–24.

[74]See People v. Stevens, 597 N.W.2d 53, 62 (Mich. 1999) (holding evidence admissible because "it would have been inevitably discovered . . . had the police adhered to the knock-and-announce requirement").

[75]467 U.S. 431 (1984).

[76]Murray v. United States, 487 U.S. 533, 542 (1988).

[77]Nix, 467 U.S. at 443–44.

knock-and-announce violations, except the Michigan Supreme Court and the Seventh Circuit, had rejected it.

Therefore, I thought *Hudson* was about two things: the importance of maintaining an effective deterrent so that police would respect the knock-and-announce rule; and, more abstractly, the proper scope of the inevitable discovery exception to the exclusionary rule. What I did not realize was that the case would put the exclusionary rule itself into play.

But for some bad timing, my understanding of the case almost certainly would have prevailed. When the case was first argued on January 9, 2006, it seemed clear that at least five members of the Court agreed that *Stevens* represented an indefensible extension of the inevitable discovery doctrine that would, if accepted, render the knock-and-announce rule meaningless. Unfortunately, one of those five justices was Sandra Day O'Connor, who was replaced by Samuel Alito in February.[78] Two months later, the Court ordered the case reargued.

At the re-argument on May 18, 2006, it became clear to me for the first time that the case was no longer about the knock-and-announce rule or the inevitable discovery doctrine when Justice Scalia asked me, in a series of questions, why the threat of internal police discipline would not convince officers to comply with the

---

[78]See, e.g., Charles Lane, Court Eases "No Knock" Search Ban, Wash. Post, June 16, 2006, at A1 ("[O'Connor's] comments at argument suggested she favored Breyer's view"). During that first oral argument, Justice O'Connor remarked to the assistant solicitor general who was arguing for the United States as amicus curiae on behalf of Michigan, "So, if the rule you propose is followed, then every police officer in America can follow the same policy [of ignoring the knock-and-announce rule]. Is there no policy of protecting the homeowner a little bit and the sanctity of the home from this immediate entry?" Transcript of Oral Argument at 59, Hudson v. Michigan, 126 S. Ct. 2159 (2006) (No. 04-1360) (Jan. 9, 2006). There is further evidence that a majority of the Court was prepared to rule in favor of Hudson after the first argument. Chief Justice Roberts has apparently followed his predecessors' policy of assigning at least one majority opinion to each member of the Court during each sitting. Since Justice Breyer did not author a majority opinion from the January sitting, it is a fair inference that he was initially assigned the majority opinion in *Hudson*, especially since he authored the dissent on behalf of four justices after the case was reargued. See also Linda Greenhouse, Court Limits Protection Against Improper Entry, N.Y. Times, June 16, 2006, at A28 ("Justice Breyer's dissenting opinion was clearly drafted to speak for a majority that was lost when Justice Sandra Day O'Connor left the court shortly after the first argument in January").

knock-and-announce rule.[79] When I responded that such a notion contradicts the very premise of *Mapp v. Ohio*,[80] the seminal 1961 case in which the Court extended the exclusionary rule to the states because other remedies had proven worthless at deterring Fourth Amendment violations, Justice Scalia replied, "*Mapp* was a long time ago. It was before section 1983 was being used, wasn't it?"[81]

Less than a month later, the Court issued its decision in *Hudson*. Writing for five members of the Court, Justice Scalia began his analysis with a lengthy discussion of the history of the exclusionary rule and its "costly toll upon truth-seeking and law enforcement objectives."[82] Turning to the knock-and-announce rule, the Court noted that the rule protects residents and police from violence that may occur when residents mistake the police for criminals, preserves private property from unnecessary destruction, and allows residents an opportunity to compose themselves and prepare for a police entry.[83] After reciting these interests, however, Justice Scalia concluded, "What the knock-and-announce rule has never protected, however, is one's interest in preventing the government from seeing or taking evidence described in a warrant. Since the interests that *were* violated in this case have nothing to do with the seizure of the evidence, the exclusionary rule is inapplicable."[84]

A moment's thought should reveal just how jaw-dropping this statement is. *None* of the interests protected by the Fourth Amendment is about preventing the government from seizing one's contraband or criminal evidence. Indeed, by definition, a person has no right to keep contraband or criminal evidence. Instead, the very point of the exclusionary rule is to safeguard the interests that are protected under the Fourth Amendment by taking away the incentive the police would have to violate those interests in order to obtain contraband or evidence. Thus, under Justice Scalia's reasoning, drugs seized from a person who has been illegally detained

---

[79]Transcript of Oral Argument at 31–33, Hudson v. Michigan, 126 S. Ct. 2159 (2006) (No. 04-1360) (May 18, 2006).

[80]367 U.S. 643 (1961).

[81]Transcript of Oral Argument, *supra* note 79, at 32.

[82]Hudson, 126 S. Ct. at 2163 (internal quotation marks and citation omitted).

[83]*Id*. at 2165.

[84]*Id*. (emphasis in original).

and searched should not be suppressed because the rules governing lawful arrest are designed to protect people from the indignities and inconvenience of arrest, not to protect anyone's possessory interest in narcotics.[85] Similarly, obscene material seized from a home following a warrantless entry should not be suppressed because the warrant requirement protects a homeowner's right against unlawful intrusions, but not his right to possess obscenity.[86]

Having completely recast the exclusionary rule as a narrow remedy that applies only when the evidence seized is of the type that the constitutional protection was designed to protect, Justice Scalia then turned squarely to the argument that exclusion is necessary to deter officers from routinely violating the knock-and-announce rule. With a reference to *Mapp*, he wrote, "We cannot assume that exclusion in this context is necessary deterrence simply because we found that it was necessary deterrence in different contexts and long ago. That would be forcing the public today to pay for the sins and inadequacies of a legal regime that existed almost half a century ago."[87]

So, exactly how have times changed since 1961, when *Mapp* was decided? In two key respects, according to Justice Scalia. First, it is easier to sue the police than it was in those days because of the availability of statutory remedies such as 42 U.S.C. § 1983.[88] In response to the fact that none of the parties in *Hudson* had found a single case in either state or federal court in which anyone recovered anything other than nominal damages for a knock and announce violation, Justice Scalia wrote, "we do not know how many claims have been settled, or indeed how many violations have occurred that produced anything more than nominal injury."[89] Thus, having assumed away the inconvenient lack of evidence that the police have ever been successfully sued for a knock and announce violation,

---

[85]But see, e.g., Ybarra v. Illinois, 444 U.S. 85 (1979) (suppressing narcotics found on bar patron illegally detained and searched).

[86]But see Mapp, 367 U.S. at 660 (suppressing obscene material seized from home following warrantless entry).

[87]126 S. Ct. at 2167.

[88]*Id.*

[89]*Id.*

Justice Scalia concluded, "As far as we know, civil liability is an effective deterrent here, as we have assumed it is in other contexts."[90]

Justice Scalia's second important post-*Mapp* change "is the increasing professionalism of police forces, including a new emphasis on internal police discipline."[91] Without a trace of irony, Justice Scalia proceeded to cite a study from criminologist Samuel Walker for the proposition that there have been "wide-ranging reforms in the education, training, and supervision of police officers" since the days of *Mapp*.[92]

It was left to Professor Walker to point out in an op-ed article that Justice Scalia "twisted my main argument to reach a conclusion the exact opposite of what I spelled out in this and other studies."[93] Professor Walker explained:

> [T]he Warren court in the 1960s played a pivotal role in stimulating these reforms. For more than 100 years, police departments had failed to curb misuse of authority by officers on the street while the courts took a hands-off attitude. The Warren court's interventions (*Mapp* and *Miranda* being the most famous) set new standards for lawful conduct, forcing the police to reform and strengthening community demands for curbs on abuse. Scalia's opinion suggests that the results I highlighted have sufficiently removed the need for an exclusionary rule to act as a judicial-branch watchdog over the police. I have never said or even suggested such a thing. To the contrary, I have argued that the results reinforce the Supreme Court's continuing importance in defining constitutional protections for individual rights and requiring the appropriate remedies for violations, including the exclusion of evidence.[94]

For the reasons stated by Professor Walker, Justice Scalia's argument that increased police professionalism obviates the need for the exclusionary rule is equivalent to a claim that we should dismantle the

---

[90]*Id.* at 2167–68 (citations omitted).

[91]*Id.* at 2168.

[92]*Id.* (quoting S. Walker, Taming the System: The Control of Discretion in Criminal Justice 1950–1990, at 51 (1993)).

[93]Samuel Walker, Scalia Twisted My Words, L.A. Times, June 25, 2006, available at http://www.latimes.com/news/opinion/commentary/la-oe-walker25jun25,0,5718124.story?coll=la-news-comment-opinions (last checked August 7, 2006).

[94]*Id.*

gun towers at the state prison because escape attempts have dropped dramatically since the towers were built.

Ultimately, then, the Court held that exclusion of evidence was unjustified for a knock and announce violation because the interests protected by that rule are not offended by the seizure of evidence found after a violation and because exclusion is no longer necessary to assure compliance with that rule.[95] Before returning to the question of what this holding portends for the knock-and-announce rule and the exclusionary rule, it is necessary to examine the concurring opinion of Anthony Kennedy, who provided the fifth vote for that holding.

B. The Strange Concurrence of Anthony Kennedy

The first paragraph of Justice Kennedy's concurring opinion contains two sentences that make me wonder, in all seriousness, whether he actually read Justice Scalia's majority opinion before he signed on to it. First, according to Justice Kennedy, "The Court's decision should not be interpreted as suggesting that violations of the [knock and announce] requirement are trivial or beyond the law's concern."[96] One can only wonder how a reader could interpret this passage from Justice Scalia's majority opinion as anything but a trivialization of the knock-and-announce rule: "Many would regard [the right not to be subjected to physical abuse and the Sixth Amendment right to counsel] as more significant *than the right not to be intruded upon in one's nightclothes.*"[97]

---

[95]Justice Scalia finished his opinion with a section in which he claimed that the outcome was consistent with three of the Court's prior decisions. Hudson, 126 S. Ct. at 2168–70 (Scalia, J.) (citing and discussing Segura v. United States, 468 U.S. 796 (1984); New York v. Harris, 495 U.S. 14 (1990); and United States v. Ramirez, 523 U.S. 65 (1998)). This section of Justice Scalia's opinion did not constitute the opinion of the Court because Justice Kennedy did not agree with this analysis and therefore did not join this section. *Id.* at 2171 (Kennedy, J., concurring) (declining to join Part IV of Justice Scalia's opinion because "I am not convinced that *Segura v. United States* and *New York v. Harris* have as much relevance here as Justice Scalia appears to conclude") (citations omitted).

[96]*Id.* at 2170 (Kennedy, J., concurring). See also *id.* ("It bears repeating that it is a serious matter if law enforcement officers violate the sanctity of the home by ignoring the requisites of a lawful entry. Security must not be subject to erosion by indifference or contempt.").

[97]*Id.* at 2167 (emphasis added).

Second, according to Justice Kennedy, "the continued operation of the exclusionary rule, as settled and defined by our precedents, is not in doubt."[98] How, then, is the reader to interpret the Court's conclusion that excluding evidence today would be punishing the public "for the sins and inadequacies of a legal regime that existed almost half a century ago," and the lengthy discussion about how things have changed since *Mapp* was decided?[99]

What makes Justice Kennedy's concurrence so difficult to fathom is that *he provided the fifth vote* for the portions of Justice Scalia's opinion trivializing the knock-and-announce rule and casting doubt on the continuing vitality of the exclusionary rule. If he disagreed with those portions of Justice Scalia's opinion, one would think that he would have written an entirely separate opinion concurring in the result. Instead, he signed on to those portions of Justice Scalia's opinion, thus creating a majority for the propositions (if not the holdings) that the knock-and-announce rule is simply about the right to pull on one's nightclothes and that the exclusionary rule is an outdated concept.

The remaining five paragraphs of Justice Kennedy's short concurrence do not help matters much. According to Justice Kennedy, Hudson's claim for exclusion fails as a simple matter of causation; that is, the failure to knock and announce did not cause the evidence to be found.[100] But this argument is nothing more or less than the inevitable discovery argument (the evidence would inevitably have been found even if the violation had not occurred) without the crucial requirement that there be a source independent of the police violation that would have found the evidence.

C. *"Knock, Knock. Who's There? Not the Police, We Don't Knock Anymore:"[101] The Death of an Ancient Privacy Protection*

Before turning to the broader implications of the *Hudson* decision, I think it worthwhile to briefly eulogize the knock-and-announce

---

[98]*Id.* at 2170 (Kennedy, J., concurring).

[99]See *supra* notes 87–92 and accompanying text.

[100]See Hudson, 126 S. Ct. at 2170–71 (Kennedy, J., concurring) ("Under our precedents the causal link between a violation of the knock-and-announce requirement and a later search is too attenuated to allow suppression"); *id.* at 2171 ("In this case the relevant evidence was discovered not because of a failure to knock-and-announce, but because of a subsequent search pursuant to a lawful warrant").

[101]I do not know who authored this joke, but several versions were apparently widely distributed by e-mail in the days after the *Hudson* decision. I thank the many people who forwarded it to me.

rule. A eulogy is appropriate because I do not believe anyone can seriously deny that the knock-and-announce rule is now dead in the United States.

It is true that police departments will still probably play lip service to the rule. But no sane police officer serving a search warrant will bother to comply with the knock-and-announce rule. Some officers might continue to shout "Police, search warrant!" before bursting through the door, just as the officers did in *Hudson*, in order to protect themselves from being mistaken for criminal intruders. But, after *Hudson*, there is no rational reason for an officer to wait for a resident to answer the door before performing an entry. There is essentially no chance that an officer who performs such a precipitous entry will be successfully sued.[102] As for the possibility trumpeted by Justice Scalia that such an officer might be subjected to internal police discipline,[103] I can only say that I have never heard of a police officer being disciplined for a knock-and-announce violation, and I am sure that I never will.

But why should any law-abiding citizen care about the death of the knock-and-announce rule? After all, how likely is it that a decent person will be subjected to a police raid?

The answer is that it is not at all unlikely that an innocent person will be present when the police come suddenly bursting through the door. In his recent comprehensive report on the rise of paramilitary policing in the United States, Radley Balko described seventy-two cases since 1995 in which police officers subjected completely innocent people to terrifying and humiliating paramilitary-style raids only to discover that they had raided the *wrong residence*.[104] While there is no national tracking of such "wrong door" raids, there is no doubt that such occurrences are not especially rare. Indeed, there is an entire American Law Reports (ALR) annotation devoted to the subject of search warrants bearing incorrect addresses, with citations to over 200 state and federal appellate cases, many of them involving raids carried out at the wrong residences.[105]

---

[102]See *supra* notes 79–81 and accompanying text.

[103]Hudson, 126 S. Ct. at 2168.

[104]Radley Balko, Overkill: The Rise of Paramilitary Police Raids in America 43–63 (Cato Institute 2006).

[105]Jay M. Zitter, Error, in Either Search Warrant or Application for Warrant, as to Address of Place to be Searched as Rendering Warrant Invalid, 103 A.L.R.5th 463 (2002).

Even when the police search the correct address, there is an excellent chance that innocent persons will be present in the residence. The standard of probable cause requires the police to show only that there is a "fair probability that contraband or evidence of a crime will be found at a particular place"[106] in order to obtain a search warrant. Since this standard is so low, it is not surprising that the information on which the police rely to obtain a warrant often turns out to be wrong; that is, the police do not find what they are looking for when they carry out the search.[107]

Finally, even if the police do have the right address and the contraband or evidence is present, there is a very good chance that innocent people, such as children or elderly relatives, will be present. Indeed, the Court has long recognized that the police may execute search warrants on premises owned and occupied by people who are not suspected of wrongdoing at all, so long as there is reason to believe that contraband or evidence of crime will be found there.[108]

After *Hudson*, all or virtually all search warrants will be carried out without giving the residents, innocent or not, a chance to answer the door or prepare themselves for the entry. That means, as a practical matter, that there will be more innocent people like Alberta Spruill who will die of heart attacks brought on by a terrifying police entry,[109] and there will be thousands more who will be terrified without dying. There will also be many more innocent people like Cynthia Chapman, who was naked in her shower when the police

---

[106]Illinois v. Gates, 462 U.S. 213, 238 (1983).

[107]There are no national records kept documenting the success rate of police searches. A few newspapers have conducted studies of local police departments and have found that many searches come up empty. See, e.g., Kevin Flynn & Lou Kilzer, No-Knocks Net Little Jail Time, Rocky Mountain News, March 12, 2000 (on file with author) (finding 146 no-knock raids in Denver in 1999 resulted in criminal charges in only 49 cases). See also Balko, *supra* note 104, at 26–27 (discussing studies from various jurisdictions showing police raids often turn up no evidence or result in no charges).

[108]See, e.g., Zurcher v. Stanford Daily, 436 U.S. 547, 556 (1978) ("The critical element in a reasonable search is not that the owner of the property is suspected of crime but that there is reasonable cause to believe that the specific 'things' to be searched for and seized are located on the property to which entry is sought").

[109]New York City police officers raided Ms. Spruill's apartment with a no-knock warrant, only to discover that they were at the wrong address. William K. Rashbaum, Report by Police Outlines Mistakes in Ill-Fated Raid, N.Y. Times, May 31, 2003, at A1.

came charging into her home,[110] who will suffer a humiliating loss of privacy because of *Hudson*. And there will be thousands more Americans who will see their doors destroyed because the police will no longer wait even ten or fifteen seconds for someone to open it.

For some eight hundred years, the knock-and-announce rule has protected English and American citizens from such indignities. I mourn its passing in the United States.

D. Increased Police Professionalism and the Coming End of the Exclusionary Rule

It was, of course, the evident hostility to the exclusionary rule permeating Justice Scalia's opinion for the Court that attracted the most attention to the decision in *Hudson*.[111] If, as Justice Scalia claimed, *Mapp* is merely a relic from "a legal regime that existed almost half a century ago,"[112] and the police today reflexively respect constitutional rights because of "increasing professionalism" and an "effective regime of internal discipline,"[113] then the exclusionary rule would seem to be an unnecessary and excessive remedy for any kind of constitutional violation.

Until *Hudson* was decided, I am not aware of any scholar who seriously believed that the exclusionary rule was in danger of being overruled. In the weeks since that decision, everyone in the field believes that it is now crystal clear that the rule will become a historical relic if one more like-minded justice joins the Court.

Indeed, it even seems possible that the Court could overrule the exclusionary rule with its current composition. Although Justice Kennedy insisted in the first paragraph of his concurring opinion that the "continued operation of the exclusionary rule, as settled

---

[110]See Balko, *supra* note 104, at 48 (discussing Chapman's case). Chapman was also the victim of a wrong door raid.

[111]See, e.g., Linda Greenhouse, Court Limits Protection Against Improper Entry, *supra* note 78, at A28 ("The majority opinion was sufficiently dismissive of the exclusionary rule as to serve as an invitation to bring a direct challenge to the rule in a future case"); Charles Lane, Court Eases "No Knock" Search Ban, *supra* note 78, at A1 (noting that Justice Breyer argued in dissent that majority approach would "roll back the use of the exclusionary rule to enforce the Fourth Amendment in areas where it has long been recognized").

[112]Hudson v. Michigan, 126 S. Ct. 2159, 2167 (2006).

[113]*Id.* at 2168.

and defined by our precedents, is not in doubt,"[114] he joined the very parts of Justice Scalia's opinion that cast doubt on the exclusionary rule. If he really believes in the continuing vitality of the exclusionary rule, it is an absolute mystery to me why he would cast the crucial fifth vote for an opinion that openly declared war on the exclusionary rule.[115]

The hot question that is being asked in the solicitor general's office and in state attorney general offices across the country is: "when will the time be ripe to take down the exclusionary rule in *toto*?" To put it more concretely, if a challenge is brought now, which Justice Kennedy will be there? The Justice Kennedy who signed on to Justice Scalia's opinion denigrating the exclusionary rule, or the Justice Kennedy who tried (but failed) to take it all back in his concurrence? Will there be a retirement among the *Hudson* dissenters so that President Bush (or, perhaps, his successor) can appoint another justice hostile to the exclusionary rule?

I am quite confident that a state prosecutor or attorney general will bring a direct challenge to the entire exclusionary rule to the Court within the next year. That is, a certiorari petition will be filed in a state criminal case that will concede that a clear constitutional violation occurred, such as failure to obtain a warrant before searching a house, but that will argue that *Mapp* should be overruled and that the evidence found after the violation should therefore be admitted.[116]

The hard question is what the Court will do with that certiorari petition. Perhaps the uncertainty in Justice Kennedy's position will cause both the other four justices in the *Hudson* majority and the four justices in the *Hudson* dissent to vote to deny the petition. On

[114]*Id.* at 2170 (Kennedy, J., concurring).

[115]I am not the only one who was mystified by Justice Kennedy's concurrence. See Greenhouse, *supra* note 78, at A28 ("One puzzling aspect of the decision was a concurring opinion by Justice Kennedy, who said that he wished to underscore the point that 'the continued operation of the exclusionary rule, as settled and defined by our precedents, is not in doubt.' Nonetheless, he signed the part of Justice Scalia's opinion that suggested that the exclusionary rule rested on an increasingly weak foundation").

[116]I think it less likely that such a petition will be filed in a federal case, because the solicitor general will probably refrain from taking that position until it is abundantly clear that there is a majority on the Court in favor of abolishing the exclusionary rule.

the other hand, if the justices who dissented in *Hudson* are confident that Justice Kennedy meant what he wrote in his concurrence, perhaps they would vote to grant certiorari in such a case in the hope of getting a fresh precedent reaffirming *Mapp*. But granting certiorari is risky because a single change in the Court's personnel while the case is pending could change the result, just as a change in the Court's makeup changed the outcome in *Hudson*. By the same token, the four justices in the *Hudson* majority (other than Justice Kennedy) might well vote to grant certiorari in a direct challenge to *Mapp*, either because they are convinced that Justice Kennedy will be on their side or because they believe that there is likely to be a new justice in their camp before the case is decided.

There are, in short, a lot of variables that make it impossible to predict the future of the exclusionary rule. But there is no doubt after *Hudson* that the exclusionary rule is back in play and could well be overruled within the next few years.

Like I said, I never saw it coming.

Finding Bickel Gold in a *Hill* of Beans
*Douglas A. Berman**

"First, do no harm," is a common aphorism for the medical profession. If the Supreme Court was judged by this principle, its work in *Hill v. McDonough*[1] might lead some to urge revoking the justices' licenses. The Court's decision to consider Clarence Hill's challenge to Florida's lethal injection protocol resulted in widespread legal confusion and the disruption of executions nationwide. The Court's subsequent ruling in *Hill* raised more legal questions than it answered and ensured that death row defendants would continue to disrupt scheduled executions by pursuing litigation over lethal injections protocols.

But, though harmful to the orderly administration of capital punishment, the Supreme Court's work in *Hill* has its virtues. The Court's consideration of Hill's claims has brought greater (and long needed) scrutiny to the particulars of lethal injection protocols. And the narrow ruling in *Hill* presents a valuable opportunity for other institutions to grapple more fully with the difficult issues raised by any method of state killing.

Consequently, *Hill* might be lauded for reflecting Professor Alexander Bickel's wise insight that the Supreme Court ought sometimes seek to avoid resolution of certain constitutional claims. Professor Bickel suggested that the Supreme Court should, in some settings, avoid definitive resolution of certain constitutional questions to allow other (more democratic) branches of government to take a second look at important issues.[2] But, for the *Hill* decision to produce

---

*William B. Saxbe Designated Professor of Law, Moritz College of Law at the Ohio State University.

[1] 126 S. Ct. 2096 (2006).

[2] See Alexander Bickel, The Least Dangerous Branch 111–98 (1962) (chapter discussing at length "the passive virtues"); see also Guido Calabresi, A Common Law for the Age of Statutes 16–30 (1982) (discussing Bickel's visions of and suggestions for constitutional adjudication).

a kind of Bickel gold, legislators and executive officials must take up the Supreme Court's invitation to start doing a better job regulating how the state kills.

I. The Long and Winding Road up to *Hill*

A. The Not-So-Modern Development of a Modern Execution Method

The historical evolution of execution methods in the United States is a fascinating story with many twists and turns.[3] But this dynamic story turned somewhat monotonous about twenty years ago: starting in the 1980s, nearly every capital jurisdiction began to move away from diverse execution techniques—ranging from hanging and firing squads to the electric chair and the gas chamber—and embraced lethal injection as a more "humane" method of execution.[4] Almost all of the more than 600 executions carried out over the last decade have been by lethal injection, and thirty-nine of the forty capital jurisdictions in the United States now rely on lethal injection as their primary or sole means of putting condemned defendants to death.[5]

The nearly uniform embrace of lethal injection might suggest that this method of execution has been developed and refined to ensure it is the soundest way to kill a condemned defendant. But, as colorfully detailed in a recent article in the *Austin American-Statesman*, the origins of lethal injection as an execution method is hardly inspiring:

> [Oklahoma] State Rep. Bill Wiseman, a Republican from
> Tulsa, suggested that there had to be a better way to execute

[3] Professor Deborah Denno has done the most thoughtful and thorough recent writings about the evolution of execution methods. See, e.g., Deborah W. Denno, Lethally Humane? The Evolution of Execution Methods in the United States, in America's Experiment with Capital Punishment: Reflections on the Past, Present, and Future of the Ultimate Penal Sanction 693 (James R. Acker et al. eds., 2d ed. 2003); Deborah W. Denno, When Legislatures Delegate Death: The Troubling Paradox Behind State Uses of Electrocution and Lethal Injection and What It Says About Us, 63 Ohio St. L.J. 63, 124 (2002).

[4] See Human Rights Watch, So Long as They Die: Lethal Injections in the United States 9–20 (Apr. 2006).

[5] See Denno, When Legislatures Delegate Death, *supra* note 3, at 84–85 and Appendix 1; see also John Gibeaut, It's All in the Execution: Prosecutors Fear Limitless Civil Rights Complaints Over Lethal Injection Procedures, ABA Journal, Aug. 2006, at 17, 18 (noting that of the "38 states with the death penalty, 37 use lethal injection, as do the federal government and the military"). Nebraska is the one state that still relies exclusively on the electric chair as its execution method.

criminals than electrocution, a process that had fallen out of public favor because it was increasingly viewed as brutal and violent. Wiseman consulted doctors, who refused to help, citing their oath to save lives, not take them. He got the same response from scientists and other medical professionals. "I muttered to colleagues that it looked as if I would need to find a veterinarian to tell me how to 'put down' condemned prisoners," Wiseman recalled in a 2001 article in The Christian Century magazine.

Enter A. Jay Chapman, Oklahoma's state medical examiner, a doctor who had been responsible for pronouncing inmates dead after electrocutions in Colorado. Chapman had no pharmacological training, just an opinion and a willingness to help. During a meeting with Wiseman, he dictated what was to become the new national template: "An intravenous saline drip shall be started in the prisoner's arm, into which shall be introduced a lethal injection consisting of an ultra-short-acting barbiturate in combination with a chemical paralytic agent.". . . Chapman was quoted as saying in [a recent] report. "I didn't do any research. . . . It's just common knowledge. Doctors know potassium chloride is lethal."[6]

The widespread affinity for lethal injection appears even more troubling given how execution protocols have been adopted and implemented throughout the United States. A recent report from Human Rights Watch has this disturbing summary of the development and application of lethal injection procedures:

> The three-drug sequence was developed in 1977 by an Oklahoma medical examiner who had no expertise in pharmacology or anesthesia and who did no research to develop any expertise. Oklahoma's three-drug protocol was copied by Texas, which in 1982 was the first state to execute a man by lethal injection. Texas's sequence was subsequently copied by almost all other states that allow lethal injection executions. Drawing on its own research and that of others, Human Rights Watch has found no evidence that any state seriously investigated whether other drugs or administration methods would be "more humane" than the protocol it adopted.

[6]See Mike Ward, Death Penalty's Drug Cocktail Rooted in Texas: Other States Adopted Method Chosen with Little Scientific Basis, Austin American-Statesman, May 28, 2006, available at www.statesman.com/news/content/news/stories/local/05/28execute.html.

> Corrections agencies continue to display a remarkable lack of due diligence with regard to ascertaining the most "humane" way to kill their prisoners. Even when permitted by statute to consider other drug options, they have not revised their choice of lethal drugs, despite new developments in and knowledge about anesthesia and lethal chemical agents. They continue to use medically unsound procedures to administer the drugs. They have not adopted procedures to make sure the prisoner is in fact deeply unconscious from the anesthesia before the paralyzing second and painful third drugs are administered.[7]

Writing in a similar vein, Professor Deborah Denno has spotlighted problems with execution procedures attributable to "vague lethal injection statutes, uninformed prison personnel, and skeletal or inaccurate lethal injection protocols. When some state protocols provide details, such as the amount and type of chemicals that executioners inject, they often reveal striking errors, omissions, and ignorance about the procedure."[8]

B. New Scrutiny of Lethal Injection Protocols and a Surprising Grant

As lethal injection became the prevailing method of execution, some commentators questioned the purported humaneness of the standard three-drug protocols,[9] and some death row defendants raised a variety of (unsuccessful) legal challenges to these protocols in state and federal courts.[10] But a 2005 article in the British medical journal *The Lancet* invigorated new public and constitutional scrutiny of lethal injection as a method of execution. *The Lancet* article, which reported the results of the postmortem analysis of executed prisoners, reached this conclusion:

[7] See Human Rights Watch, *supra* note 4, at 2.

[8] See Deborah Denno, Death Bed, 124 TriQuarterly J. 141, 144 (2006); see also Denno, When Legislatures Delegate Death, *supra* note 3, at 105–28 (arguing that lethal injection as a method of execution violates the Eighth Amendment's prohibition of cruel and unusual punishments).

[9] See Adam Liptak, Critics Say Execution Drug May Hide Suffering, N.Y. Times, Oct. 7, 2003, at A1; Amnesty International, Lethal Injection: The Medical Technology of Execution (Jan. 1998), at http://web.amnesty.org/library/Index/ENGAC T500011998?open&of = ENG-TWN#LAB (last checked August 15, 2006).

[10] See Denno, When Legislatures Delegate Death, *supra* note 3, at 100–05 (details some of the unsuccessful challenges to lethal injection protocols up through 2002).

> Failures in protocol design, implementation, monitoring and
> review might have led to the unnecessary suffering of at
> least some of those executed. Because participation of doctors
> in protocol design or execution is ethically prohibited, ade-
> quate anesthesia cannot be certain. Therefore, to prevent
> unnecessary cruelty and suffering, cessation and public
> review of lethal injection is warranted.[11]

The Lancet article received considerable media attention and
became the focal point for new court challenges by death row defendants. Defendants due to be executed by lethal injection asserted
that *The Lancet* article provided new and compelling evidence that
the standard three-drug lethal injection protocol violated the Eighth
Amendment's prohibition of cruel and unusual punishment.
Throughout 2005, however, lower state and federal courts continued
to reject death row defendants' assertions of constitutional flaws in
lethal injection protocols.[12]

As his execution date approached, Clarence Hill was just another
death row prisoner having little success arguing that the standard
lethal injection protocol was unconstitutional. Convicted and sentenced to die in the 1980s, Hill had challenged his death sentence
on various grounds in state and federal court for over two decades.
After a November 2005 death warrant finally scheduled his execution for January 24, 2006, Hill filed another state motion for post-
conviction relief that, inter alia, cited *The Lancet* article and demanded
public records concerning Florida's lethal injection procedures. On
January 17, 2006, a week before Hill's scheduled execution date,
Hill's state lawsuit was resolved when the Florida Supreme Court
ruled that *The Lancet* study was insufficient to justify reconsidering
its prior decision that Florida's lethal injection protocol was constitutionally sound.[13]

---

[11] G. K. Leonidas, et al., Inadequate Anesthesia in Lethal Injection for Execution,
The Lancet, Vol. 365 (9468), April 16, 2005, at 1412.

[12] See, e.g., Bieghler v. State, 839 N.E.2d 691 (Ind. 2005); Abdur'Rahman v. Bredesen,
181 S.W.3d 292 (Tenn. 2005); Baze v. Rees, No. 04-CI-01094 (Ky. Cir. Ct. July 8, 2005);
Brown v. Crawford, 408 F.3d 1027 (8th Cir. 2005).

[13] Hill v. Florida, 921 So. 2d 579 (Fla. 2006) (relying heavily upon *Sims v. State*, 754
So. 2d 657 (Fla. 2000)). Notably, Justice Anstead authored a partial dissent in *Hill v.
Florida* explaining why he believed *The Lancet* article justified providing Hill with an
evidentiary hearing in the trial court to explore more fully the soundness of Florida's
lethal injection procedures. *Id.* at 586–87 (Anstead, J., concurring in part and dissenting
in part).

After his lack of success in the state courts, and with his scheduled execution date only days away, Hill brought his claims to federal court by filing a civil rights action under 42 U.S.C. § 1983. The district court concluded that Hill's action was procedurally barred as a successive habeas petition, and the Eleventh Circuit affirmed that ruling in a decision rendered only hours before Hill was scheduled to be executed.[14] Significantly, both the district court and the Eleventh Circuit rejected Hill's attempt to bring his claim as a section 1983 action by relying heavily on a 2004 ruling by the Eleventh Circuit,[15] even though the Supreme Court had subsequently ruled in *Nelson v. Campbell*[16] that section 1983 actions could be used for challenging some aspects of lethal injection protocols.

Because Hill's arguments in lower courts had failed, and because the Supreme Court in the past had regularly denied review in cases challenging lethal injection protocols, Florida officials began the state's execution process soon after the Eleventh Circuit rejected Hill's appeal. At roughly 6 p.m. on January 24, 2006, Hill was strapped to a gurney and IV lines were run into his arms as the execution team awaited the expected denial of Hill's appeal to the Supreme Court. Hill was required to lay on the gurney for an hour anticipating his execution while everyone wondered why final word was slow to come from the Supreme Court.[17]

Finally, Justice Anthony Kennedy, acting on behalf of the Court, issued a stay to allow the Supreme Court more time to consider Hill's claims. Initial word about Hill's case hinted that the Court might be interested in the merits of his Eighth Amendment challenge to Florida's lethal injection protocol. But it subsequently became clear that the Court granted certiorari only to address the procedural question of whether Hill should have been permitted to pursue a section 1983 claim to challenge Florida's execution methods even after he had exhausted his habeas rights.[18]

[14] See Hill v. Crosby, 437 F.3d 1084 (11th Cir. 2006).

[15] See *id.* at 1084–85 (discussing reliance on *Robinson v. Crosby*, 358 F.3d 1281 (11th Cir. 2004)).

[16] 541 U.S. 637 (2004).

[17] See Tamara Lytle & John Kennedy, Top Court Halts Killer's Execution, Orlando Sentinel, Jan. 26, 2006, at A1.

[18] See Lyle Denniston, Court to Hear Florida Death Penalty Case, SCOTUSblog (Jan. 25, 2006), at http://www.scotusblog.com/movabletype/archives/2006/01/court_to_hear_f.html.

C. *Questions and Confusion Following the Grant in* Hill

It was hard to understand why the Supreme Court granted certiorari and full argument in the *Hill* case on only the narrow question of whether a section 1983 action could be used to challenge the constitutionality of a method of execution. The Court's unanimous 2004 ruling in *Nelson v. Campbell*[19] seemed to clarify that a challenge to the constitutionality of an execution method could be brought as a section 1983 action. Of course, lower federal courts had rebuffed Hill's efforts to challenge Florida's execution protocol via a section 1983 action, but the Eleventh Circuit's ruling did not mention *Nelson* and relied heavily on a pre-*Nelson* circuit precedent. The Supreme Court certainly had reason to be troubled by the Eleventh Circuit's failure to address *Nelson*, but some form of summary reversal and remand, citing *Nelson*, would have been sufficient to ensure Hill's claim was considered on the merits below.

By choosing to grant certiorari and schedule argument in *Hill*, the Supreme Court created extraordinary uncertainty about the constitutionality of a standard execution method used by nearly every capital jurisdiction in the country. The unique attention given to Hill's seemingly routine case suggested that the justices, perhaps troubled by the article in *The Lancet* and accounts of botched executions, had concluded that standard lethal injection protocols were constitutionally problematic. After all, if Hill's substantive constitutional claim was sure to be unavailing on the merits—as lower courts nationwide had repeatedly concluded—why would the Supreme Court be unduly concerned that Hill's claim was rejected in the proper procedural posture? It was hard to understand why the Supreme Court, with its limited time and docket, would care about the procedural issues in *Hill* unless some justices saw merit in his substantive constitutional attack on Florida's lethal injection protocol.

Though the Supreme Court's approach to *Hill* may have been puzzling, the consequences of the certiorari grant quickly became clear. First, the Supreme Court's grant in *Hill*, together with a related stay entered in another Florida capital case, produced a de facto moratorium on executions in Florida: Governor Jeb Bush announced

[19] 541 U.S. 637 (2004).

that the Court's actions would keep him from signing any more death warrants until these lethal injection challenges were resolved.[20]

Second, the Court's work in *Hill* had a profound nationwide ripple effect on lethal injection litigation and on state efforts to carry out scheduled executions. Richard Dieter, the executive director of the Death Penalty Information Center, observed after the Supreme Court granted certiorari in *Hill* that any lawyer representing a defendant on death row should be "filing something just like Clarence Hill as we speak."[21] And many lower courts around the nation responded quickly and dynamically to new filings from death row prisoners facing execution.[22] In February, the Eighth Circuit stayed a scheduled Missouri execution to allow more time for a lethal injection challenge.[23] In California, a federal district judge ordered revisions to the state's lethal injection process, and an execution had to be postponed indefinitely because California could not find doctors willing to assist with the execution.[24] In Ohio and Delaware, federal district

[20] See Alex Leary & Chris Tisch, Bush: Death Warrants on Hold, St. Petersburg Times, Feb. 2, 2006, at 5B.

[21] See Phil Long & Lesley Clark, Supreme Court Halts Execution, Agrees to Examine Civil Rights Claim, Knight Ridder Newspapers, Jan. 25, 2006, available at www.fadp.org/news/ts-20060125 (last checked August 15, 2006).

[22] A complete account of all the lethal injection litigation that followed the *Hill* grant could fill many volumes. The Death Penalty Information Center has chronicled most of the major highlights on a special section of its website. See Death Penalty Information Center, Special Webpage on Lethal Injections, at http://www.deathpenaltyinfo.org/article.php?did=1686&scid=64 (last visited Aug. 14, 2006) [hereinafter DPIC Lethal Injections Page]. In addition, the Death Penalty Clinic at the University of California Boalt Hall School of Law has maintained a web page entitled "Resources Regarding Challenges to Lethal Injection" at https://www.law.berkeley.edu/clinics/dpclinic/resources.html, which includes a state-by-state collection of materials relating to recent lethal injection litigation.

[23] See Taylor v. Crawford, 445 F.3d 1095, 1097–98 (8th Cir. 2006). The Missouri litigation has continued through and after the Supreme Court decided *Hill*, and the District Court for the Western District of Missouri recently ordered a halt to all executions in the state until the state significantly modified its execution procedures. See Mike Nixon, Execution Ruling Sets up Change in Missouri's Future, Daily Record (Kansas City, Mo.), July 11, 2006, available at http://findarticles.com/p/articles/mi_qn4181/is_20060711/ai_n16527562.

[24] Litigation over exactly how California needs to change its execution protocol is still on-going. See Order Reflecting Stipulation of Parties to Continue Hearing to September, in Morales v. Woodard, No. 5:06-cv-00219-JF (N.D. Cal. Apr. 27, 2006), available at https://www.law.berkeley.edu/clinics/dpclinic/Lethal%20Injection%20Documents/California/Morales/Morales%20Dist%20Ct/Order%20to%20Continue.pdf (last checked August 15, 2006).

judges stayed executions scheduled for April and May based on challenges to the lethal injection process in these states.[25] Federal execution plans were also disrupted by the *Hill* litigation: a federal district judge barred the Federal Bureau of Prisons from executing three defendants scheduled to be executed in May as a result of their challenges to the federal system's lethal injection process.[26]

But while court actions delayed or fully blocked scheduled executions in many jurisdictions, other states moved forward with lethal injections while *Hill* was pending before the Supreme Court. In North Carolina, a federal judge ordered monitoring of the state's lethal injection process by medically trained personnel, and the state completed a scheduled execution in April after arranging for a doctor to monitor a machine indicating the defendant's degree of consciousness during the lethal injection process.[27] Similarly, legal challenges brought by many defendants did not block executions in the three states that have historically made the greatest use of the death penalty. Texas, Oklahoma, and Virginia collectively carried out more than a dozen executions using standard lethal injection protocols while *Hill* was pending before the Supreme Court.[28] Many defendants executed while *Hill* was pending appealed their cases to the Supreme Court, but the justices repeatedly refused to intervene without giving any explanation for granting or upholding stays in some cases and denying stays in others.

Judge Boyce Martin, commenting in one of many cases subject to last-minute litigation over lethal injection protocols while the *Hill* case was pending,[29] summarized the legal mess that *Hill* helped create:

[25] See DPIC Lethal Injections Page, *supra* note 22.

[26] *Id.*

[27] See Brown v. Beck, No. 5:06-CT-3018-H (E.D.N.C. Apr. 17, 2006); see also Patrick O'Neill, Execution As Science Experiment, The Independent (Raleigh, NC), Apr. 26, 2006, at www.indyweek.com/gyrobase/Archive?author=oid%3A13853 (last checked August 15, 2006).

[28] See DPIC Lethal Injections Page, *supra* note 22. Notably, in mid-May, the Texas Court of Criminal Appeals stayed one execution because of the defendant's challenge to the lethal injection process, but that stay was lifted only two days later. See Pamela A. MacLean, Lethal Injection Stays Inconsistent in U.S., The Legal Intelligencer, May 23, 2006, at 4.

[29] Alley v. Little, No. 3:06-0340, 2006 WL 1454740 (M.D. Tenn. May 11, 2006), vacated, 2006 WL 1313365 (6th Cir. May 12, 2006), reh'g en banc denied, 447 F.3d 976 (6th Cir. 2006).

> [T]he dysfunctional patchwork of stays and executions going on in this country further undermines the various states' effectiveness and ability to properly carry out death sentences. We are currently operating under a system wherein condemned inmates are bringing nearly identical challenges to the lethal injection procedure. In some instances stays are granted, while in others they are not and the defendants are executed, with no principled distinction to justify such a result. This adds another arbitrary factor into the equation of death and thus far, there has been no logic behind the Supreme Court's decision as to who lives and who dies. . . .

> No doubt the march toward death is powerful. Currently, however, the march is anything but orderly. The current administration of the death penalty in light of the pending decision of *Hill* is more like a march in dozens of different directions. . . . The arbitrariness of death penalty administration is not ameliorated by the fact that *Hill* involves . . . "a procedural matter." Rather, administration of the death penalty can only be made more arbitrary by the possibility that after *Hill*, some current death row inmates may be able to show in court that the practice of lethal injection violates the Eighth Amendment's prohibition of cruel and unusual punishment, while other currently similarly situated inmates will have already been put to death through a method deemed to violate the Constitution. . . .[30]

II. A Ruling Not Worth a *Hill* of Beans?

A. A Dynamic Oral Argument Followed by a Bland Ruling

The Supreme Court heard full argument in *Hill* in late April. The questions at oral argument suggested the justices were interested in exploring the basic soundness of standard lethal injection protocols. Questioning of counsel was not confined to the narrow procedural issue raised in the case; the justices asked broad questions about the Eighth Amendment and different execution methods.[31] For example, Justice Scalia asked Hill's counsel whether the Eighth Amendment

[30] Alley v. Little, 447 F.3d 976, 977–78 (6th Cir. 2006) (Martin, J., dissenting from the denial of rehearing en banc).

[31] See generally Transcript of Oral Argument, Hill v. McDonough, 126 S. Ct. 2096 (2006) (No. 05-8794), (Apr. 26, 2006), available at http://www.supremecourtus.gov/oral_arguments/argument_transcripts/05-8794.pdf.

requires a painless execution,[32] and Justice Stevens asked the state's counsel why Florida's legislature regulated how pets are euthanized but did not regulate lethal injection protocols.[33] In a summary of the *Hill* argument, reporter Linda Greenhouse made this astute observation:

> Although the question before the court was the procedural one of how a challenge to lethal injection can be raised by a death row inmate who has exhausted the normal course of appeals, the intense argument showed that it was not easy to separate procedure from substance, at least with phrases like "excruciating pain" hanging in the courtroom air.[34]

In short, oral argument raised the prospect that fundamental issues surrounding the constitutionality of standard lethal injections protocols might be addressed in *Hill*. But the Court's oral argument bark proved more compelling than its ruling's bite.

On June 12, 2006, the Supreme Court overruled the Eleventh Circuit Court of Appeals and allowed Hill to proceed with his civil rights challenge to Florida's lethal injection process.[35] Despite the "intense" oral argument covering lots of ground, Justice Kennedy's opinion for the unanimous Court disposed of the case as a straightforward application of prior precedent. The Court's milquetoast opinion starts by stating that "Hill's suit . . . is comparable in its essentials to the action the Court allowed to proceed under § 1983 in *Nelson*."[36] Then, after a laborious review of the procedural history in *Hill* and the Court's prior work in *Nelson*, the opinion simply reiterates that challenges to execution protocols can be brought as section 1983 actions: "In the case before us we conclude that Hill's § 1983 action is controlled by the holding in *Nelson*. Here, as in *Nelson*, Hill's action if successful would not necessarily prevent the State from executing him by lethal injection."[37]

---

[32] *Id.* at 13.

[33] *Id.* at 36–37.

[34] See Linda Greenhouse, Supreme Court Hears Case Involving Lethal Injection, N.Y. Times, Apr. 27, 2006, at A18.

[35] Hill v. McDonough, 126 S. Ct. 2096 (2006).

[36] *Id.* at 2100.

[37] *Id.* at 2102.

After narrowly resolving the merits, the Court briefly addresses prosecutors' concern that lethal injection litigation brought through section 1983 actions could be used as a tactic to delay executions. Here is part of the Court's response to the practical problems raised by its ruling in *Hill*:

> Filing an action that can proceed under § 1983 does not entitle the complainant to an order staying an execution as a matter of course. Both the State and the victims of crime have an important interest in the timely enforcement of a sentence. Our conclusions today do not diminish that interest, nor do they deprive federal courts of the means to protect it.
>
> We state again, as we did in *Nelson*, that a stay of execution is an equitable remedy. It is not available as a matter of right, and equity must be sensitive to the State's strong interest in enforcing its criminal judgments without undue interference from the federal courts. . . .
>
> After *Nelson* a number of federal courts have invoked their equitable powers to dismiss suits they saw as speculative or filed too late in the day. Although the particular determinations made in those cases are not before us, we recognize that the problem they address is significant. Repetitive or piecemeal litigation presumably would raise similar concerns. The federal courts can and should protect States from dilatory or speculative suits, but it is not necessary to reject *Nelson* to do so.
>
> The equities and the merits of Hill's underlying action are also not before us. We reverse the judgment of the Court of Appeals and remand the case for further proceedings consistent with this opinion.[38]

B. *Questions and Continued Litigation*

With due respect to the Supreme Court, its work in *Hill* is more likely to infuriate capital litigators than to illuminate future lethal injection litigation. *Hill* authorized any and every death row prisoner to challenge applicable execution protocols in federal court through section 1983 actions. But *Hill* provided no guidance whatsoever regarding how the merits of these actions should be examined. In

---

[38] *Id.* at 2104 (citations and quotations omitted).

addition, the Court did not address the potentially complicated interplay of lethal injection challenges brought as section 1983 actions and those brought in state court or in federal habeas actions. As one report on *Hill* observed:

> The justices granted perhaps thousands of death row inmates a significant new avenue for collateral appeal considerably less restrictive than the usual petition for a writ of habeas corpus. . . . But the justices also left the lower courts with precious little guidance on how to determine which section 1983 cases to hear and which ones to send packing. . . . By extending the possibility of a civil rights suit to routine procedures, such as the one at issue in *Hill*, the court in effect invited nearly all the nation's 3,370 death row inmates to vie for another day in court.[39]

Though *Hill* briefly spoke to some practical concerns surrounding last-minute lethal injection claims, the Court's magniloquent discussion is somewhat maddening given the Court's own work in *Hill*. If, as the *Hill* Court says, "[b]oth the State and the victims of crime have an important interest in the timely enforcement of a sentence," why did the Supreme Court take nearly five months to issue an opinion that does little more than reaffirm a recent precedent? And if "[r]epetitive or piecemeal litigation" impacts this "important interest," shouldn't the Supreme Court have just taken up the "equities and the merits of Hill's underlying action"?

In short, *Hill* presents itself as a cautious opinion, but the Supreme Court's approach to *Hill* and other lethal injection litigation has displayed a kind of recklessness concerning how lower courts would have to decipher and respond to the Court's opaque work. By taking up *Hill*, the Court ensured that constitutional uncertainty would envelop standard lethal injection protocols; by delivering a narrow opinion, the Court provided little help for lower courts caught up in tumultuous litigation over these protocols. There are many confounding substantive and procedural issues on the other side of *Hill*; lower courts must sort through these critical issues:

(1) What are the appropriate standards for examining and adjudicating an Eighth Amendment claim lodged against a particular execution method?

---

[39] John Gibeaut, More Inmates Likely to Contest Lethal Injection, ABA Journal E-Report, June 16, 2006, at http://www.abanet.org/journal/ereport/jn16inject.html.

(2) How should a section 1983 action challenging an execution method take account of prior challenges brought in state court or in a federal habeas action?

(3) Should a federal habeas court decline to consider challenges to standard execution methods now that such claims can be regularly brought as section 1983 actions?

(4) Is *The Lancet* article, which only suggests a *risk* of a painful death, sufficient evidence to make out an Eighth Amendment claim against standard lethal injection protocols?

(5) What obligations might a state have under the Eighth Amendment to improve its execution method or to investigate and utilize more humane methods of execution?

(6) When exactly can and should a death row defendant bring a section 1983 action against a lethal injection protocol, and what particular considerations should influence whether a stay is justified?

In light of these and other questions raised, but not resolved, by the Court's work in *Hill*, it is not surprising that litigation over lethal injection protocols has continued. And, as was true during *Hill*'s pendency, the results of this litigation vary state by state, case by case. A few weeks after *Hill* was decided, a federal judge in Arkansas granted a stay of execution and a preliminary injunction to allow further investigation into the constitutionality of the state's execution protocol.[40] But only days earlier, Oklahoma's highest criminal court unanimously declared that state's standard lethal injection protocol to be constitutionally sound.[41] Tellingly, *Hill* did not significantly impact these lethal injection cases, and *Hill* did not promote greater

[40] See DPIC Lethal Injections Page, *supra* note 22.

[41] Malicoat v. Oklahoma, 137 P.3d 1234 (Okla. 2006). In the final paragraph of a separate opinion, Judge Lumpkin in *Malicoat* expressed what might be a common sentiment concerning lethal injection challenges by death row defendants: "I find Appellant's request to be spared the imposition of his legally imposed punishment because it might cause him to suffer or experience pain unpersuasive (and rather ironic) as his murderous acts have been the cause of the ultimate pain and suffering for the victim and her family." *Id.* at 1239–40 (Lumpkin, J., concurring in part and dissenting in part).

order or consensus concerning how lethal injection claims were being brought and resolved nationwide.[42]

III. Finding Bickel Gold in a *Hill* of Beans?

As lethal injection litigation continues to roil state execution efforts and embroil federal courts, it is easy to be critical and cynical about the Court's work in *Hill*. The justices clearly recognized the broader issues at stake in *Hill*, but the Court's ruling revealed an eagerness to dodge the toughest questions raised by constitutional challenges to standard lethal injection protocols.[43] After *Hill*, lethal injection litigation remains chaotic, confused, and convoluted, and the Supreme Court arguably did more harm than good in *Hill*. Proponents of capital punishment have to be troubled that *Hill* initially inspired, and then did not help resolve, litigation-driven de facto moratoriums on executions now in place in numerous states. Opponents of capital punishment have to be troubled that *Hill* did not require Texas and some other active death penalty states to review their lethal injection protocols as they move forward with executions. Moreover, anyone genuinely interested in federalism, or sentencing consistency, or orderly government has to find the frantic, patchwork litigation still taking place nationwide after *Hill*—which necessarily involves the stressful and inefficient expenditure of the time and energies of lower courts and lots of lawyers—unseemly and counterproductive to the sound operation of criminal justice systems.

But Professor Debby Denno, a leading expert on lethal injection protocols and execution methods generally, has suggested reasons to be more positive about *Hill*:

> First, it's unanimous (and the oral arguments gave some suggestion that it wouldn't be unanimous if it was favorably

---

[42]See DPIC Lethal Injections Page, *supra* note 22; see also John Gibeaut, It's All in the Execution, *supra* note 5, ABA Journal, August 2006, at 17 (noting prosecutorial concerns that *Hill* fails to provide any "significant guidance on how trial courts can stop litigation that could continue forever by allowing inmates to refocus their complaints every time a state changes its execution protocol").

[43]In addition, while *Hill* was pending, the Supreme Court denied certiorari in a case coming from Tennessee, *Abdur'Rahman v. Bredesen*, which presented directly questions concerning the constitutionality of standard lethal injection protocols. See Warren Richey, At High Court, No Rush to Resolve Conflicts over Lethal Injection, Christian Science Monitor, May 22, 2006, at 2.

decided and even indicated that the case might not be affirmatively decided). Second, . . . section 1983 doesn't require
inmates to jump through as many procedural hoops and has
a potentially richer field of case law for them to draw upon
in their arguments. Next, the issue raised in *Hill* is broader
than that raised in *Nelson*. *Nelson* concerned a 1983 challenge
of a cut down procedure based in part on Nelson's own
deteriorating veins. Cut down procedures were rare in 2004
and they are even rarer now. But the use of chemicals prompt-
ing Hill's challenge is generic to every lethal injection in the
country; in other words, every state uses the same three
chemicals that Hill challenged and there was no mention
of Hill's particular anatomical limitations (nor were they
relevant). While the Court did not address head on the substantive aspects of lethal injection, it does mention the fact
that Hill's challenge concerns "a foreseeable risk of gratuitous and unnecessary pain." If the Court thought the issue
were totally frivolous, the case wouldn't have garnered
their attention.

I think *Hill* validates the lethal injection issue and clarifies
its importance both to attorneys and to courts. It sends a
message that departments of corrections ([DOC]) are going
to continue to be scrutinized and perhaps spotlighted more
than in the past. Incrementally, the [DOC]'s are being pres-
sured to alter their protocols or to switch to another method.
While in the grand scheme of things this movement today
may not seem like a big deal, I think it's useful to remember
that the Court has directed more attention to lethal injection
in the last two years than it has to any other method of
execution in the last 110 years. Put in context, seemingly
small steps are magnified.[44]

Though Professor Denno's initial points about *Hill* might only please
death penalty opponents, her final insights spotlight the jurispruden-
tial gold that might be found buried in *Hill*. As Professor Denno
suggests, the Supreme Court's new attentiveness to execution methods sends a powerful message to all death penalty jurisdictions—
namely that, through section 1983 actions, federal courts can and

[44]See Posting of Douglas A. Berman, Sentencing Law and Policy Blog, Insights on
Hill from THE Expert (June 12, 2006), at http://sentencing.typepad.com/sentencing
_law_and_policy/2006/06/insights_on_hil.html (quoting e-mail from Deborah
Denno).

will be independently scrutinizing execution protocols and thereby shining light on death penalty procedures long shrouded in secrecy.

As detailed in Part I above, the development and administration of lethal injection protocols have often been haphazard and sloppy. Internal state reviews of standard lethal injection protocols have often been non-existent or perfunctory. Valuably, the Supreme Court's decision to hear the *Hill* case led to lethal injection protocols receiving much greater (and long needed) scrutiny not only from lower courts, but also from public policy groups and the media. And the *Hill* decision did confirm that challenges to standard lethal injection procedures could be brought through section 1983 actions, which essentially ensures that every capital jurisdiction's execution methods will continue to be put under the microscope.

Moreover, and perhaps even more valuably, the narrow ruling in *Hill* presents other institutions with an important new opportunity to confront directly the difficult issues raised by any execution method. The particulars of any process of state killing necessarily implicate complicated medical issues and intricate administrative concerns. Courts presented with constitutional challenges to particular execution methods—especially in last-minute litigation brought by prisoners with swiftly approaching execution dates—are not well suited to sorting through alternative execution technologies, debatable medical evidence, and the administrative issues that states face in carrying out scheduled executions. Though federal courts may effectively play a watch-dog role ensuring that unreasonable execution methods are not utilized, it is unwise and unseemly for individual federal district judges to be tasked with developing detailed regulations to govern state execution procedures. The Supreme Court's circumscribed work in *Hill* perhaps reveals that the justices felt that particular revisions and improvements to lethal injection protocols should be pioneered by other, more democratically responsive and accountable branches of government.

In short, a nugget of gold to be found in *Hill* flows from its effectuation of Professor Alexander Bickel's recommendation that the Supreme Court sometimes resist broad constitutional rulings. Bickel proposed that the Supreme Court sometimes avoid definitive resolution of contentious constitutional questions in order to allow other (more democratic) branches of government to take a second look at important issues. Bickel suggested that the Supreme Court, by utilizing various decision-avoiding techniques, could avoid premature resolutions of critical issues that would benefit from further exploration by the political branches of government and by the public at large.[45] Writing in a similar vein, Professor Cass Sunstein has more recently touted "decisional minimalism"—judicial efforts to keep judgments "shallow and narrow"—as a means to foster democratic processes.[46] Sunstein has suggested that minimalist adjudication by the Supreme Court is "democracy-forcing" and thus valuable as a means to "leave open the most fundamental and difficult constitutional questions [and] also . . . promote democratic accountability and democratic deliberation."[47]

As detailed above, the Court's narrow ruling in *Hill* has enabled and essentially invited other governmental branches to give more focused attention to the legal, policy, and practical issues surrounding lethal injection protocols. Rather than begin micromanaging execution protocols, the Supreme Court in *Hill* has encouraged other legal institutions to respond to identified problems in a way that might entirely eliminate the need for a contentious constitutional decision or should at least help frame the constitutional issue in more precise terms.

Encouragingly, corrections officials in a few states have started to rise to the challenge that remains on the other side of *Hill*. Only a few weeks after *Hill*, Ohio prison officials announced changes in the state's lethal injection process,[48] and corrections officials in other states have also responded to lethal injection litigation by proposing

---

[45] Professor Bickel's most famous first account of his vision of the "passive virtues" that the Supreme Court should utilize was in a 1961 article in the *Harvard Law Review*. See Alexander M. Bickel, The Supreme Court, 1960 Term—Foreword: The Passive Virtues, 75 Harv. L. Rev. 40 (1960). Professor Bickel expanded his ideas into a book the following year. See Bickel, *supra* note 2.

[46] See Cass R. Sunstein, One Case At a Time: Judicial Minimalism on the Supreme Court 3–4 (1999); Cass R. Sunstein, The Supreme Court, 1995 Term—Foreword: Leaving Things Undecided, 110 Harv. L. Rev. 6, 6–7 (1996).

[47] Sunstein, Leaving Things Undecided, *supra* note 46, at 6.

[48] See Alan Johnson, Ohio Changing Lethal Injection Process, Columbus Dispatch, June 28, 2006. Though on-going lethal injection litigation surely played a role in Ohio's changes to its lethal injection protocol, another contributing factor was the problems that delayed the May execution of a condemned prisoner for more than an hour as prison officials scrambled to find a suitable vein for completing the lethal injection process. See *id.*

alterations in their lethal injection programs.[49] Though these changes may only be motivated by a desire to avoid or thwart constitutional litigation, they still represent a positive first step toward a sounder approach to the administration of capital punishment.

But, disconcertingly, a central institutional player in our nation's systems of government has not yet gotten involved. Despite headline-making lethal injection litigation raging in numerous states, not a single state legislature has even conducted hearings on standard lethal injection protocols to explore whether sounder execution methods might be developed. Legislatures could—and, in my view, should—at the very least hold public hearings to examine the range of medical and administrative issues raised by lethal injection protocols. Conflicting and evolving medical evidence about lethal injection protocols is being presented in federal district courts around the country, and individual federal judges are being asked to assess whether complicated procedures are medically and practically sound. In some instances, federal judges feel compelled to issue detailed regulations that a state must follow to proceed with executions. In a country committed to democratic rule, these life-and-death judgments ought to be carefully considered in the first instance by legislatures, not by individual judges.

As Justice Stevens noted during the *Hill* oral argument, many states have legislatively regulated how animals can be killed. It is odd and disconcerting that the killing of humans does not get at least an equal measure of legislative attention. The legislative inaction is especially disappointing because an improved execution process appears achievable. A recent *New York Times* article reports that "medical experts say the current method of lethal injection could easily be changed to make suffering less likely."[50] Yet, as that article further notes, even though "[s]witching to an injection method with less potential to cause pain could undercut many of the lawsuits,

[49]See Tom McNichol, Why the Reputations of "Humane" Execution Methods Keep Dying Out, San Francisco Chronicle, June 18, 2006, available at www.sfgate.com/cgi-bin/article.cgi?file/chronicle/archive/2006/06/18/INGAUJDQMS1.DTL (noting that "California has proposed altering its three-drug lethal injection protocol . . . to ensure [a condemned prisoner] isn't conscious when the paralyzing and heart-stopping drugs are injected").

[50]Denise Grady, Doctors See Way to Cut Suffering in Executions, N.Y. Times, June 23, 2006, at A1.

... so far, in this chapter of the nation's long and tangled history with the death penalty, no state has moved to alter its lethal injection protocol."[51]

Though one can surely fault state legislatures for failing to investigate and better regulate execution protocols, the (non)actions of our nation's legislature also deserves criticism. The national significance of disrupted state capital justice is arguably of great moment. Especially if one credits evidence that the death penalty deters—and recall that President Bush and other death penalty supporters in Congress have long justified an affinity for capital punishment by claiming the death penalty "saves lives"—a major disruption in the administration of the death penalty could put the innocent lives of potential murder victims at risk. Beyond deterrence concerns, uncertainty surrounding scheduled executions dramatically affects the personal fate of death row defendants and the emotional state of the family members of both murder victims and those scheduled to be executed.

But while many lives hang in the balance, Congress has not even begun to explore what it might be able to do to address the medical and legal issues surrounding lethal injection protocols. Whatever one's views on the death penalty, the haphazard litigation over lethal injection has to be considered a national disgrace. As spotlighted above, neither proponents nor opponents of the death penalty can be pleased with the frantic, patchwork, and discrepant lethal injection litigation playing out in courtrooms nationwide. And this litigation necessarily requires—and will continue to require—the stressful and inefficient expenditure of the time and energies of lower courts and hundreds of lawyers and will continue to be counter-productive to the sound operation of criminal justice systems.

Notably, in early 2005, members of Congress worked through a weekend to pass legislation to impact the litigation surrounding the possible removal of Terri Schiavo's feeding tube. Though the Schiavo law did not prevent removal of Terri Schiavo's feeding tube, the entire episode revealed that Congress and President Bush believe that the fate of a single citizen can be a matter of national importance and that swift legislative intervention may be appropriate when contentious life-and-death issues are unfolding in the states.

[51] Id.

In the life-and-death setting of lethal injection protocols, Congress could, at the very least, hold hearings to explore the range of medical issues raised by *The Lancet* article and other recent research on execution methods. Congress could also, of course, weigh in on the merits by adopting a particular protocol for federal executions or by encouraging states to adopt a particular new lethal injection protocol. Though there are pros and cons to all possible congressional interventions, the essential question is whether Congress should continue to sit on the sidelines while life-and-death issues unfold in a haphazard way through litigation in various federal courts.

Legislative inaction in the wake of *Hill* is not only disappointing, but also telling. It has become common sport for politicians and commentators to assail justices and judges for intervening in significant policy debates that seem more the province for legislative action. In *Hill*, the Court was perhaps attentive to these concerns when it decided to dodge the most contentious issues presented by the ongoing lethal injection litigation. Other branches of government must now demonstrate that they can and will soundly govern in this controversial area now that the Supreme Court has indicated that, for the time being, it will stay out of the way. If other branches don't step up, not only will the model of constitutional adjudication suggested by Bickel and Sunstein suffer a blow, but complaints of judicial activism will ring even more hollow.

Missed Opportunities in *Independent Ink*

Joshua D. Wright*

The Supreme Court's opinion in *Illinois Tool Works Inc. v. Independent Ink, Inc.*[1] is unequivocally good for consumers and eminently sensible. The decision rejects the presumption of antitrust market power in patent tying cases. The presumption is at odds with the longstanding consensus among antitrust scholars,[2] Congress,[3] and the antitrust agencies[4] that patents do not confer antitrust monopoly power. There is virtually no authority defending the proposition, and rightly so. While some have argued that the Court's previous decisions never created a presumption that patents confer market power, that particular debate is largely academic at this point.[5] The

*Assistant Professor, George Mason University School of Law. The George Mason Law and Economics Center generously provided financial support. I thank Daniel Crane and Bruce Kobayashi for comments and Brandy L. Wagstaff for research assistance. All errors are my own.

[1]Illinois Tool Works Inc. v. Independent Ink, Inc., 126 S. Ct. 1281 (2006), rev'g 396 F.3d 1342 (Fed. Cir. 2005).

[2]See, e.g., 10 Philip E. Areeda et al., Antitrust Law ¶ 1737a (2d ed. 2004); 1 Herbert Hovenkamp et al., IP and Antitrust: An Analysis of Antitrust Principles Applied to Intellectual Property Law § 4.2 ("an intellectual property right does not confer a monopoly"); Richard A. Posner, Antitrust Law 97–98 (2d ed. 2001) ("most patents confer too little monopoly power to be a proper object of antitrust concern").

[3]See 35 U.S.C. § 271(d)(4), (5) (amending patenting laws to mandate proof of market power in the tying product in the patent misuse context).

[4]See U.S. Department of Justice and Federal Trade Commission, Antitrust Guidelines for the Licensing of Intellectual Property § 2.2 (Apr. 6, 1995) (enforcement agencies will "not presume that a patent, copyright, or trade secret necessarily confers market power upon its owner").

[5]See, e.g., Brief for the United States as Amicus Curiae Supporting Petitioners at 18–25, Illinois Tool Works Inc. v. Independent Ink, Inc., 126 S. Ct. 1281 (2006) (No. 04-1329); Kevin D. McDonald, Moving Forward While Facing Backward: Illinois Tool Rejects the Presumption of Market Power in Tying Cases, 20(3) Antitrust 33 (Summer 2006), for an exposition of this view. Also unsatisfied with the holding, though for different reasons, McDonald also characterizes *Independent Ink* as an "opportunity lost." Specifically, McDonald criticizes the decision for failing to provide guidance with respect to the law of tying: "If Justice Stevens had devoted half the time and energy he lavished on defending his own dictum from *Hyde* to explicating the law

333

presumption has already done its damage. Courts have relied upon its wisdom, casting a shadow of unwarranted litigation risk over the competitive decisions of firms with intellectual property rights.

Justice Stevens' opinion for the unanimous Court should be applauded for taking an important step towards aligning a perplexing and muddled tying jurisprudence with economic sense and empirical reality. When the well-earned round of applause comes to an end, however, *Independent Ink* also represents a missed opportunity to clarify antitrust doctrine with respect to competitive conduct that facilitates price discrimination.[6] This essay explores this missed opportunity in greater detail, arguing that while Justice Stevens' opinion exhibits an undeniable interest in aligning modern antitrust jurisprudence with the consensus view of economists, it does not finish the job. Specifically, the economic logic underlying the Court's result also supports the conclusion that price discrimination does not imply antitrust market power and, without more, is not an antitrust problem because it does not threaten to reduce consumer welfare in a manner which antitrust policy can improve upon. By failing to endorse the economic logic with which the Court sought to harmonize doctrine, the Court missed a tailor-made opportunity to simultaneously rid antitrust doctrine of a nonsensical presumption and the misguided view that price discrimination is anticompetitive or involves monopoly-type welfare losses associated with the artificial reduction of output.

Part I briefly reviews the Supreme Court's analysis rejecting the presumption of market power in patent tying cases. Part II relies upon the substantial economic literature analyzing competitive price

of tying and how a presumption of market power undermines it, we might have twice the guidance." *Id.* at 38. See also Kevin D. McDonald, Why the Presumption of Market Power in Patent Tying Cases Never Existed, and Won't Much Longer, Paper Presented at ABA Section of Antitrust Law Spring Meeting (Feb. 16, 2006).

[6] It is worth noting at the outset of this essay that I do not refer to price discrimination only in the sense prohibited by the Robinson-Patman Act, *i.e.*, the same product sold to different consumers at different prices. Rather, I refer to all forms of price discrimination ranging from coupons and quantity discounts to the practice of charging consumers "effectively" different prices relative to marginal cost. For instance, in the classic example of the tied sale of razor blades to the razor, where the seller lowers the price of the razor and increases the price of the blades, high intensity users pay a higher price for the package relative to marginal cost. While the economic insights regarding price discrimination in Part II apply to all forms of price discrimination, Robinson-Patman liability is outside the scope of this essay.

discrimination and builds the foundation for the primary claim of this essay set forth in Part III: a consumer welfare-oriented antitrust regime should ignore competitive conduct facilitating price discrimination unless it is independently capable of causing competitive harm. To be sure, such conduct would not enjoy absolute immunity from antitrust enforcement. For example, a tying arrangement or refusal to deal might raise barriers to entry and cause an anticompetitive effect by allowing a dominant firm to maintain its monopoly. The economic point is that this harm has nothing to do with price discrimination, and conflating price discrimination with monopolistic exclusion threatens to deter a substantial amount of procompetitive conduct.

I. *Illinois Tool Works Inc. v. Independent Ink, Inc.*

Independent Ink involves a classic example of a metering tie. A subsidiary of Illinois Tool Works, the Trident division, manufactures a patented printhead to print bar codes on product cartons. Trident licenses its patented printheads to original equipment manufacturers on the condition that they purchase non-patented ink from Illinois Tool. Independent Ink, Inc., is a rival distributor and supplier of ink and ink products and brought suit alleging that Illinois Tool Works engaged in an unlawful tying arrangement in violation of section 1 of the Sherman Act and monopolization under section 2 of the Sherman Act.[7]

The district court granted Illinois Tool's motion for summary judgment on all antitrust claims because there was no allegation of market power in the sale of the "tying" good and no evidence of actual market power.[8] The Federal Circuit reversed with respect to the section 1 claims, holding that "where the tying product is patented or copyrighted, market power may be presumed rather than proven."[9]

The Supreme Court granted certiorari to "undertake a fresh examination of the history of both the judicial and legislative appraisals of tying arrangements . . . informed by extensive scholarly comment and a change in position by the administrative agencies charged with enforcement of the antitrust laws."[10] The Court framed the

---

[7]126 S. Ct. at 1284–85.

[8]Independent Ink, Inc. v. Trident, Inc., 210 F. Supp. 2d 1155, 1173 (C.D. Cal. 2002).

[9]396 F.3d 1342, 1348 (Fed. Cir. 2005). The Federal Circuit argued that the presumption was required under prior Supreme Court precedent. *Id.* at 1348–49 ("*International Salt* and *Loew's* make clear that the necessary market power to establish a section 1 violation is presumed.").

[10]126 S. Ct. at 1285.

issue presented as "whether the presumption of market power in a patented product should survive as a matter of antitrust law despite its demise in patent law."[11]

Justice Stevens' opinion is largely devoted to identifying the origin of the presumption in a case about patent misuse, *Motion Picture Patents Co. v. Universal Film Manufacturing Co.*,[12] and arguing that the presumption "migrated" from patent law to antitrust law in *International Salt Co. v. United States*,[13] upon urging from the United States that tying arrangements involving patented products were indeed per se violations of the Sherman Act. Having identified the source of the presumption's migration into antitrust jurisprudence, the Court noted that in 1988 Congress had eliminated the presumption in the same patent misuse context[14] before concluding that "it would be anomalous to preserve the presumption in antitrust after Congress has eliminated its foundation."[15]

The Court's conclusion that plaintiffs must demonstrate proof of market power in patent tying cases is not surprising in light of the overwhelming and virtually undisputed weight of authority against the presumption. There are, however, two particularly notable aspects of the opinion worth addressing before turning to the larger issue of the antitrust analytics of price discrimination.

The first is that the Court rejected a more subtle version of the argument that patents confer market power raised by Independent Ink with the help of Professors Barry Nalebuff, Ian Ayres, and Lawrence Sullivan ("Nalebuff") as amici.[16] The Nalebuff argument claims that an alternative and more narrowly tailored presumption, found in neither patent nor antitrust cases, remained appropriate despite the weight of scholarly commentary to the contrary. Specifically, Nalebuff argues that the presumption of market power remains appropriate for metering arrangements or "requirements ties," *i.e.*, those tying arrangements involving a patented tying good and the purchase of unpatented goods over a period of time, because they

[11]*Id.* at 1284.

[12]243 U.S. 502 (1917).

[13]332 U.S. 392 (1947).

[14]35 U.S.C. § 271(d)(5).

[15]126 S. Ct. at 1291.

[16]Brief of Professors Barry Nalebuff, Ian Ayres, and Lawrence Sullivan as Amici Curiae in Support of Respondent, Illinois Tool Works Inc. v. Independent Ink, Inc., 126 S. Ct. 1281 (2006) (No. 04-1329) [hereinafter "Nalebuff Brief"].

allow the patent holder to charge different prices to heavy and light users of the unpatented good. Economists generally refer to tying arrangements that require the purchase of a complementary good as "metering ties," because they allow the seller to charge lower package prices to those who use the product less intensely and, conversely, higher package prices relative to costs for high intensity users. Examples of "metering" are common in the modern economy: computers and punch cards, razors and razor blades, video game consoles and video games, and, of course, printers and ink.

Nalebuff argues that this sort of price discrimination associated with metering "is strong evidence of market power."[17] It is not. I will address the flaws in the economics of this argument in Part II. Ultimately, the Court properly rejects this argument, but solely on the grounds that the legal foundation for the antitrust presumption, *International Salt*, did not rely on the use of a requirements tie in presuming market power.[18] This legal response is technically correct. Indeed, *International Salt* applied no presumption and there was no argument that the defendant actually possessed market power. However, Justice Stevens' doctrinalist response is particularly disappointing in light of the second notable characteristic of the opinion: a not-so-subtle desire to align tying jurisprudence with the economic literature.

Justice Stevens' opinion repeatedly informs us that the Court's analysis is consistent with both scholarly commentary and the consensus view of economists. In rejecting the logic behind the presumption, the Court notes that "[o]ur imposition of this requirement accords with the vast majority of academic literature on the subject,"[19] and that "the vast majority of academic literature recognizes that a patent does not necessarily confer market power."[20] The Court also appeals to the growing economic literature recognizing that price discrimination of the type associated with metering ties occurs in fully competitive markets and correctly notes that neither price discrimination nor supracompetitive package pricing are sufficient

[17]*Id.* at 27.

[18]126 S. Ct. at 1292.

[19]*Id.* at 1291 n.4 (citing 10 Areeda et al., *supra* note 2, at ¶ 1737a; Kenneth J. Burchfiel, Patent Misuse and Antitrust Reform: "Blessed be the Tie?," 4 Harv. J.L. & Tech. 1, 57 & n.340 (1991); 1 Herbert Hovenkamp et al., *supra* note 2, at § 4.2a; William M. Landes & Richard A. Posner, The Economic Structure of Intellectual Property 374 (2003)).

[20]*Id.* at 1292.

conditions for antitrust market power.[21] Finally, the passage that most clearly signals the Court's desire to align tying jurisprudence with economic analysis appears toward the end of the opinion:

> Congress, the antitrust enforcement agencies, and most economists have all reached the conclusion that a patent does not necessarily confer market power upon the patentee. Today, we reach the same conclusion, and therefore hold that, in all cases involving a tying arrangement, the plaintiff must prove that the defendant has market power in the tying product.[22]

The Court was undoubtedly sincere regarding its desire to incorporate the consensus view of economists and scholars into tying jurisprudence. This effort was largely successful and it is worth taking a moment to congratulate the Court for reaching a proconsumer result supported by both economic logic and principles of sound antitrust policy. Virtually all antitrust and intellectual property scholars view the presumption as unequivocally misguided both in theory[23] and as an empirical matter.[24] The presumption improperly

---

[21]*Id.* (citing William J. Baumol & Daniel G. Swanson, The New Economy and Ubiquitous Competitive Price Discrimination: Identifying Defensible Criteria of Market Power, 70 Antitrust L.J. 661, 666 (2003); 9 Areeda et al., *supra* note 2, at ¶ 1711; Landes & Posner, *supra* note 19, at 374–75).

[22]*Id.* at 1293.

[23]To my knowledge, there is no single legal or scholarly authority defending the presumption on theoretical grounds. An exchange between Kathleen Sullivan, on behalf of the respondent, and the Court is telling:

> Ms. Sullivan: The patent presumption, not a rule, is a sensible rule of thumb for capturing the wisdom that patents used to enforce requirements ties are more likely than not to show market power. That's what they're intended to do through barriers to entry, and that's what they have done. In fact, the petitioners and Government have been able—unable to show a single procompetitive tie.

> Chief Justice Roberts: Are you conceding that the presumption makes no sense outside of the requirements metering context?

> Ms. Sullivan: Mr. Chief Justice there could be a sensible argument that you should always presume requirements ties to indicate market power. That's not the law, and we don't urge it here . . . .

> Justice Stevens: I'm kind of curious what your answer is to the Chief Justice's question.

> (Laughter).

Transcript of Oral Argument at 43–44, Illinois Tool Works Inc. v. Independent Ink, Inc., 126 S. Ct. 1281 (2006) (No. 04-1329).

[24]See, e.g., F.M. Scherer, The Value of Patents and Other Legally Protected Commercial Rights Panel Discussion (1984), in 53 Antitrust L.J. 535, 547 (1985) ("studies

shifted a substantial burden to antitrust defendants without the power to impact market conditions, thus chilling welfare enhancing competition.[25]

If the opinion's goal was to harmonize tying jurisprudence with the economic literature and empirical reality, however, the success was both undeniable and incomplete. While the Court reached a sound result from an economic perspective, the Court avoided use of economic logic in reaching its holding, relying instead solely upon analysis of prior precedent and changes in patent law.[26] This choice is not without its costs. Most significantly, by failing to expressly adopt the economic principles underlying its holding, the Court missed an opportunity to clarify antitrust policy in an area of growing importance: competitive price discrimination.[27] Importantly, the economic consensus referenced by the Court supports the rejection of the presumption precisely because it rejects the notion that price discrimination implies antitrust market power. That is, the ability to price discriminate simply does not imply the ability to influence market prices or conditions.

II. The Economics of Competitive Price Discrimination

Price discrimination involves a firm taking advantage of different elasticities of demand for the same goods by charging different prices relative to marginal cost.[28] Demand elasticities may vary for similar goods across several different margins. For instance, interpersonal price discrimination involves different prices charged to different

---

suggest that the vast majority of all patents confer very little monopoly power"); John R. Allison et al., Valuable Patents, 92 Geo. L.J. 435, 437 (2004).

[25]Chief Justice Roberts and Justice Kennedy recognized this effect of the presumption at oral argument despite attempts to frame the impact of the presumption as de minimis because it was simply a rebuttable presumption with respect to a single element of a tying claim. Transcript of Oral Argument, *supra* note 23, at 34–36.

[26]The Court's analysis places considerable weight on the changes in patent law, framing the issue before the court as whether the presumption "should survive as a matter of antitrust law despite its demise in patent law." 126 S. Ct. at 1284.

[27]For instance, the *Antitrust Law Journal* recently dedicated a symposium issue to this topic. See 70 Antitrust L.J. 593 (2003).

[28]See, e.g., Hal R. Varian, Price Discrimination, in Handbook of Industrial Organization 597 (Richard Schmalensee & Robert D. Willig eds., 1989).

consumers, whereas intrapersonal price discrimination involves different prices on units sold to the same consumer, such as a quantity discount.

There are other ways to classify forms of price discrimination. Most students of economics are no doubt familiar with Pigou's classification of price discrimination into "degrees."[29] Under third-degree discrimination, customers are segmented according to these differing demand elasticities and each group is charged a single profit-maximizing price. Second degree discrimination, by contrast, involves a single profit maximizing price which varies by elasticity. First degree price discrimination, which Pigou argued (along with second degree discrimination) was rarely if ever observed in the real world,[30] involves the manufacturer varying the price to each consumer in order to extract the maximum surplus.

Price discrimination, especially of the second- and third-degree variety, is extremely common in real world markets characterized by intense competition. Despite its ubiquity in competitive product markets of all varieties, price discrimination has proven a particularly stubborn problem for antitrust. The problem involves a number of fundamental questions. Does price discrimination imply market power? Does it imply antitrust monopoly power? What is the difference between the two, if any? Does price discrimination in competitive markets harm consumers? Each of these questions must be answered in order to design a sensible antitrust response to competitive price discrimination. Recent analyses of price discrimination by economists and antitrust scholars provide the answers.[31] This

---

[29] A.C. Pigou, The Economics of Welfare (1920).

[30] *Id.* at 244.

[31] See, e.g., Benjamin Klein & John Shepherd Wiley, Competitive Price Discrimination as an Antitrust Justification for Intellectual Property Refusals to Deal, 70 Antitrust L.J. 599, 608–10 (2003); William J. Baumol & Daniel G. Swanson, The New Economy and Ubiquitous Competitive Price Discrimination: Identifying Defensible Criteria of Market Power, 70 Antitrust L.J. 661 (2003); Michael E. Levine, Price Discrimination Without Market Power, 19 Yale J. Reg. 1 (2002); Lars A. Stole, Price Discrimination and Imperfect Competition, in Handbook of Industrial Organization (December 22, 2003), available at http://gsblas.uchicago.edu/papers/hio-distrib.pdf; Mark Armstrong & John Vickers, Competitive Price Discrimination, 32 Rand J. Econ. 579 (2001); Severin Borenstein, Price Discrimination in Free-Entry Markets, 16 Rand J. Econ. 380 (1985); Kenneth S. Corts, Third Degree Price Discrimination in Oligopoly: All-Out Competition and Strategic Commitment, 29 Rand J. Econ. 306 (1998).

burgeoning economic literature sets the foundation for the policy claims in Part III by dispelling some commonly invoked myths about price discrimination. Specifically, this literature demonstrates that the power to discriminate does not derive from market power as the term is used in antitrust law, that economists and antitrust law do indeed mean something different by "market power," that recent attempts to reconcile this tension are not useful, and that competitive price discrimination does not generally involve pernicious welfare effects.

A. *Price Discrimination Requires Only the Absence of Perfect Substitutes*

Competitive price discrimination will occur wherever product differentiation exists since all that is required for a firm to have the potential to charge differential prices is the absence of perfect substitutes deriving from any source.[32] Real world markets are characterized by exactly such product differentiation. Firms sell products with unique characteristics, whether the source of that uniqueness derives from a protected trademark, locational advantages, taste, packaging, quality, or any number of seller- or customer-specific factors.[33]

The important economic point is that price differentials can be expected to persist in equilibrium in competitive markets characterized by differentiated products. A leading treatise of the economics of price discrimination explains that a sufficient condition for price discrimination without long run market power is "some short run source of market power that allows prices to remain above marginal cost, such as a fixed cost of production."[34] Any source of customer brand-specific preference is sufficient to enable the firm to price discriminate.

A comparison with the model of perfect competition is useful to illustrate this point. Under perfect competition, all firms face perfectly elastic demands and therefore any deviation from marginal

[32]See Stole, *supra* note 31, at 1 n.2.

[33]See Timothy J. Muris, Improving the Economic Foundations of Competition Policy, 12 Geo. Mason L. Rev. 1, 28 (2003) ("Most real world markets, even those for relatively 'homogenous' products and a market structure inconsistent with significant market power, exhibit significant price variation. These price differences do not prove that the firms have market power.").

[34]Stole, *supra* note 31, at 1 n.2.

cost pricing causes demand to fall to zero. The reason why the firm in the perfectly competitive market of textbooks does not have this power is because the model assumes that all products are homogenous. Therefore, any attempted deviation from marginal cost pricing, even by one penny, will result in a loss of sales to rival firms offering perfect substitutes. Obviously, this assumption does not correspond with the real world, where firms compete by offering imperfect substitutes, products that are somewhat unique and differentiated across a wide spectrum of characteristics. Each of these firms, and virtually all in the economy, has the ability to charge prices above marginal cost because they offer unique products.

B. *Economists Define Market Power as the Ability to Set Price Above Marginal Cost Because They Use Perfect Competition as a Competitive Benchmark*

Price discrimination implies market power for economists because it involves some sales above marginal cost. In fact, above marginal cost pricing is the standard definition for market power in economics textbooks, which measures a firm's market power by its own-elasticity of demand.[35] This definition of market power explicitly adopts the perfectly competitive model as the competitive benchmark. In this world, firms cannot price discriminate because they face a perfectly horizontal demand. In real world markets, however, products can be expected to be differentiated on some margin. Some consumers will prefer the taste of Coca-Cola over Pepsi, or to drive to the gas station nearest the freeway entrance rather than to other locations, or to purchase groceries from a supermarket with a reputation for high quality produce. When a firm offering a differentiated product increases its price, sales will decrease, but not fall to zero. Once we allow for the reality of product differentiation between competitive firms, the model of perfect competition no longer applies. The perfectly competitive model is rendered inapplicable as a useful benchmark for antitrust analysis since virtually each seller in a real world market has the ability to price discriminate.

---

[35]Own-price elasticity of demand refers to the responsiveness of quantity demanded as a function of a change in price. Dennis W. Carlton & Jeffrey M. Perloff, Modern Industrial Organization 610 (3d ed. 2000) ("A firm ... has market power if it is profitably able to charge a price above that which would prevail under competition, which is usually taken to be marginal cost.").

C. *Market Power in Economics is Fundamentally Different than Market Power in Antitrust Law*

Benjamin Klein and John Wiley persuasively argue that market power in economics (the ability to price discriminate or price above marginal cost) is a phenomenon distinct from market power in antitrust,[36] though antitrust law sometimes conflates the two by adopting an own-elasticity of demand definition of market power. Klein and Wiley carefully document this confusion and diagnose the root cause as the mistaken view that market power in economics is the same phenomenon as market power in antitrust law.[37] It is not.

Market power in economics derives from the ability to deviate from marginal cost pricing, a power that comes from any source of product differentiation, *i.e.,* a trademark, reputation, relationship with buyers, taste, or location. The monopoly power required to trigger a violation of the antitrust laws refers to a different sort of power—the power to control *market* prices. Klein and Wiley demonstrate that, contrary to the classic analysis by Landes and Posner,[38] antitrust law should, and generally does, define market power, though sometimes ambiguously, in terms of the ability of a firm to influence market conditions rather than focusing on the firm's own-elasticity of demand.[39]

A commonly cited and relied upon definition of market power in antitrust law, adopted by the Supreme Court in *Jefferson Parish*, is that "market power exists whenever prices can be raised above levels that would be charged in a competitive market."[40] Market power under the antitrust law is therefore only identical to market power in economics if the case law can reasonably be understood as endorsing the view that prices charged in competitive markets are always equal to marginal cost, as would prevail under perfect

---

[36]Klein & Wiley, *supra* note 31, at 624–33.

[37]*Id.* at 624–29 (citing prominent antitrust scholars such as Phillip Areeda, Donald Turner, Robert Bork, Richard Posner, and Lawrence Sullivan as endorsing the proposition that the ability of a firm to price discriminate is evidence of significant monopoly power).

[38]William M. Landes & Richard A. Posner, Market Power in Antitrust Cases, 94 Harv. L. Rev. 937, 977 (1981).

[39]Klein & Wiley, *supra* note 31, at 629–30 & n.73 (collecting cases).

[40]Jefferson Parish Hosp. Dist. No. 2. v. Hyde, 466 U.S. 2, 27 n.46 (1984).

competition.[41] As Klein and Wiley point out, it is difficult to reconcile this view with the language from the Cellophane case rejecting the notion that a firm's ability to control its own prices resulting from product differentiation determines whether it has market power:

> [O]ne can theorize that we have monopolistic competition in every nonstandardized commodity with each manufacturer having power over the price and production of his own product. However, this power that, let us say, automobile or soft-drink manufacturers have over their trademarked products is not the power that makes an illegal monopoly. Illegal power must be appraised in terms of the competitive market for the product.[42]

It is clear that the definition of market power for the purposes of antitrust law is the ability to influence market prices and output, a power that is not usefully defined as a function of the firm's own-elasticity of demand. The question of antitrust market power is one of selecting an appropriate competitive benchmark to compare current market conditions. A firm's ability to price discriminate, and therefore its own-elasticity of demand, is only suggestive of antitrust market power if the competitive benchmark is perfect competition, which would require a finding that antitrust market power exists in virtually every firm in our modern economy characterized by competition between firms offering differentiated products.

One obvious exception to the "market conditions-based" definition of antitrust market power derives from the Supreme Court's analysis in *Eastman Kodak Co. v. Image Technical Services*.[43] While *Kodak* acknowledges that antitrust market power has been defined as "the ability of a single seller to raise price and restrict output," the definition adopted in *Jefferson Parish*, the Court ultimately adopts a strikingly different "consumer lock-in" conception of antitrust market power.[44] This definition allows for post-contractual evaluation of antitrust market power rather than analyzing the choices

---

[41]See Klein & Wiley, *supra* note 31, at 630–31.

[42]*Id.* at 630 (citing United States v. E.I. du Pont de Nemours & Co., 351 U.S. 377, 393 (1956)).

[43]504 U.S. 451 (1992).

[44]See, e.g., Benjamin Klein, Market Power in Aftermarkets, 17 Managerial & Decision Economics 143 (1996).

available to the buyer at the time of the relevant decision. This "lock-in" definition allows for antitrust market power to be found, at least under some conditions, in a single seller's brand, independent of firm market share and control over market conditions. The power to hold up "locked-in" consumers in proprietary aftermarkets is no different than the power a landlord has over a tenant after a competitive lease arrangement is signed.[45] While *Kodak's* alternative "lock-in" definition of market power is the exception rather than the rule in antitrust analysis, and has been limited to certain aftermarket tying cases, it would be inaccurate to suggest that the "market conditions-based" definition of market power is applied universally.

D. *Price Discrimination Does Not Imply Antitrust Market Power— Not Even a Little Bit of Market Power*

Antitrust scholars recognizing that the ability to price discriminate does not *necessarily* imply antitrust market power have sensibly attempted to reconcile the own-price elasticity definition of market power with the reality that most firms in our economy wield this power without the ability to influence market conditions. While these efforts are commendable, they have resulted in increased confusion regarding the role of antitrust in governing competitive price discrimination. The most commonly invoked attempt to reconcile economic market power with antitrust market power is the claim that price discrimination implies economic market power, but not to a degree sufficient to create antitrust market power.[46] That is, the

---

[45]The landlord and tenant example, and an antitrust analysis of aftermarket tying arrangements, appears in Benjamin Klein, Market Power in Antitrust: Economic Analysis After Kodak, 3 S. Ct. Econ. Rev. 43 (1993).

[46]A second attempt to reconcile the own-price elasticity definition of market power with antitrust law is to add the caveat that price discrimination implies market power only in markets with entry barriers. See generally Jonathan B. Baker, Competitive Price Discrimination: The Exercise of Market Power Without Anticompetitive Effects (Comment on Klein and Wiley), 70 Antitrust L.J. 643 (2003). Baker adopts the view that while price discrimination always proves market power, such power can be exercised without anticompetitive effects in markets with free entry. Klein and Wiley persuasively respond that in many industries characterized by brand names and intellectual property, entry is not likely to be free, but it is generally accepted that the presence of these assets does not imply the existence of market power. Benjamin Klein & John S. Wiley, Market Power in Economics and in Antitrust: Reply to Baker, 70 Antitrust L.J. 655, 656–57 (2003).

two phenomena are distinguished by a matter of degree and not kind. For instance, the 2002 edition of a leading treatise states:

> Proving price discrimination in selling or leasing identical (or nearly identical) products can usefully show the existence of market power if cost differences (or their absence) are readily determinable. But price discrimination seldom shows the amount of market power, and many instances of price discrimination are quite consistent with robust but imperfect competition. As a result, price discrimination evidence has very limited utility for proving power.[47]

No less an antitrust luminary than Judge Richard Posner adopts this reconciliation of the legal and economic definitions of market power. While conceding on the one hand that it would be "a profound mistake" to conclude that every firm facing a downward sloping demand curve has monopoly power in the sense meant by antitrust laws, Posner argues that this is only because these firms face "almost horizontal" demand curves.[48] Klein and Wiley correctly point out that Posner reaches the right result for the wrong reasons by adopting the unrealistic model of perfect competition as a benchmark.[49]

A downward sloping demand curve, the demand facing a firm whose rivals offer imperfect substitutes, does not imply antitrust market power. Nor does this power, which enables the firm to price discriminate, imply a level of antitrust market power "too small" to be concerned with for antitrust purposes. Economic market power and the monopoly power that is the concern of the antitrust laws are separate and distinct phenomena. What of Judge Posner's argument that firms which have the power to price discriminate do not have antitrust market power only if they face "almost horizontal" demand? A firm with trivial market share and the ability to price discriminate may well face significantly inelastic demand if its unique characteristics appeal strongly to a small set of buyers.

---

[47]2A Phillip E. Areeda et al., Antitrust Law ¶ 517, at 127–28 (2d ed. 2002); see also Landes & Posner, *supra* note 38, at 939 ("A simple economic meaning of the term 'market power' is the ability to set price above marginal cost .... But the fact of market power must be distinguished from the amount of market power.").

[48]Richard A. Posner, Antitrust Law 83 (2d ed. 2001); see also In re Brand Name Prescription Drugs Antitrust Litigation, 186 F.3d 781, 786–87 (7th Cir. 1999).

[49]Klein & Wiley, *supra* note 31, at 627–28.

Consider the market for the sale of men's colognes. Colognes are differentiated across a number of dimensions: brand names, smell, look, packaging, and others. "Michael Jordan Cologne for Men," for example, likely faces a significantly downward sloping demand curve and charges a price significantly above the marginal cost of producing the cologne, but has a trivial share of the total market for men's colognes. The seller of the Michael Jordan brand cologne undoubtedly has the power to engage in price discrimination, for example by offering quantity discounts or coupons. Loyal fans of Michael Jordan may constitute a very small fraction of the men's cologne market but be very loyal to the brand because of an affinity for the former basketball superstar. Michael Jordan brand cologne is of no antitrust concern because it does not have the ability to influence market conditions, not because it faces an "almost horizontal" demand curve.

Conversely, one might imagine a hypothetical cologne monopolist with 95% share facing more elastic demand than Michael Jordan Men's Cologne because consumers are attracted to the characteristics of the product but are not as fiercely brand-loyal as Michael Jordan's fans. Both firms have the ability to price discriminate, but only the firm with the more elastic demand might possibly possess control over market conditions. One simply cannot rank the degree of antitrust market power according to a firm's elasticity of demand. The fundamental economic point is that the ability to price discriminate is not evidence of some "degree" of influence over market conditions. Indeed, the ability to price discriminate is irrelevant to the power to control market conditions that is the *raison d'etre* of modern antitrust.

The same analysis applies to the presence of a patent, such as the one held by Illinois Tool Works. Rather than conferring market power, a patent merely allows a firm to exclude competitors from selling identical products. Patents do not ensure that the firm does not compete against a significant number of substitutes, but guarantee that those substitutes will be imperfect.[50] In other words, a patent

---

[50]Justice O'Connor makes this distinction, joined by three other concurring justices, in *Jefferson Parish*. 466 U.S. 2, 37 n.7 (1984) ("A common misconception has been that a patent or copyright, a high market share, or a unique product that competitors are not able to offer suffice to demonstrate market power. While each of these three factors might help to give market power to a seller, it is also possible that a seller in these situations will have no market power: for example, a patent holder has no market power in any relevant sense if there are close substitutes for the patented product."). Accord 1 Hovenkamp et al., *supra* note 2, § 4.2, at 4–9 ("a patent grant

guarantees merely that the firm, like virtually all others in the economy, will face a downward sloping demand since rivals will be unable to duplicate the product in the marketplace for some fixed period of time. The patented product may garner a small share of the market but have an intensely loyal following and thus face highly inelastic demand. Alternatively, the patented product may succeed in obtaining a dominant market share but face competition from an imperfect substitute with a more loyal following consisting of less price sensitive customers. The patent wielding monopolist will face more elastic demand despite greater control over market conditions. For the same reason that patents do not confer antitrust market power, neither does the power to price discriminate, since both derive from the same source: the lack of perfect substitutes.

E. Price Discrimination Does Not Generally Involve Pernicious Welfare Effects

The conventional mantra for those advocating strict antitrust scrutiny of price discrimination is the well-known economic analysis which concludes that the total welfare effects of third-degree price discrimination are ambiguous. From a static perspective, this analysis makes some intuitive sense: some buyers receive lower prices (and purchase higher quantities) while other buyers receive higher prices (and purchase lower quantities) and therefore the net impact of price discrimination on output is ambiguous. Indeed, standard models of price discrimination in the economic literature demonstrate that an increase in aggregate output is a necessary condition for price discrimination to increase welfare under monopoly.[51] This conventional welfare analysis is of limited utility for several reasons.

The first is because most aftermarket metering agreements do not involve what Pigou classified as third-degree price discrimination. Recall that third-degree price discrimination refers to the practice of breaking buyers into distinct groups and setting a profit maximizing price for each group, resulting in one price for each group. But

creates an antitrust 'monopoly' only if it succeeds in giving the exclusive right to make something for which there are not adequate market alternatives, and for which consumers would be willing to pay a monopoly price").

[51]See, e.g., Hal Varian, Price Discrimination and Economic Welfare, 75 Am. Econ. Rev. 870 (1985). For a survey of the analysis of the welfare effects of price discrimination generally, see Stole, *supra* note 31.

aftermarket metering arrangements, like those involved in *Independent Ink*, do not involve third-degree price discrimination. Rather, Illinois Tool Works' arrangement involved a single price for printers and ink which allowed it to vary the total package price across each unit sold to each buyer according to the intensity of use in an attempt to capture the maximum surplus. Klein and Wiley point out that aftermarket metering arrangements, the most common example of price discrimination in antitrust analysis, are much more appropriately described as second-degree price discrimination.[52]

A comparison to "perfect" or first-degree price discrimination is useful. Perfect price discrimination refers to the ability of a seller to vary the price across each unit to each consumer in order to extract all consumer surplus. It is well known that perfect price discrimination generates outcomes where industry output is identical to that which would prevail under perfect competition, where price equals marginal cost. Second-degree price discrimination in the metering context is therefore an approximate form of perfect price discrimination. So why do Klein and Wiley contend that aftermarket metering falls into this category rather than the "welfare-ambiguous" class of third-degree discriminatory arrangements? The answer is because aftermarket metering, like perfect price discrimination, involves an attempt to collect the maximum for each unit sold to each buyer by metering the intensity of the package demand. High intensity users pay a higher package price and lower intensity users pay a lower package price, with the seller collecting varying levels of consumer surplus from each type of user. Klein and Wiley describe the relationship the following way:

> The essential economic determinant of how closely a manufacturer using an aftermarket metering arrangement can approximate the output increases of perfect price discrimination is the accuracy of the meter in measuring intensity of package demand above the non-discriminating price.[53]

The welfare effects of perfect price discrimination are unambiguous from a static perspective: producer surplus and output increase while consumer surplus decreases. The more surplus the seller is

[52]Klein & Wiley, *supra* note 31, at 612–13.
[53]*Id.* at 613.

able to extract with the metering device, the greater the output increasing effect of the discriminatory arrangement.

The second failure of the conventional welfare analysis is that it ignores important dynamic welfare effects that are unambiguously welfare increasing. The increase in producer surplus predicted by the conventional price discrimination analysis provides incentives for additional investment in innovation and other competitive investments such as increasing product variety, expanding retail outlets, or research and development. Klein and Wiley summarize the static and dynamic welfare effects of aftermarket metering arrangements as likely to enhance efficiency.[54] Investments made to enhance the ability to price discriminate are not socially wasteful, rent-dissipating expenditures. Rather, these investments are best seen as part of the competitive process as firms attempt to attract consumers through offering valuable products, services, and amenities.

Finally, the conventional welfare analysis ignores the possibility that price discrimination intensifies competition and therefore increases consumer welfare for *all* consumers. Recent models analyze the competition-intensifying impact of price discrimination and challenge the result that price discrimination necessarily involves losses to some consumers.[55] The economic intuition behind these models is that price discrimination is a competitive tool that allows firms to compete for *all consumers* on different segments of the demand curve by offering a menu of prices rather than competing only for the marginal consumer with uniform pricing. Competitive price discrimination therefore leads to lower profits and lower prices. Thus, an examination of these static welfare effects suggests that third-degree price discrimination is at least welfare neutral relative to uniform pricing.

Economics provides no single universal welfare theorem for all arrangements involving price discrimination.[56] It is certainly true

[54] *Id.* at 619.

[55] See, e.g., Corts, *supra* note 31.

[56] There is another important dimension upon which welfare results might vary in addition to those already mentioned. The economics literature distinguishes between price discrimination to final consumers as opposed to intermediate buyers. In the former, it has been shown that nonlinear pricing schedules may be welfare superior to uniform pricing under general conditions. See, e.g., Robert D. Willig, Pareto-Superior Nonlinear Outlay Schedules, 9 Bell J. Econ. 36 (1978). However, these welfare results do not necessarily apply to intermediate goods market. See, e.g., Michael

that some consumers are worse off under some discriminatory arrangements, and that sometimes those losses will outweigh the gains to other consumers. However, even an analysis of the static welfare effects of competitive price discrimination can involve benefits to all consumers. Because the standard welfare analysis ignores important dynamic effects as well as the possibility that the practice intensifies competition generally, and both effects unambiguously increase consumer welfare, consumers are likely to benefit from the practice.

Even if some discriminatory arrangements theoretically involve a net welfare loss, it is necessary to distinguish these welfare losses from those caused by an artificial reduction in output. As discussed in Part III, antitrust policy should distinguish between welfare losses associated with competitive attempts to increase output by attracting consumers and monopolistic attempts to reduce market output.

F. A Reply to Nalebuff, Ayres, and Sullivan: Metering Ties Facilitating Price Discrimination Are Not Evidence of Market Power

Independent Ink and its amici curiae, Professors Barry Nalebuff, Ian Ayres, and Lawrence Sullivan, argued that the presumption was appropriate for metering ties because they involve price discrimination that "is strong evidence of market power." As discussed, the Court rejected this argument largely on legal grounds. However, the Court did not ignore the economic merits of the Nalebuff brief altogether, noting that it was "not persuaded that the combination of [price discrimination and an above-market price for the tied package]

Katz, The Welfare Effects of Third Degree Price Discrimination in Intermediate Good Markets, 77 Am. Econ. Rev. 154 (1984); Janusz A. Ordover & John C. Panzar, On the Nonlinear Pricing of Inputs, 23 Int. Econ. Rev. 659 (1982). The weaker welfare results in the case of intermediate goods might suggest to some that greater antitrust scrutiny is warranted where price discrimination occurs in intermediate goods markets, such as *Independent Ink*. However, the shortcomings of the standard welfare analysis generally apply in the case of intermediate goods as well. For instance, the weaker welfare results in intermediate goods markets do not account for dynamic consumer welfare benefits. In addition, as I argue in Part III.A, the potential for negative welfare effects arising from price discrimination does not justify antitrust intervention because the effects do not arise from the power to control market conditions, and such a policy would necessitate micro-management of competition between firms. Antitrust does not, and should not, be responsible for determining which forms of competitive price discrimination such as offering coupons or quantity discounts result in net welfare losses. I thank Bruce Kobayashi for bringing this issue to my attention.

should give rise to a presumption of market power when neither is sufficient to do so standing alone."[57] The Court adopts the view that:

> [W]hile price discrimination may provide evidence of market power, particularly if buttressed by evidence that the patentee has charged an above-market price for the tied package, it is generally recognized that it also occurs in fully competitive markets.[58]

While the Court was correct to reject the Nalebuff proposal, it reaches the right conclusion for the wrong reasons. The Court incorrectly asserts that price discrimination, without more, implies at least "some" evidence of market power. As discussed, this view adopts the own-price elasticity definition of antitrust market power that does not stem from the ability to control market conditions and adopts the unrealistic scenario of perfect competition as a competitive benchmark.

Nalebuff's assertions that metering arrangements imply antitrust market power and are likely to reduce consumer welfare are both incorrect, but not because price discrimination implies a degree of market power too small to warrant antitrust concern. Rather, the Nalebuff argument is incorrect because it conflates the ability to price discriminate with the ability to influence market conditions and asserts that the practice is likely to harm consumers.

Nalebuff's assertion that metering implies market power is also incorrect. The reason that Nalebuff mistakenly concludes that metering is evidence of market power is because they expressly adopt the view that "the amount of price discrimination a firm can impose is related to its market power."[59] Following this logic, Nalebuff argues that the fact that Trident was able to charge customers 2.5 to 4 times the price offered by Independent Ink for ink indicates a "substantial degree of price discrimination and hence market power."[60] We have already seen the fallacy of assuming this sort of relationship between elasticity of demand and antitrust market power. The ability to price discriminate does not imply antitrust market power because the

---

[57]126 S. Ct. 1281, 1292 (2006).

[58]*Id.* (citation omitted).

[59]Nalebuff Brief, *supra* note 16, at 24.

[60]*Id.*

latter requires the ability to control market conditions. The power to price discriminate is not equivalent to the ability to control market conditions, nor is it a related phenomenon to a lesser degree.

The welfare effects of aftermarket metering arrangements like the one involved in *Independent Ink* also do not support Nalebuff's claims. Nalebuff argues that "[t]he act of price discrimination via tied sales creates a harm to consumers."[61] While the authors concede that price discrimination can expand output and improve efficiency in some cases, they argue that "there is no reason to believe that price discrimination is efficient" and emphasize that "there is no general result that suggests that imperfect price discrimination improves efficiency, even treating consumer surplus and producer profits equally."[62] The last statement is correct as a technical matter, but proves nothing. The possibility that price discrimination reduces consumer welfare is not very useful. The same literature generally recognizes that price discrimination does not always reduce efficiency or harm consumers and increasingly recognizes that price discrimination is a part of the competitive process. As discussed, this welfare analysis also ignores the consumer welfare-enhancing dynamic effects associated with price discrimination as producers earn additional profits and make significant additional investments and innovations that benefit consumers.

Perhaps most importantly, even if one were to accept the static welfare analysis, the analysis does not support Nalebuff's position regarding the presumption of market power. The modern economics literature is full of results establishing that nearly all forms of conduct may or may not be efficient depending on the circumstances. The burden of proof on the issue of market power for every single one of these practices, however, is placed on the plaintiff. The possibility that some subset of discriminatory arrangements may reduce static consumer welfare does not imply that the burden of proof with respect to market power should be placed on the defendant in this case.

The fallacy of the relationship between price discrimination and antitrust market power is a significant problem for antitrust. It is crucial to keep distinct the concepts of economic market power and

[61]*Id.* at 17.
[62]*Id.* at 19–20.

antitrust market power, despite the temptation to reconcile and unify the two with appeals to "degrees" or entry conditions. Antitrust in a world where price discrimination does imply antitrust market power will find violations in the most mundane marketing arrangements, *e.g.*, the use of supermarket grocery coupons, movie theater senior citizen discounts, or quantity discounts on Michael Jordan's Cologne. Attempts to reconcile this tension with appeals to entry conditions, or dismissing these situations as involving some, but "not enough," market power to warrant antitrust concern, are convenient but ultimately misguided answers to this problem. The more accurate, and appropriate, policy response is to adopt a definition of market power that takes seriously the notion that such power refers to the ability of the monopolist to change competitive conditions in the market.

As I argue in Part III, an integral part of such a policy response is for antitrust to ignore competitive price discrimination without separate evidence of the exercise of antitrust market power.

III. Competitive Price Discrimination Should Not Be an Antitrust Problem

Modern antitrust scholars have emphasized a desire to ground policy in the empirical realities of real world markets. The Supreme Court has expressed a similar preference for antitrust rules that reflect empirical reality.[63] *Independent Ink* represents an important step forward in this regard. However, the empirical reality—that the modern economy involves markets nearly universally characterized by product differentiation and competitive price discrimination—has yet to be fully recognized by antitrust doctrine. The link between these two is clear: patents confer a right to exclude which guarantees only the absence of perfect substitutes, which is all that is required to price discriminate. Rather, price discrimination is a normal part of the competitive process in the modern economy, and consumers would benefit from an antitrust regime that abandoned any inferences of anticompetitive effect associated with the practice.

[63]See, e.g., Eastman Kodak Co. v. Image Technical Servs., Inc., 504 U.S. 451, 466–67 (1992) ("Legal presumptions that rest on formalistic distinctions rather than actual market realities are generally disfavored in antitrust law . . . . In determining the existence of market power . . . this Court has examined closely the economic reality of the market at issue.").

Justice Stevens' opinion in *Independent Ink* explicitly recognizes that price discrimination occurs in competitive markets and that is not a sufficient condition for market power.[64] The opinion also properly rejects the view, expressed by the Nalebuff brief, that price discrimination associated with metering arrangements is more likely than not to generate consumer welfare losses.[65] These are excellent starting points for a more sensible antitrust policy. However, once it is recognized that price discrimination does not confer monopoly power, and does not generally produce anticompetitive effects, only one additional step is required to illustrate that competitive price discrimination should remain outside the domain of modern antitrust enforcement. *Independent Ink* thus represents an opportunity foregone for the Court to clarify the confused but critical antitrust jurisprudence governing practices that facilitate price discrimination by embracing the economic logic behind its rejection of the market power presumption.

A. Antitrust Law Should Not Prohibit the Potential Negative Welfare Effects Arising from Price Discrimination

Price discrimination does not generally reduce consumer welfare when one appropriately accounts for all static and dynamic welfare effects. While some discriminatory arrangements involve gains to all consumers, it is also certainly possible for a discriminatory arrangement to result in net losses for consumers. So why should antitrust ignore these arrangements altogether rather than identifying and prosecuting those cases involving negative net welfare effects?

There are two very good reasons to refrain from such detailed welfare analyses. One is conceptual and the other is pragmatic in nature.[66] Conceptually, it is essential to understand that any net consumer welfare losses arising out of competitive price discrimination do not involve monopoly power and therefore do not arise out of an artificial restriction of output. The hallmark of modern antitrust enforcement is the prevention of the exercise of monopoly power to the detriment of consumers. Even in the case that net consumer

---

[64]126 S. Ct. at 1292.

[65]*Id.*

[66]See Klein and Wiley, *supra* note 31, at 619–21.

welfare decreases as a result of a discriminatory arrangement, the losses are simply not the sort of losses that the antitrust laws are designed to protect against. As Klein and Wiley argue:

> Antitrust law should not, however, involve a determination of which consumers gain and which lose when a firm enforces a discriminatory pricing arrangement with a refusal to deal. It is also not the role of antitrust to determine, for example, that there are too many restaurants in the economy or that restaurants are of too diverse a variety because of price discrimination. We look to the unsupervised competitive market process and not to antitrust law to settle such issues.[67]

The pragmatic reason is that such a test would involve an unacceptable risk of false positives.[68] Because arrangements facilitating price discrimination generally improve the welfare of some consumers while other consumers lose, such an analysis would require the calculation of net welfare effects. This is an extremely demanding task to require of courts and would require consumer specific data, which is difficult to obtain, as is the measurement of the dynamic welfare benefits already discussed.

B. Conduct Involving the Exercise of Monopoly Power May Be Attacked Whether or Not it Involves a Discriminatory Arrangement

One might be skeptical that ignoring competitive price discrimination might result in unnecessary immunity from antitrust scrutiny for monopolists utilizing discriminatory arrangements to exclude rivals and injure competition. Such harm, which results from the exercise of monopoly power, is precisely what the antitrust laws are designed to prevent and should not be immunized. Of course, immunizing competitive price discrimination, and therefore removing from the domain of antitrust enforcement conduct that may harm welfare only because of its discriminatory effects, does not grant a free pass to monopolists exercising their power to the detriment of consumers.

To the contrary, conduct involving price discrimination, such as aftermarket tying arrangements, quantity discounts, refusals to deal,

---

[67] *Id.* at 620.
[68] *Id.* at 620–21.

or other arrangements may lead to anticompetitive effects by creating or maintaining antitrust market power, that is, the power to control market conditions. Under these limited circumstances, conduct facilitating price discrimination should be subject to the enforcement of the antitrust laws. The important analytical point is that any anticompetitive effects from the separate, monopolistic conduct should be analyzed separately from the welfare effects of price discrimination.

IV. Conclusion

It is well known and universally accepted that intellectual property rights rarely confer monopoly power in the antitrust sense. Just as plainly, the power to price discriminate does not necessitate a finding of monopoly power. *Independent Ink* should be applauded for incorporating the first proposition into antitrust doctrine by rejecting the patent presumption. This is no small event for antitrust doctrine. Consumers will benefit from this decision as intellectual property holders engage in the competitive process with less unwarranted fear of antitrust liability.

Perhaps just as importantly, *Independent Ink* also represents a missed opportunity to clarify the role of antitrust enforcement in policing competitive conduct which facilitates price discrimination without threatening welfare losses associated with the exercise of true monopoly power. While the Court embraced the notion that competitive price discrimination, such as the metering arrangement adopted by Illinois Tool Works, does not require market power, the Court did not embrace the economic logic supporting its holding rejecting the patent presumption. Because patent rights only grant the power to price discriminate, an ability shared by nearly every firm in our modern economy facing a downward sloping demand curve, the Court could have correctly rejected the view that price discrimination confers antitrust market power.

The failure to broadly and universally reject the claim that price discrimination confers antitrust market power is not without its costs. The misleading notion that competitive contracting processes facilitating price discrimination imply antitrust market power still exists in many arenas of antitrust jurisprudence. For example, the Court's analysis in *Kodak* leaves open the possibility that firms like Illinois Tool Works will face similar claims easily reconstituted as aftermarket tying cases involving "consumer lock-in," rather than invoking the patent presumption. The substitution towards "consumer lock-in" cases from patent presumption-based claims demonstrates yet another reason why *Independent Ink* must be viewed as a missed opportunity.

The persistent conflation of the concepts of economic market power and antitrust market power creates an antitrust policy which finds some degree of antitrust market power in nearly every firm in the economy. Competitive price discrimination is not a problem deserving of antitrust scrutiny. Price discrimination is generally consumer welfare enhancing when one accounts for the dynamic effects associated with product differentiation investments designed to attract more consumers. Further, even when the net welfare effect of a discriminatory arrangement is negative, these welfare losses are not the result of an artificial reduction in output and are nearly impossible to measure. Any negative welfare effects associated with competitive price discrimination do not involve the exercise of monopoly power, and the antitrust laws are not designed to micromanage the competitive process to find and prohibit those arrangements which help some consumers but hurt others. In the rare case where the discriminatory arrangement is adopted by a monopolist, rather than a competitive firm with the ability to price discriminate, and creates an anticompetitive effect, the antitrust laws should attack the conduct. The important point is that the competitive harm in these cases has nothing to do with price discrimination and everything to do with the exercise of monopoly power.

Product differentiation is the hallmark of firms in our modern economy. Intellectual property rights allow firms to exclude competitors from offering perfect substitutes, and therefore to price discriminate. While it is difficult to make any form of discrimination sound good, I have attempted to demonstrate here that it typically accrues to the benefit of consumers and, in any event, is part of the normal competitive process and not a function of monopolistic power. Rather, it is a power held by every restaurant, landlord, corner gas station, supermarket, and small firm in the economy. Because price discrimination is profitable, we can expect firms in our modern economy to invest substantial resources not only in product differentiation, but also in finding methods to price discriminate. This is no need for competitive concern, as these investments are motivated by the competitive process, not monopoly power, and take the form of providing benefits to consumers. The pervasive nature of price discrimination underlines the importance of understanding its role in the normal competitive process. *Independent Ink* demonstrates that while antitrust law has come a long way in terms of economic sophistication, it has not yet fully incorporated lessons from the economic literature regarding competitive price discrimination, and this failure threatens consumer welfare by associating anticompetitive inferences with an inherently competitive practice.

Looking Ahead: October Term 2006

Peter B. Rutledge*

October Term 2006 will be the first full opportunity for Court-watchers to assess the impact of recent changes in the Court's membership. It will be Chief Justice Roberts' second full term and Justice Alito's first. It also will provide the first full term in which to assess whether Justice Kennedy will reclaim his role as "swing justice." Accompanying these changes in the Court's personnel will be a docket full of interesting cases on topics such as the constitutionality of racial diversity programs, abortion, environmental law, punitive damages, and criminal procedure.

Consistent with prior contributions to this series, this essay offers readers a critical overview of what to expect during October Term 2006 at the U.S. Supreme Court. Given the potentially important shifts in the Court's personnel and the consequences of those shifts for the Court's voting blocs, the essay first analyzes the general effect of these shifts in membership, especially the impact of Chief Justice Roberts and Justice Alito as well as the increased importance of Justice Kennedy. The second portion of the essay examines the major cases on the Court's docket for October Term 2006 and places them in context of these changes in the Court's membership.

I. Changing Personnel and the New Voting Dynamics

This part of the essay addresses the impact of changes in the Court's personnel. It considers the impact of Chief Justice Roberts, Justice Alito, and Justice Kennedy.

*Associate Professor of Law, Columbus School of Law, Catholic University of America. I would like to thank the Cato Institute, especially Mark Moller, for the invitation to submit this essay. Veryl Miles, Dean of the Law School, provided generous financial support for my research this summer. Maureen Smith and Barney Ford, both students at the Law School, provided excellent research assistance. Steve Young, a reference librarian at the Law School, helped to track down materials on the Supreme Court. Julie Kendrick, an assistant at the Law School, helped with the production of the manuscript (including suffering through my chicken scratches on the first draft).

A. Chief Justice Roberts

The impact of Chief Justice Roberts is two fold: his impact as chief and his impact as a justice. The chief justice has often been described as the first among equals.[1] That is, with respect to the bread-and-butter work of the Court, he possesses certain institutional prerogatives, mostly by tradition.[2] Otherwise, he has no more power to influence an outcome than any other justice. This is especially true when he is in the minority, whether on a certiorari petition, a stay application, or a decision of the Court. In three respects, though, Chief Justice Roberts has had or has the potential to have an impact on the Court in his capacity as chief justice.[3]

First, Chief Justice Roberts has, to a point, achieved a greater degree of consensus on the Court. During his confirmation hearings, Chief Justice Roberts expressed his desire to achieve greater judicial consensus, which was a matter of particular importance at the time in light of recent splintered decisions at the Court such as the Ten Commandments cases.[4] As part of this desire to achieve consensus,

---

[1]Denis Steven Rutkus & Lorraine H. Tong, Congressional Research Service, The Chief Justice of the United States: Responsibilities of the Office and Process for Appointment, at Summary-1 (CRS Report for Congress RL 32821) (September 12, 2005).

[2]On the statutory responsibilities of the chief justice, see *id.* at CRS-4–CRS-7.

[3]A fourth deserves brief mention but does not warrant full treatment. Some accounts suggest that the chief justice also has influenced the dynamics of the justices' conferences, where they discuss certiorari petitions and their votes on cases. Whereas Chief Justice Rehnquist allegedly ran those conferences on a fairly tight schedule, Chief Justice Roberts allegedly has loosened those restrictions and, thereby, occasioned greater debate among the justices. See, e.g., Linda Greenhouse, In the Roberts Court, More Room for Argument, N.Y. Times, May 3, 2006, at A19; Linda Greenhouse, New Leaders, Tough Issues for Court in Transition, N.Y. Times, Sept. 30, 2005, at A1. The justices' conferences remain entirely private, so, until a justice retires and makes his papers publicly available, these speculations are extremely hard to verify through objective means.

[4]Confirmation Hearing on the Nomination of John G. Roberts, Jr. to be Chief Justice of the United States Before the S. Comm. on the Judiciary, 109th Cong. 371 (2005), available at 2006 WL 86787 (F.D.C.H.) [hereinafter Transcript of Roberts Confirmation Hearings] ("Well, if I am confirmed, I think one of the things that the Chief Justice should have as a top priority is to try to bring about a greater degree of coherence and consensus in the opinions of the Court. . . . I think the Court should be as united behind an opinion of the Court as it possibly can."); *id.* at 303 ("I do think, though, it's a responsibility of all the Justices, not just the Chief Justice, to try to work toward an opinion of the Court . . . . I do think the Chief Justice has a particular obligation

Chief Justice Roberts has commented favorably on the subject of judicial minimalism, famously quipping at Georgetown University's Law School this year: "If it is not necessary to decide more to dispose of a case, in my view it is necessary not to decide more."[5]   In several respects, Chief Justice Roberts already has succeeded in his efforts at consensus building. In October Term 2005, the Court decided nearly fifty percent on its docket without dissent, a significant uptick over recent terms.[6] This past term, the Court decided sixteen cases by five-vote majorities, far fewer than in its most recent terms.[7] Of all the justices who sat during the entire term, Chief Justice Roberts was most often in the majority—both across all cases and in split decisions.[8] Notably, some of these consensus decisions included areas where Court watchers had predicted pitched battles. The Court handed down unanimous decisions in cases involving the constitutionality of the Solomon Amendment, New Hampshire's abortion law, restrictions on abortion protests, standing in dormant Commerce Clause cases, the death penalty, and religious freedom.[9]

Of course, the chief justice's efforts at building consensus did not always succeed. Indeed, given the controversial nature of many cases on the Court's docket, it is hardly surprising that, so long as

---

to try to achieve consensus consistent with everyone's oath to uphold the Constitution, and that would certainly be a priority for me if I were confirmed.").

[5]Cass R. Sunstein, The Minimalist, L.A. Times, May 25, 2006, at B11, available at http://www.law.uchicago.edu/sunstein-minimalism-roberts.html (last visited July 30, 2006).

[6]Rebecca Cady, Georgetown University Law Center Supreme Court Institute, Supreme Court of the United States: October Term 2005 Overview 1 (June 30, 2006) [hereinafter Georgetown Overview]. Any statistical account of activity at the Supreme Court must make certain methodological assumptions such as how to count consolidated cases, how to treat per curiam opinions, and how to treat partially joined opinions for purposes of determining voting affinities. While several sources exist, this essay utilizes the statistics of (and the methodological assumptions contained in) the Georgetown Overview for the current term and some of my own research for prior terms.

[7]*Id.*

[8]*Id.* at 7–8.

[9]See Rumsfeld v. Forum for Academic and Institutional Rights (FAIR), 126 S. Ct. 1297 (2006); Ayotte v. Planned Parenthood of N. New England, 126 S. Ct. 961 (2006); Scheidler v. N.O.W., Inc. 126 S. Ct. 1264 (2006); DaimlerChrysler Corp. v. Cuno, 126 S. Ct. 1854 (2006); Hill v. McDonough, 126 S. Ct. 2096 (2006); and Gonzales v. O Centro Espirita Beneficente Uniao do Vegetal, 126 S. Ct. 1211 (2006).

the Supreme Court permits separate opinions, justices will continue to write them. In several cases, in areas such as environmental law, voting rights, and campaign finance, the Court was unable to achieve a majority.[10] Perhaps the most extreme disappointment in this regard was the Texas redistricting case, where one virtually needs an instructional manual to understand the holding:

> Kennedy, J., announced the judgment of the Court and delivered the opinion of the Court with respect to Parts II-A and III, in which Stevens, Souter, Ginsburg, and Breyer, JJ., joined, an opinion with respect to Parts I and IV, in which Roberts, C. J., and Alito, J., joined, an opinion with respect to Parts II-B and II-C, and an opinion with respect to Part II-D, in which Souter and Ginsburg, JJ., joined. Stevens, J., filed an opinion concurring in part and dissenting in part, in which Breyer, J., joined as to Parts I and II. Souter, J., filed an opinion concurring in part and dissenting in part, in which Ginsburg, J., joined. Breyer, J., filed an opinion concurring in part and dissenting in part. Roberts, C. J., filed an opinion concurring in part, concurring in the judgment in part, and dissenting in part, in which Alito, J., joined. Scalia, J., filed an opinion concurring in the judgment in part and dissenting in part, in which Thomas, J., joined, and in which Roberts, C. J., and Alito, J., joined as to Part III.[11]

In the coming term, watch for Chief Justice Roberts to continue to strive for consensus—or at least greater clarity—in the Court's decisions.

Second, watch also how the chief justice assigns opinions. In some potentially controversial cases, he assigned the opinion to himself and achieved either a unanimous opinion or unanimity in judgment, suggesting that he has sought to use the opinion assignment process to build consensus.[12] Yet not all his opinion assignments seem geared to consensus. In some, rather than assigning the opinion to a "swing" justice, who might be inclined to resolve the case on narrower, more

[10]See Rapanos v. United States, 126 S. Ct. 2208 (2006); League of United Latin American Citizens v. Perry, 126 S. Ct. 2594 (2006) [hereinafter LULAC]; and Randall v. Sorrell, 126 S. Ct. 2479 (2006).

[11]LULAC, 126 S. Ct. at 2604.

[12]See Rumsfeld v. FAIR, 126 S. Ct. 1297 (2006); Gonzales v. O Centro Espirita Beneficiente Uniao do Vegetal, 126 S. Ct. 1211 (2006); and DaimlerChrysler Corp. v. Cuno, 126 S. Ct. 1854 (2006).

minimalist grounds, he has instead assigned the opinion to a justice who was bound to write a far broader opinion. The starkest example from the past term was *Hudson v. Michigan*,[13] where the Court held that the exclusionary rule did not apply to violations of the Fourth Amendment's knock-and-announce requirement.[14] Justice Scalia's opinion for the Court rested on broad reasoning that is not easily confined to the knock-and-announce context (and could therefore foreshadow a broader scaling back of the exclusionary rule).

Third, watch the size of the docket. During the Rehnquist Court, the size of the Court's argument docket shrunk.[15] At his confirmation hearings, Chief Justice Roberts indicated that he believed the Court could increase the size of its docket.[16] This past term did not mark a significant shift in the docket size, and the Court only decided seventy-five cases after argument, consistent with the relatively small docket in recent years.[17] Of course, in two respects, it is difficult to attribute that statistic to Chief Justice Roberts—a portion of the docket had been set before he became chief justice and, at conference, he only has a single vote whereas certiorari requires four.[18] Perhaps more tellingly, though, the Court only has twenty-nine cases on its docket for October Term 2006, far fewer than have been on its docket at comparable points in prior years.[19] Until a justice's vote sheets are released in the national archives decades from now, we can only speculate why this might be the case: perhaps cert-worthy cases are not reaching the Court; perhaps Chief Justice Roberts is having difficulty persuading his brethren of the desirability of taking more cases; or perhaps the chief justice himself is having second thoughts

[13]126 S. Ct. 2159 (2006).

[14] See, e.g., *id.* at 2165.

[15]See David M. O'Brien, A Diminished Plenary Docket, 89 Judicature 134 (Nov.-Dec. 2005), available at http://www.ajs.org/ajs/publications/Judicature_PDFs/OBrien_893.pdf (last visited July 30, 2006).

[16]Transcript of Roberts Confirmation Hearing, *supra* note 4, at 337 ("I do think there is room for the court to take more cases. They hear about half the number of cases they did 25 years ago. There may be good reasons for that that I will learn if I am confirmed, but just looking at it from the outside, I think they could contribute more to the clarity and uniformity of the law by taking more cases.").

[17]See Peter Bowman Rutledge & Nicole L. Angarella, An End of Term Exam: October Term 2003 at the United States Supreme Court, 54 Cath. U.L. Rev. 151, 240 (2004).

[18]Robert L. Stern, et al., Supreme Court Practice 336 (8th ed. 2002).

[19]Georgetown Overview, *supra* note 6, at 25.

about the desirability of increasing the docket. The coming term will provide additional indications of whether the chief justice is able to increase the docket.

Apart from his impact in his capacity as first among equals, Chief Justice Roberts' impact as a voting justice has been relatively straightforward. He generally has aligned himself with the views of Justices Scalia and Thomas on most issues, including executive power, criminal law, and the Commerce Clause.[20] In terms of voting affinity Chief Justice Roberts voted with Justice Scalia 86.4% of the time, the second-highest voting affinity after the Scalia-Thomas affinity (86.8%).[21] By contrast, he aligned least frequently with Justice Stevens.[22] One major exception to this trend came in *Padilla v. Hanft*.[23] In that case, the Court denied certiorari, and Chief Justice Roberts joined an opinion by Justice Kennedy respecting the denial of certiorari.[24] In that opinion, also joined by Justice Stevens, Justice Kennedy expressed some concern over how Padilla's transfer could frustrate habeas review and noted the "fundamental" separation of powers considerations raised by the case.[25] As described below in Part II, the coming term offers several opportunities to test whether the voting alliance between Chief Justice Roberts and Justices Scalia and Thomas will continue to stick.

B. Justice Alito

The coming term also will provide further insights into the impact of Justice Alito. Compared to Chief Justice Roberts, Justice Alito provides a far more limited data set (he voted in only thirty-six cases the past term). In those cases, however he voted most frequently with Chief Justice Roberts.[26] By contrast, he voted with Justice Stevens

[20]See Georgia v. Randolph, 126 S. Ct. 1515 (2006); House v. Bell, 126 S. Ct. 2064 (2006); Hamdan v. Rumsfeld, 126 S. Ct. 2749 (2006); Gonzales v. Oregon, 126 S. Ct. 904 (2006).

[21]Georgetown Overview, *supra* note 6, at 9. Other studies suggest that the voting alliance between Chief Justice Roberts and Justice Scalia was the highest on the Court. See Tom Goldstein, The First Voting Statistics, Scotusblog (June 28, 2006), available at www.scotusblog.com/movabletype/archives/2006/06/the_first_votin.html.

[22]Georgetown Overview, *supra* note 6, at 9.

[23]See Padilla v. Hanft, 423 F.3d 386 (4th Cir. 2005), cert. denied, 126 S. Ct. 1649 (2006).

[24]See 126 S. Ct. at 1649–50 (Kennedy, J., concurring).

[25]*Id.* at 1650.

[26]Georgetown Overview, *supra* note 6, at 9.

only 41.2% of the term, by far the lowest voting affinity of the Court of any pair of justices.[27] While one should not read too much into these statistics due to the limited data set, several data points suggest the emergence of a Roberts-Scalia-Thomas-Alito voting bloc. In the 5-4 cases decided by the Court this past term, those four justices voted together six times. Another telling indicator came in three cases reargued after his confirmation. In each, Justice Alito voted with the Roberts-Scalia-Thomas bloc.[28] As with Chief Justice Roberts, there are a few, low-level counter-trends. In his first vote following confirmation, Justice Alito declined to vacate a stay in a capital case (contrary to the views of Justices Scalia and Thomas).[29] Additionally, he parted company with Justice Scalia in *United States v. Gonzalez-Lopez*,[30] which held that depriving a criminal defendant of the counsel of his choice represented structural error.[31] As discussed below in Part II, the coming term presents several occasions where the Roberts-Alito bloc can have a significant impact on the course of the Court's jurisprudence.

C. Justice Kennedy

Since he joined the Court in 1988, Justice Kennedy has shared with Justice O'Connor the power of serving as "swing justice" on most issues. During her last five terms on the bench, Justice O'Connor was in the majority most often in 5-4 decisions.[32] Prior to that, Justice Kennedy regularly was most often in the majority in such close cases.[33] When Justice O'Connor announced her retirement, Court watchers predicted the solidification of Justice Kennedy's position as the swing justice.[34]

---

[27]*Id.*

[28]See Garcetti v. Ceballos, 126 S. Ct. 1951 (2006); Hudson v. Michigan, 126 S. Ct. 2159 (2006); and Kansas v. Marsh, 126 S. Ct. 2516 (2006).

[29]See Rutherford v. Crosby, 126 S. Ct. 1190 (2006).

[30]126 S. Ct. 2557 (2006).

[31]See *id.* at 2566 (Alito, J., dissenting).

[32]Rutledge & Angarella, *supra* note 17, at 157.

[33]*Id.*

[34]See, e.g., Charlie Savage, With Alito, Kennedy would have pivotal role, Boston Globe, Nov. 4, 2005, at A3; Orin S. Kerr, O'Connor's Successor Will Likely Be a Swinger, L.A. Times, July 3, 2005, at M1.

October Term 2005 largely confirms this prediction and suggests that Justice Kennedy perhaps even relishes the role a bit.[35] Somewhat surprisingly, among the justices who sat for the entire term, Justice Kennedy ranked behind Chief Justice Roberts among justices in the majority in split decisions (i.e., those decided by five-vote majorities).[36] But in "high-profile" cases (i.e, those involving major issues of constitutional law or otherwise expected to spark significant disagreement among members of the Court), he was by far most frequently in the majority and wrote the majority opinion most often.[37] In several close cases, Justice Kennedy parted from a Roberts-Scalia-Thomas(-Alito) bloc and provided the critical vote joining a Stevens-Souter-Ginsburg-Breyer bloc.[38] In others, he wrote separate opinions—either concurring or concurring in the judgment—effectively providing the governing rule for the case.[39] The coming term presents further opportunities to test whether Justice Kennedy will solidify his role as the "swing justice" in close cases.

This section has identified some of the major trends at the Court brought about by the changes in membership that can be expected to influence the coming term. The next section identifies some of the critical cases on the Court's docket and analyzes how the changing voting dynamics at the Court can influence the outcome of those cases.

II. Key Cases on the Docket

As noted above, the Court currently has twenty-nine cases on its argument docket for October Term 2006. In this brief essay, it is impossible to discuss all of them in adequate depth. This part highlights some of the more important ones—in areas including punitive

[35]See, e.g., Drew C. Ensign, Comment, The Impact of Liberty on Stare Decisis: The Rehnquist Court from Casey to Lawrence, 81 N.Y.U. L. Rev. 1137, 1165 (2006); Andrew Cohen, The Kennedy Court: The Real Power Lies With Kennedy's Swing Vote, CBS News (July 4, 2006), at http://www.cbsnews.com/stories/2006/07/04/opinion/courtwatch/main1774288.shtml.

[36]Georgetown Overview, *supra* note 6, at 8.

[37]*Id.*

[38]See Hamdan v. Rumsfeld, 126 S. Ct. 2749, 2799 (2006) (Kennedy, J., concurring); Georgia v. Randolph, 126 S. Ct. 1515 (2006).

[39]See Hudson v. Michigan, 126 S. Ct. 2159, 2170 (2006) (Kennedy, J., concurring); Rapanos v. United States, 126 S. Ct. 2208, 2236 (2006) (Kennedy, J., concurring).

damages, abortion, affirmative action, environmental law and criminal procedure. It places these cases in the context of the voting dynamics described above.

A. Punitive Damages

During the confirmation hearings on Justices Roberts and Alito, various commentators expressed the hope that the Court would take more "business" cases.[40] In *Philip Morris USA v. Williams*,[41] the Supreme Court answers that call and again takes up the constitutional limits on punitive damages awards. Ten years ago, in *BMW of North America v. Gore*, the Supreme Court set forth the modern-day framework for those limits.[42] *Gore* required that punitive damages awards be measured against three "guideposts": the reprehensibility of the defendant's conduct, the proportionality between the punitive damages award and the harm to the plaintiff, and a comparison of the punitive damages award to other civil or criminal penalties.[43] More recently, in *State Farm Mutual Automobile Insurance Co. v. Campbell*, the Court further expounded on those limits.[44] At bottom, the Court in *State Farm* held that the reprehensibility guidepost permits, at most, only a limited consideration of lawful out-of-state conduct and that a 145:1 ratio between punitive and compensatory damages was "excessive."[45]

Williams arises out of a widow's tort suit against the cigarette manufacturer following her husband's death for lung cancer. After a trial, a jury awarded the widow approximately $821,000 in compensatory damages (subsequently remitted to approximately $521,000) and $79.5 million in punitive damages. Following extensive appellate proceedings (including a vacatur and remand by the U.S. Supreme Court in light of *State Farm*), the Oregon Supreme Court upheld the $79.5 million punitive award.[46]

---

[40]See, e.g., Ronald A. Cass & Kenneth W. Starr, In Case You Missed It: The Supreme Court's Business, Wall St. J., Oct. 20, 2005, at A14.

[41]No. 05-1256.

[42]517 U.S. 559 (1996).

[43]*Id.* at 574–75.

[44]538 U.S. 408 (2003).

[45]*Id.* at 422, 424–26.

[46]Williams v. Philip Morris, Inc., 127 P.3d 1165, 1171 (2006) (summarizing history of the case).

As it comes to the Supreme Court, *Williams* presents two basic issues: (1) the relationship between the various *Gore* guideposts and (2) whether the Constitution permits a jury to consider non-party conduct as it awards punitive damages. The first issue presents the recurring problem in any legal doctrine that turns on a multi-factor test: what does one do when the factors cut in different directions? Here, for example, the proportionality guidepost suggests that the punitive damages award (more than 150 times the remitted compensatory damages) exceeded the constitutional limit (the Supreme Court previously had suggested that a 4:1 ratio was "close to the constitutional line.")[47] But can such a ratio be justified when the defendant's conduct is particularly reprehensible under the first *Gore* guidepost?

The second issue re-raises an issue that the Court addressed, but did not squarely resolve, in *State Farm*. *State Farm* suggested that a jury could not, in its award, punish a defendant for conduct that affects non-parties,[48] but it was unclear whether this limitation applied to all conduct involving non-parties or only dissimilar conduct. The Oregon Supreme Court applied the narrower reading, a limitation that did not bar consideration of harm suffered by other smokers due to Philip Morris's alleged conduct.[49] If *Williams* rejected this interpretation and erected a broader bar, that could have a profound effect on the admissibility of evidence during the damages phase of a case.

Apart from the interesting doctrinal questions presented by *Williams*, the case also presents an opportunity for Chief Justice Roberts and Justice Alito to shape the jurisprudence in this area. Here, the fault lines among the other justices are a bit unconventional. Justices Scalia and Thomas have repeatedly expressed their view that *Gore* was wrongly decided and that the Due Process Clause does not constrain the size of punitive damages awards.[50] Justice Ginsburg likewise disagreed with *Gore* and the Court's post-*Gore* jurisprudence

---

[47]State Farm, 538 U.S. at 425. See also Pacific Mutual Life Ins. Co. v. Haslip, 499 U.S. 1, 23 (1991).

[48]State Farm, 538 U.S. at 423–24.

[49]Williams, 127 P.3d at 1175–76.

[50]See Gore, 517 U.S. at 598 (Scalia, J., dissenting). See also State Farm, 538 U.S. at 429 (Scalia, J., dissenting).

but on federalism grounds—viewing the *Gore* doctrine as an unjustified federal intrusion into matters traditionally committed to the states.[51] By contrast, Justices Stevens, Kennedy, Souter, and Breyer all have subscribed to some constitutional limits on the size of punitive damages awards. This leaves Chief Justice Roberts and Justice Alito as the swing votes in the case. Neither of them during their time on the federal appellate bench had an occasion to express a view on the scope of the doctrine. Thus, if they both joined the Scalia-Thomas-Ginsburg wing, *Williams* has the potential to cut back on the limits articulated in *Gore* and *State Farm*. As a case coming from a state trial court, the case presents a particular opportunity for Justice Ginsburg to advance her federalism arguments and perhaps, in doing so, persuade one or two of the new justices.

B. Abortion

Two cases on the docket this year—*Gonzales v. Carhart*[52] and *Gonzales v. Planned Parenthood*[53]—invite the Court to consider again the constitutionality of laws restricting abortion, here the federal Partial Birth Abortion Act.[54] Such issues are not new for the Court. In *Stenberg v. Carhart*,[55] the Court invalidated a Nebraska law that prohibited one type of late-term abortion known as "dilation and extraction" (D&X).[56] One of the Nebraska statute's flaws, according to the *Stenberg* Court, was its failure to include an exception that would allow D&X where necessary to protect the mother's health. Last term, *Ayotte v. Planned Parenthood of Northern New England*[57] presented the Roberts Court an opportunity to reconsider whether the Constitution requires abortion regulations to contain a "maternal health" exception. But the Court in *Ayotte* clearly declined to "revisit [its] abortion precedents today," instead resolving the case on a narrower ground—namely that the lower court had crafted too broad a remedy by invalidating the entire statute.[58]

---

[51]Gore, 517 U.S. at 607 (Ginsburg, J., dissenting).
[52]No. 05-380
[53]No. 05-1382.
[54]Pub. L. No. 108-105, 117 Stat. 1201 (codified at 18 U.S.C. § 1531 (2006)).
[55]530 U.S. 914 (2000).
[56]*Id.* at 950–51.
[57]126 S. Ct. 961 (2006).
[58]*Id.* at 964–65.

The two cases currently on the Court's abortion docket likely will resurrect the debate in *Stenberg* and *Ayotte* over the constitutional requirement for a maternal health exception. The federal law, enacted in response to *Stenberg*, prohibits two types of late-term abortions—D&X and dilation and evacuation (D&E). While the federal act, like the Nebraska act, does not include a maternal health exception, the statute includes specific findings that attempt to justify this decision.[59] The Nebraska statute lacked such findings. Notwithstanding the differences, federal appellate courts in both cases, the Eighth Circuit in *Gonzales v. Carhart*[60] and the Ninth Circuit in *Gonzales v. Planned Parenthood*,[61] invalidated the federal statutes. In his petitions for writs of certiorari, the solicitor general framed the question in terms of whether the federal law was unconstitutional due to its failure to include a maternal health exception.

The Court's treatment of the two petitions is noteworthy. In *Gonzales v. Carhart*, the Court held the petition pending its decision in *Ayotte*, rejecting the solicitor general's suggestion that the Court grant the petition. Instead, the Court granted the petition after deciding *Ayotte*. Thereafter, in *Gonzales v. Planned Parenthood*, the Court again rejected the solicitor general's suggestion about how to treat the petition. Here, the solicitor general suggested that the Court hold the petition until it had resolved *Gonzales v. Carhart*. Contrary to that suggestion, the Court this time granted the petition.

What explains the Court's treatment of these petitions and repeated rejections of the solicitor general's suggestions? As to its decision to hold *Gonzales v. Carhart* for *Ayotte*, rather than grant it, two are possible. First, as already noted, *Ayotte* presented an opportunity for the Court to display rare consensus on an abortion case (perhaps illustrative of Chief Justice Roberts's philosophy of judicial minimalism); in light of the 5-4 decision in *Stenberg*, such consensus would have been impossible if the Court had also considered *Gonzales v. Carhart*. Second, deferral on *Gonzales v. Carhart* means that Justice Alito, rather than Justice O'Connor, will address the major question whether the Constitution requires a maternal health

[59]Pub. L. No. 108-105, *supra* note 54, at § 2.

[60]Carhart v. Gonzales, 413 F.3d 791 (8th Cir. 2005).

[61]Planned Parenthood Federation of America v. Gonzales, 435 F.3d 1163 (9th Cir. 2006).

exception. This is potentially quite significant, for Justice O'Connor joined the majority in *Stenberg* whereas Justice Kennedy dissented. This means that, if Justice Alito (and Chief Justice Roberts) joined Justices Scalia, Thomas, and Kennedy, potentially five votes exist to uphold the federal statute. This would depend, as well, on whether Justice Kennedy remains committed to his views expressed in *Stenberg* or, instead, follows *Stenberg* in reliance on stare decisis. Thus, this case presents one of the starkest examples where the new voting dynamics of the Roberts Court will shape the doctrine.

What about the Court's decision to grant the petition in *Gonzales v. Planned Parenthood* rather than hold it? This is particularly curious: both petitions presented precisely the same question, and the Court's order granting certiorari did not reframe the question or order the parties to address additional issues. Nonetheless, again, two explanations are possible. One is that the Court saw *Gonzales v. Planned Parenthood* as an opportunity to address additional constitutional challenges to the federal law. These include whether the federal law imposed an "undue burden" on a woman's decision whether to have an abortion and whether the law was void for vagueness. This reason is at least a bit dubitable, for the solicitor general expressly conceded that the respondents in *Gonzales v. Carhart* properly preserved these issues below and, thus, the Court could consider them in that case.[62] Another, more likely, reason why the Court may have granted the petition in *Gonzales v. Planned Parenthood* is to consider again the remedial questions at issue in *Ayotte*. The Ninth Circuit's decision contained a richer discussion of whether, in light of *Ayotte*, to invalidate the federal law in its entirety.[63] By contrast, the Eighth Circuit decided *Gonzales v. Carhart* before the Supreme Court decided *Ayotte* and, thus, naturally lacks consideration of this more recent jurisprudence.

Of course, we will only know the answer to this question after the Court hands down its opinion in *Gonzales v. Planned Parenthood*, but the opinion (particularly its author) will be quite revealing. In particular, if Chief Justice Roberts is in the majority, it may well reveal something about his use of the opinion-assignment power.

[62]Petition for Writ of Certiorari, Gonzales v. Planned Parenthood Federation of America, Inc. (No. 05-1382).

[63]435 F.3d at 1184–91.

If he assigns the opinions to a justice who would like to expressly overrule *Roe* and *Casey* (like he did in *Hudson* in the context of the exclusionary rule), these decisions might contain broad language presaging a broader shift in the Court's abortion jurisprudence. By contrast, if he assigns the opinion to a justice with more moderate (perhaps minimalist) views, then the opinion likely will lack such broad language and signal the Court's reluctance to reconsider its past abortion decisions.

C. Affirmative Action

Two cases this term—*Meredith v. Jefferson County Board of Education* ("*Meredith*")[64] and *Parents Involved in Community Schools v. Seattle School District #1* ("*Parents Involved*")[65]—present the Court with an opportunity to consider the constitutionality of programs that use race to determine a student's assignment to a public high school. The Court most recently addressed related issues two terms ago in *Gratz v. Bollinger*,[66] which involved the University of Michigan's undergraduate admissions system, and *Grutter v. Bollinger*,[67] which involved the University's law school admissions system. Those decisions were criticized for sending conflicting signals over the constitutional contours of affirmative action programs.[68] In some respects, that criticism was unfair. Both decisions shared certain common conclusions. In those cases the Court held: (1) that affirmative action admissions programs constituted race-based classifications subject to strict scrutiny, and (2) that diversity (at least in the context of higher education) was a "compelling state interest" that could justify a race-based classification.[69] In other respects, though, the criticism was justified. The decisions parted company on a core issue—namely whether the admissions programs were "narrowly tailored" to advance the state's interest. While the two admissions programs differed in certain respects (such as how race factored into the admissions process), these distinctions surely were slender reeds

---

[64]No. 05-915

[65]No. 05-908.

[66]Gratz v. Bollinger, 539 U.S. 244 (2003).

[67]Grutter v. Bollinger, 539 U.S. 306 (2003).

[68]See, e.g., Rachel F. Moran, Of Doubt and Diversity: The Future of Affirmative Action in Higher Education, 67 Ohio St. L.J. 201, 202 (2006).

[69]Gratz, 539 U.S. at 270; Grutter, 539 U.S. at 325.

on which to distinguish the cases and particularly difficult to justify as a matter of constitutional principle. The different results in *Gratz* and *Grutter* came under harsh criticism as examples of the Court's confusing, patchwork jurisprudence that failed to provide clear guidance to lower courts and policymakers.[70] In a passage that has been the subject of much criticism, Justice O'Connor's majority opinion in *Grutter* announced famously that "[w]e expect that 25 years from now, the use of racial preferences will no longer be necessary to further the interest approved today."[71] As Justice O'Connor provided the swing vote in the two cases, there was a plausible argument that the outcomes seemed to turn on little more than Justice O'Connor's personal policy preferences.

Enter, then, *Meredith* and *Parents Involved*. *Meredith* concerns a challenge to Jefferson County, Kentucky's school assignment system. Under that system, which has existed in some form since a 1975 desegregation order, students can indicate their preferred school, but the school district assigns them based on a formula that ensures that the African American student population at each school is between 15% and 50%.[72] While the school district maintains that most students receive one of their top-two choices, some parents complain that the assignment system has not worked—it imposes educational disadvantages on their children and creates logistical problems for students who in some cases must travel several hours per day to and from school. *Parents Involved* concerns a challenge to the Seattle School District's program for assigning students to high schools; under that system, the school district considers race as one of several factors in assigning students to schools, particularly where the school district deems the school to be "racially imbalanced."[73] Under that system, the school district had excluded qualified white applicants who otherwise satisfied the admissions criteria for special "magnet" or other high-achieving schools.

[70]See Suzanne B. Eckes, Race-Conscious Admissions Programs: Where Do Universities Go From Gratz and Grutter?, 33 J.L. & Educ. 21, 21 (2004), available at http://www.findarticles.com/p/articles/mi_qa3994/is_200401/ai_n9383333. See also David Faigman, Laboratory of Justice: The Supreme Court's 200-Year Struggle to Integrate Science and the Law (2004).

[71]Grutter, 539 U.S. at 343.

[72]McFarland v. Jefferson County Public Schools, 330 F. Supp. 2d 834, 842 (W.D. Ky. 2004)

[73]Parents Involved in Community Schools v. Seattle School Dist., No. 1, 426 F.3d 1162, 1169 (9th Cir. 2005). Specifically, under the program, the school district first

These cases present the first opportunity for the Court, following Justice O'Connor's retirement, to address not only the scope of *Gratz* and *Grutter* but also the continued viability of *Grutter*. Both cases present common themes: (1) whether *Gratz*'s holding that diversity is a compelling state interest extends to admissions preferences in secondary school assignments/admissions, and (2) how to apply the narrow tailoring requirement after *Gratz* and *Grutter*. Unlike the abortion cases, though, these twin cases present distinct questions that explain more clearly why the Court granted both petitions. Most centrally, the petition in *Meredith* could be read to ask the Court to overrule *Grutter* and *Gratz*.[74]

Apart from the interesting doctrinal questions, these cases also will provide important evidence on the shifting vote dynamics on the Court. As in the abortion cases, in *Gratz* and *Grutter* Justice Kennedy aligned himself with Justices Thomas and Scalia. Consequently, if Chief Justice Roberts and Justice Alito share this view, a majority of the Court would exist to cabin or, even, overrule *Grutter*. Even more than the abortion cases, *Meredith* and *Parents Involved* present one of the first opportunities for Chief Justice Roberts and Justice Alito to signal their views on matters of stare decisis. Like the abortion cases, *Meredith* and *Parents Involved* present another test of how Justice Kennedy might position himself as the swing vote—will he hew to his views in *Gratz* and *Grutter* or, instead, back away from them, either through factual distinctions between the cases or in reliance on stare decisis? Finally, as with the abortion cases, assuming Chief Justice Roberts is in the majority, these cases will provide an important insight into his use of the opinion-assignment power—whether to assign the opinions to justices likely to signal broad shifts in the Court's Equal Protection jurisprudence or, instead, to minimalists less inclined to overrule prior precedent.

D. Environmental Law

Massachusetts v. Environmental Protection Agency[75] presents one of those classic cases where popular discussions of the issues mask

---

considers whether the student has a sibling in the school; it then considers race; thereafter, it considers accessibility to the student's home; finally it utilizes random assignment.

[74]*Meredith* also presents the question whether the district court exceeded its remedial powers in its design of the Jefferson County School District's "managed" assignment system.

[75]No. 05-1120.

some of the subtle underlying questions of legal doctrine. Popularly, the case is understood as the "greenhouse gas case,"[76] the product of a multi-year effort (stretching back before the change in presidential administrations) by a coalition of states, cities, environmental groups, and others ("the environmental petitioners") to force the Environmental Protection Agency to regulate greenhouse gases. Legally, the case involves complex issues of standing, statutory interpretation, and administrative law.

Back in 1999, the environmental petitioners asked the EPA to regulate carbon dioxide and other greenhouse gases under section 201(a)(1) of the Clean Air Act. Section 201(a)(1) directs the EPA administrator to "prescribe . . . standards applicable to the emission of any air pollutant from [cars] which, in his judgment, cause, or contribute to, air pollution which may reasonably be anticipated to endanger public health or welfare."[77] During the notice-and-comment period on the petition, the National Research Council, an arm of the National Academy of Sciences, issued a report concluding that "causal linkage" between greenhouse gases and global warming "cannot be unequivocally established."[78] Following this report, the EPA concluded that the input received during the notice and comment period did not seriously alter the National Research Council's conclusions. Legally, then, the EPA could not conclude that greenhouse gases "cause, or contribute to, air pollution."

The environmental petitioners then sought review of the EPA's decision in the D.C. Circuit. In a badly divided panel opinion, the court dismissed the petitions. Two judges (Randolph and Tatel) believed that the Court should reach the merits—Judge Randolph made the unusual assumption that the plaintiffs had established standing (at least to survive summary judgment), whereas Judge Tatel concluded definitely that at least one plaintiff had standing.[79] A different pair of judges (Randolph and Sentelle) agreed that the EPA acted reasonably in its decision not to regulate (Judge Sentelle,

---

[76]See, e.g., Warren Richey, High court to hear 'greenhouse' case, Christian Science Monitor, June 27, 2006, at 10.

[77]42 U.S.C. § 7521(a)(1).

[78]Committee on the Science of Climate Change, National Research Council, Climate Change Science: An Analysis of Some Key Questions 17 (2001).

[79]See, e.g., Massachusetts v. EPA, 415 F.3d 50, 56 (D.C. Cir. 2005); *id*. at 64–67 (Tatel, J., dissenting).

unlike Randolph and Tatel, concluded that the plaintiffs did not establish standing).[80]

As it comes to the Supreme Court, the case is curious in several respects. Here, as in the abortion cases, the Court bucked the recommendation of the solicitor general, who had recommended denying certiorari. More notably, the case turns traditional federalism principles on its head. Whereas most federalism debates involve state governments objecting to federal encroachment, here some states are affirmatively asking the federal government to regulate a matter (admittedly, though, other states oppose the requested involvement). Finally, to add to the comedy, the responsible federal agency, in an exceptional example of bureaucratic self-restraint, is taking the view that it lacks the authority to provide the sought-after regulation.[81]

Apart from these curiosities, the case presents several interesting doctrinal issues. Some concern standing. There is some doubt whether any of the environmental petitioners can satisfy the injury and redressability requirements set forth in *Lujan v. Defenders of Wildlife*.[82] While the environmental petitioners submitted extensive documentation on the health and environmental impacts of greenhouse gases, at bottom their complaint bears the hallmarks of the types of generalized grievances that standing doctrine does not tolerate (interestingly, Judge Tatel, who dissented in the D.C. Circuit panel opinion, concluded that a state, the Commonwealth of Massachusetts, had standing).[83] A determination by the Supreme Court that any of the environmental petitioners had standing in this case might mark an important new boundary to *Lujan*'s sometimes strict standing requirements.

The case also presents an interesting question about how a court should address standing questions that are intimately intertwined with the merits. A few terms ago, the Court in *Steel Co. v. Citizens*

---

[80]*Id*. at 56–59 (Randolph, J.); *id*. at 60–61 (Sentelle, J., dissenting in part and concurring in part).

[81]Notably, in the course of the administrative proceedings in 2003, the EPA general counsel withdrew a memorandum, drafted by his predecessor under President Clinton, that had concluded that the Clean Air Act did authorize the EPA to regulate climate change. *Id*. at 54.

[82]504 U.S. 555 (1992).

[83]415 F.3d at 67 (Tatel, J., dissenting).

for a Better Environment[84] chided lower federal courts for eliding difficult standing questions and, instead, assuming standing in order to dispose of the case on more straightforward merits-related reasons.[85] The decision created both frustration and confusion among lower federal courts as they sought to sort out the order in which they had to decide jurisdictional and merits issues in a case.[86] Recognizing the tensions that this case presents with *Steel Company*, Judge Randolph took the exceptional step of relying on the D.C. Circuit's statutory standing cases. He concluded that, notwithstanding doubts about any environmental petitioner's standing, the petitioners had, in his opinion, put forth enough information to defeat summary judgment motion on standing, thereby justifying a decision on the merits.[87] Watch to see whether the Court uses this case as an opportunity further to gloss *Steel Company*'s order of inquiry.

Finally, the case presents another foray by the Court into the scope of the nation's major environmental laws. Court-watchers will recall that, last term, a badly divided Court in *Rapanos v. United States*[88] addressed the scope of the Clean Water Act, with the justices disagreeing over the precise "nexus" that a particular waterway or wetland had to have in order to qualify for regulation under the act. Here, Justice Kennedy provided the swing vote, concurring in the plurality's judgment but articulating reasoning that, in some respects, aligned him more closely with the dissent.[89] If the Court reaches the merits, one can expect another pitched battle, with Justice Kennedy likely in the middle, over the scope of the Clean Air Act.

E. Criminal Procedure

The Court's docket consistently has included a large number of criminal cases, and October Term 2006 is no exception.[90] Three in

---

[84]523 U.S. 83 (1998).

[85]*Id.* at 93–101.

[86]See, e.g., Ruhrgas AG v. Marathon Oil Co., 526 U.S. 574 (1999) (addressing confusion in the Fifth Circuit over application of *Steel Co.*).

[87]415 F.3d at 55–56.

[88]See *supra* note 10.

[89]See *supra* note 39 and accompanying text.

[90]See Ornaski v. Belmontes, 414 F.3d 1094 (9th Cir. 2005), cert. granted, 126 S. Ct. 1909 (2006) (No. 05-493); Toledo-Flores v. United States, 149 Fed. Appx. 241 (8th Cir. 2005), cert. granted, 126 S. Ct. 1652 (2006) (No. 05-7664); Whorton v. Bockting, 399 F.3d 1010 (9th Cir. 2005), cert. granted, 126 S. Ct. 2017 (2006) (No. 05-595); Carey v. Musladin, 427 F.3d 653 (9th Cir. 2005), cert. granted, 126 S. Ct. 1769 (2006) (No. 05-

particular warrant brief mention here—*Cunningham v. California*,[91] *Burton v. Waddington*,[92] and *Whorton v. Bockting*.[93] *Cunningham* and *Burton* both involve the Sixth Amendment jury right as detailed in the Supreme Court's earlier decisions in *Apprendi v. New Jersey*[94] and *Blakely v. Washington*.[95] *Apprendi* held that the Sixth Amendment jury guarantee requires that a jury, not a judge, find any fact (apart from recidivism) that increases the statutory maximum penalty for a crime.[96] *Blakely* extended this holding to invalidate Washington's state sentencing scheme, under which judicial fact-finding could increase a defendant's sentence within a presumptive range that was within the statutory maximum.[97] (*Blakely* was the critical case in the doctrinal developments that resulted in the Supreme Court's decisions in *Booker* and *Fanfan* that invalidated mandatory application of the United States Sentencing Guidelines).[98]

Cunningham involves a challenge under the *Apprendi-Blakely* line of cases to California's Determinate Sentencing Law.[99] Under that law, generally, a convicted defendant is sentenced to one of several "terms" (upper, middle, or lower), all of which are within the statutory maximum penalty. California's law instructs that the judge "shall" select the middle term unless he finds, by a preponderance of the evidence, that aggravating circumstances warrant imposition of the "upper" term (or mitigating circumstances justify imposition of the "lower" term). In this case, following Cunningham's conviction for continuous sexual abuse of a child under the age of 14, the

---

785); United States v. Resendiz-Ponce, 425 F.3d 729 (9th Cir. 2005), cert. granted, 126 S. Ct. 1776 (2006) (No. 05-998); People v. Cunningham, No. A103501, 2005 Cal. App. Unpub. LEXIS 3383 (Cal. App. 1st April 18, 2005), cert. granted, 126 S. Ct. 1329 (2006) (No. 05-6551); Burton v. Waddington, 142 Fed. Appx. 297 (9th Cir. 2005), cert. granted, 126 S. Ct. 2352 (2006) (No. 05-9222); and James v. United States, 172 Fed. Appx. 144 (11th Cir. 2005), cert. granted, 126 S. Ct. 2913 (2006) (No. 05-9264).

[91] No. 05-6551.

[92] No. 05-9222.

[93] No. 05-595.

[94] 530 U.S. 466 (2000).

[95] 542 U.S. 296 (2004).

[96] See Apprendi, 530 U.S. at 490.

[97] See Blakely, 542 U.S. at 304–05.

[98] See United States v. Booker, 543 U.S. 220 (2005).

[99] Cal. Penal Code § 1120.

trial judge determined that various "aggravating factors" justified sentencing Cunningham to the "upper term" of 16 years (rather than the "middle term" of 12 years).[100] At issue before the Supreme Court is whether this four-year upward enhancement under the Determinate Sentencing Law contravenes the *Blakely* doctrine.

While both sides have plausible arguments, Cunningham's is probably stronger as a matter of doctrine. His argument is straight-forward—that under the Determinate Sentencing Law the defendant is subject to an increased punishment based on judicial fact-finding. *Blakely*, however, forbids this practice and, instead, requires the jury to find any facts (apart from the fact of a prior conviction) that increase the sentence, even when that sentence is within the statutory maximum. California advances two main arguments in response. First, it argues that, unlike the scheme in *Blakely*, California's law (as authoritatively interpreted by its supreme court) permits, but does not require, the judge to enhance the sentence.[101] Through this argument, California tries to align its sentencing scheme with the residual federal guidelines scheme following *Booker* (where judges are not obligated to apply the guidelines but, apparently, must consult them in an effort to impose a reasonable sentence within the statutory maximum). Second, California also argues that sentences in its scheme are "based on the verdict" whereas in *Blakely* the sentencing judge could not depart from the presumptive range without additional factfinding.

Whatever the outcome, the case potentially has important doctrinal consequences. If the Supreme Court strikes down the California sentencing law, such an anti-federalist broadening of the *Blakely* principle would call into doubt several other states' determinate sentencing schemes.[102] If the Supreme Court upholds the California scheme, that decision would supply a bookend to the *Apprendi-Blakely* doctrine. It also would provide Congress a model of how to bring the federal guidelines into compliance with the Sixth Amendment.

---

[100]People v. Cunningham, 2005 Cal. App. Unpub. LEXIS 3383, at *2, *20, *30–31 (Cal. App. 1st April 18, 2005) (describing facts and California sentencing scheme).

[101]See People v. Black, 113 P.3d 534, 543 (Cal. 2005).

[102]See, e.g., State v. Gomez, 163 S.W.3d 632, 656 (Tenn. 2005); State v. Lopez, 123 P.3d 754, 768 (N.M. 2005).

Burton involves the broader question whether *Blakely* applies retroactively. Generally, under the Court's retroactivity jurisprudence, new procedural rules do not apply to convictions that were final at the time the Court announced the decision (a final conviction is one where the Court has denied certiorari on direct review or the time for filing a certiorari petition on direct review has expired).[103] The Court first asks whether the rule was "new" (that is, was it "dictated by prior precedent"). If the rule is not new, then it can apply retroactively. If the rule is new, then it generally will not apply retroactively unless the case falls under one of two exceptions: (1) it constitutes a watershed rule of criminal procedure or (2) the rule places certain conduct beyond criminal sanction.[104]

In this case, Burton was convicted in a Washington state court of rape, robbery, and murder. Burton was sentenced to forty-seven years imprisonment, twenty-one years higher than the ordinary sentence under Washington's guidelines in effect at the time. Those guidelines, however, permitted the trial judge to make an upward adjustment, and the trial judge did so in this case.[105] After Burton's conviction became final, the Supreme Court invalidated the Washington scheme in *Blakely*. Thus, unless *Blakely* applied retroactively, Burton could not benefit from the decision (he could, however, benefit from *Apprendi*, which was decided before his conviction became final). Doctrinally, therefore, the questions are whether (1) *Blakely* is new (or, instead was "dictated" by *Apprendi*) and, if *Blakely* is new, whether (2) it announced a watershed rule of criminal procedure?

Here, the decision to grant certiorari is curious in light of the Court's recent retroactivity jurisprudence. In recent years, the Court generally only has granted certiorari in non-capital habeas corpus cases either where there is a deep split among the federal courts of appeals over a question of habeas corpus law or where the state is seeking review of an adverse judgment. In this case, the petition effectively conceded the unanimity among federal appellate courts

---

[103]See Schriro v. Summerlin, 542 U.S. 348, 351–52 (2004); Teague v. Lane, 489 U.S. 288, 301 (1989).

[104]See Schriro, 542 U.S. at 351–52. In dicta, *Schriro* arguably modified this second exception—characterizing it as a type of "substantive" rule rather than an exception to the general prohibition against retroactive application of new procedural rules. *Id.* at 352 n.4.

[105]Burton v. Waddington, 142 Fed. Appx. 297, 299–300 (9th Cir. 2005).

that *Blakely* was not retroactive and could identify only a weak split at best with two state appellate decisions.[106] While it is always difficult to read the tea leaves in a decision to grant certiorari, the Court's order suggests that (a) it saw the case as an opportunity to fill the docket, (b) the case provided a good vehicle to resolve an issue that the Court eventually would have to settle, or (c) some justices genuinely believed that the lower courts were misreading its cues about *Blakely*'s retroactivity.

Some language in the Court's prior decisions suggests that it did in fact believe that *Apprendi* dictated *Blakely* and, thus, *Blakely* was not a new rule. For example, the Court in *Blakely* described the case as requiring it "to apply the rule we expressed in *Apprendi*."[107] Likewise, according to the Court, *Apprendi* reflected "longstanding tenets of common-law criminal jurisprudence."[108] These principles were moreover "acknowledged by courts and treatises since the earliest days of graduated sentencing."[109] The Court might stitch together each of these doctrinal threads to support a holding that *Blakely* was not a "new" rule and, thus, could apply to the issue in *Burton*.

Even more than *Cunningham*, the consequences of *Burton* could be enormous. Affirmance would work little mischief, as it would merely validate the unanimous views of the lower federal courts. Reversal, however, would reopen potentially thousands of sentences entered under schemes created prior to the Supreme Court's rule in *Blakely*. The federalism and finality costs of such a decision, in terms of reopened convictions, could be potentially staggering: it would all but ensure a flood of new habeas corpus petitions in

---

[106]The petition cited a decision from the Tennessee Supreme Court and the Colorado Court of Appeals. See Petition for Certiorari at 7–8, Burton v. Waddington (No. 05-9222) (citing State v. Gomez, 163 S.W.3d 632 (Tenn. 2005); State v. Johnson, 121 P.3d 285 (Colo. Ct. App. 2005)). The first decision involved a direct appeal and, therefore, at best only provides dictum on the retroactivity issue. The second, presently under review by the Colorado Supreme Court, does conflict with the unanimous view of the federal appellate courts but does not satisfy the standards for certiorari set forth in Supreme Court Rule 10.

[107]542 U.S. at 301.

[108]*Id.*

[109]*Id.*

state and federal courts, seeking to reopen sentences entered in contravention of *Blakely*.

Like *Burton, Bockting* involves the retroactivity of a recent constitutional decision that finds its genesis in an unusual alignment of justices. Court-watchers will recall that in *Crawford v. Washington*[110] the Supreme Court overruled *Ohio v. Roberts* and held that, subject to a few historically rooted exceptions, the Confrontation Clause prohibits the introduction of a witness's out-of-court testimonial statements unless the witness is unavailable and the defendant has had a prior opportunity to cross examine the witness.[111] That decision had its genesis in views originating with Justice Thomas and strongly resisted by Chief Justice Rehnquist, Justice O'Connor, and Justice Kennedy.[112]

In this case, Bockting was on trial for sexual abuse charges. The critical pieces of evidence admitted against him were the child-victim's statements to a detective.[113] Under *Crawford*, such evidence would be inadmissible, but Bockting's conviction became final before the Supreme Court handed down *Crawford*. Nonetheless, the Ninth Circuit held that *Crawford* applied retroactively. In its retroactivity analysis, the Ninth Circuit conceded that *Crawford* announced a new rule (undoubtedly right in light of *Crawford*'s overruling of prior precedent).[114] Nonetheless, it concluded that *Crawford* announced a "watershed rule of criminal procedure" and, thus, applied to convictions that were final at the time the Supreme Court decided the case.[115] Unlike *Burton*, there is little mystery surrounding why the Supreme Court took this case. The Ninth Circuit's holding on the "watershed" point created a clear conflict among the federal appellate courts.[116]

Doctrinally, the case will provide the Court another opportunity to gloss the meaning of the exceptions under which new procedural

[110]541 U.S. 36 (2004).

[111]*Id.* at 67–68.

[112]See the opinions in Lilly v. Virginia, 527 U.S. 116 (1999), and Justice Thomas's separate opinion in White v. Illinois, 502 U.S. 346 (1992).

[113]Bockting v. Bayer, 399 F.3d 1010, 1012 (9th Cir. 2005).

[114]*Id.* at 1015–16.

[115]*Id.* at 1020–21.

[116]Compare Brown v. Uphoff, 381 F.3d 1219, 1226–27 (10th Cir. 2004) (concluding *Crawford* is not a watershed decision).

rules can apply retroactively. In its recent decision of *Schriro v. Summerlin*,[117] a bare majority of the Court held that *Ring v. Arizona* did not apply retroactively and, in doing so, narrowly defined the "watershed rule" exception.[118] *Schriro* held that such a rule must be one "without which the likelihood of an accurate conviction is seriously diminished."[119] The four *Schriro* dissenters (Stevens, Souter, Ginsburg, Breyer) may see *Bockting* as an opportunity to push back on *Schriro*. Yet they may find it difficult to pick up a fifth vote here. Justice Kennedy joined the *Schriro* majority. While two members of the *Schriro* majority (Justices Scalia and Thomas) were among *Crawford*'s staunchest advocates,[120] they also supported *Ring* yet did not find it retroactive. *Schriro*, thus, demonstrates that these two justices are reluctant to apply new constitutional rules retroactively even where they may support the underlying rule. That leaves only Chief Justice Roberts and Justice Alito, neither of whom has indicated a strong preference for a robust retroactivity jurisprudence.

Conclusion

October Term 2006 already promises to provide important indicators of the future direction of the Court. Some of the complex cases described above, especially *Massachusetts v. EPA*, will test the chief justice's ability to achieve consensus. Others such as the abortion and affirmative action cases may reveal how he will use the opinion-assignment power (when in the majority) to shape the doctrine. *Williams* will provide important insights into the impact of Chief Justice Roberts and Justice Alito in an area of the doctrine important to business interests. And everyone will be watching whether Justice Kennedy continues to position himself in the middle of these close cases as he did last year. With a relatively small docket to date and with cases such as the constitutionality of the search of Congressman Jefferson's office and the terrorist surveillance program looming on the horizon, no doubt more cases testing these dynamics will fill the docket in the months to come.

[117]See *supra* note 103.

[118]Schriro v. Summerlin, 542 U.S. 348, 358 (2004). In *Ring*, the Court held that the Sixth Amendment precluded imposition of the death penalty based on judicial fact finding. Ring v. Arizona, 536 U.S. 484, 609 (2002).

[119]See Schriro, 542 U.S. at 352.

[120]See Lindh v. Murphy, 521 U.S. 320 (1997); Gilmore v. Taylor, 508 U.S. 333 (1993); and Brecht v. Abrahamson, 507 U.S. 619 (1993).

Contributors

Douglas A. Berman is an associate professor of law at the Ohio State University Moritz College of Law. He received his A.B. from Princeton University and his J.D. from Harvard Law School, where he was the editor and Developments Office Chair of the *Harvard Law Review*. After graduation, Professor Berman served as a law clerk for the Honorable Jon O. Newman and then for the Honorable Guido Calabresi, both on the United States Court of Appeals for the Second Circuit. Professor Berman is the co-author of a casebook, *Sentencing Law and Policy: Cases, Statutes and Guidelines*, published by Aspen Publishers; has served as an editor of the *Federal Sentencing Reporter* for nearly ten years; and also now serves as co-managing editor of the *Ohio State Journal of Criminal Law*. Professor Berman is the sole creator and author of the widely-read and widely-cited web log, *Sentencing Law and Policy*, which has the distinction of being the first blog cited by the U.S. Supreme Court and has been cited in at least four federal circuit opinions, nearly a dozen federal district court opinions, and in dozens of law reviews.

Dale Carpenter is the Julius E. Davis Professor of Law at the University of Minnesota Law School, where he teaches and writes in the areas of constitutional law, the First Amendment, sexual orientation and the law, and commercial law. He also serves as an editor of *Constitutional Commentary*. Professor Carpenter received his B.A. degree in history, *magna cum laude*, from Yale College in 1989. He received his J.D., with honors, from the University of Chicago Law School in 1992. At the University of Chicago he was editor-in-chief of the *University of Chicago Law Review*; the recipient of the D. Francis Bustin Prize for excellence in legal scholarship; and the recipient of a John M. Olin Foundation Scholarship for Law and Economics. Professor Carpenter clerked for the Honorable Edith H. Jones of the United States Court of Appeals for the Fifth Circuit from 1992 to 1993. After his clerkship, he practiced as an associate at Vinson &

Elkins in Houston and Howard, Rice, Nemerovski, Canady, Falk & Rabkin in San Francisco. He is a frequent television, radio, and print commentator on constitutional law and the First Amendment.

Brannon P. Denning is an associate professor of law at Samford University's Cumberland School of Law in Birmingham, Alabama. Prior to joining the Cumberland School of Law in 2003, Professor Denning taught at the Southern Illinois University School of Law in Carbondale, Illinois, for four years. During the summer of 2005, he was a visiting professor at the University of Tennessee College of Law. Professor Denning has written extensively on the Commerce Clause, the Dormant Commerce Clause doctrine, the constitutional amending process, the confirmation process, the Second Amendment, and on foreign affairs matters. His articles have appeared in the *American Journal of International Law, Constitutional Commentary, Foreign Affairs*, the *Minnesota Law Review*, the *William and Mary Law Review*, and the *Wisconsin Law Review*, among other journals and periodicals. He has also collaborated with Yale law professor Boris I. Bittker on a treatise on the Commerce Clause and is co-editor of a one-of-a-kind coursebook on gun control and gun rights. Professor Denning earned a B.A. in political science, *magna cum laude*, from the University of the South in Sewanee, Tennessee. He received a J.D., *magna cum laude*, from the University of Tennessee in 1995, and an LL.M. from Yale University in 1999.

Martin S. Flaherty received his B.A. from Princeton, M.A. and Masters in Philosophy from Yale, and J.D. from Columbia. Professor Flaherty was a book review and articles editor of the *Columbia Law Review* and currently serves as the chair of the Committee on International Human Rights for the Association of the Bar of the City of New York. He served as law clerk to the Honorable John J. Gibbons of the United States Court of Appeals for the Third Circuit, and to Justice Byron White. Professor Flaherty has been a visiting professor at the China University of Political Science and Law and at the National Judges College in Beijing. Additionally, he serves as a professor of law and co-director of the Joseph R. Crowley Program in International Human Rights, at Fordham Law School in New York. Professor Flaherty's principal subjects of study are constitutional law and history, international human rights, and public international law.

Richard W. Garnett received his B.A. in philosophy, *summa cum laude*, from Duke University in 1990, and his J.D. from Yale Law School in 1995. He served as senior editor of the *Yale Law Journal* and as editor of the *Yale Journal of Law & the Humanities*. After graduation, he clerked for Chief Judge Richard S. Arnold of the United States Court of Appeals for the Eighth Circuit, and then for Chief Justice William H. Rehnquist. He practiced law for two years at the Washington, D.C., law firm of Miller, Cassidy, Larroca & Lewin, specializing in criminal-defense, religious-liberty, and education-reform matters. His areas of research interest and expertise include school choice, church/state relations, religion in the public square, free speech and expressive association, free exercise of religion, federalism and criminal law, and the death penalty.

Allison R. Hayward is an assistant professor at George Mason University School of Law. Her areas of interest include campaign finance, Internet regulation, government ethics, and related fields. She has been published in a variety of magazines and journals, including *National Review*, the *Weekly Standard*, *Reason*, the *Journal of Law and Politics*, and the *Election Law Journal*. Ms. Hayward graduated from Stanford University with degrees in political science and economics, and received her law degree from the University of California, Davis. She clerked for Chief Judge Danny J. Boggs of the United States Court of Appeals for the Sixth Circuit; was an associate at Wiley, Rein & Fielding in Washington, D.C.; and of counsel at Bell, McAndrews & Hiltachk in Sacramento, California. She also served as the in-house attorney at the National Republican Congressional Committee, and on the staff of the Senate Special Investigation of the 1996 Federal Election Campaigns, chaired by Senator Fred Thompson (R-TN). Most recently, she was chief of staff and counsel to Commissioner Bradley A. Smith of the Federal Election Commission. Before attending law school, Professor Hayward served as staff in the California legislature and managed a legislative campaign. Ms. Hayward lives in McLean, Virginia, with her husband and two children. She also authors *Skeptic's Eye*, a blog at www.skepticseye.com.

Mark Moller is a senior fellow in constitutional studies at the Cato Institute and the editor-in-chief of the *Cato Supreme Court Review*. Mr. Moller earned his B.A., *magna cum laude*, from Duke University

389

in 1994, a J.D. with honors at the University of Chicago Law School in 1999, and an LL.M in common law legal history and theory (first class honors) from the University of Cambridge in 2000. After graduation, he practiced law at Gibson, Dunn & Crutcher LLP for three years, with a focus on complex class litigation and appellate litigation. He is the author of *The Rule of Law Problem: Unconstitutional Class Actions and Options for Reform* (*Harvard Journal of Law and Public Policy*) and the forthcoming Chevron *and Class Action Lawmaking* (*Texas Journal of Law and Politics*). Mr. Moller's commentary has appeared in a variety of publications, including the *Washington Post*, *Slate*, *Reason*, *Legal Times*, and *Legal Affairs*. He frequently comments on the Supreme Court on television and radio.

David A. Moran is the associate dean at Wayne State University Law School in Detroit, where he has been a member of the faculty since 2000. He regularly teaches classes in criminal law, criminal procedure, and evidence, and he occasionally teaches a seminar on the causes of wrongful criminal convictions. He has been voted "Teacher of the Year" by the law school students six times. A native of Oklahoma, Dean Moran holds a master's degree in theoretical physics from Cornell University, a master's degree in mathematics from Cambridge University, and a J.D., *magna cum laude*, from the University of Michigan Law School. After serving as a law clerk for the Honorable Ralph B. Guy, Jr., of the United States Court of Appeals for the Sixth Circuit, he was a staff attorney with the State Appellate Defender Office in Detroit from 1992–2000, where he represented some 200 indigent criminal defendants on appeal, including six defendants who were exonerated by new evidence. He is on the board of directors of the Michigan Innocence Project, and he helped draft the legislation that permits Michigan inmates to seek DNA testing to prove their innocence. He has argued five times before the United States Supreme Court since 2003. In June 2005 the Court ruled in his favor in *Halbert v. Michigan* and held that states must provide attorneys for indigent criminal defendants who wish to appeal their sentences after pleading guilty.

Roger Pilon is vice president for legal affairs at the Cato Institute. He holds Cato's B. Kenneth Simon Chair in Constitutional Studies and is the founder and director of Cato's Center for Constitutional

Studies. Established in 1989 to encourage limited constitutional government at home and abroad, the Center has become an important force in the national debate over constitutional interpretation and judicial philosophy. Mr. Pilon's work has appeared in the *New York Times, Washington Post, Wall Street Journal, Los Angeles Times, Legal Times, National Law Journal, Harvard Journal of Law and Public Policy, Notre Dame Law Review, Stanford Law and Policy Review, Texas Review of Law and Politics,* and elsewhere. He has appeared, among other places, on ABC's *Nightline,* CBS's *60 Minutes II,* National Public Radio, Fox News Channel, CNN, MSNBC, and CNBC. He lectures and debates at universities and law schools across the country and testifies often before Congress. Before joining Cato, Mr. Pilon held five senior posts in the Reagan administration, including at State and Justice. He has taught philosophy and law and was a national fellow at Stanford's Hoover Institution. Mr. Pilon holds a B.A. from Columbia University, an M.A. and a Ph.D. from the University of Chicago, and a J.D. from the George Washington University School of Law. In 1989 the Bicentennial Commission presented him with the Benjamin Franklin Award for excellence in writing on the U.S. Constitution. In 2001 Columbia University's School of General Studies awarded him its Alumni Medal of Distinction.

Larry E. Ribstein is the Mildred Van Voorhis Jones Chair at the University of Illinois College of Law. He is a scholar in the areas of unincorporated business entities, partnerships, limited liability companies, corporate and securities law, choice of law, ethical rules, and uniform laws. His books include *Unincorporated Business Entities, Business Associations* (with Letsou), *Bromberg and Ribstein on Partnership, Bromberg and Ribstein on LLPs and RUPA, Ribstein & Keatinge on Limited Liability Companies, The Constitution and the Corporation* (with Butler), and *The Sarbanes-Oxley Debacle* (with Butler). He has also served as editor of the *Supreme Court Economic Review.* His more than 100 articles include *Are Partners Fiduciaries?* (*Illinois Law Review*) (voted among the top ten corporate and securities articles in 2005), *Market v. Regulatory Responses to Corporate Fraud* (*Journal of Corporation Law*), *Opting Out of Fiduciary Duties: A Response to the Anti-Contractarians* (with Butler) (*Washington Law Review*), *Economic Analysis of Uniform State Laws* (with Kobayashi) (*Journal of Legal Studies*), *From Politics to Efficiency in Choice of Law* (with O'Hara) (*University of*

Chicago Law Review), *Ethical Rules, Agency Costs and Law Firm Structure* (*Virginia Law Review*), and *Takeover Defenses and the Corporate Contract* (*Georgetown Law Journal*).

Peter (Bo) Rutledge is an associate professor of law at the Columbus School of Law, Catholic University of America. He received his B.A. in Government, *magna cum laude*, from Harvard Univerity, his M. Litt. in Applied Ethics from the University of Aberdeen (Scotland), and his J.D. with high honors from the University of Chicago, where he was a member of the Order of the Coif. After law school, Professor Rutledge clerked for the Honorable J. Harvie Wilkinson of the United States Court of Appeals for the Fourth Circuit and Justice Clarence Thomas of the Supreme Court of the United States. Following his clerkships, Professor Rutledge spent four years in private practice in Europe and Washington, D.C., where his specialties included international arbitration, international litigation, and appellate litigation. Since entering the academy, Professor Rutledge has written extensively on topics including criminal procedure, international arbitration, international litigation, and the Supreme Court. He currently is completing his first book, *International Civil Litigation in the United States* (4th ed.) (with Gary B. Born), due to be published this fall by Aspen. In addition to his academic work, Professor Rutledge advises clients and lawyers on matters before the U.S. Supreme Court and the lower federal courts in the areas of his expertise. He is a regular commentator in print and broadcast media on these subjects as well.

Ilya Somin is an assistant professor at George Mason University School of Law. His research focuses on constitutional law, property law, and the study of popular political participation and its implications for constitutional democracy. Professor Somin previously served as the John M. Olin Fellow in Law at Northwestern University Law School in 2002–2003. In 2001–2002, he clerked for the Honorable Judge Jerry E. Smith of the United States Court of Appeals for the Fifth Circuit. Professor Somin earned his B.A., *summa cum laude*, at Amherst College; M.A. in political science from Harvard University; and J.D. from Yale Law School.

Nadine Strossen is the president of the American Civil Liberties Union (ACLU) and a professor of law at New York Law School, where she teaches courses on constitutional law, international human rights, and individual rights. She has served as president of the ACLU since 1991 and was the first woman to do so. She received her A.B. from Harvard College, Phi Beta Kappa, and her J.D., *magna cum laude*, from Harvard Law School, where she was editor of the *Harvard Law Review*. Professor Strossen has published in numerous scholarly legal journals including, among others, the *Harvard Journal of Law and Public Policy*, *Cornell Journal of Law and Public Policy*, *New York Law School Law Review*, *Cornell Law Review*, and the *Yale Journal of Law and Feminism*. She has contributed chapters or articles to at least eighteen edited works such as *The Reader's Companion to U.S. Women's History* (Houghton Mifflin Co. 1998), *The Warren Court, A Retrospective* (Oxford University Press 1996), and *Benchmarks: The Great Controversial Supreme Court Cases* (Ergmans 1995). Professor Strossen also has been published in such leading national periodicals as the *New York Times*, *Washington Post*, *USA Today*, *The New Yorker*, and the German weekly, *Der Spiegel*. Among her many distinctions and awards is being named one of the *National Law Journal's* "100 Most Influential Lawyers in America."

Joshua D. Wright is an assistant professor of law at the George Mason University School of Law and a graduate of the UCLA School of Law, where he was a managing editor of the *UCLA Law Review*. Professor Wright also holds M.A. and Ph.D. degrees in economics from UCLA. Professor Wright served as a law clerk to the Honorable James V. Selna, United States District Court, Central District of California. His research focuses on the law and economics of the competitive process for product distribution, including slotting allowances, category management, payola, and other marketing relationships. Professor Wright's teaching interests include antitrust, contracts, law and economics, and quantitative methods. He has taught courses in law and economics at Pepperdine University Graduate School of Public Policy and at UCLA. Professor Wright is a regular contributor to *Truth on the Market*, a weblog dedicated to academic commentary on law, business, and economics.

John Yoo is a professor of law at the University of California, Berkeley, School of Law (Boalt Hall), where he has taught since 1993. He received his B.A., *summa cum laude*, in American history from Harvard University. He received his J.D. from Yale Law School, where he was an articles editor of the *Yale Law Journal*. He clerked for Judge Laurence H. Silberman of the United States Court of Appeals of the D.C. Circuit. After joining the Boalt faculty in 1993, Professor Yoo clerked for Justice Clarence Thomas of the United States Supreme Court. He served as general counsel of the United States Senate Judiciary Committee from 1995–96. From 2001–03, he served as a deputy assistant attorney general in the Office of Legal Counsel at the United States Department of Justice, where he worked on issues involving foreign affairs, national security, and the separation of powers. Professor Yoo has been a visiting professor at the University of Chicago and the Free University of Amsterdam, and he held the Fulbright Distinguished Chair in Law at the University of Trento, Italy, in 2006. He has received research fellowships from the University of California, Berkeley, the Olin Foundation, and the Rockefeller Foundation, and is a visiting scholar at the American Enterprise Institute. Professor Yoo also has received the Paul M. Bator Award for excellence in legal scholarship and teaching from the Federalist Society for Law and Public Policy. He is the author of *The Powers of War and Peace: The Constitution and Foreign Affairs after 9/11* (University of Chicago Press 2005) and the forthcoming *War By Other Means: An Insider's Account of the War on Terrorism* (Atlantic Monthly Press 2006). He is currently working on a book on the American presidency.

ABOUT THE CATO INSTITUTE

The Cato Institute is a public policy research foundation dedicated to the principles of limited government, individual liberty, free markets, and private property. It takes its name from *Cato's Letters*, popular libertarian pamphlets that helped to lay the philosophical foundation for the American Revolution.

Despite the Founders' libertarian values, today virtually no aspect of life is free from government encroachment. A pervasive intolerance for individual rights is shown by government's arbitrary intrusions into private economic transactions and its disregard for civil liberties.

To counter that trend, the Cato Institute undertakes an extensive publications program that addresses the complete spectrum of policy issues. It holds major conferences throughout the year, from which papers are published thrice yearly in the *Cato Journal*, and also publishes the quarterly magazine *Regulation* and the annual *Cato Supreme Court Review*.

The Cato Institute accepts no government funding. It relies instead on contributions from foundations, corporations, and individuals and revenue generated from the sale of publications. The Institute is a nonprofit, tax-exempt educational foundation under Section 501(c)(3) of the Internal Revenue Code.

ABOUT THE CENTER FOR CONSTITUTIONAL STUDIES

Cato's Center for Constitutional Studies and its scholars take their inspiration from the struggle of America's founding generation to secure liberty through limited government and the rule of law. Under the direction of Roger Pilon, the center was established in 1989 to help revive the idea that the Constitution authorizes a government of delegated, enumerated, and thus limited powers, the exercise of which must be further restrained by our rights, both enumerated and unenumerated. Through books, monographs, conferences, forums, op-eds, speeches, congressional testimony, and TV and radio appearances, the center's scholars address a wide range of constitutional and legal issues—from judicial review to federalism, economic liberty, property rights, civil rights, criminal law and procedure, asset forfeiture, tort law, and term limits, to name just a few. The center is especially concerned to encourage the judiciary to be "the bulwark of our liberties," as James Madison put it, neither making nor ignoring the law but interpreting and applying it through the natural rights tradition we inherited from the founding generation.

CATO INSTITUTE
1000 Massachusetts Ave., N.W.
Washington, D.C. 20001